FILM SCRIPTS ONE

D1500788

FILM SCRIPTS ONE

Edited by
George P. Garrett
O. B. Hardison, Jr.
Jane R. Gelfman

Applause Theatre & Cinema Books
An Imprint of Hal Leonard Corporation

First Applause printing 2013 by arrangement with Ardent Media Inc.
Copyright © 1971 by Meredith Corporation

All rights reserved. No part of this book may be reproduced in any manner whatsoever, including information storage, or retrieval, in whole or in part (except for brief quotations in critical articles or reviews), without written permission from Ardent Media Inc. For information, contact info@ardentmediainc.com or fax 1-212-861-0998.

Distributed by Applause Theatre & Cinema Books
An Imprint of Hal Leonard Corporation
7777 West Bluemound Road
Milwaukee, WI 53213

Trade Book Division Editorial Offices
33 Plymouth St., Montclair, NJ 07042

Acknowledgments:
Henry V Film script for Shakespeare's HENRY V (1944) by courtesy of The Rank Organisation.
The Big Sleep Film script for Raymond Chandler's THE BIG SLEEP (1946), based on the novel of the same name copyright 1939 by Raymond Chandler, by permission of Helga Green and United Artists Corporation.
A Streetcar Named Desire Photoplay of A STREETCAR NAMED DESIRE (1951) reprinted by permission of International Famous Agency, Inc. Copyright 1951 by Tennessee Williams. All rights reserved.

These film scripts in their present form are designed for the reading public only. All dramatic rights are fully protected by copyrights and no public or private performance—professional or amateur—may be given.

Originally published by Appleton-Century-Crofts/Meredith Corporation in 1971
Reprinted by Irvington Publishers Inc. in 1989

Front cover design by Mark Lerner

Printed in the United States of America

The Library of Congress has cataloged the Irvington Publishers Inc. printing as follows:

Film scripts / edited by George P. Garrett, O.B. Hardison, Jr.,
 Jane R. Gelfman
        p.   cm.
  Reprint. Originally published: New York: Appleton-Century-Crofts, 1971-
      1. Motion picture plays. I. Garrett, George P., 1929-
II. Hardison, O.B. III. Gelfman, Jane R.
PN1997.AIG25 1989
791.43'75—dc19
                                     89-2004
                                      CIP

ISBN 978-1-4803-4203-3

www.applausebooks.com

CONTENTS

v

FILM SCRIPTS ONE

INTRODUCTION

The first movie in the modern sense of the word was made by the Thomas A. Edison laboratories and shown in the unlikely location of West Orange, New Jersey, on October 6, 1889. It was produced by the marriage of Edison's sprocket-controlled motion picture camera with the new nitrocellulose film developed by George Eastman of Rochester, New York. Because the early Edison movies had to be viewed individually, through a peephole exhibiting device, they remained curiosities. During the early 1890s attempts were made by Major Woodville Latham, Louis and Auguste Lumière, Thomas Armat, and others to wed Edison's films to the magic lantern to permit film showings for large audiences. Armat's projector was put in regular use at Koster and Bial's music hall in New York City on April 23, 1896. In spite of a series of ills, including a disastrous fire in a Paris theater that killed some 180 spectators, legal battles by Edison over foreign patent rights, and various attempts to regulate the new industry by monopoly control, motion pictures flourished. The final step in the emergence of the modern film industry was taken by Edwin S. Porter, an Edison cameraman, in 1903. Dissatisfied with the vaudeville acts and sporting events that were the staple of early film, Porter made a narrative film crowding as many thrills as possible onto a standard thousand-foot reel. *The Life of an American Fireman* was sufficiently successful to justify a second effort, which emerged as *The Great Train Robbery* (1903). This film was the first commercially important narrative movie. When it opened in 1905 in a theater specifically designed for film showing and dubbed the *nickelodeon* on the basis of the five-cent admission price, the film industry was fairly launched on its amazing twentieth-century career.

For the first decade of the new century the movie industry was dominated by eastern producers (the Motion Picture Patents Company licensed by Edison). A group of independents using French equipment soon arose to challenge the monopoly of Edison's "movie trust." Partly as a result of competition, the independents moved to Southern California, where labor was cheap, the terrain varied, and the climate mild, an important consideration at a time when almost all movies were made outdoors. In 1911 the Nestor film company, under David Horsley, leased a studio site on Sunset Boulevard in Hollywood, and by the end of the year some fifteen companies had followed suit.

During the decade from 1910 to 1920, Hollywood became the film capital of the world. Cecil B. De Mille, Jesse Lasky, Samuel Goldwin, D. W. Griffith, Charlie Chaplin, Douglas Fairbanks, Sr., and a host of others came to Hollywood during this period and were to remain dominant for years to come, some, like De Mille and Goldwin, until after World War II. It was during this decade that movies found their audience. Regarded by intellectuals as crude popular entertainment, they quickly became the cultural staple for the unwashed millions. As success strengthened the financial position of the theater owners and Hollywood studios, movies challenged the supremacy of almost every form of popular entertainment—fiction, Victorian stage melodrama, and vaudeville—except sports. An awkward symbiosis, in some ways closer to an armed truce than peaceful coexistence, eventually developed between Hollywood and the legitimate theater, but movies badly upset the economy of stage drama. Touring companies were broken up. Smalltown theaters were everywhere converted into moving picture houses. Only the large cities—eventually, only New York—continued to support a vital stage drama. Many of the refugees from legitimate drama, of course, later found their way to Hollywood.

During the twenties and thirties movies reigned supreme in the mass entertainment field, and Hollywood was the undisputed center of world cinema. After World War I, while Europe's picture-making capacity was disrupted, the American industry quickly, and with little additional cost, peddled prints of its films abroad. By 1925, American films had captured 95 percent of the British market, 70 percent of the French, and 68 percent of the Italian; elsewhere the situation was much the same.[1]

The "Hollywood approach" was the hard sell. Hollywood producers based their work on what paid off at the box office, not on what film directors or critics claimed would make great art. They gave the public what the public wanted—slick photography, fast-paced plots, action for the men, and tear-soaked sentiment for the ladies. "Eventually two kinds of film

---

[1] Thomas H. Guback, *The International Film Industry: Western Europe and America Since 1945* (Bloomington: Indiana University Press, 1969), pp. 8–9; supporting references here omitted.

would dominate the screen: the peep show and the chase. As primitive tribes described them to Hortense Powdermaker, 'kiss-kiss' and 'bang-bang' stories are right for the screen." [2]

So successful was Hollywood that after 1915, the date of D. W. Griffith's *Birth of a Nation*, the film industry in England, France, Germany, and Italy never offered serious competition. But, in spite of Hollywood's unchallenged position in America as well as Europe through the twenties and thirties, the market at home still accounted for most of its income. [3] As the world's screen capital, it could afford to be as provincial and inward-looking as the country itself. To accommodate ever-larger audiences, enormous cathedrals or palaces of film were built in the major cities. The forerunner of these citadels was Mitchell Mark's Strand, opened in New York in 1914, with a seating capacity of 3,000. In the twenties the cathedral/palaces rivalled in glitter and luxury the fabled opera houses of Paris, Vienna, and Milan. The Roxy Theater in New York, for example, cost some $8,000,000 and had a seating capacity of over 6,000. But every small town had its moviehouse of some sort, and throughout America, Saturday night became almost synonymous with "going to the movies." Meanwhile, in addition to satisfying the popular craving for entertainment, movies created something like an American equivalent of European royalty. The star system fed the public on dreams of glamour, embodied in such popular idols as Theda Bara, Lillian Gish, Rudolph Valentino, Greta Garbo, William S. Hart, and others, whose exploits were followed obsessively not only on the screen but also in the gossip columns of newspapers and in the screen magazines that were by-products of the star system.

The introduction of sound in 1928 greatly increased the range of artistic effects possible in movies. At the same time it created a group of artistic problems that are still unresolved in the 1970s. Sound tended to nationalize movies. The silents spoke the universal language of visual imagery. Their few subtitles could easily be translated into French, Thai, Hindustani, or what have you, with no leakage of meaning. Talkies, however, relied heavily on rapidly spoken dialogue and often on fairly subtle vocal nuances. This was particularly true in their early years when directors tended to stress sound at the expense of image simply because sound was new, and when many Broadway plays—together with many actors—were translated bodily from the legitimate stage to film. To sell such films abroad it was necessary either to add subtitles or to dub in native-language dialogue. Neither expedient was satisfactory. Subtitles are a poor substitute for the spoken word. They can never translate more than a fraction of what is spoken in fast dialogue. And, of course, they make the unwarranted as-

[2] Roy Huss and Norman Silverstein, *The Film Experience: Elements of Motion Picture Art* (New York: Dell, 1969), p. 15; citing Hortense Powdermaker, *Hollywood: The Dream Factory* (Boston: Little, Brown, 1950), p. 14.
[3] Guback, p. 9.

sumption that the audience is literate! Dubbed dialogue, while better than subtitles, is also awkward. The actors who do the dubbing are usually poorly paid hacks. The dialogue itself is often crudely translated. Perhaps most distressing, the words on the sound track seldom correspond to the lip movements of the actors on the screen, a situation that undercuts, if it does not destroy, the dramatic illusion. Thus, in spite of the growing international character of the film industry, the serious viewer still suffers an annoying distortion and dislocation if he must experience, say, Michelangelo Antonioni's *L'Eclisse* (1961), which is set in contemporary Rome, under the amplification of an English-language sound track. Equally disturbing, on the other hand, is an encounter with the same director's *Blow-up* (1967), which is set in London of today, in any tones other than those of British English.

More fundamental, sound brought with it the unanswerable question of whether movies are a visual or a verbal art. The accident of limited technology forced the directors of the silent era to concentrate on the visual aspect of film. They explored a remarkable range of techniques for telling stories visually. In the opinion of many students of film, sound caused a regression in film technique that lasted until after World War II. Sound made it too easy to tell a story. Cinematic techniques that were commonplace to producers like Griffith and actors like Chaplin were replaced by stale devices imported from Broadway along with playscripts and actors. Not until after World War II, when a new breed of filmmakers formed by the realities of invasion, military defeat, and economic collapse made its vision felt, was Hollywood shaken out of its complacency.

While Hollywood continued to dominate world cinema between the two world wars, Europeans did produce many films that gained international attention either for their intrinsic qualities or innovative techniques. Sergei Eisenstein, the great Russian director, is a towering figure both in the art of making films and of analyzing principles of cinematography. Several of his films, notably *Potemkin* (1925), *Alexander Nevsky* (1938), and *Ivan the Terrible* (1944–46), have had worldwide influence. The silent, *The Cabinet of Dr. Caligari* (1919), by the Austrian director Robert Wiene, remains a classic of expressionism in the theater adapted to film while *The Blue Angel* (1930), a talking picture directed by Josef von Sternberg and starring Marlene Dietrich and Emil Jannings, remains a classic of harsh realism, social and psychological, which was inspired by the disillusionment that pervaded Germany in the last years of the Weimar Republic. Among the French, René Clair produced charming, socially cutting, film fantasies like *À nous la liberté* (1932) and *The Ghost Goes West* (1938); and Marcel Pagnol revealed with tender luminosity in *La Femme de boulanger* (1938) and a trilogy—*Marius* (1929), *Fanny* (1931), and *César* (1936)—complexities of feeling among the petty bourgeoisie of provincial France.

But it was not until 1945, following World War II, that European cinema began to challenge Hollywood and the economic situation for American producers began to change completely. In such films as Rossellini's *Open City* (1945), De Sica's *Shoe Shine* (1946), and his *Bicycle Thief* (1948), Italian filmmakers achieved sensitive but unsentimental renderings of the physical and emotional realities of German occupation, American liberation, and the struggle to rebuild a peacetime society with habits and outlooks conditioned by years of learning how to survive only from moment to moment. This new spirit of filmmaking, *cinéma vérité* (or direct cinema), came as a refreshing new perspective for American audiences when experienced against their own long exposure to Hollywood's vision, subsidized by our government, of a world at war. The newsreel-like verisimilitude of scenes shot on location where local inhabitants played the lesser roles was a radical break with the controlled and insulated environment of the sound studio and its professional actors.

This new and less-expensive procedure opened the door for shooting other films—from British comedies to Scandinavian psychocinedramas—out-of-doors. As the impressionists liberated painting during the last quarter of the nineteenth century by taking their canvases out of the studio and into the fields and streets, European directors led a similar revolution in filmmaking out of necessity after World War II. *Cinéma vérité* also restored to the directors some of the preeminence they had enjoyed during the silent era. They thus opened the way for such meditative, director-dominated films as *8½*, *Last Year at Marienbad* (1962), *Juliet of the Spirits* (1964), and *Blow-up*. French cinema has also been influential, though perhaps experimental, beginning with the postwar classic *Les enfants du Paradis* and extending through the *nouvelle vague* movement of the 1960s. Many isolated but major contributions have also come from Japanese and Scandinavian filmmakers, most notably Akira Kurosawa and Ingmar Bergman.

During the sixties British and American filmmakers began to draw on continental techniques. *A Hard Day's Night* (1964) is a brilliant English contribution which manages the difficult task of carrying its unorthodox techniques so lightly that they seem entirely natural expressions of the dominant tone of exuberant, uninhibited play. In the United States, as the photographic industry produced less cumbersome and expensive cameras and more light-sensitive film, a new kind of movie, one of *personal statement*, emerged. "Underground"—or "independent" as most of them preferred to be called—filmmakers could dissent "radically in form, or in technique, or in content, or perhaps in all three" from the offerings of commercial cinema, and all for an outlay of about a thousand dollars.[4] In the fifties

[4] Sheldon Renan, *An Introduction to the American Underground Film* (New York: Dutton, 1967), p. 17.

and sixties a subculture whose important personages included Stan Brakhage, Kenneth Anger, Stan VanDerBeek, and Andy Warhol established themselves as the heirs of an earlier generation of avant-gardists and experimentalists such as Jean Cocteau (*Le sang d'un poète,* 1930) and Luis Buñuel (*Un chien andalou,* 1928).

The response of the major American studios to the new freedom has been slow, but there are signs of change, principally in the form of more flexible use of visual strategies—jump-cuts, flash cuts (forward or backward), slow and accelerated motion, form cuts, zoom-freezes, and the like. *Petulia* (1968), *The Graduate* (1967), *The Wild Bunch* (1969), and *The Landlord* (1970) are excellent films which illustrate this tendency, and they doubtless indicate the direction of much future development. Whatever the case, the pressure on Hollywood to experiment is constant, especially (and ironically) from the screen of commercial television, which feeds heavily on Hollywood's past to keep its viewers awake and watching between plugs for automobiles, beer, and carpets. To compete, the motion picture industry, which is increasingly worldwide in every respect, must either seek a different audience from television or offer the average addict of the tube a positive inducement to leave his living room with its easy chair, ash tray, and nearby supply of cold beer for the privilege of spending from two to five dollars for a *new* movie.

The future of commercial filmmaking is now being shaped by pressures from several, and often conflicting, directions. In terms of revenues for a new feature film "just four countries in Western Europe—the United Kingdom, Italy, France, and West Germany—can yield almost half of the domestic [i.e., United States] gross for a film." [5] Indeed, as early in the postwar years as 1953, Hollywood producers conceded, through Eric Johnston, their industry spokesman, that "9 out of 10 United States films cannot pay their way on the domestic market alone." Simultaneously with greater dependence on foreign markets, other important economic shifts have occurred at home and abroad. Moviegoing in the United States, as reflected in average weekly attendance at theaters, is "but slightly more than half the 1941 figure, while population growth in the intervening years has stretched the imbalance." [6] Even though admission prices have risen steeply, they do not offset the loss of volume. In addition, the suppression of the "block-booking" system by forced separation of Hollywood's production facilities from its distribution outlets through action of the federal government (1948) early deprived major Hollywood studios of assured domestic showcases for each of their products, whatever their individual cinematic or other merits.

Since then, a number of forces are at work to push and shove the world's film capital into its future. Increasingly, "one centrally located, fully equipped permanent facility" makes little economic sense because

[5] Guback, p. 4.
[6] Guback, p. 3.

of high labor costs in the United States when compared with the rest of the world; access to remote corners of the world for airborne men and equipment becomes ever easier; an improved technology offers better and more portable cameras and more sophisticated editing equipment as well as film stock that is both more sensitive to light and less sensitive to extremes in climate; a new generation of filmmakers are as concerned about experimenting with the technical and psychological aspects of the medium as they are in exploring a variety of social themes; major studios are steadily absorbed by vast financial conglomerates which, though sensitive to costs and attentive to balance sheets, are insensitive to Hollywood's traditions and indifferent to established patterns of production.[7]

In addition to all of these pressures, American capital investment, starting in the early 1950s, has gone abroad and offered to national film industries, which welcomed aid from the United States, financial backing of production costs and the guarantees of an international distribution system for completed films. In two decades the rest of the world has, for better or worse, increasingly lost its independence. In other words, the internationalization of the film industry under American auspices has inevitably meant the diminishing of "chances for diversity and different points of view." Film, however, which is "not only a business commodity but a vehicle of communication . . . , is important not only for what it says but for what it does not say. The boundaries of human experience . . . expand or contract on the basis of what people have presented to them." [8]

The purpose of this thumbnail sketch of the history of film is not to outline or even block out a subject whose dimensions are so large that they are still partly unexplored. Rather, it is to document the basic contention of the present anthology: that film is not *an* art form of the twentieth century, it is *the* art form of the twentieth century. If sculpture was the glory of Periclean Greece, architecture of Augustan Rome, painting of Renaissance Italy, and drama of Elizabethan England, cinema has been both the major contribution of America to world culture and the dominant mode of world culture itself for the last fifty years.

In its brief history, the film has assimilated the photograph variously filtered and focused, motion near and far, sound from one or several directions, color in all of its subtle gradations, screens of great breadth both indoors and out, and lenses that give a visceral feeling of depth and movement. Within these expanding dimensions, filmmakers have elaborated techniques of transition and dislocation from frame to frame which dissolve rigidities of time and space as its audiences know them in everyday life. As a result, the tension achievable in film between order and chaos, between control and chance—which lies at the heart of every art regardless

---

[7] "Movies Leaving 'Hollywood' Behind," *The New York Times* (May 27, 1970), p. 36.
[8] Guback, pp. 203, 4; see also pp. 94–95.

of its media—is more dynamic and capable of greater complexity than in any other art. Film is far from exhausting its possibilities for artistic triumphs.

In the years since World War II a new medium and industry, television, has emerged not only to challenge established patterns of filmmaking and moviegoing but also to create intricate and reciprocal relations with cinema. Even a partial profile of the mutual impact of film and television on each other would take us too far afield from our primary concern, feature films and their scripts. But certain aspects, some of which we have already discussed, should be noted in passing. The advent of television in the United States has coincided with a reduction in selected subjects, especially newsreels and weekly serials, at moviehouses and their reintroduction in contemporary forms on home screens. Television has also relied heavily on films of the thirties through the sixties from its sister industry in order to sustain the commercial messages of its own advertisers. And, in the postwar years, while the large Hollywood production companies have redefined themselves—lost their chains of tied moviehouses, dismantled their sound stages, and dissolved the star system—commercial television has formed three major networks with affiliated stations across the country, fostered its own production facilities, and created its own stellar personalities—the hosts of its talk, news, and variety shows. At the present time, the internationalism that the film industry has gradually achieved since 1945 is only just becoming possible for television, thanks in part to the broadcast potential of transmission satellites.

The place of film in twentieth-century culture can be demonstrated in another, equally dramatic way. The average nineteenth-century child was illiterate. He was effectively isolated from the culture of the dominant class. As he matured, his entertainment, when he could afford it, consisted of dance-hall reviews, vaudeville, and, occasionally, a melodrama by Dion Boucicault or one of his imitators. Conversely, middle- and upper-class children were brought up on books. They were introduced to the world of art through the printed page. As adults they consumed a constant fare of novels, some good, most bad or indifferent. Theater and opera were significant, but the novel formed the core of the cultural life of the literate population. The modern child, by contrast, is exposed to the visual world of movies and television long before he can read. There is no class distinction in this exposure. It is experienced equally by rich and poor, and it becomes more rather than less intense as the typical modern child matures. College students read more than the general public, but it has been estimated that in the United States a typical freshman has seen twenty movies for every book he has read—and this does not include an average of some 15,000 hours of exposure to television by age 18! [9] After college, the student tends

[9] *Man and the Movies,* ed. W. R. Robinson (Baton Rouge: Louisiana State University, 1967), pp. 3–4.

to fall back into habits like those of the population in general, which means that he reads less, while his consumption of movies and television remains constant or increases. Clearly, film and television now form the cultural medium in which twentieth-century men—from the illiterate to the affluent—are immersed.

The consequences of the dominance of film and television as twentieth-century culture media have often been discussed. Marshall McLuhan feels we are being (or have been) pushed abruptly into a new phase of world culture, the post-Gutenberg era. Sounds and images, rather than printed words, shape our imaginative apprehension of the surrounding world. Sounds and images are not only far richer than printed words, they are also less "linear"—less dominated by the sequential logic of the sentence or paragraph or chapter—less constrained by the need to avoid redundancy or contradiction, and far more accessible since they do not assume literacy. McLuhan's theories imply that the printed word may be growing archaic: that some day the reading of printed books may be an antiquarian pursuit, a little like reading books written in Greek and Latin.

Whatever the future of the printed word, today's educational curricula are shaped around it to a degree that seems exaggerated on the secondary level and nearly obsessive on the college and university level. The higher-education establishment does obeisance to the printed word as devoutly as primitive tribes worship the idols of gods. While harmless in the area of the physical sciences, this behavior is questionable in the area of the humanities. Our literature departments boast of their concern for relevance—for significant examination of every aspect of modern culture. They actively encourage the study of modern fiction, modern poetry, modern drama, and modern criticism. Yet a Martian, after taking the "modern lit." curriculum at a typical American college, might emerge with no other knowledge of cinema than the vague realization that from time to time earthlings of the twentieth century went (probably furtively) to certain entertainments called movies. He might realize that plays and novels were occasionally made into movies, but he would have no inkling of the influence that movies have had on twentieth-century drama and fiction. At best, he would conclude that movies were a minor diversion appealing chiefly to the lower classes, the illiterate, the vulgar, the naive, the deviant.

Granted that film is the cultural medium characteristic of our age, that its neglect has been unfortunate, and that a proper understanding of its values and achievements would enrich studies of twentieth-century fiction, drama, and poetry, not to mention studies of modern psychology and sociology—the question remains: how does one study film?

In general, three approaches to film are possible: the technical, the historical, and the aesthetic. The technical is perhaps the most common one. Presently, some 850 courses on film are being taught at American colleges. The majority are technical in orientation. They are usually taught in departments of radio-television-film, of drama, and of speech, by individuals who are interested in how films are made.[10] Their common feature is their stress on making films—on script writing, photography, film acting, and film direction and editing. They are valuable, but they tend to be professionally oriented. In other words, they are primarily for those who hope to find a career (or, at least, an avocation) in film. They bear the same relation to the study of film that courses in creative writing bear to courses in literature and literary criticism, with the difference that, being much more technical, they are more numerous and less standardized in content.

No one who is interested in film can afford to be ignorant of the technical side of filmmaking, but the limitations of the technical approach should be recognized. One does not need to know how to write a novel in order to appreciate a good one once it is written: to respond to it, to observe its artistry, its literary relations, its form, and its thematic and historical significance. The same holds true for the study of film. Most films are made to be appreciated by audiences who could not care less about how they are made. Occasionally we have a technical *tour de force* like *The Cabinet of Doctor Caligari*, Cocteau's *Orpheus* (1949), or *Blow-up;* but the sheer cost of making a major film means that all but a few experimental directors use technique functionally—a point equally illustrated by Alfred Hitchcock's thrillers and Ingmar Bergman's meditative studies of the human psyche. Hitchcock and Bergman are both masters of film technique, and their technique is always part of their expression. Never present for its own sake, it serves as the medium of our vision, and, while we are members of an audience, we need be no more conscious of it *as technique* than the botanist examining plant cells is conscious of the complex arrangement of lenses that makes his observations possible.

The historical approach to film is also well-defined. Like the technical approach, it offers a valuable, even essential, body of information to the student. Although less common than the technical approach, it appears widely in the curriculum in the form of courses on "The History of Film," "The Silent Film Era," and the like. Historical courses are organized on analogy to the standard courses in the history of literature. Like the "surveys of English lit.," they tend to emphasize chronology, biography, and historical context, and to concentrate on early landmarks—the silent era—rather than later achievements. Their limitation is intrinsic to their approach. They are necessarily oriented toward history rather than toward the achievement of individual films.

The battle begun in the 1930s between historical scholars and the new critics of literature has given way to a generally peaceful coexistence. We recognize that there were (and are) important verities on both sides. In general, however, the basic contentions of the new critics have been established. We accept the idea that the study of literature is primarily a study

[10] *Film Study in Higher Education*, ed. D. C. Stewart (Washington, D.C.: American Council on Education, 1966), pp. 164–67.

of works of literature, not of dates, genres, influences, or biographies. This is why the old-fashioned sophomore literature survey has been replaced at most schools by courses in literary appreciation or literary masterpieces.

Surely, the same principles should apply to the study of film. It should be oriented toward our interest in ourselves and the culture within which the self is defined. The emphasis should be on individual films. Their artistic and cultural significance, rather than their technique or relation to the history of film, should receive first priority. Beyond that, if the films are considered in chronological order, the approach will take on an historical coloring; if they are considered by genres like the Western, the thriller, or the social documentary, the coloring will be formalist; if they are approached in terms of theme, the coloring will be sociological, philosophical, or theological. Some such coloration is inevitable and proper. It supplements the aesthetic approach, as long as it does not threaten to compromise examination of individual films.

To examine a film with the same care and thoroughness as a novel or a poem is difficult. The authoritative text of a film is the master print on which all prints made for commercial distribution are based. In the first place, the master print is never available. All films that are shown commercially and for educational purposes are later prints, and these are often edited silently to conform to local censorship laws, time requirements, and the like. Since many master prints have been lost, the later prints now available may or may not be edited versions, and for many early films, there is no way of knowing what the original really was.

Such bibliographical problems need not concern the average viewer. He can assume that the print of the film which he sees is reasonably close to the master print unless warned otherwise. His problem is of a different order. It stems from the fact that films are dynamic. They move. And as they move they convey more information than the human mind can retain. An experienced critic can pick up an impressive amount of detail from a single viewing of a film, but even the best observer has his limits and they are soon reached. The viewer of a film is the witness of a complex but significant series of events. We know how fallible even the most intelligent witnesses can be from the conflicting testimony that is always generated by a sensational public event. A vivid case in point is provided by the assassination of President Kennedy. We have to recognize the same propensity to error in ourselves. Yet the study of film demands accurate recall not only of what happened but what was said, how it was said, and—film being visual as well as verbal—how it was conveyed in images. That is, we certainly need to know that the hero married the heroine in the last reel. Depending on the aspect of the film that catches our interest, we may also need to know whether or not the butler was wearing gloves, whether the father drove a Ford or a Chevrolet, whether the heroine's costume in the first reel was red to foreshadow the sunset in the last, or whether there was a cut, a fade, or a dissolve from the chapel to the mountains. Moreover, if we wish to discuss our observations, we need some means of verifying them. If we disagree on the color of the heroine's costume, for example, the only way to decide who is right is to go to the film or an authoritative substitute.

Apparently, the ideal way of solving this problem is through movie archives and a viewing machine like the movieola, which permits the observer not only to see the film but to stop the action on a given frame, reverse it, and begin again. Comprehensive film archives would make it possible to document discussions of film in the same way that discussions of poems and novels are documented. An archive would have the further advantage of allowing interested critics to view films as often as necessary to refine and extend their observations.

But this solution, though ideal, is at present impracticable. No archive can accommodate the large numbers of individuals interested in film, and even if it could, the constant use of films quickly destroys them. A much more practical solution is to coordinate viewing of films with reading of scripts. Unlike reels of film, a script is easily portable; it can be read anywhere; it resists wear; notes can be written in its margins; and it is not "time bound," that is, it does not move continuously forward. If the critic comes to the last scene and wants to compare it to the first, he can simply turn back. Although a film can be reversed, the process is time-consuming, particularly if it has to be repeated several times.

Evidently, if film is to be studied as a cultural form in something of the same way that we study poetry, fiction, and drama, the script is a necessary adjunct to viewing the film. Note that it is an adjunct, not a replacement. A faithful copy of the master print must remain the final, authoritative text for the public at large. Normally, however, it is seen only once. At best it can be seen two or three times since rental schedules are fixed and viewing facilities (not to mention the time of the viewer) are limited. The script, which can be read as preparation for viewing the film, can also be annotated while the memory of the film is still fresh, reviewed easily and conveniently as often as needed, and can serve as documentation in resolving doubts about the filmmaker's intentions.

Note, too, that the importance here assigned the script does not imply that film is primarily verbal. The relative importance of image and word is a question in film aesthetics that will probably be debated as long as the question of what Aristotle meant by catharsis. The only assertion being made here is that if film is to be given its proper place in the study of modern culture, then viewing must be supplemented by use of scripts. In fact, a shooting script of the sort included in the present anthology often contains comments and revisions that call attention to effects that might otherwise be missed.

A final word may be useful concerning the scripts selected for the present volume. Silent films are not represented because they had no scripts in the modern sense of the term. Foreign films are excluded because they necessarily lead to awkward—usually misleading—compromises. Anyone who has read a translated script will be aware that its dialogue usually bears little relation to the dialogue in the film. The translator who provides subtitles works directly from the original shooting script, but within the economies of space and time in the footage. Many foreign films today are shown with dubbed-in dialogue. The alternative to a translation is thus a script transcribed from the English dialogue of a dubbed-in sound track. Such a script is next to worthless since the quality of the acting—the tonality, expression, gestures, and the like—was dictated by the nature of the *original* dialogue as well as the linguistic and cultural inheritance of the director and actor, not the words chosen by the English-language editor because they happen to fit the lip movements on the screen.

The scripts selected are entirely from the period between 1945 and 1970. The complicated legal status of prewar scripts makes permission to print difficult to obtain, and, evidently, many shooting scripts have been lost because they were not thought to have any intrinsic value. This limitation is not, however, without advantages. Hollywood's most vital periods were the silent era and the period following World War II. Postwar films are generally more serious in theme, more flexible in technique, and, of course, more directly relevant to contemporary life than their prewar forerunners. Since this anthology is intended for the study of film as an art form rather than the history or technique of film, the basis of the selection has been the quality and intrinsic interest of the film itself. Each selection attracted the serious attention of reviewers and critics when it originally appeared; and each still repays thoughtful critical analysis. Given the abundance and excellence of English and American films during the period covered, no more than a sampling of them can be offered. But an effort has been made to represent the more important types—comedy, satire, costume-movie, social criticism, psychological study, thriller, and fantasy—as well as the more important ways in which a story comes to the screen—from a novel or short story, from a drama, from television, and from an original screen play. Although every reader will inevitably miss several of his favorites, the editors believe that each film selected has a legitimate claim for inclusion.

Most of the scripts are shooting scripts; that is, they represent the written version of a story as it was available to director, actors, and cameraman before and during the making of the film itself. Because shooting scripts differ from dramatic scripts, a brief discussion of their characteristics will be helpful.

Place and Use of the Script

The true text of any film is the film itself, or, more strictly speaking it is the final negative, called the *master film*, from which all prints are made.

The relationship between a shooting script and a finished film is complex and depends upon a large number of variables, mostly upon the intentions and practices of the director. Some of the most outstanding directors, Alfred Hitchcock, for example, work with most explicit and detailed scripts and follow the script with much the same precision as a builder does the blueprints of an architect. (Hitchcock, of course, always works very closely with his writer at every step of the way in preparing his own kind of script.) Other directors prefer a loosely defined scenario so that they have a maximum amount of margin for revision and improvisation during the shooting stage. Some cineasts believe, quite wrongly, that many contemporary pictures are made without scripts. In general, this is simply not true, although the form of the script may vary widely from neatly bound scripts to pencilled scribblings done moments before shooting or even during the shooting of a scene. Granted the powerful aesthetic influence of *cinéma vérité* in our time, which some critics see as a new development in the medium and others as a return to the classical purity of improvisation that characterized the making of many of the greatest silent films, the fully developed script remains a key step in the creation of most films.

To be sure, a certain kind of film, increasingly popular and becoming well-known, dispenses with the rigidities of conventional plot and conventional story line, in favor of working out, directly before the camera, improvisations, ad lib dialogue, and even events or happenings. A conventional script obviously serves little or no purpose in such a scheme. In addition, as the old, arbitrary lines of distinction between fiction and nonfiction, fable and fact, continue to break down, even the feature-length documentary film will be affected by this new creative energy. The work of the American filmmaker Fred Wiseman is an excellent example. Using his team of cameramen to record actual people engaged in actual events, he might once have been called a documentary filmmaker, and judged by old-fashioned standards and classifications. Today he is regarded simply as a filmmaker. His *Titicut Follies* (1967), *High School* (1968), *Law and Order* (1969), and *Hospital* (1970) are, indeed, documentaries taken on the scene at particular times and places and using real people, not actors. Yet these films are also examples of advocacy reporting, designed to make strongly felt social and political points. He exercises the filmmaker's art in choosing to film the events that support his views and feelings and also in the most careful editing of the film to make "reality" coincide with his personal vision. He is thus as much a deliberate fabulator as any other filmmaker, an honest and engaged artist for whose work the old distinctions between "fiction" and "nonfiction" are largely irrelevant. But his method, at least in these films, precludes the use of any ordinary script.

Allowing for notable exceptions, however, it is still generally true that all feature films intended to be shown to audiences in theaters have a script. They may differ in form and format. The script may exist in many copies, available and known to all concerned, or it may be the private property of only a few key figures in the production process. But there is almost always a script, and that script precedes the making of the film.

The process of filmmaking and the unique nature of the medium are such that a script may be considered as raw material for the finished product. It helps to initiate the process of making, serves as a guide to director, actors, and technicians, and is then finally, to a greater or lesser degree, expendable. To the student of cinema, however, a script can be of real value. Close reading of it, in conjunction with an attentive viewing of the film, will demonstrate a great deal, which otherwise might be difficult to learn, about the nature of this twentieth-century art form. And such a procedure can offer substance for the purposes of query, discussion, and debate, the give-and-take and discovery that is learning.

The primary value of using shooting scripts in the study of films is that this method reflects honestly the first critical phase in the process of filmmaking. Although the outlines have been publicly available for a full half-century and have changed only slightly and very gradually during all that time, the process of making pictures is surprisingly little known. Or, when known, it is all too often ignored. Critics and reviewers are, for their own reasons, frequently indifferent to the process of making; or, what is perhaps less defensible, sometimes imply a very different sort of process than the one actually followed by the makers of films. Audiences, even some of the most appreciative and sophisticated, are frequently unfamiliar with the basics of the craft. This ignorance may be partially advantageous; for films, perhaps more than any other art form, depend almost as much upon sleight-of-hand, upon the magicians's art, for their effect upon the viewer as they do upon what is literally shown and seen. Often what is not shown, but is instead evoked in and imagined by the audience, is as viable as what is really shown. Good film shows us a great deal, but we perceive more than what is shown. From Eisenstein to Hitchcock to McLuhan and including the young filmmakers and cinema buffs around the world, directors and producers of films as well as critics and scholars of the art have sought to define theoretically and to name and classify the elements that combine to create the aesthetic effects of film. Their explorations, especially those of the makers of films, are a fascinating subject for research and study and are extremely important in the cultivation of a finer cinematic sensibility. The views of these men, although not to be ignored or slighted, in theory and practice, are far from definitive, whether they be interpreted singly or in any combination. The rules of the game, as even a slight reading of items listed in the bibliography will show, keep changing. One of the surest signs of vitality is the resistance of film art to every attempt at definitive classification, even the most subtle and persuasive. A rudimentary knowledge and general familiarity with the basic steps in the process of making a film should, however, at least serve to increase one's sense of appreciation, to refine one's taste and judgment rather than strip the cinematic experience of its human magic.

And that is the aim of this collection of scripts: to give the reader a means of seeing how films evolve from words to something else and, ideally, something much more than a script, namely, a complex of images, arranged in careful sequence, supported by sound and by music, dramatized by actors, and controlled by the intelligence and sensibility of a director.

Although most scripts are much transformed in the sequential processes of shooting and editing, the ideal of filmmakers, from producer to prop man, is to translate the script into the language and idiom of cinematography and to realize in doing so the script's full potential. This goal is an elusive one at best because of the nature of the process of making films and the many variables involved. All of the artists, craftsmen, and technicians who work at the making of a picture bring to it both skill and creativity. Each is a maker who seeks by his own skills to create something new and good. But even the best results have never given us "perfect" films, only truly fine films whose magic succeeds in spite of their imperfections.

A film script, even when published with care to reflect in detail the copy provided by the film's proprietors, is at best a verbal outline, a blueprint of what one sees and experiences in viewing a film. It is in no way a substitute for the actual experience of seeing a clear, unbutchered print of the film. But as an aid to memory, it helps us recall what we have already experienced as an ordering of meaningful sights and sounds.

Although the script writer is a valuable contributor to the total experience of a film, he is only one of many. Insofar as a single controlling sensibility unifies the entire process and experience, it is always that of the director. The director, of course, cannot possibly do everything himself or know in detail everything necessary to make a moving picture. But he, in the last analysis, is held responsible for all that happens or fails to happen. In recent years, especially with the decline of the large corporate producers in Hollywood, we have come to perceive this fact more clearly. The director's name rather than that of the producer or his imprint is the one we associate with a film in allotting praise or blame. In a very real sense the French critics of our time have been more accurate than innovative in naming the director of a picture its *auteur*. No full and easy analogy, however, quite explains the role of the director. His function is at once that of quarterback, orchestra conductor, building contractor, trail boss, company commander, and, sometimes, lion tamer—the latter image amusingly exploited by Fellini in 8½. The director rules, benevolently or despotically, over a little kingdom. The writer, though absolutely essential to the process and especially to the beginning of it, remains his majesty's loyal servant.

This book contains several sorts of film scripts in a variety of formats. Most are final shooting scripts, that is, examples of the very form which director, cast, and crew worked with when a film first went into production. In many cases additions and deletions and rearrangements and revisions of material take place during the period of shooting the film and, again, during the period of editing the film. Freedom and flexibility are basic characteristics of the creative process of filmmaking. The possibilities for revision are always present when a scene is being filmed, and equally so in the cutting room and laboratory as the film is being edited and polished into its finished form. The final shooting script is the first part of the production process, but it should be remembered that even in this form a script has usually been through many stages already and has been much revised.

Two scripts in this entire collection are not precisely final shooting scripts: those of *Henry V* (1944) and *The Pumpkin Eater* (1964). Each of these British scripts is designated, in British film terminology, as a *release screenplay*. That is to say, each has been more or less adjusted to conform as closely as possible to the edited film, its basic camera angles and shots, its frames and footage. These screenplays, in comparison with final shooting scripts, offer a fuller description of sound and music devices, present many more separate camera shots, and include such elements of the finished and released film as the full title and credits. Necessity requires the inclusion of these release screenplays; for, unlike their American counterparts, it is not the custom of British production companies to preserve copies of the earlier versions of scripts on file. We are most fortunate, however, thanks to the writers themselves, to have obtained rare versions of the shooting scripts of *A Hard Day's Night* (1964) and *Darling* (1965) for this collection. Yet even these release screenplays are somewhat different from and fall short of what is generally known as the *final* official form of a film script—the *combined continuity*. Created by a specialist (usually designated as *script girl*) who follows the shooting and editing of a film from beginning to end, based entirely upon the completed and commercially released form of the film, with all of the separate camera shots listed and all details of footage and running time of individual shots and scenes, etc., carefully recorded, a combined continuity is at once a sort of chart or graph of a finished film and the very last *word* of the film. Close as these two British release screenplays are to what is seen in the films, they are not combined continuities; and differences exist between them and the films. The alert student will note slight changes in each of them.

All of the other scripts in this collection are final shooting scripts. If the release screenplay comes near the end of the process of filmmaking, a final shooting script represents a true beginning. It is the demarcation point—many filmmakers would call it "the point of no return," the place where the production of the film really begins. From there on it goes first before the cameras, then, perhaps most crucially of all, into the movieola of the film editor to be cut and arranged before the finished film is to be projected upon a screen. Next to the director the film editor has, in a literal and physical sense, more control over what will be seen by an audience than anyone engaged in the making of a picture. The director remains responsible for the results and thus supervises the editing process closely. Some directors are engaged in the cutting and editing of a film in all details. Others prefer to give their film editor considerable freedom and to act in a critical capacity, viewing sections of the film in the projection room and offering general advice, suggestions, and criticism as, bit by bit, the whole film is put together. (Sometimes the screenwriter is called upon to participate at this stage as well.) The film editor, of course, is a highly professional craftsman, often an experienced artist in his own right. How he works with the director and others, and how much the actual labor is overseen and divided is a subtle matter involving diplomacy, tact, and personal relationships. Theoretically, in any event, the director has the last word in this area and is held responsible for the quality of the editing.

The Process of Filmmaking

In the beginning someone has an idea for making a picture. Once this "someone" was almost always a producer. Now, increasingly, it is a director, a writer, or occasionally a star who initiates the process. As witnessed by the scripts in this collection, the idea, the source of original inspiration for a movie, may come from almost anywhere—a novel or short story, a play for stage or television, another film old or new, something from the newspapers or magazines, or something that has captured an artist's attention and can lead to an original screenplay. However the idea may begin, it soon becomes a *property*. This term, though unfortunate in its connotations, is almost universally used by filmmakers and is used in a neutral rather than a pejorative sense. In any case, the original desire and intention to create a film becomes a matter of real property when a producer involves himself by means of an option or outright purchase of film rights.

Enter the writer (if he has not arrived already) to set about building a story and writing a script. Whether the picture is an adaptation or an original screenplay, as soon as a producer is involved, commerce begins to make its claims. The making of all pictures to be shown in theaters, where audiences buy tickets of admission, is an elaborate (and sometimes lucrative) business as well as an art. Each year the cost of making films increases. The producer must be able to raise the capital necessary to make the film from one or more sources. Perhaps, under ideal circumstances and blessed with a reputation for success, he can tentatively arrange the financing, sign options with leading actors and the right director, and gather the essential elements of the crew on the strength of the property alone. But sooner or later, and usually sooner, he will need a script to present to both potential backers and key coworkers before any firm commitments can be made, contracts signed, and a budget and production schedules devised. The writer thus comes in early. If he is lucky he stays late and sees the picture through production.

A very large number of projects, begun with high hopes and much enthusiasm, never reach the point of a workable script, one that is satisfactory to everyone who must be satisfied. A large percentage of properties never become films. And a very large number of the films we see have had more than one screenwriter and many preliminary versions and drafts of the script. Only writers whose material is actually used in the film receive *film credit*, even though a number of writers may have worked on the property earlier.

For simplicity and assuming ideal circumstances, let us imagine one writer working on a script. It should also be understood that though the stages described here are customary and conventional, they vary considerably according to the experience and reputation of the writer and his personal relationship with the producer and the director. Usually the writer will first produce a brief *synopsis* that is basically a literary outline of how he proposes to deal with the story in cinematic terms. If this proves satisfactory, he then writes a *treatment*, a much longer and detailed development of the synopsis, an extended outline of the potential script. The treatment is still more or less literary in form, descriptive rather than dramatic, though it may very well include some individual scenes done in dramatic form and with some dialogue.

Many filmmakers find the treatment a vital stage in the development of script into film. A commonplace among filmmakers says, "If it isn't in the script, it won't be in the picture." What is not meant, of course, by this aphorism is the picture's style, direction, cinematography, cutting, or any matter of filmmaking technique. What is meant is what has always concerned writers as storytellers—structure, character, motivation, tone, etc. Some filmmakers themselves apply this rule of thumb to the treatment and swear that if a script—and hence the film—takes a wrong turn, the flaw can be found in the treatment.

Following the treatment comes the *first draft screenplay*, now employing one of the conventional formats used for film scripts. These forms, as you will see, have slight differences, but there are some general things that apply to all the shooting scripts in this collection. A script is broken down into separate units. Usually, though not always, these are numbered sequentially, and are called *master scenes*. These units may be many or relatively few in number, depending on the detail called for in order to help the translation of dialogue and action as written into camera frames, angles, depth-of-field, transitions, sound, etc. Compared to continuities all scripts are sparse in this kind of explicit direction. A master scene is, then, simply a single dramatic unit at a single location or setting. Within this unit any number of shots and camera angles may be used to shoot many feet of film—versions of the same scene from a variety of angles and points of view. Though the method is changing, the traditional one still employed by most directors requires that all actions in a given master scene be shot at least five times (sometimes the number can be as high as twelve) in order to insure proper *coverage* of the scene. The purpose here is not only to allow for different readings on the part of actors or, say, different lighting conditions, but to provide the director and the film editor with enough footage of the same basic dramatic unit so that they may cut and splice with a maximum of freedom and choice. In the cutting, which comes later, they may well use and juxtapose frames and pieces from all the separate versions of a photographed master scene. This rule does not apply easily, of course, to scenes (or entire films) based upon spontaneity and improvisation.

In addition to specifying a sequence of master scenes and calling for certain specific camera angles in the cinematography of a film, the writer may or may not specify the use of certain kinds of transitions from one unit to the next. Transitions from one scene to the next, from one piece of film to the next, are the concern of the editor. It is not properly a part of the writer's job to tell director, cameraman, or editor how to do theirs; nor will they heed his suggestions to the disadvantage of the film or the inhibition of their own talents. There are a number of reasons, however, why a writer will offer some directions, camera angles, and transitions in his script. First, he will do so in order to make clear a point within his proper area of concern—a story or plot point, a bit of characterization, a structural device, or, perhaps, an occasional suggestion as to the rhythm of a scene or sequence of shots. For the rhythm of a film is intricately wedded to its dramatic structure. Unless elapsed time, for example, is being used functionally for suspense, as in *High Noon* (1952), film is not concerned with what we call "real" time. Instead one has a sense of continual present, a sense that is created by the rhythm of the film. Context may make two scenes of approximately the same footage seem radically different. One may appear slow and lyrical whereas the other may seem jagged, jazzy, and quick. With a full awareness that his views are largely speculative suggestions and may frequently be ignored, the writer is within his rights in dealing with these elements. His views may give director, cameraman, or editor a clearer idea of the intent and inner quality of the script. He will be at fault only in persuading himself that his own visualization of the finished film ought to be binding on the director, actors, and technicians.

There is also another value in the writer's use of at least a few technical devices in his script. Although the script is mainly intended to lead towards the creation of the film, it must be read by a great many people, some very knowledgeable in cinematic technique, others less so. In addition to being examined by the cast and crew, the script is read by bankers and financial backers, by lawyers and talent agents and casting agents, by potential distributors, sometimes even by the owners of theaters, and by publishers and journalists, etc. And each of these readers must be given a sense of the finished film, enough detail to imagine, however, vaguely, the style, form, and content of the film itself. Whether or not the details are ever used as they are indicated in a shooting script depends upon many things, but clearly one function of the script writer, though it is secondary, is to produce a readable film script.

The writer writes his first draft screenplay and the drafts and versions that follow with the criticism, encouragement, and, to an increasing degree as he comes closer to the final shooting script, the collaboration of others who will be making the picture.

The *production manager* worries about the budget, tries to eliminate what seem to him unnecessary scenes and characters wherever possible. And he arranges his own *sequence* for the shooting of the picture, a sequence designed to use talent, sets, material, etc., as efficiently as possible. Almost all pictures made these days, anywhere is the world, are shot *out of sequence* because of the enormous expense of making films. The actual sequence of production and shooting thus hardly ever parallels the sequential structure of the script. Major parts, the leads, have the whole script to study and, with the help of the director, can, even out of proper order, build a character. The minor actors with bit parts are frequently given only *sides*, that is, those specific pages of the script which involve them. They are thus much more dependent on the director. Producer, director, actors, production manager, cameraman, editor, art director, set dresser, and even the prop man, these and many more all have legitimate interests and concerns, and they may exert a considerable influence before the final shooting script is ready.

Once the picture goes into production, collaboration is increased both because more people are involved at that stage and because of the necessity of meeting a fairly strict schedule, within the terms of a fixed budget. If the writer continues on the job, working through the period of production, he will make many changes on the spot to fit unforeseen circumstances. If he does not, there will be changes anyway. Like the diagram of a football play, the script, though well-conceived and planned, does not always work out on the ground exactly as anticipated.

Revision and repeated possibilities for revising, changing, and rearranging occur in every stage of the filmmaking process. Everyone involved has to make constant choices. With liberty to choose and change comes an increased responsibility. For often the choices that must be made are not clear-cut, not between good and bad, but, like many political choices, are decisions between imperfect options for the sake of expediency and in hope and faith that results may serve to justify what is finally decided.

Hence, everyone involved in the making of a film, and not least of these the writer, must always allow for the unexpected and for the possibility of change throughout the entire production. Even then, with the production finished and "in the can," the possibilities of change and (sometimes) improvement remain. Many films are slightly revised following their first previews. Some are revised even later, after their initial premiere openings and in response to reviews. One of the most famous of American filmmakers, the late Irving Thalberg (who served as the model for the producer in F. Scott Fitzgerald's last and unfinished novel, *The Last Tycoon*) is frequently quoted as describing the filmmaking process: "Pictures are not made, they are remade."

Sometime after the final shooting script is finished, the picture goes into actual production, following the shooting schedule. There are rehearsal periods (and, usually, subsequent changes) sometimes before the shooting begins, and always on the set during daily shooting. Scene by scene, the material to be shot is rehearsed until the director is ready to photograph the scene. Then, with everything in place, lighting arranged, camera and sound equipment ready to record, there is the *take*. There may be many takes before the director is satisfied and signifies that a particular take is a *print*. As the shooting schedule progresses the director and editor are regularly viewing the prints called *rushes* or *dailies* as they are delivered from the photographic laboratory. Always bearing in mind their aim of assembling the best possible scenes, they study the prints to decide if it is necessary (and possible) to reshoot sequences that seem to have failed.

When the shooting schedule has been completed and most of the cast and crew are gone, then the stage of full-scale editing commences. It is an intense time which, by traditional rule of thumb, is at least equal to the time spent shooting. All the prints must now be assembled into a single form, a sort of rough draft of the film called the *work print* or *rough cut*. Some figures will give an indication of the magnitude of the task facing the editor and the director. The average feature film runs approximately ninety minutes or, in footage, 8,100 feet of film. It is not unusual for the director and editor to have at least 200,000 feet of prints to work with, from which the film must be composed. And it is also common to have on hand another 100,000 feet of film which represent prints put aside in reserve but not yet discarded during the daily viewing of the rushes. These reserve prints are called *bolds*.

Now the director and editor begin the task of composing and arranging all of this material, through constant revision, into the order and form of the rough cut. When the rough cut is ready, the director can for the first time know with some degree of accuracy how long his film, in its present stage, runs. It is not uncommon for a rough cut to be very long indeed, sometimes an hour or even several hours too long for a feature film. When this is the case, a process of cutting back and simplifying begins. In editing, whole scenes from the script can be shortened or, in some cases, ruthlessly eliminated as being, in terms of the context of the entire picture, no longer necessary. Whole scenes and even larger blocks of script material can be easily rearranged. Both sequence and structure are relatively flexible again.

When the director and the producer are satisfied with the work print, more work still remains to be done. Although this custom is changing, the services of the *composer* are called upon at this late stage. He views the work print, studies the script, then writes music for the picture, which is arranged, performed, and recorded. The contribution of music to the total experience of the film can be enormous. From the beginning, even before the advent of sound, when pianos accompanied the silent pictures in theaters, music has been an integral part of the aesthetic experience of movies. The full implications and possibilities of the use of music in support of and conjunction with all the elements of the film are only now being systematically explored and understood. At least it is clear to all that composer and musicians make a really major creative contribution to the totality of a film.

With the music ready and recorded and all the various sound effects (for example, the ringing of a doorbell, traffic noise, a jet passing overhead, train and boat whistles, etc.) on hand, then, music, dialogue and sound effects are *mixed* by a careful and complicated electronic process to become the *sound track*, a permanent part of the *negative* and, thus, of the *composite print* made from it. At that point the film is done, the picture is finished and ready to be previewed and put into release.

From this oversimplified account of the making of a film several basic generalizations can be drawn:

(a) Filmmaking is complex and collaborative to an extent beyond any of our other media or art forms.

(b) The writer has a critical part to play in the collaboration, for he makes what is at once a blueprint for and the raw material of the finished film. But nonetheless his part is only one among many.

(c) The script is only the first tentative draft text of the film. The extent to which it is followed, closely or freely, literally or with much embellishment, depends on many variable factors.

(d) The effect of the finished film as experienced by an audience is simultaneous, a happening in which all the individual parts, done separately and in bits and pieces, come together at once. Only in the film, and to a lesser extent in the shooting script from which it evolved, is this unity possible.

(e) The making of pictures is a process allowing for many stages of revision, for an extraordinary number of choices to be made. Choices, even bad choices, are exercises of reason. Filmmaking becomes, by definition, one of the most rational art forms man has known. The writer shares in this process, and there is a reason for everything in his script. But in the end, since a film must evoke emotional and imaginative responses from the audience, all the reasons of the makers of the film become means to an end, tools to accomplish a task.

Perhaps the finest picture concerned with the process of filmmaking is Fellini's *8½*, in which the protagonist is a gifted director trying to make a picture. Although he fails in his intention, he does succeed in creating the picture we have seen. At the end, the next-to-last scene of the film, the director and his writer sit in a lonely car and the writer, most reasonably, tells him all of the reasons why he has failed. The writer's arguments are irrefutable. Except . . . except precisely at that point a mind reader, a kind of magician who had appeared much earlier in the film, reappears and summons the director to come and do his proper job. The characters from all of the story's episodes reappear at once and, following the instructions of the director, come together hand in hand in a beautiful dance. As they fade out and we are left to confront a dark screen, the truth brightens at the last: out of all the confusion and chaos of this collaborative enterprise, out of all the choices and reasons, good and bad, comes something marvelous, a kind of magic. All the craft of filmmaking conspires to strive towards what Alexander Pope called "a grace beyond the reach of art."

Films are the art form of our tribe, our modern cave paintings. To study the script and to see the film is only the beginning, a preliminary stage in acquiring a finer appreciation of the medium and a greater refinement of taste and judgment. It is fitting and proper to begin where the filmmakers begin, with the script, and to retrace, partly by the evidence and partly by educated surmises, their journey to the final destination of the finished film.

Film Terms in Context

The grammar and syntax of film are not verbal. In the complete cinematic experience words play a part, a very small part, in the form of dialogue. And words are important in the creation of film, beginning with the written script. But when creators, critics, and scholars speak of the *language* of film they are very seldom referring to words. Rather they are speaking of all aspects of cinematic technique as they apply to the making of films and as they are part of the aesthetic experience of the finished film. Though the language of film is essentially nonverbal, a *vocabulary* for film exists to describe the steps taken in the making of films and the effects of films upon appreciative viewers.

The terminology associated with film is complex at its best and esoteric at its worst. It is often confusing to the uninitiated when it is not apparently contradictory. A classic example is the word *montage*. Originally it was the French filmmaker's technical term for the entire process of editing. Great Russian theorists and filmmakers, notably Lev Kuleshov, Vsevolod Pudovkin, and Eisenstein, pioneers of film art, took over the term and changed its meaning. It replaced for them what they had earlier called *the American cut* and was used more strictly to describe both their theory and practice of the art of rapid cutting. (See below for definition of a *cut*.) Because the art and critical theory of these men, and others who followed, have been extremely influential and remain so today, their definitions and classifications of montage are widely used. At the same time, however, American filmmakers incorporated the term montage to describe a very different thing, and their definition is also current and is sometimes called for in scripts. They used the word to describe a series of shots rapidly *dissolving* (see below) over each other. Today the word is used in either sense. Its meaning depends upon context.

The shifting values of montage, both denotative and connotative, are typical of many words in the glossary of film. Context tends to make meaning clear even when there is disagreement about the precise definition. Critics and reviewers, looking at films from the point of view of the effect of the experience of viewing, use their own words and definitions, some of these used exclusively in this critical language. Scholars and specialists in the history of film art are often inclined to use other words, or to use more common words within the limits of special connotation. Makers of films, usually quite aware of both these "dialects," have another vocabulary to describe the technical details of making. They can communicate to each other easily enough, even across the barriers of national language, as witnessed by the fact that in our time international pictures made by multilingual casts and crews are not a novelty. A great many terms in the filmmaker's lexicon are thus more or less meaningless to all those outside of the craft. Fortunately, an appreciative student of film art need not master a very large vocabulary of technical terms at the outset to speak to the basic aspects of scripts or finished films. From an understanding of some of the elementary terms and experience with the things they signify, the student of film can go on to increase his knowledge and refine his understanding through reading the work of outstanding historians, critics, and filmmakers.

In recent years, precisely the years covered by the volumes of *Film Scripts*, it has been the custom of filmmakers to hire writers of all kinds— dramatists, novelists, poets, journalists—to write screenplays. Most of these writers at least begin their association with filmmaking without any previous experience, except for the great, common, shared experience of moviegoing. The days of great production studios, each with its building where a corps of full-time script writers was kept busy, are gone for good. A writer is generally hired to work on one particular project. The common experience of the beginner, frequently described by these writers in interviews and written accounts of their experience, has been doubt at the ability to master the form of the medium, a doubt followed by a sense of surprise and relief that the fundamentals of the vocabulary of filmmaking are not so complex as to demand years of expert experience.

The purpose here is to offer a limited glossary needed for the reading of these scripts and the viewing of the films which came from them. (A full glossary will be found in the back of the book.) Some terms have already been isolated and defined in the preceding section. Others are briefly defined and discussed below.

Those readers who wish to seek out deeper and more inclusive working definitions and examples, will find them in a number of readily accessible books.

(a) *The Filmviewer's Handbook* by Emile G. McAnany, S.J., and Robert Williams, S.J. (Glen Rock, N.J.: Paulist Press, 1965). The chapter entitled "The Language of Film" (pp. 42–69) offers excellent and precise definitions of many terms in a general introduction to the subject.

(b) *A Grammar of the Film* by Raymond Spottiswoode (Berkeley, Calif.: University of California Press, 1965). The chapter "Definitions" (pp. 42–53) offers some useful definitions, though some of his terminology is eccentric when seen beyond the context of this volume.

(c) *A Dictionary of the Cinema* by Peter Graham (New York: A. S. Barnes, 1964). Essentially a brief listing of people in films, this book does offer some definitions of film terms and, notably, some of the special terms used by British and European filmmakers.

(d) *People Who Make Movies* by Theodore Taylor (New York: Doubleday, 1967). Though intended for younger readers, this introduction is exceptionally clear and fine in its coverage of many parts of the filmmaking process. Basic terms, together with examples, are used throughout the text. A brief but accurate glossary is appended.

(e) *Behind the Screen: The History and Techniques of the Motion Picture* by Kenneth MacGowan (New York: Delacorte Press, 1965). This massive compendium of information gives examples and illustrations by a distinguished producer and deals with all aspects of picture-making. Pages 333–501, concerned in depth with technical aspects of filmmaking, present a great many useful terms with full, accurate definitions.

The scene as unit

The opening unit of the script *High Noon,* the first capitalized section, incorporating scenes 1–8 in a descriptive passage, is a useful example. Its format is conventional enough to be called standard.

1–8 EXT. OUTSKIRTS OF HADLEYVILLE–DAY

First, the numbering indicates that eight separate shorter "scenes" are here incorporated into one unit. This device, which is somewhat literary, is designed to make the script more readable at the outset, to set the tone and style before any reader contends with the difficulty of trying to visualize and imagine a large number of separate scenes, 426 in all, many of which are to be very short, individual shots. In the capitalized identification the abbreviation "EXT." establishes that the shooting of the scene is *exterior,* outdoors. The abbreviation "INT." would have established an *interior* location, a setting within some structure. Though this identification may seem so obvious as to be silly to the reader, it serves both a narrative purpose in the script and a technical purpose in making the film. A number of important members of the crew, for example the production manager and the cameraman, not to mention a host of minor functionaries, use this information at a quick glance in their preparation for a scene. Since a film can seldom be shot in the order and sequence of scenes found in the script, the production manager must devise a schedule in which exterior scenes, or nearby parts of them, can be used in a single shooting sequence. At the same time he must be ready not to lose a full day's shooting on account of weather. In the event of rain, for example, he has ready a *backup schedule,* or alternate shooting plan that uses interior sets. These sets must be in order and ready, lighting and sound facilities available, and other members of the cast alert to be called. The script and the schedule also give the cameraman and his crew or *unit* some of the basic information they need to work efficiently. Their equipment for outdoor shooting, the size and composition of the crew, will be different than for interior work.

Because the action of *High Noon* takes place within a small span of time and entirely by daylight, the convention "DAY" is not repeated after the initial heading. In other scripts, however, this traditional direction is frequently used, either regularly with each separate scene, wherever context requires it, or the information is necessary for the crew. Very often scenes supposedly set at night are photographed during the day since the illusion of darkness can be created by the use of appropriate lens and filters as well as by the type and the quality of the film. If the scene must in fact be shot at night, then the proper artificial illumination must be on hand.

Occasionally a more specific direction will be found, such as "DAWN," "TWILIGHT," or "DAY FOR NIGHT," the latter calling explicitly for the daylight shooting of a night scene. These notations tell the cameraman and his unit the kind of light qualities they must capture on film.

The scene

Generally, the breakdown of scenes, headed by the capitalized line and separated by space from other scenes, is determined not only by place, but also by the primary *setup* of the camera and other equipment necessary for shooting. Although all of this equipment cannot easily be displaced in most instances from one setting to another, within a single setting the camera is readily movable. A scene combines, therefore, the physical setting and the primary placement of camera and equipment. In all of the scripts different "scenes" occur from time to time within the larger scene. These separate units, which are part of the same setting and sequence of action, can be used to identify a new and specific setup or to isolate a particular kind of shot.

The filmmaking technique of Alfred Hitchcock is an exception to the rule. Hitchcock prepares, simultaneously with the preparation of the final shooting script, an elaborate and detailed series of sketches (rather like an oversize comic strip) visualizing the film-to-be scene by scene. These sketches are called *continuity sketches.* Script and continuity sketches together, and coordinated as to camera angles and shots, are the material upon which the production of the film is based. Many other directors use continuity sketches as a part of their working strategy, for at least parts of a film, as a guide to the shooting and editing of difficult scenes and transitions. (See "Editorial Terms" below.)

Camera shots

Many kinds of shots are possible, but basically all of them are variations upon a few standards.

Three are defined by proximity of the camera to the subject, whether literally by distance or by use of special lenses. These shots—*long, medium,* and *close*—are only relative and not specific measures. The long shot includes details of an entire setting. Its subject may be on the horizon, for example, a distant ship, the buildings of a city, an expanse of open country, or it may be as close as, say, fifty yards. In order to emphasize great distance, an *extreme long shot* is sometimes called for. A medium shot is of a distance to include, if necessary, a group of two or more people and at least part of the surroundings. A close shot, also called *closeup,* focuses closely on its subject in isolation. It may be of the face or hands of a character or of some single object. Close shots, of course, can be photographed quite separately, even at another time and place, and inserted later in the action of a sequence. For further definition close shots may be *extreme* or *tight* on the one hand or a *medium close shot,* which is indefinite in scope, but nearer at hand than a standard medium shot and at the same time not so tight as the standard closeup.

Two other shots, in which the proximity may vary, are usually included in the five basic shots. They are the *two-shot,* or *group shot* if more than two characters are involved, and the *over-shoulder* shot. The first, at whatever distance, focuses attention on two characters or the group. Sometimes the cameraman is asked in this context to center attention on one of the characters by *featuring* or *favoring*. The over-shoulder shot is, in fact, a variation of the two-shot or group shot; for, in the foreground is the back of the head of one character and in the background we see what the character sees.

Occasionally other kinds of shots are called for, which the context makes clear. For example, a *full shot* does not specify distance, merely that the shot should be fully inclusive of the subject.

In scripts the term *montage* is sometimes used to describe a shot. It then signifies a "series of rapid dissolves," which was mentioned earlier, and involves both cameraman and editor in its creation.

A *stock shot* is a shot or sequence not filmed specifically for the picture but taken from the stock of available footage of any given subject or event. A frequently used stock shot is that of a commercial jet taking off or landing.

A *process shot* is a shot in which actors in the foreground play out a scene in front of a screen that is itself filled with a photograph or movie. The most familiar conventional example occurs in traffic scenes. The characters are photographed in the shell of a stationary automobile while a film of traffic, visible through the rear window, gives the impression of movement and traffic. Process shots may also be used to give the impression of some background or setting far from the studio and set where the actors are being photographed.

Camera angles

In addition to the specific kind of shot sometimes explicitly called for in a script, camera angles may be stated. Just as in the case of shots, these suggestions by the writer will be actually followed by the director and cameraman only insofar as they are deemed valid and functional.

The camera may photograph from certain basic *angles* and, as well, it may shoot from a particular *point of view* (usually abbreviated POV). Point of view need not include the observing character, whose presence on the screen would constitute an over-shoulder shot. A character, for example, looks up; the next shot, made as if to represent what he sees, is of a buzzard in the sky.

Camera angles can be reduced to three principal types: a *regular* or standard angle, unnamed and unspecified since it is assumed to be taken from the camera as set up, straight up and down; a *high angle* (looking from above); and a *low angle* (looking up).

Occasionally the angle is assumed and the direction *shooting up* or *shooting down* is given. The high angle is sometimes simply described as a *high shot*.

Camera and movement

In shooting a camera may be either *fixed* or *moving*.

A fixed camera is set up at one spot. But a fixed camera can nevertheless be used to create a sense of movement or action.

The fixed camera can *tilt*, be moved upward or downward on its single axis while shooting.

And the fixed camera can *pan*. The word is a contraction of the original term used—*panoramic shot*. It is a pivotal movement, usually lateral, made by turning the camera on its axis from one side or part of a scene or setting to another.

Two other customary movements of a fixed camera are the *zoom* and the *whip*.

The zoom is achieved by lens adjustment during photographing so that, without any break, the camera may move (*zoom in*) to a quick closeup of a particular subject.

The whip is a variation on the pan. The camera, focused on one object in a scene, is suddenly and swiftly moved (whipped) to focus upon another subject.

But, since the earliest days, it has not been necessary to depend exclusively upon a fixed camera. The camera may be moved while shooting in what are called *moving* or *running* shots.

One method of moving the camera is by means of a *dolly*. Mounted upon a short set of tracks or a level platform with wheels, the camera can be moved along to follow action, and it can *pull back* from or *come in* on the action. A *crab dolly* is a small platform on wheels designed to move in any direction.

More extensive movement over a larger area than can be accomplished by dollying is achieved by mounting the camera on a platform on a car or truck or other moving vehicle for what are called *trucking* or *tracking* shots. A well-known example of extensive tracking, praised by some critics and censured by others, is to be seen in Olivier's direction of the Battle of Agincourt in *Henry V*.

Still another form of using a mobile camera is by means of the *crane* or *boom*. A small camera platform is set at the end of a long crane, and the crane may be moved up and down or laterally across a set.

Another basic photographic effect, increasingly popular in recent times, is most often described as the use of a *hand-held* camera. The term is most accurately used to differentiate the filmic qualities obtained by a small camera held in the hands while shooting from those created by a standard studio camera which is balanced, level, and set on its tripod, a dolly, or platform. Ironically, the results of the hand-held camera, rather like that of home movies, can be duplicated by more conventional (and more expensive) camera setups. Combined by laboratory work with grainy prints of high or low key, the camera work appears to be less smooth and even in the recording of subjects and action. What is deliberately achieved is a certain urgent and amateurish quality, associated in the minds of the contemporary audience with the verisimilitude of newsreels and documentaries and, as well, with the art films of certain prominent European directors in the immediate postwar years, the *réalismo* of Roberto Rossellini and Vittorio De Sica, for example. The effects of the hand-held camera seem more "realistic" however they are manufactured, and call attention to the cameraman's struggle and the immediacy of his work. Because of the artifice of film techniques, however, these effects may in fact be as "artificial" as those usually associated with only the highest standards of cinematography.

Editorial terms

The process of editing, which has already been mentioned, is highly technical and requires specialized study and experience. Some basic editorial techniques should, however, be understood by any student of film. One of these is the method of *transition* from one unit of film or larger sequence to another. Although the screenwriter must concern himself to some extent with the transitions, his part is marginal and limited to suggestions. For the editing of a film is exclusively the director's concern and that of his editor, or *cutter* as he is usually called by filmmakers.

There are essentially three kinds of transitions, with variations and, in some cases, different ways of accomplishing the same effect. The three forms of transition are the *cut*, the *dissolve*, and the *fade*.

The cut is, quite simply, a break or cut in the film. A sequence of images photographed from the same setup and angle is literally cut off, then spliced to another sequence. Cutting is, inevitably, continuous in a film, so frequent a pattern that we seldom notice it—unless it is the intention of the editor and the director that we should. The use of the word cut is somewhat confused by a number of other definitions of the term. For example, a cut may be used to describe a single strip of film. Many filmmakers call shots cuts, as in "Let's have a cut of the charging Indians here." And cut may mean *take out* or *add to*.

Professionals have no difficulty with this burden of possible meaning because context makes the particular case clear. But in terms of transitions, some examples may be in order. One of the most frequent cuts occurs when a character in an exterior setting starts to open a door to go into an unseen interior. We see him turn the handle of the door and start inside. The next shot will likely be a *reverse*, taken from within the interior set. The door is opening and he is coming in. Another common example of the conventional direct cut is frequently found when two characters are in conversation. At the outset we may see them both together in a two-shot. Then we cut back and forth from their separate faces as they speak to each other and react.

For the most part we do not consciously notice simple cuts. We imaginatively supply the missing connections and, so long as we are engaged in the viewing of the film, the action may seem smooth and continuous. Part of our reaction comes from experience and the habit of response; for the fundamentals of cutting have remained much the same since the days of D. W. Griffith. In *Birth of a Nation* he effectively used five-second shots, cut and joined together, in many places to establish a pattern for future editing.

Equally conventional is the use of the cut for a special effect in unexpected circumstances. An excellent example of the cut, used for humor, occurs in the fine Italian comedy *Big Deal on Madonna Street* (1959). Vittorio Gassman, arrested and awaiting trial, confidently reassures his weeping girl friend that he has an excellent lawyer and that the prosecution has no case against him. Nothing to worry about. From his smiling self-assurance there is a *direct cut* to a line of convicts, Gassman among them, marching doubletime around the yard of a penitentiary.

A *dissolve* or *lap dissolve* is a different sort of transition, sometimes called a *special effect* because it involves laboratory work. It is a process of superimposition by which one image gradually vanishes to be simultaneously replaced by another image without any perceptible fading of the light. The result is often a graceful sort of transition, traditionally used to indicate shifts of time and place without appearing to break the continuity of the film.

A variation on the dissolve is the *swish-pan*, a very swift dissolve which seems to be the result of camera movement, but is in fact a laboratory process.

A fade, used within the film as a transition, begins as a *fade out*. Both light and images fade into darkness and the screen goes (briefly) black. Following that a new image slowly *fades in*. Traditionally a fade acts as a definite break in the action of a film, somewhat analogous to the use of the curtain in the proscenium theater. It is also traditional to begin a script with the direction "Fade In" and to end it with "Fade Out."

There are a number of variations which can be used in lieu of a dissolve or fade. One is the *wipe*, in which the scene we are watching appears literally to be wiped away or erased from the screen, horizontally, vertically, or diagonally.

The *flip* is an effect in which a frame of film and its images appear to be flipped over like a card, either horizontally or vertically, to be replaced by another frame of images.

One of the oldest means of transition in the history of filmmaking, once widely used before the fade was possible, but still in use today, is the *iris*. As in fades, we *iris out* or *iris in*. The effect of irising out may occur in one of two ways. Either, within the frame, black seems to come from all sides diminishing the area of the image seen so that the image itself appears to recede or dwindle until it vanishes; or a single spot of black in the frame may appear to grow larger, going outward in all directions until the entire frame is dark. To iris in is to reverse the process.

The extent to which any of these editorial devices of transition—or, for that matter, the full variety of camera shots and angles—is employed depends, of course, on such things as current cinematic fashion and the nature and treatment of the subject of a script and a film. It also depends in large part upon the taste and aesthetic predilections of the director. On the one hand is Richard Lester, who opened up a full, rich bag of tricks, and most appropriately, to enliven *A Hard Day's Night*, whose shooting script gives very little indication of the style of the finished film. On the other hand is Billy Wilder; his scripts for *Some Like It Hot* (1959) and *The Apartment* (1960) are almost equally bare of explicit or suggested directions to cameraman or editor. Although Wilder is no stranger to the use of tricks, witness his *Sunset Boulevard* (1950), he has long been outspoken against depending too much on techniques to do the work of actors and directors. Kenneth MacGowan quotes him as saying: "If the scene is well directed from the point of view of its feelings, the camera can be set down, forgotten, and allowed to record." Wilder is, as ever, more careful than he seems at first glance. While he proposes limitations on the camera as writer-director, Wilder does not place limits upon the techniques of the editor.

Sound

Though sound as a part of motion pictures was technically possible much earlier, it did not become commercially feasible until the mid-1920s, and silent films continued to thrive until 1930. With the advent of sound as an integral part of the film art, this element became a part of the editor's general responsibility. In preparing the sound track, he has a number of technicians to help him. A *sound crew*, which works during the shooting of the picture, usually consists of a *mixer*, a *recordist*, and a *sound boom man*. Once the editing process begins a *sound effects editor* and a *music editor* are usually on hand in addition to a number of mixers who work on the final synchronization of all sounds and images in creating the composite print.

For a beginning, the editor has at his disposal the sound crew's original recordings taken during shooting. When synchronized with the rough cuts these recordings comprise the *wild track*. Where dialogue needs correction and better quality, which is often the case, the actors redo their lines in a controlled sound studio where *off-screen* or *voice over* dialogue is also added. This process of recording in synchronization with the film is called *dubbing* or *looping*. The opposite procedure, the deletion of sound effects or unwanted noises, is called *dialing out*.

The technical resources and possibilities of filmmaking, as even this brief glossary makes clear, are enormous. The greatest problem facing all of a film's creators is to choose among all of the possibilities the most efficient and most suitable means. The director, aided and advised by other artists, bears final responsibility for the choices made.

The writer's special responsibility is to create a script which, whatever its format, speaks to the needs of all the cast and crew, points directions by suggestion, and yet leaves each artist and technician free to create within the framework of his own competence. Within this context the technical terms of filmmaking should be understood. The value in application can be measured only by close viewing of films.

A Note on the Text of These Scripts

In preparing *Film Scripts* for publication, the editors have tried to present, as closely as is reasonable and possible, the version of each script acquired in the form in which it originally came to them. Because no two are precisely the same in all details, the special characteristics of each are mentioned in the appropriate headnote.

All of the American scripts included here are final shooting scripts. Some were more "finished" and "clean" than others; some contained pencilled revisions, made on the spot during the process of making.

In order to facilitate comparative study of word and image, the following conventions have been observed in reproducing facsimile versions of the scripts:

Deletions (of a passage, line, speech, direction, etc.) are indicated by asterisks plus any end punctuation.

New passages are underlined with dashes. Where there was a deletion involved this is likewise indicated by asterisks.

Deleted material is given in the form of annotation at the foot of the page. Large brackets have been placed around each continuous deletion. Small brackets are used to indicate changes in material that was later discarded.

The purpose here is not to provide a description or analysis of bibliographical changes; for the true bibliography of a film would chiefly be concerned with the text of the film—the master film and the prints made from it. But since revisions, even of the final shooting script, are parts of the process of making a film, these changes are indicated where evidence of them in the script was decipherable.

The most important revisions and changes, however, are manifest in the difference between the script and the finished film. The reader, who should also be a viewer, may wish to keep his own notes, perhaps in the margin of the text, on the basis of his own seeing of the film. This anthology can thus lead the reader/viewer to a better and more detailed understanding of the process of filmmaking. For, by having the script in handy and readable form, he not only has points of reference for testing his own memory of a screening but also, at least in a number of cases, a base line for questioning the possible function and purpose of some of the filmmaker's visions and revisions.

HENRY V

1944—A Two Cities Film; released
in the United States by United Artists
Director Laurence Olivier
Script Laurence Olivier and Reginald Beck
Source Shakespeare's *Henry V*
Stars Laurence Olivier, Renee Anderson, Robert Newton

Henry V was written by Shakespeare in 1599 to celebrate the English spirit as embodied in the near-legendary English king who, after a miraculous conversion from madcap and prodigal, became conqueror of France and idol of his subjects. The play, although unabashedly patriotic, reveals perhaps a few hints of criticism by Shakespeare in such details as Henry's motive for beginning the war in France, his treatment of French prisoners after Agincourt, and his uneasy knowledge that his claim to the English throne is tainted. The action is epic, so much so that it overflows the limits of the Elizabethan stage. Shakespeare's Chorus apologizes for this in the opening speech of the play:

> O for a Muse of fire, that would ascend
> The brightest heaven of invention,
> A kingdom for a stage, princes to act
> And monarchs to behold the swelling scene!
> Then should the warlike Harry, like himself,
> Assume the port of Mars; and at his heels,
> Leash'd in like hounds, should famine, sword, and fire
> Crouch for employment. But pardon, gentles, all,
> The flat unraised spirits that hath dar'd
> On this unworthy scaffold to bring forth
> So great an object. Can this cockpit hold
> The vasty fields of France? Or may we cram
> Within this wooden O the very casques

That did affright the air at Agincourt?
O pardon! since a crooked figure may
Attest in little place a million;
And let us, ciphers to this great accompt,
On your imaginary forces work.

The play does strain the resources of the theater. This very characteristic makes it ideally suited for film.

Both the patriotism and epic sweep of the action made *Henry V* a natural choice for Olivier. Filmed during the Second World War, after England had suffered through her "finest hour," the production faced severe economic shortages. Only a patriotic film, useful for propaganda both at home and abroad, could justify the choice of technicolor and the lavish use of talent, time, and money evident in *Henry V*. Dedicated to "The Men of the Royal Air Force," the film was explicitly intended as a contribution to the war effort. As such, it is one of the most brilliant propaganda films ever made.

Because the original motive for Shakespeare's play and for the film version of it are closely parallel, Olivier's chief contribution to the script was to cut the play's dialogue to the length of the average movie. The result is one of the best—some would say the best—film adaptations of Shakespeare, an adaptation that has continued to delight spectators long after World War II has become history. The filming of the Battle of Agincourt is a piece of pure visual poetry. The settings for the French court, modeled on late medieval miniatures such as those found in the *Book of Hours* of the Duc de Berri, are exquisitely stylized without being coy or quaint. The introductory scenes in the Globe theater, besides enhancing the film's educational value, provide an unorthodox but highly successful technique for awakening the spectator's imagination gradually to the magic of the later scenes.

To their credit, most reviewers of the film recognized its excellence immediately. Perhaps the most interesting comment was made by P. Mosdell in the *Canadian Forum* of October, 1946. While praising Olivier's success, Mosdell wrote, "*Henry V* is not particularly significant in the history of cinema." Sergei Eisenstein's *Alexander Nevsky*, Mosdell felt, was cinema from beginning to end, superbly done; while *Henry V* was a film of a play. The comparison with Eisenstein's masterpiece, also an epic film which celebrates another national spirit, is unquestionably apt. It raises the question of whether Shakespeare's plays can be transferred to film without such extensive revision that the movie becomes an original production. For the British, the answer has been an emphatic yes, as proved by Olivier's *Hamlet* (1948) and *Richard III* (1955) and by the films made during the sixties by Peter Brook and the Royal Shakespeare Company of London.

On the other hand, the answer of directors like Franco Zeffirelli is largely no in his *The Taming of the Shrew* (1967) and the far more successful *Romeo and Juliet* (1968). Depending on lyrical use of the camera for effects that Shakespeare achieved through speech, Zeffirelli preserves Shakespeare's plot but ruthlessly eliminates his dialogue. Whatever the ultimate answer to the question, American reviewers were unanimous in their praise. In a review titled "Miracle" published in the *New Yorker* (June 22, 1946), John McCarten prophesied correctly that Olivier would be the dominant figure in the postwar movement to transfer Shakespeare to the screen.

The Script The script is a continuity or release script. It describes the film as it has been completed in contrast to a shooting script, which precedes the making of the film. No revisions are evident since all changes were made before the continuity was written. Several abbreviations are used. LS, CS, MLS, and MCS stand for long, close, medium long, and middle close shot. L and R stand for left and right stage. CU and MCU stand for closeup and middle closeup, and bg and fg mean background and foreground. Note the technique of incorporating credits in the script proper and the fact that the instructions for sound are kept on the right, while dialogue and camera instructions are on the left. Two items, frame numbers and the footage of each frame, have been deleted.

Credits See script, *pp. 40–41, 135–36.*

Awards Henry V was seventh on the 1946 "Ten Best Pictures" list compiled by *Film Daily,* and the New York Film Critics' Poll cited Olivier for the best male performance of the year.

FADE IN: -- CENSOR TITLE.

FADE IN: -- EAGLE LION PRESENTS   FADE OUT:
                                                  BELLS
                                                  DISSOLVE TO:

                    A TWO CITIES FILM
                     In Technicolour

                  Made at D. & P. Studios

Recorded on   Colour Director Natalie Kalmus
Western Electric
Mirrophonic   Associate Joan Bridge.
Sound system.
                                                  FADE OUT.
                                                  BELLS STOP.

FADE IN.

                 To the Commandoes and Airborne Troops of
                           Great Britain.

The spirit of whose ancestors it has been humbly attempted to recapture
in some ensuing scenes this film is dedicated.

                                                  FADE OUT.

FADE IN -- TITLE   MUSIC STARTS.

                 A LAURENCE OLIVIER PRODUCTION.

                                                  DISSOLVE TO:

TITLE 2.

                 A paper bill fluttering towards camera out
                 of the sky. It hits the camera and reads: --

                    The Chronicle History of

                    KING HENRY THE FIFTH

              with his battle fought at Agincourt in France

                              by

                       Will Shakespeare

                      will be played by

The Lord Chamberlain's Men

at the

GLOBE PLAYHOUSE

THIS DAY THE FIRST OF MAY 1600.

DISSOLVE TO:

L.S. Aerial View of London in 1600. CAMERA TRACKS BACK to reveal the
City in extreme L.S. then TRACKS in to centre first the Bear Playhouse
and then the Globe Playhouse. A flag is being hoisted up the Standard
of this Playhouse.

C.S. The Globe Playhouse Flag unfurling and fluttering.

MUSIC STOPS.

M.C.S. Man in Globe Playhouse on small platform at foot of flagpole.
He tightens the flag rope and makes it secure. He blows two fanfares.
CAMERA TRACKS DOWN TO Orchestra Gallery below him.

ORCHESTRA STARTS TO PLAY.

CAMERA PANS LEFT to show people filling the top gallery of theatre.
CAMERA continues panning round and down to the second gallery. A girl
drops a handkerchief out of picture.

M.L.S. THE THIRD GALLERY. A man catches the handkerchief. CAMERA PANS
LEFT to the ground floor entrance where the people are coming in. An
orange Seller steps down into the theatre.

M.S. The Orange Girl walking into the Theatre offering her wares,
CAMERA PANS LEFT with her and TRACKS SLOWLY BACK to reveal the auditorium in L.S. with the stage in background. A prompter gives a signal
to the Orchestra to play a fanfare.

MUSIC STOPS.

M.L.S. Low angle shot the Orchestra Gallery. Man blows a FANFARE.

L.S. AUDITORIUM WITH STAGE IN B.G. A boy comes through the curtains on
to the stage and holds a board up to the audience.

M.C.S. SIDE ANGLE OF THE BOY. He swings the board to camera on which
is written --

The Chronicle History of
HENRY THE FIFTH
with his battle fought at Agin Court.

L. HIGH ANGLE SHOT FROM THE TOP GALLERY. Audience in f.g. The boy on
the stage swings the board and exits through the curtains. Chorus enters and bows. Audience applauds.

CHORUS: O for a Muse of fire

M.C.S. Chorus.

                              That would ascend
            The brightest heaven of invention:

He walks R. CAMERA PANS with him.

            A kingdom for a stage, princes to act,
            And monarchs to behold the swelling scene!

He walks L. CAMERA PANS with him.

            Then should the warlike Harry, like himself,
            Assume the port of Mars, and at his heels
            Leash'd in like hounds, should famine, sword and fire,
            Crouch for employment.

He walks R. to the centre of the stage CAMERA PANS with him.

                    But pardon, gentles all,
            The flat unraised spirits, that hath dared,
            On this unworthy scaffold to bring forth
            So great an object.
            Can this cockpit hold
            The vasty fields of France? or may we cram
            Within this wooden O the very casques
            That did affright the air at Agincourt?

He walks to camera speaking directly to it in C.U.

            On your imaginary forces work.

                              MUSIC STARTS.

CAMERA TRACKS BACK.

            Suppose within the girdle of these walls
            Are now confin'd two mighty monarchies

Whose high, upreared, and abutting fronts
The perilous narrow ocean parts asunder.
Piece out our imperfections with your thoughts;
Think, when we talk of horses, that you see them,
Printing their proud hoofs i' the receiving earth
For 'tis your thoughts that now must deck our kings,

CAMERA TRACKS BACK TO leave Chorus and Stage In M.L.S.

Carry them here and there; jumping o'er times;
Turning the accomplishment of many years
Into an hour-glass:

MUSIC STOPS

for the which supply
Admit me Chorus to this history:
Who, prologue-like, your humble patience pray,
Gently to hear, kindly to judge our play.

He bows and pulls the Stage Curtain aside.

MUSIC STARTS.

A boy with a board steps forward and shows this board to the audience.

M.C.S. The boy with the board on which reads: --

Ante chamber in King Henry's Palace.

CAMERA TRACKS UP to Stage Balcony above him. Through curtains at the back the Archbishop of Canterbury and the Bishop of Ely enter and bow.

AUDIENCE APPLAUDS

Canterbury sits down at the table and studies a paper. He bangs his fist.

MUSIC STOPS.

CANTERBURY: My lord, I'll tell you, that same bill is urg'd,
Which in the eleventh year of the last king's reign
Was likely to have been against us pass'd,
But that the scambling and unquiet time
Did push it out of further question.

ELY: But how, my lord, shall we resist it now?

CANTERBURY: It must be thought on; if it pass against us,
We lose the better half of our possession:

CANTERBURY (Cont'd)
>For all those temporal lands, which men devout
>By testament have given to the church,
>Would they strip from us: Thus runs the bill.

ELY: This would drink deep.

                                    AUDIENCE LAUGHS.

CANTERBURY: 'Twould drink the cup and all.

                                    AUDIENCE LAUGHS.

ELY: But what prevention?

CANTERBURY: The king is full of grace, and fair regard.

ELY: And a true lover of the holy church.

CANTERBURY: The courses of his youth promis'd it not.
>Since his addiction was to courses vain,
>His companies unletter'd, rude and shallow,
>His hours fill'd up with riots, banquets, sports,
>And never noted in him any study.

ELY: And so the Prince obscur'd his contemplation
>Under the veil of wildness, which grew
>No doubt like the summer grass, fastest by night.

                                    AUDIENCE LAUGHS.

CANTERBURY: The breath no sooner left his father's body,
>But that his wildness, mortified in him,
>Seem'd to die too; Sir John Falstaff

                                    AUDIENCE CHEERS.

L.S. High Angle Shot of Audience cheering.

CANTERBURY: (off)
>   . . . and all
>His company along with him

M.S. CANTERBURY and ELY.

CANTERBURY: . . . he banished,

L.S. High angle shot of Audience.

AUDIENCE GROANS.

M.S. Canterbury and Ely.

CANTERBURY: (contd).
Under pain of death not to come near his person,

L.S. High angle shot of Audience.

AUDIENCE BOOES.

CANTERBURY: (off) By ten mile;

M.C.S. CANTERBURY. He stands up.

CANTERBURY: Yea, at the very moment,
Consideration like an angel came,
And whipp'd the offending Adam out of him;
Never was such a sudden scholar made;
Never came reformation in a flood,
As in this king.

M.C.S. ELY.

ELY: We are blessed in the change.

AUDIENCE JEERS.

ELY walks L. and joins Canterbury. CAMERA PANS WITH HIM.

ELY: But, my good lord;
How now for mitigation of this bill
Urg'd by the commons? Doth his majesty
Incline to it, or no?

They sit down.

CANTERBURY: He seems indifferent;
Or rather swaying more upon our part.
For I have made an offer to his majesty,
As touching France, to give a greater sum
Than ever at one time the clergy yet
Did to his predecessors part withal.

ELY: How did this offer seem receiv'd, my lord?

CANTERBURY: Of good acceptance of his majesty;
Save that there was not time enough to hear,

CANTERBURY (Cont'd)
        As I perceive his grace would fain have done,
        Of his true titles to some certain dukedoms,
        And generally to the crown and seat of France,
        Deriv'd from Edward, his great grandfather.

ELY: What was the impediment that broke this off?

CANTERBURY: The French ambassador upon that instant
        Crav'd audience;

                            AUDIENCE CHUCKLES.

CANTERBURY looks pointedly L. of screen.

        . . . and I think the hour is come
        To give him hearing, is it four o'clock?

M.S. THE PROMPTER'S CORNER.
The prompter gets up from his chair and peers through a grille in the
door at the side of the stage.

          BELL RINGS THREE TIMES THEN A FOURTH.

M.S. CANTERBURY and ELY on the balcony.

ELY: It is.

CANTERBURY rises from his chair.

CANTERBURY: Then we go in, to know his embassy:
        Which I could with a ready guess declare,
        Before the Frenchman speak a word of it.

He goes out.   MUSIC STARTS.

ELY: I'll wait upon you, and I long to hear it.

                          AUDIENCE TITTERS.

ELY gathers up their documents and follows Canterbury.

C.U. THE STAIRS FROM THE BALCONY BACKSTAGE. CANTERBURY and ELY come
down the stairs. CAMERA TRACKS BACK to reveal the actors getting ready
for their entrances. A boy crosses to a fellow youngster to try on a
wig.

M.C.U. The two boys try out their headgear, one of whom has been shaving prior to playing Mistress Quickly.

M.S. BACKSTAGE.
English herald and four soldiers take up positions for stage entrance
          FANFARE.

They exit and actors playing the Earls of Salisbury and Westmoreland exit right.   FANFARE.

They are followed by Exeter and Gloucester. The actor playing King Henry V. enters left in C.U.
          MUSIC STOPS.
He coughs.
          MUSIC STARTS.
CAMERA PANS with him as he goes through door on to stage. Audience visible in b.g.
          AUDIENCE APPLAUDS.
Henry bows to audience.
          MUSIC STOPS.

HENRY: Where is my gracious Lord of Canterbury?

EXETER enters left.

EXETER: Not here in presence.

HENRY: Send for him, good uncle.

HENRY exits left and EXETER signals HERALD to fetch the Archbishops. Herald walks up to camera.

C.U. BACKSTAGE.
Ely is robing for his entrance. He drinks beer with a fellow-actor.

WESTMORELAND: Shall we call in the ambassador, my liege?

C.U. Herald signals to Henry:
Ely to get ready to enter stage.

HENRY: Not yet, my cousin; we would be resolv'd,
      Before we hear him, of some things of weight
      That task our thoughts, concerning us and France.

M.S. BACKSTAGE.
Canterbury comes up and ushers Ely into position.
Canterbury exits right CAMERA PANNING with him.
Ely follows.

M.S. THE FRONT OF THE STAGE.
Canterbury enters his hand raised in blessing. CAMERA PANS WITH HIM to
reveal stage in L.S. Henry is seated on his throne surrounded by his
court. He bows to Canterbury.

CANTERBURY: God and his angels guard your sacred throne
                And make you long become it!

HENRY: Sure we thank you.

Ely enters in a flurry and Henry acknowledges him.
                                        AUDIENCE LAUGHS.

HENRY: Sure, we thank you.
                My learned lord, we pray you to proceed
                And justly and religiously unfold
                Why the law Salique, that they have in France,
                Or should or should not bar us in our claims.

M.C.S. Henry rises from his throne and steps down from it. CAMERA
TRACKS BACK with him.

HENRY: We charge you in the name of God take heed
                How you awake the sleeping sword of war:
                For never two such kingdoms did contend
                Without much fall of blood, whose guiltless drops
                Do make such waste in brief mortality.

CANTERBURY: Then hear me, gracious sovereign, and you peers,
                That owe your lives, your faith, and services
                To this imperial throne. There is no bar
                To make against your highness' claim to France.
                But this, which they produce from Pharamond.

Canterbury takes a document from Ely and quotes . . .

CANTERBURY: 'In terram Salicam mulieres ne succedant':
                'No woman shall succeed in Salique land!'
                Which Salique land the French unjustly glose
                To be the realm of France.
                Yet their own authors fully affirm
                That the land Salique lies in Germany,
                Between the floods of Sala and of Elve:

Ely hands him another document. CAMERA PANS with Canterbury as he
walks to the left.

CANTERBURY: Where Charles the Great having subdued the Saxons,
                    There left behind and settled certain French;
                    Who, holding in disdain the German women
                    For some dishonest manners of their life,
                    Establish'd there this law;

                                    AUDIENCE TITTERS.

He turns and walks back to centre stage. CAMERA PANS with him. He
continues walking to the right to stop at the edge of the stage.

CANTERBURY: To wit, no female
                  Should be inheritrix in Salique land:
                  Which in this day in Germany called Meisen
                  Then doth it well appear, the Salique law
                  Was not devised for the realm of France
                  Nor did the French possess the Salique land,
                  Until Four hundred one and twenty years
                  After defunction of . . .

He looks at his document and signals Ely to bring another.

M.C.S. Ely hands another document to Canterbury. CAMERA PANS left to
right with him.
                                AUDIENCE TITTERS.

CANTERBURY: . . . King Pharamond
                  Idly suppos'd the founder of this law,
                  King Pepin, which depos'd Childeric,
                  Did as heir general, being descended of Blithild,

Canterbury hands the paper back to Ely. He slaps Ely's hand as another
document is proffered. CAMERA PANS right to left with Canterbury. He
has to return to Ely for the paper and snatches it from him and Ely
throws the remainder in the air.
                                AUDIENCE TITTERS.

C.U. Canterbury finds documents are falling about his ears . . .

CANTERBURY: Which was daughter to . . .
                                AUDIENCE LAUGHS.

M.C.S. Ely points to the papers on the floor. CAMERA PANS down to
papers and Canterbury's hand comes into picture.

M.S. Canterbury picks up the paper. Henry is beside him, and tries to
interrupt. Canterbury turns left and the CAMERA PANS with him and back
again as he walks right, back to the king.

CANTERBURY: . . . King Clothair,
                Make claim and title to the crown of France.
                Hugh Capet also, who usurp'd the crown
                . . . Charles the duke of Lorraine, sole heir male
                Of the true line and stock of . . .

Canterbury holds out his hand for another paper.

                                        AUDIENCE TITTERS.

M.C.S. Ely points to the floor.

                                        AUDIENCE LAUGHS.

C.U. Canterbury's hand comes into picture, but his wrist is seized by
Henry, who picks up the next paper. CAMERA PANS up to two-shot of
them.

CANTERBURY: . . . . Charles the Great,
                Could not keep quiet in his conscience,
                Wearing the crown of France, till satisfied
                That fair . . .

M.C.S. Ely looks for the paper.

                . . . that fair

                                        AUDIENCE LAUGHS.

L.S. Audience laughing.

                . . . that fair

M.S. Exeter, Canterbury and Henry kneeling on the floor. Ely is standing beside Exeter, Canterbury has found the paper. Ely finds him another. Henry and Exeter get to their feet.

CANTERBURY: . . . Queen Isabel, his grandmother,
                Was lineal of the . . . the Lady Ermengare,
                Daughter to Charles the foresaid duke of Lorraine:
                So that, as clear as is the summer's sun

                                        AUDIENCE LAUGHS.

                . . . all appear
                To hold in right and title of the female:
                So do the kings of France unto this day.

CANTERBURY (Cont'd)
>Howbeit, they would hold up this Salique law
>To bar your highness claiming from the female.

Henry and Exeter help Canterbury to his feet. CAMERA TRACKS into M.C.S.
as Henry interrupts Canterbury.

HENRY: May I with right and conscience make this claim?

CANTERBURY: The sin upon my head, dread sovereign!

Ely holds up a Bible for Canterbury.

>For in the book of Numbers it is writ,
>When the son died, let the inheritance
>Descend unto the daughter.

EXETER: (off) Gracious Lord, stand for your own.

C.U. Exeter.

EXETER: Look back into your mighty ancestors:
>Go, my dread lord, to your great-grandsire's tomb,
>From whom you claim; invoke his warlike spirit
>And your great-uncle's, Edward . . .

C.U. Henry.

EXETER: (off) . . . the Black Prince.

SALISBURY: (off) Your brother kings and monarchs of . . .

M.C.S. Salisbury and Westmoreland. CAMERA PANS with Salisbury as he
walks to the left.

>. . . the earth
>Do all expect that you should rouse yourself
>As did the former lions of your blood.

Westmoreland walks up to camera.

WESTMORELAND: They know your grace hath cause and means, and might;
>So hath your highness, and more loyal subjects,
>Whose hearts have left their bodies here in England,
>And lie pavilion'd in the fields of France.

A hand taps him on the shoulder. CAMERA PANS left to reveal Canterbury.

CANTERBURY: O let their bodies follow my dear liege
              With blood and sword and fire, to win your right;
              In aid whereof . . .

CAMERA PANS as Ely joins Canterbury.

CANTERBURY: . . . we of the spirituality
              Will raise your highness such a mighty sum
              As never did the clergy at one time
              Bring in to any of your ancestors.

C.U. Henry.

HENRY: Call in the messengers sent from the Dauphin.
                                                  FANFARE.

L.S. Canterbury and Ely stand aside as Henry walks to the throne.

HENRY: Now we are well resolv'd and, by God's help,
              And yours, the noble sinews of our power,
              France being ours, we'll bend it to our awe,
              Or lay these bones in an unworthy urn,
              Tombless, with no remembrance over them.
                                                  FANFARE.

M.C.S. English Herald, French Herald enter through door at side of
stage, followed by the French Ambassador, the Duke of Berri and two
pages carrying a casket. CAMERA TRACKS back to reveal the stage in
long shot.

HENRY: Now are we well prepar'd to know the pleasure
              Of our fair cousin Dauphin; for we hear
              Your greetings is from him, not from the king.

MONTJOY: May't please your majesty to give us leave
              Freely to render what we have in charge
              Or shall we sparingly show you far off
              The Dauphin's meaning, and our embassy?

HENRY: We are no tyrant, but a Christian king,
              Therefore with frank and with uncurbed plainness
              Tell us the Dauphin's mind.

The French Ambassador bows.

AMBASSADOR: Thus then in few;

M.C.S. French Ambassador.

AMBASSADOR: . . . Your highness, lately sending into France,
Did claim some certain dukedoms, in the right
Of your great predecessor, King Edward the third.
In answer of which claim, the prince our master
Says that you savour too much of your youth,
He therefore send you fitter for your study.
This tun of treasure;

The two pages carry the casket round to the front of the throne.
CAMERA PANS LEFT with them.

AMBASSADOR: . . . and, in lieu of this,
Desires you let the dukedoms that you claim
Hear no more of you. This the Dauphin speaks.

Henry leans over to Exeter on his left.

HENRY: What treasure, uncle?

Exeter opens the casket and closes it quickly.

EXETER: Tennis balls, my liege.

                   AUDIENCE GIGGLES.

C.U. Henry seated on his throne.

HENRY: We are glad the Dauphin is so pleasant with us,
His present, and your pains, we thank you for;

CAMERA TRACKS back and Henry springs to his feet.

        When we have match'd our rackets to these balls,
We will, in France, by God's grace, play a set
Shall strike his father's crown into the hazard.
Tell him, he hath made a match with such a wrangler
That all the courts of France will be disturb'd
With chases.

Henry steps down from the throne and walks camera right in M.S. CAMERA
PANS with him.

        And we understand him well,
Now he comes o'er us with our wilder days,
Not measuring what use we made of them,
But tell the Dauphin we will keep our stage.
Be like a king, and show our sail of greatness,
When we do rouse us in our throne of France:

He turns and walks back to centre stage. CAMERA PANS with him.

> And tell the pleasant Prince, this mock of his
> Hath turned these halls to gun-stones and his soul
> Shall stand sore-charged, for the wasteful vengeance
> That shall fly with them: for many a thousand widows.

He walks camera left. CAMERA PANS with him.

> Shall this his mock out of their dear husbands:
> Mock mothers from their sons, mock castles down:
> Ay some are yet ungotten and unborn
> That shall have cause to curse the Dauphin's scorn.

He turns and walks camera right to stage centre and back to his throne, turning to camera when he reaches it. CAMERA PANS with him and TRACKS BACK to L.S.

> But this lies all within the will of God,
> To whom we do appeal, and in whose name
> Tell you the Dauphin, we are coming on . . .
> To venge us as we may, and to put forth
> Our rightful hand in well hallow'd cause.
> So get you hence in peace;
>   . . . and tell the Dauphin
> His jest will savour but of shallow wit,
> When thousands weep more than did laugh at it.
> Convey them with safe conduct. Fare you well.

> AUDIENCE APPLAUDS.

Henry bows to the applause as French Ambassador and Heralds exit on the right. Henry goes to sit down on his throne.

M.C.S. Henry sits down on his throne, Exeter standing on the left.

EXETER: This was a merry message.

Henry rises and takes off his crown. He walks camera left. CAMERA PANS with him. He stops in front of stage exit door.

HENRY: We hope to make the sender blush at it.
               Therefore, let our proportions for those wars
               Be soon collected and all things thought upon
               That may with reasonable swiftness add
               More feathers to our wings: for, God before,
               We'll check this Dauphin at his father's door.

Henry bows and goes out through the door

             MUSIC STARTS.
             AUDIENCE APPLAUDS.

M.S. Chorus comes through the other door and draws the curtain across
the inner stage. CAMERA PANS left to right with him. He turns and
walks up to camera; CAMERA PANS right to left with him. He throws
open his arms as he starts speaking.

            MUSIC AND APPLAUSE STOP

CHORUS: Now all the youth of England are on fire,
       And silken dalliance in the wardrobe lies;
       Now thrive the armourers, and honour's thought
       Reigns solely in the breast of every man:
       They sell the pasture now, to buy the horse,
       Following the mirror of all Christian kings,
       With winged heels, as English Mercuries,

Chorus throws up his hands and starts to walk away from camera. CAMERA
PANS left with him until he stands in L.S. He throws up his hands
again.

       For now sits Expectation in the air,
       And hides a sword, from hilts, unto the points,
       With crowns imperial, crowns and coronets,
       Promised to Harry, and his followers.
       Linger your patience on, for, if we may,
       We'll not offend one stomach with our play.

            AUDIENCE APPLAUDS.

He bows and goes out through the door behind him. Two stage hands
enter with bundles of rough grass. They look skywards.

            ROLL OF THUNDER.

L.S. Clouds covering the sun.

L.S. HIGH ANGLE SHOT of the theatre audience. It starts to rain and
some of the audience go home. A boy with a billboard appears on the
balcony in foreground.

       NOISE OF RAIN AND OF AUDIENCE GRUMBLING.

M.C.S. Front-angle of boy displaying billboard to audience. He stands
it on a bracket on left of screen, bows and exits through curtains

behind him. CAMERA PANS with him, then CAMERA TRACKS in to the balcony
and curtains. Nym pokes his head through the curtains and furtively
climbs over the balcony and drops out of picture.

AUDIENCE REACTS TO NYM'S ENTRANCE.

C.U. Nym drops into picture. Bardolph is standing on left of picture.

MUSIC STOPS.

BARDOLPH: Wellmet, Corporal Nym.

Nym gets up from the floor of the stage. CAMERA PANS up to reveal
Bardolph in M.C.S. CAMERA TRACKS BACK as Bardolph steps forward.

NYM: Oh, good morrow, Lieutenant Bardolph.

BARDOLPH: What, are Ancient Pistol and you friends yet?

NYM: For my part, I care not; I say little: but
              when time shall serve . . .

Nym prods Bardolph's arm. Camera PANS L. to R. as Bardolph walks round
Nym.

BARDOLPH: I will bestow a breakfast to make you friends,
              and we'll all go three sworn brothers to France:
              let it be so, good Corporal Nym.

NYM: Well, I cannot tell.

BARDOLPH: Oh, it is certain, Corporal, that he is
              married to Nell Quickly, and certainly she
              did you wrong for you were betrothed to her.

Nym prods Bardolph's arm.

NYM: Things must be as they may; men may sleep,
              and they may have their throats about them
              at that time, and some say, knives have edges.
              Well, I cannot tell.

Bardolph shudders. Nym crosses in front of Bardolph, L. to R.

MUSIC STARTS

BARDOLPH: Here comes Pistol and his wife; good
              corporal, good corporal, be patient here.

Bardolph ushers Nym L. to R. to the side of the stage.

AUDIENCE APPLAUDS.

L.S. GLOBE THEATRE STAGE with audience in f.g. Pistol and Mistress Quickly come through door in L. background. CAMERA TRACKS in to them as Pistol flourishes his hat.

M.C.S. Audience at the lip of the stage applauding ecstatically.

M.C.S. Pistol flourishing his hat. CAMERA PANS with him L. to R. up to Bardolph.

BARDOLPH: How now, mine host Pistol?

MUSIC STOPS.

Pistol steps back in disgust.

PISTOL: Base tike, call'st thou me host?

AUDIENCE LAUGHS.

Now by this hand I swear I scorn the title;

He walks camera L. to Mistress Quickly.

And nor shall my Nell keep lodgers.

AUDIENCE LAUGHS.

M.S. Nym crosses his legs and rubs his hands smugly.

MISTRESS QUICKLY: (off)
            No, by my troth, not long.

M.C.S. Mistress Quickly and Pistol.

            For we cannot lodge and board a dozen
            or fourteen gentlewomen that live
            honestly by the prick of their needles,
            but it will be thought we keep a bawdy
            house, straight!

Pistol leads her by the hand over to Nym. CAMERA PANS right with them.

PISTOL: (he slaps Nym on the shoulder) Oh hound of
            Crete, think'st thou my spouse to get?

PISTOL (Cont'd)
> I have, and I will hold my honey queen and
> there's enough. Go to.

NYM:
> I will prick your guts a little, and that's
> the truth of it.

> AUDIENCE LAUGHS.

PISTOL: Ha!

Mistress Quickly runs to the lip of the stage.

MISTRESS QUICKLY:
> Well a day, Lady, we shall have wilful murder
> and adultery committed.

Bardolph comes in screen left.

> AUDIENCE LAUGHS.

BARDOLPH: Good corporal, good lieutenant, offer nothing
> here.

Nym draws his sword.

NYM: Pish!

PISTOL: Pish to thee, Iceland dog! Thou prick-ear'd
> cur of Iceland!

> AUDIENCE LAUGHS.

Mistress Quickly walks back to Nym.

MISTRESS QUICKLY:
> Good corporal Nym, show thy valour, put up the
> sword.

She helps him to sheath his sword.

NYM: I will cut thy throat one time or other in
> fair terms.

Pistol draws and brandishes his sword. He comes down to lip of stage
then back to the group again. CAMERA PANS R. then L. with him.

> AUDIENCE LAUGHS.

PISTOL: Ha! I can take! Now Pistol's cock is up and
               flashing fire will follow.

Bardolph draws his sword.

BARDOLPH: Hear me, hear me what I say; he that
               strikes the first stroke, I'll run him up to
               the hilt, as I'm a s-s-s-soldier.

Pistol walks away from the group. CAMERA PANS left with him. He
addresses theatre audience.

PISTOL: An oath of mickle might, and fury shall abate.

                                     AUDIENCE LAUGHS.

Pistol turns round to camera right.

BOY: (off) Mine host Pistol . . .

M.S. Low angle shot of the boy on the balcony.

BOY: . . . you must come to Sir John Falstaff.

Pistol comes in to picture on the left, Mistress Quickly on the right,
followed by Bardolph.

               and you hostess; he's very sick and
               would be bed. Good Bardolph, put thy
               nose between the sheets, and do the
               office of a warming-pan.

BARDOLPH: Away you rogue!

BOY: Faith, he's very ill.

The boy leaves the balcony. CAMERA PANS DOWN to leave the three below
in M.C.S.

MISTRESS QUICKLY:
               By my troth, the king has kill'd his heart.
               Good husband come home presently.

                                     MUSIC STOPS.

Mistress Quickly goes out left. Bardolph takes Pistol by the arm and
leads him over to Nym. CAMERA PANS R. with them.

BARDOLPH: Come, shall I make you two friends? We must
                go to France together: why the devil should
                we keep knives to cut one another's throats?

PISTOL: Let floods o'erswell, and fiends for food
                howl on!

NYM: You'll pay me the eight shillings I won of
                you at betting?

PISTOL: Base is the slave that pays.

                                        AUDIENCE LAUGHS.

NYM: Now that will I have: that's the humour of it.

PISTOL: (he draws his sword)
                As manhood shall compound: push home.

                                        AUDIENCE LAUGHS.

Bardolph draws his sword.

BARDOLPH: By this sword, he that makes the first thrust,
                I'll kill him: By this s-s-sword I will.

                                        AUDIENCE LAUGHS.

Pistol moves over to L. forefront of stage and addresses theatre audience. CAMERA PANS LEFT with him.

M.S. Bardolph and Nym.

BARDOLPH: Corporal Nym, an thou wilt be friends, be
                friends, an thou wilt not, why, then, be
                enemies with me too. Prithee, put up.

Bardolph slaps Nym's sword with his own. Pistol comes into picture,
screen left.

M.C.S. Mistress Quickly on the Balcony. Low angle shot.

MISTRESS QUICKLY:
                As ever you come of women come quickly to
                Sir John.
                                        MUSIC STARTS:

He's so shak'd of a burning contigian

MISTRESS QUICKLY (Cont'd)
            fever, it's lamentable to behold. Sweet men,
            come to him.

She beckons them, then goes through the curtains behind her. CAMERA
TRACKS BACK to reveal Bardolph, Pistol and Nym looking up at the
balcony.

NYM: The king hath run bad humours on the knight.

Pistol lays his right hand on Nym's shoulder.

PISTOL: Nym, thou hast spoke the right, his heart
              is fracted and corroborate.

BARDOLPH: The king is a good king, but it must be as it
              may; he passes some humours.

Pistol takes a step forward.

PISTOL: Let us condole the knight . . . for lambkins,
              we will live.

He turns round to face the camera, and places a hand on Bardolph's and
Nym's shoulders. They turn round to camera. AUDIENCE APPLAUDS. As
the audience applauds they bow and flourish their hats. CAMERA TRACKS
right back to reveal the theatre in L.S. The three make their exit
through a door on screen left, as attendants sweep away the rushes on
the floor and Chorus pulls across the proscenium arch a curtain depict-
ing Southampton.

M.C.S. Chorus standing on left of screen in front of the Southampton
curtain. He steps forward to address the theatre audience.

                                      MUSIC STARTS

CHORUS: Linger your patience on and we'll digest
              The abuse of distance; force a play;
              The king is set from London, and the scene
              Is now transported, gentles, to Southampton.
              There is the playhouse now, there must you sit,
              And thence to France . . .

Chorus walks back and indicates the curtains. He goes out of picture
left. CAMERA TRACKS up to the curtain and we:

                                      DISSOLVE TO:

MED. L.S. SOUTHAMPTON, exactly as depicted on the curtain. CAMERA

TRACKS ON, then PANS L. to reveal in L.S. the stern of a ship, and Southampton quay. The Archbishop of Canterbury is giving benediction to Henry and his knights. Henry rises.

CHORUS: (off)
                . . . shall we convey you safe,
                And bring you back charming the narrow seas,
                To give you gentle pass; and here till then,
                Unto Southampton do we change our scene.

M.C.S. Henry steps down to the deck. CAMERA TRACKS with him as he walks to the mast.

                                MUSIC STOPS.

HENRY: Now sits the wind fair.

He turns and walks back to group of noblemen. CAMERA TRACKS L. with him.

                Uncle of Exeter,
                Set free the man committed yesterday,
                That rail'd against our person.
                We consider it was the heat of wine that set him on,
                And, on his wiser thought, we pardon him.

EXETER: That's mercy, but too much security.

WESTMORELAND: Let him be punish'd,sovereign, less example
                Breed by his sufference more, of such a kind.

HENRY: Oh let us yet be merciful.

He turns to Canterbury just behind him.

                  We doubt not now
                But every rub is smoothed, on our way.

L.S.
Henry mounts the gangplank.

HENRY: Then forth dear countrymen;

                              SOLDIERS CHEER.

Henry steps ashore, followed by Canterbury and the Nobles. He walks along the quay to a table. CAMERA TRACKS L. with him.

HENRY (Cont'd) . . . let us deliver
          Our puissance into the hand of God,
          Putting it straight in expedition.
          Cheerly to see,

                                  SOLDIERS CHEER.

    . . . the signs of war advance

                                  SOLDIERS CHEER.

Henry takes a seal and stamps a paper on the table.

          No King of England, if not King of France

He turns and walks away from CAMERA followed by Canterbury and the
nobles.

                                  MUSIC STARTS.

                                  DISSOLVE TO:

C.U. BOAR'S HEAD INN SIGN, at night.

CHORUS: (off)   still be kind,
           And eke out our performance with your mind!

                                  DISSOLVE TO:

L.S. THE BOAR'S HEAD INN:
CAMERA TRACKS BACK a short distance as an upper window is opened by
Mistress Quickly. CAMERA TRACKS FORWARD up to, and through the window.
An old man is lying in bed in the room inside. Mistress Quickly is by
the bed. She goes out through a door on the right of picture.
Falstaff, the old man, struggles and sits up in bed.

FALSTAFF: God save thy Grace -- King Hal -- my royal Hal,
           God save thee my sweet boy:
           My King, my Jove, I speak to thee my heart.

CAMERA TRACKS SLOWLY IN to Falstaff, till he is in close up during
Henry's speech.

HENRY: (off and distant)
           I know thee not, old man, fall to thy prayers.
           How ill white hairs become a fool and jester!
           I have long dreamed of such a kind of man,
           So surfeit swelled, so old and so profane,

HENRY (Cont'd)

        But being awaked I do despise my dream.
        Reply not to me with a foolish jest,
        Presume not that I am the thing I was;
        For God doth know, so shall the world perceive
        That I have turned away my former self
        So shall I those that kept me company.

Falstaff sinks back onto the pillow, fumbling convulsively with the sheets.

CLOSE UP. Low Angle shot of Falstaff in profile. Mistress Quickly is at the bedside.

                        DISSOLVE TO:

M.L.S. OUTSIDE THE BOAR'S HEAD INN.
The street door on R. of screen opens and Nym, the Boy, Bardolph and Pistol come out. They walk over to a cart on L. of screen and stand and sit around it. CAMERA PANS with them. They are followed by Mistress Quickly. CAMERA TRACKS forward as she walks over to Pistol and touches his arm.

                        MUSIC STOPS

MISTRESS QUICKLY:

        Prithee, honey-sweet husband, let me bring
        thee to Staines.

Pistol rouses himself.

PISTOL: No: for my manly heart doth yearn.
        Bardolph be blithe: Nym, rouse they vaulting veins:
        Boy, bristle thy courage up, for Falstaff.
        He is dead and we must yearn therefore.

BOY: Well, Sir John is gone, God be with him!

Mistress Quickly sits down on a stool.

BARDOLPH: Would I were with him wheresome'er he is
        either in heaven, or in hell!

CAMERA TRACKS VERY SLOWLY up to Mistress Quickly.

MISTRESS QUICKLY:

        Nay, he's not in hell: he's in Arthur's
        bosom, if ever a man went to Arthur's bosom.

MISTRESS QUICKLY (Cont'd)
>He made a finer end, and went away an it
>had been any christom child: parted e'en
>just betwixt twelve and one, e'en at the
>turning o' the tide: when I saw him fumble
>with the sheets, and play with flowers, and
>smile upon his fingers' end, I knew there
>was no way but one: for his nose was as
>sharp as a pen and he babbled of green
>field. 'How now, Sir John?' quoth I: "What
>man? Be o' good cheer! '; so he cried out,

CAMERA HAS STOPPED TRACKING, and leaves Mistress Quickly in M.C.U.

MISTRESS QUICKLY:
>(contd) . . . "God, God, God!" three or four
>times: and I, to comfort him, bid him he
>should not think on God: I hop'd there was no
>need to trouble himself with any such thoughts
>yet: so he bade me lay more clothes on his
>feet: I put my hand in the bed, and felt
>them, and they were as cold as any stone:
>then I felt to his knees,

She touches Pistol's knee, and CAMERA TRACKS SLOWLY BACK TO GROUP SHOT again.

>and they were as cold as any stone, and so
>upwards and upwards, and all was cold as any
>stone.

Nym wipes his nose.

NYM: They say he cried out for sack.

MISTRESS QUICKLY:
>Ay, that he did.

BARDOLPH: And for women.

MISTRESS QUICKLY:
>Ay, that he did not.

BARDOLPH: Ay, that he did! And he said they were
>devils incarnate.

BOY: He said once, the devil would have him about
>women.

MISTRESS QUICKLY:
>He did in some sort, indeed handle women;
>but then he was rheumatic: he spoke of the
>whore of Babylon.

BOY:
>Do you not remember, he saw a flea stand
>on Bardolph's nose, and said it was a black
>soul burning in hell-fire?

BARDOLPH:
>Well, the fuel is gone that maintained that fire:
>that's all the riches I got in his service.

Nym stirs and picks up his helmet.

NYM:
>Shall we go? The king will be gone from
>Southampton.

Pistol rouses himself.

PISTOL:
>Come, let us away.

He turns R. to Mistress Quickly.

>My love, give me thy lips.
>Look to my chattels and my moveable.
>Go, clear thy crystals.

He turns to Nym, Bardolph and the Boy.

>. . . Yoke-fellows in arms,
>Let us to France, like horse-leeches, my boys,
>To suck, to suck, thy very blood to suck!

He signals to Bardolph.

>Touch her soft lips and part.

MUSIC STARTS.

BARDOLPH:
>Farewell, hostess.

Bardolph kisses Mistress Quickly and goes out R., putting on his helmet.
Nym moves to go. Pistol growls at him.

PISTOL:
>Huh!

Nym turns to say goodbye to Mistress Quickly. He kisses his hand to
her.

NYM: I cannot kiss, that's the humour of it; but
                       adieu.

Pistol embraces his wife.

PISTOL: Let housewifery appear: keep close I thee
                       command.

He goes out R. The Boy runs forward to Mistress Quickly, and she
kisses his head. The boy runs out R.

L.S. THE STREET UP FROM THE BOAR'S HEAD.
Pistol and Company are walking up it. Pistol turns and waves his
helmet.

PISTOL: Farewell, farewell, divine Zenocrates --
                       Is it not passing brave to be a King
                       And ride in triumph through Persepolis!

Mistress Quickly comes into picture in L. f.g. As Pistol turns and
continues up the street. Mistress Quickly looks L. up to Falstaff's
window. CAMERA PANS up in same direction to centre on the window. The
curtain is drawn across it as we:

                                             FADE OUT.

                                             MUSIC STOPS.

The voice of Chorus is heard over a black screen.

CHORUS: Thus with imagin'd wing our scene flies
                       swift as that of thought.

                                             MUSIC STARTS.

C.U. Chorus against a black b.g. is FADED IN slowly. CAMERA TRACKS
SLOWLY BACK TO leave Chorus in extreme L.S.

CHORUS: Suppose that you have seen
                       The well appointed King at Hampton Pier
                       Embark his royalty; and his brave fleet
                       Play with your fancies; and in them behold
                       Upon the hempen tackle ship-boys climbing;
                       Hear the shrill whistle, which doth order give
                       To sounds confus'd;

A mist begins to obscure him.

CHORUS (Cont'd)
     . . . behold the threaden sails,
     Borne with the invisible and creeping wind,
     Draw the huge vessels through the furrow'd sea . . .

He extends his arms.

     Breasting the lofty surge. Oh, do but think
     You stand upon the shore and thence behold

He swings round, now back to camera, and is completely blotted out by
mist. A fleet of ships becomes visible through the mist. CAMERA
TRACKS FORWARD over them.

     A city on the inconstant billows dancing;
     Holding due course to Harfleur. Follow, follow.
     And leave your England as dead midnight, still,
     Guarded with grandsires, babies, and old women,
     For who is he, whose chin is but enrich'd
     With one appearing hair, that will not follow
     These culled and choice-drawn cavaliers to France?

          DISSOLVE TO:

LONG SHOT. The French Palace.

          DISSOLVE TO:

LONG SHOT. Inside THE FRENCH PALACE. High Angle Shot.

CHORUS: (off)
     The French, advis'd by good intelligence
     Of this most dreadful preparation
     Shake in their fear, and with pale policy,
     Seek to divert the English purposes.

CAMERA TRACKS DOWN to the ground level, and centres the French King,
Charles, who is seated at the base of a pillar. He looks nervously
screen right, then turns back again.

          MUSIC STOPS

CHARLES: Thus comes the English with full power upon us
     And more than carefully it us concerns
     To answer royally in our defences,
     Therefore you Dukes . . .

Charles points screen left . . .

CHARLES (Cont'd)
                    . . . of Berri . . .

MEDIUM CLOSE SHOT. The Duke of Berri reading at a lectern. He turns
round to look screen right.

                    . . . and of Bourbon,

CAMERA PANS DOWN to C.U. of BOURBON.

                    . . . Lord Constable . . .

CAMERA PANS UP AND RIGHT to Constable.

                    . . . and Orleans shall make forth,

CAMERA PANS RIGHT to Orleans.

CLOSE UP King Charles. He points screen left and gets to his feet.
CAMERA PANS as he walks to the left, and we see the Dauphin standing at
a window in the b.g.

KING CHARLES: (contd.)
                    And you, Prince Dauphin, with all swift despatch,
                    To line and new repair our towns of war,
                    With men of courage, and with means defendant

The King has turned round and he goes out screen right.

DAUPHIN: My most redoubted father,
                    It is most meet we arm us 'gainst the foe:

The Dauphin steps down from the window.

                    And let us do it with no show of fear,
                    No, with no more than if we heard that England
                    Were busied with a Whitsun morris dance;
                    For, my good liege, who is so idly king'd,
                    So guided by a shallow humorous youth,
                    That fear attends her not.

CONSTABLE: (off) O peace, Prince . . .

The Dauphin looks round screen left.

M.C.S. The Constable. He steps down and walks right to the Dauphin.
CAMERA PANS with him to leave them standing together. The Constable
smiled at Orleans en route.

CONSTABLE: . . . Dauphin! You are too much mistaken in this king;
                Question your grace our late ambassadors
                With what great state he heard their embassy,
                How well supplied with aged counsellors,
                How terrible in constant resolution.

DAUPHIN: Well, 'tis not so, my good lord constable,
                But though we think it so, it is no matter:
                In cases of defence, 'tis best to weigh
                The enemy more mighty than he seems.

Constable bows slightly.

CHARLES: (off)
                And he is bred out of . . .

Constable and the Dauphin look screen right.

M.C.S. Charles seated on some stone steps.

CHARLES: . . . that bloody strain
                That haunted us in our familiar paths;
                When Cressy battle fatally was struck,
                And all our Princes captured, by the hand
                Of that black name, Edward, Black Prince of Wales;

Charles shivers and crosses himself.

                This is the stem
                Of that victorious stock; and let us fear
                The native mightiness and fate of him.

                                        FANFARE.

Charles looks up startled.

L.S. LEFT HAND STAIRCASE OF THE APSE. The Dukes are seated about in the
middle foreground. A Messenger dashes in.

MESSENGER: Ambassadors from Harry King of England
                Do crave admittance to your majesty.

Charles comes into picture right foreground, his back to camera.

CHARLES: We'll give them present audience,
                Go, and bring them.

Charles points irritably at the messenger, then turns and scampers to the throne.

MUSIC STARTS

CAMERA TRACKS RIGHT with him. He sits on the throne and an attendant proffers the crown jewel casket.

M.C.S. Charles with the attendant in left foreground holding jewel case. Charles takes the crown and puts it on his head. The Dauphin comes in left. Charles, impatient, continues to regale.

DAUPHIN: Good, my sovereign.
             Take up the English short, and let them know
             Of what a monarchy you are the head.
             Self love, my liege, is not so vile a sin,
             As self-neglecting.

FANFARE

Charles and the Dauphin look left.

L.S. THE LEFT-HAND STAIRCASE OF THE APSE.
English and French heralds come up the staircase followed by Exeter and Erpingham. CAMERA TRACKS BACK as the Heralds take up positions on either side of the throne. Exeter turns to address the throne.

CHARLES: From our brother England?

EXETER: From him, and thus he greets your majesty:
             He wills you, in the name of God Almighty,
             That you divest yourself, and lay apart
             The borrowed glories, that by gift of heaven,
             By law of nature, and of nations, 'longs
             To him and to his heirs, namely the crown,
             Willing you overlook this pedigree:

Exeter indicates a document. Two messengers unfurl it and hold it up before the throne.

             And when you find him evenly deriv'd
             From his most fam'd, of famous ancestors,
             Edward the third, he bids you then resign
             Your crown and kingdom, indirectly held

Charles fingers his crown.

             From him, the native and true challenger.

C.U. Charles.

CHARLES: If not, what follows?

C.U. Exeter.

EXETER: Bloody constraint: for if you hide the crown
                Even in your hearts, there will he rake for it.
                Therefore in fierce tempest is he coming,
                In thunder and in earthquake, like a jove;
                That, if requiring fail, he will compel.
                This is his claim, his threatening, and my message;
                Unless the Dauphin . . .

He glances to right and left.

M.C.U. Charles with the Dauphin beside him. Charles edges the Dauphin
out of picture on the right.

EXETER: (off) . . . be in presence here;
                To whom expressly I bring greeting too.

Charles lays his hand on his breast, then points screen left.

CHARLES: For us, we will consider of this further:
                Tomorrow shall you bear our full intent
                Back to our brother England.

M.S. Dauphin.

DAUPHIN: For the Dauphin,
                I stand here for him: what to him from England.

Enter Exeter extreme L.

EXETER: Scorn and defiance, slight regard, contempt,
                And anything that may not misbecome
                The mighty sender, doth he prize you at.
                Thus says my King; and if your father's highness
                Do not, in grant of all demands at large,
                Sweeten the bitter mock you send this Majesty,
                He'll make your Paris Louvre shake for it.

King Charles enters L.

CHARLES: Tomorrow shall you know our mind at full.

EXETER: Dispatch us with all speed, lest that our King
                 Come here himself to question our delay;

King Charles faints.

                                          MUSIC STARTS

                                          DISSOLVE TO:

TROUBLED SEA.
                                          DISSOLVE TO:

L.S. English soldiers storming Harfleur Beach.

                                          DISSOLVE TO:

C.S. The Beach. A few soldiers are hauling a cannon ashore.

CHORUS: (off) Work, work your thoughts . . .
                 . . . and therein see a siege;
                 Behold the ordnance on their carriages
                 With fatal mouths gaping on girded Harfleur.

CAMERA TRACKS FORWARD as English Infantry appear round the cliff breach
in retreat. Henry rides round on horseback.

C.S. Henry -- he takes off helmet.

L.S. Henry rides up to his men.

HENRY: Once more unto the breach, dear friends . . .

M.L.S. Henry rides into picture L.

HENRY: . . . once more;
                 Or close the wall up with our English dead.

M.S. Henry rides into picture R.

                                          MUSIC STOPS

HENRY: In peace there's nothing so becomes a man
                 As modest stillness, and humility:
                 But when the blast of war blows in our ears,
                 Then imitate the action of the tiger:
                 Stiffen the sinews, summon up the blood,
                 Disguise fair nature with hard-flavour'd rage;
                 Then lend the eye a terrible aspect;

CAMERA IS TRACKING SLOWLY BACK TO LONG SHOT

HENRY (Cont'd)

> Let it pry through the portage of the head
> Like a brass cannon; let the brow o'erwhelm it
> As fearfully as doth a galled rock
> Oer hang and jutty his confounded base,
> Swill'd with the wild and wasteful ocean.
> Now set the teeth and stretch the nostril wide,
> Hold hard the breath, and bend up every spirit
> To his full height. On, on you noblest English!
> Whose blood is fet from fathers of war-proof;
> Fathers that, like so many Alexanders,
> Have in these parts from morn til even fought
> And sheath'd their swords for lack of argument.
> Dishonour not your mothers: now attest
> That those whom you call'd fathers did beget you.
> Be copy now to men of grosser blood,
> And teach them how to war. And you, good yeomen,
> Whose limbs were made in England, show us here
> The mettle of your pasture; let us swear
> That you are worth your breeding; which I doubt not;
> For there is none of you so mean and base
> That hath not noble lustre in your eyes.
> I see you stand like greyhound in the slips,
> Straining upon the start. The game's afoot.
> Follow your spirit; and upon this charge
> Cry, 'God for Harry, England and Saint . . .

M.S. Henry's horse rears and he rides away followed by cheering troops.

HENRY: . . . George!'

                                        MUSIC STARTS

TROOPS: (they chant)
                'God for Harry, England and Saint George!'

LONG HIGH ANGLE SHOT.
CAMERA TRACKS DOWN as Troops rush up to the breach.

M.L.S. Bardolph standing on a rock waving them on.

BARDOLPH: On! On! On! On to the breach, on to the breach.

M.C.S. Bardolph drops into picture from the rock, and takes refuge beside Pistol, Nym, the Boy.

NYM: Pray thee, corporal, stay, the knocks are
                     too hot.

PISTOL gets up, CAMERA PANS with him.

PISTOL: Ah, knocks they come and go; God's
                     vassals drop and die;
                     And the sword and shield
                     In bloody field,
                     Doth win immortal fame!
                     Ah! Ah!

He springs back as a horse leaps from the rock.

C.U. Nym and the Boy.

NYM: 'Tis honour, and that's the truth of it.

BOY: Would I were in an alehouse in London, I would
                     Give all my fame for a pot of ale, and safety.

FLUELLEN: (off) God's plud.

M.C.S. Fluellen. He pulls Nym and the Boy to their feet and kicks them
up to the breach. CAMERA PANS with the action.

FLUELLEN: . . . up to the breach you dogs! Avant, you
                     cullions!

Fluellen sees Pistol hiding behind a rock.

FLUELLEN: Ah!

PISTOL: Be merciful, great duke, to men of mould;
                     Abate thy rage, abate thy manly rage;

FLUELLEN: On, on!

He slashes at Pistol with the flat of his sword.

PISTOL: Abate thy rage . . .

                                        DISSOLVE TO:

C.U. a flaming linstock touches the powder box of a cannon which goes
off. CAMERA TRACKS WITH IT.

CHORUS: (off)
                 . . . and the nimble gunner
                 With linstock now the devilish cannon touches.

                                         DISSOLVE TO:

M.S. Wall crashing.

CHORUS: (off) And down goes all before them.

                                         DISSOLVE TO:

L.S. OUTSIDE THE BIVOUAC. Captain Gower appears.

                                         MUSIC STOPS

GOWER: Captain Fluellen!

He walks towards CAMERA which TRACKS BACK to reveal Fluellen sitting at
a table in the bivouac.

GOWER: Captain Fluellen, you must come presently
                 to the mines; the Duke of Gloucester would
                 speak with you.

FLUELLEN: To the mines! Tell you the Duke, it is not
                 so good to come to the mines! For look
                 you, the mines is not according to the
                 disciplines of war! The concavities of it
                 is not sufficient; for look you, th'
                 athversary, you may discuss unto the Duke,
                 look you, is dig't himself four yards under
                 the countermines; by Cheshu, I think he will
                 plow up all, if there is not better directions.

GOWER: The Duke of Gloucester, to whom the order
                 of the siege is given, is altogether directed
                 by an Irishman, a very valiant gentleman,
                 i' faith.

FLUELLEN: It is Captain MacMorris, is it not?

GOWER: I think it be.

FLUELLEN: By Cheshu, he is an ass, as in the world,
                 I will verify as much in his beard; he has
                 no more directions in the true disciplines

FLUELLEN (Cont'd)

        of the wars, look you, of the Roman disciplines,
        than is a puppy dog.

GOWER looks right and behind him.

GOWER: Here he comes, and the Scots captain, Captain
                Jamy with him.

FLUELLEN: Ah, Captain Jamy is a marvellous falorous
                gentleman, that is certain, of great
                expedition and knowledge in th' aunchient
                wars.

CAMERA PANS SLIGHTLY R. as Captain Jamy and MacMorris enter from R.
background.

JAMY: I say gud-day Captain Fluellen!

FLUELLEN: Good-den to your worship, good Captain James.
                Captain Jamy is a marvellous valorous
                gentleman that is certain.

Jamy laughs.

GOWER: How now Captain . . .

C.U. MacMorris.

GOWER: . . . MacMorris, have you quit the mines?
                Have the pioneers given o'er?

MACMORRIS: Oh, by the Saints, tish ill done! The work ish
                give over, the trompet sound the retreat.
                By my hand I swear . . .

CAMERA PANS as he walks L. to Fluellen.

MACMORRIS: . . . and by my father's soul, tish ill done;
                the work ish give over. I would have blowed
                up the town, so God save me, in an hour! Oh,
                tish ill done, by my hand tish ill done!

CAMERA PANS WITH HIM as he walks R. and leans his head against the
tree.

M.C.S. Jamy and Fluellen.

FLUELLEN: Captain MacMorris, I beseech you now, will
                   you voutsafe me, look you a few disputations
                   with you, partly . . .

C.U. MacMorris. He leans his head against the tree.

FLUELLEN: (off) . . . to satisfy my opinion, and partly
                   for the satisfaction, look you, of my mind . . .

M.C.S. Jamy and Fluellen.

FLUELLEN: . . . as touching the direction of the
                   military discipline that is the point . . .

JAMY: It shall be very gud, gud faith, gud captain
                   both, and I would fain hear some discourse
                   between you tway!

Jamy and Fluellen giggle together.

M.C.S. Gower and MacMorris standing behind him.

MACMORRIS: This is no time to discourse so God save me!

He walks back to Fluellen and CAMERA PANS L. with him.

MACMORRIS: The day is hot, and the weather, and the wars,
                   and the king, and the dukes; this is no
                   time to discourse, the town is beseech'd:
                   an' the trumpet call us to the breach, and we
                   talk, and by the Holy do nothing, 'tis a
                   shame for us all;
                   So God sa' me.

CAMERA PANS R. as he walks back to Gower.

MAC: . . . 'tis a shame to stand still, 'tis a
                   shame by my hand! and there is throats to
                   be cut . . .

CAMERA PANS L. as he walks back to the table and flops down on it.

MAC: . . . and works to be done and nothing ish
                   done, so help me God!

Jamy laughs and leans back.

C.U. Jamy.

JAMY: By the mess, are these eyes of mine tak
themselves to slomber, ay'll do gud service,
or ay'll lie i' the grund for it: ay, or go
to death, and ay'll pay't as valorously as I
may, that sall I surely do, that is the breff
and the long of it.

CAMERA TRACKS BACK to Jamy, Fluellen and MacMorris around the table.

FLUELLEN: Captain MacMorris, I think, look you under
your correction, there is not many of your
nation --

MAC: Of my nation? What ish my nation? Ish a
villain, and a bastard, and a knave, and a
rascal. What ish my nation? Who talks of my
nation?

FLUELLEN: Look you, if you take the matter otherwise
than is meant, Captain MacMorris, peradventure
I shall think you do not use me with that
affability as in discretion you ought to use
me, look you, being as good a man as . . .

C.U. Fluellen jumps up into picture . . .

FLUELLEN: . . . yourself, both in the disciplines of war
and the derivation of my birth and other
particularities.

MacMorris' head enters screen R.

MACMORRIS: I do not know you so good a man as myself . . .
so God save me and I will cut off your head.

CAMERA TRACKS BACK as Gower enters R.

GOWER: Gentlemen both, you will mistake each other.

JAMY: (laughs) That's a foul fault. (laughs)

A TRUMPET SOUNDS

GOWER: The town sounds a parley.

The four Captains cheer and grab their helmets.

DISSOLVE TO:

L.S. OUTSIDE THE GATES OF HARFLEUR. Henry at the head of his Army addresses the Governor on the City wall.

CAMERA TRACKS SLOWLY IN to the end of the shot.

HENRY: How yet resolves the Governor of the Town.
                This is the latest parley we'll admit.

GOVERNOR OF HARFLEUR:
                Our expectation hath this day an end:
                The Dauphin, of whom succour we entreated
                Returns us word his powers are not yet ready,
                To raise so great a siege. Therefore, dread King
                We yield our town and lives to your soft mercy:
                Enter our gates, dispose of us and ours
                For we no longer are defensible.

L.S. HIGH ANGLE SHOT. Henry at the gates of Harfleur.

HENRY: Open your gates!

M.S. Henry and Gloucester.

HENRY: Come, brother Gloucester,
                Go you and enter Harfleur; there remain,
                And fortify it strongly against the French:
                Use mercy to them all; for us, dear brother,
                The winter coming on, and sickness growing
                Upon our soldiers, we will retire to Calais.
                Tonight in Harfleur will we be your guest.
                Tomorrow for the march are we addrest.

                                        MUSIC STARTS.

Gloucester leads the English Army into Harfleur. Henry watches them
and CAMERA PANS R. as he turns and surveys the country ahead.

                                        DISSOLVE TO:

L.S. The French Palace.

                                        DISSOLVE TO:

M.C.S. The door of the Garden Terrace. The door opens and Alice followed
by the Princess Katharine come through . . .

                                        FANFARE SOUNDS.
. . . and Katharine looks over the balcony to her L.

L.S. High angle shot of Palace Courtyard. Mountjoy, escorting Exeter and Party, wait for the gates to be opened.

M.S. Mountjoy, Exeter and Party acknowledge the Princess on the balcony.

M.C.S. Katharine watching the Party leave. She turns and walks screen R.

M.S. Katharine walks down the terrace into the garden, followed by Alice.

KATHARINE: Alice, tu as été en Angleterre, et tu parles bien le langage.

ALICE: Oh! Un peu Madame.

KATHARINE: Je te prie, m'enseignez: Il faut que j'apprenne a parler. Comment appelez-vous la main en Anglois?

ALICE: La main? Elle est appelée de hand.

KATHARINE: De hand. Et les doigts?

ALICE: Les doights? Oh! ma foi, j'oublie les doights; mais je me souviendrai. Les doights? je pense qu'ils sont appelés de fingres; oui de fingres.

KATHARINE: La main, de hand, les doights, de fingres. Je pense que je suis le bon écolier; J'ai gagné deux mots d' Anglois vitement. Comment appelez-vous les ongles?

ALICE: Les ongles? nous les appelons de nails.

KATHARINE: De nails. Ecoutez; dites-moi, si je parle bien: de hand, de fingres, de nails.

ALICE: Ah! C'est bien dit, madame; et il est fort bon Anglois.

KATHARINE: Dites-moi l'anglois pour le bras.

ALICE: De arm, madame.

KATHARINE: Et le coude.

ALICE: De elbow.

KATHARINE: De elbow. Je m'en fais le répétition
de tous les mots que vous m'avez appris
dès à présent.

ALICE: Ca c'est trop difficile, madame, comme
je pense.

KATHARINE: Excusez-moi, Alice; écoutez; de
hand, de fingres, de nails, de arm,
de bilbow.

ALICE: De elbow, sauf votre honneur.

KATHARINE: O Seigneur Dieu, je m'en oublie! de
elbow. Comment appelez-vous le col?

ALICE: De neck.

KATHARINE: De nick. Et le menton?

ALICE: De chin.

KATHARINE: De sin. Le col, de nick, le menton,
de sin.

Katharine has been cutting flowers, and she moves on camera R. Alice
following her.

ALICE: Sauf votre honneur, en verité, vous
prononcez les mots aussi droit que
les natifs d'Angleterre.

KATHARINE: Je ne doute point d'apprendre, par la
grace de Dieu, et en peu de temps.

ALICE: N'avez vous pas déjà oublié ce que je
vous ai enseigné?

KATHARINE: Non, je réciterai à vous promptement:
de hand, de fingres, de mails,

ALICE: De nails, madame.

KATHARINE: De nails, de arm, de ilbow.

ALICE: Sauf votre honneur de elbow.

KATHARINE: Ainsi dis-je; de elbow, de nick, et
                de sin.

Katharine walks right away from Alice, CAMERA PANS with her.

KATHARINE: Comment appelez-vous le pied et la robe?

M.S. Alice.

ALICE: De foot, et de coun!

M.C.S. Katharine, Alice joins her. They sit down.

KATHARINE: Oh Seigneur Dieu! ce sont mots de son
                mauvais, corruptible, gros, et
                impudique et non pour les dames d'
                honneur d'user: je ne voudrais
                prononcer ces mots devant les seigneurs
                de France pour tout le monde. Foh!
                le foot et le coun! Néanmoins, je
                réciterai une autre fois ma leçon
                ensemble: de hand, de fingres, de
                nails, de arm, de elbow, de nick, de
                sin, de foot, de coun.

ALICE: Oh, Madame, c'est excellent.

KATHARINE: C'est assez pour une fois: allons-nous
                à dîner.
                                        MUSIC STARTS.

They rise and walk left to the garden gate and go through on to the
terrace. CAMERA PANS with them.

                                        FANFARE SOUNDS.

KATHARINE looks over the balcony.

M.C.S. Katharine looking over the balcony.

L.S. High angle shot of the Courtyard, Mountjoy returns through the
gate alone.

C.U. Katharine looking up to the horizon.

L.S. Essex and Party riding away in the distance.

M.C.S. Katharine turns away from balcony and walks through a door into the Palace. She is followed by Alice. CAMERA PANS with Katharine, left.

L.S. INSIDE THE FRENCH PALACE. Katharine and Alice descend the stairs to the floor of the Banqueting Hall. At a table at the back King Charles, Queen Isabel, the Dauphin, the Constable, and the Dukes of Bourbon and Orleans are seated.

CHARLES: 'Tis certain he hath pass'd the river
                Somme.

CONSTABLE: And if he be not fought withal, my lord,
                Let us not live in France; let us quit all,
                And give our vineyards to a barbarous people.

The CAMERA TRACKS IN to centre BOURBON, KATHARINE and ALICE.

BOURBON: Normans, but bastard Normans, Norman
                bastards!

Alice screams.   MUSIC STOPS.

C.S. Bourbon. He looks right. He looks left.

BOURBON: Mort de ma vie!

He stands up.   MUSIC STARTS.

M.S. Katharine and Alice walk round and take their places at table. CAMERA PANS R. with them.

M.S. The Dukes at table. Constable, Orleans and Bourbon sit down.

BOURBON: if they march along
                unfought withal, then I will sell my dukedom,
                To buy a slobbery and dirty farm,
                In that nook-shotten isle of Albion.

ORLEANS: Dieu de batailles! where have they this mettle?
                Is not the climate foggy, raw and dull,
                On whom, as in despite, the sun looks pale,
                Killing their fruit with frowns?
                And shall our quick blood, spirited with wine,
                Seem frosty?

BOURBON: By faith and honour,
                Our madams mock at us, and plainly say

BOURBON (Cont'd)

        Our mettle is bred out, and they will give
        Their bodies to the lust of English youth,
        To new-store France with bastard warriors.

Isabel screams (off)   MUSIC STOPS.

M.S. Isabel, Katharine, and Alice at table. Isabel pokes Charles in the arm on extreme R. of screen.

C.S. King Charles -- he wakes up.

CHARLES: Where is Mountjoy the herald? speed him hence,
                Let him greet England with our sharp defiance,

L.S. Charles and his court seated at table. Charles stands up.

CHARLES: (contd).
                。 。 。 Up, princes and, with spirit of honour edg'd

The three Dukes get up and come down in front of the table.

        Bar Harry England, that sweeps through our land
        With pennons painted in the blood of Harfleur:
        Go down upon him, you have power enough,
        And in a captive chariot, into Rouen
        Bring him our prisoner.

CONSTABLE: This becomes the great.
                Sorry am I his numbers are so few,
                His soldiers sick and famish'd in their march;
                For I am sure, when he shall see our army,
                He'll drop his heart into the sink of fear
                And for achievement offer us his ransom.

CHARLES: Therefore, lord constable, haste on Mountjoy.

                              MUSIC STARTS.

The three Dukes walk off left.

M.C.S. King Charles. He turns R. and walks over to the Dauphin -- the CAMERA PANS with him.

CHARLES: Prince Dauphin, you shall stay with us in Rouen.

DAUPHIN: Not so, I do beseech your majesty.

CHARLES: Be patient, for you shall remain with us.

King Charles turns left.

> Now forth, lord constable and princes all
> And quickly bring us word of England's fall.

Charles turns back to the Dauphin and kisses him.

                                        DISSOLVE TO:

EXT. PICARDY FIELDS. Mountjoy preceded by two Heralds and followed by
his Standard Bearer rides up. The Heralds sound a fanfare as Mountjoy
and Bearer ride out of picture L.

M.S. Henry surrounded by his knights, Henry steps forward as Mountjoy
and Bearer ride in Camera R.

                                        MUSIC STOPS.

MOUNTJOY: You know me by my habit.

HENRY: Well, then, I know thee: what shall
              I know of thee?

M.C.S. Mountjoy and Standard Bearer. Henry in left f.g.

MOUNTJOY: My master's mind.

HENRY: Unfold it.

MOUNTJOY: Thus says my king: Say thou to Harry
              of England: Though we seem'd dead, we
              did but slumber: Tell him we could
              have rebuk'd him at Harfleur, but that
              we thought not good to bruise an
              injury till it were full ripe. Now we
              speak upon our cue, and our voice is
              imperial. England shall repent his
              folly, see his weakness, and admire
              our sufferance. Bid him therefore
              consider of his ransom,

M.C.S. Henry. Mountjoy in R. f.g.

MOUNTJOY: (contd).
              . . . which must proportion the losses
              we have borne, the subjects we have

<u>MOUNTJOY</u> (Cont'd)
        lost, the disgrace we have digested;

C.U. MOUNTJOY.

<u>MOUNTJOY</u>:   (contd).
        For our losses, his exchequer is too
        poor; for the effusion of our blood,
        the muster of his kingdom too faint
        a number; and for our disgrace, his
        own person . . .

C.U. HENRY.

<u>MOUNTJOY</u>:   (off)
        . . . kneeling at our feet, but a weak
        and worthless satisfaction.

M.C.S. Mountjoy and Standard Bearer. Henry in left f.g.

<u>MOUNTJOY</u>:   To this add defiance; and tell him
        for conclusion, he hath betrayed his
        followers, whose condemnation is
        pronounc'd . . . so far my king and
        master. So much my office.

<u>HENRY</u>:   What is thy name? I know thy quality.

<u>MOUNTJOY</u>:   Mountjoy.

M.C.S. HENRY -- Mountjoy in R. f.g.

<u>HERALD</u>:   (aside to Henry) Mountjoy.

<u>HENRY</u>:   Thou dost thy office fairly. Turn
        thee back, and tell thy king, I do
        not seek him now; but could be willing
        to march on to Calais without impeachment.

M.C.S. Mountjoy and Standard Bearer. Henry in left f.g.

<u>HENRY</u>:   . . . for, to say the sooth, my people
        are with sickness much enfeebled, my
        numbers lessened.
        Go, therefore, tell thy master here I am;
        My ransom is this frail and worthless body;
        My army, but a weak and sickly guard;

C.U. Henry.

HENRY: Yet God before tell him we will come on
                Though France herself and such another neighbour
                Stood in our way.
                If we may pass, we will; if we be hindered
                We shall your tawny ground with your red blood
                Discolour: and so Mountjoy . . .

M.C.S. Mountjoy and Standard Bearer. Henry in left f.g.

HENRY: (contd).
                . . . fare you well.
                We would not seek a battle, as we are,
                Nor, as we are, we say we will not shun it:

C.U. HENRY.

HENRY: So tell your master.

C.U. MOUNTJOY. He flourishes his hat.

MOUNTJOY: I shall deliver so.

C.U. Henry. He takes and throws a purse of money.

HENRY: There's for thy labour, Mountjoy.

C.U. MOUNTJOY. He catches the purse and rides out R. followed by his
Standard Bearer.

MOUNTJOY: Thanks to your highness.

                                        FANFARE SOUNDS.

M.C.S. Henry and Gloucester. Henry turns to a Knight behind him . . .

HENRY: March to the bridge,

                                        DRUM ROLL STARTS.

                It now draws towards night . . .
                Beyond the river we'll encamp ourselves
                And on the morrow bid them march away.

Henry, Gloucester and the Army move off R.

                                        DISSOLVE TO:

L.S. The English Army marching wearily away from camera along the Bank
of Picardy River.

FADE OUT:

DRUM ROLL STOPS.

Over a black screen the voice of Chorus is heard.

MUSIC STARTS.

CHORUS: (off)
               Now entertain conjecture of a time
               When creeping murmur and the poring dark
               Fills the wide vessel of the universe.

FADE IN on L.S. French & English camps at night.

               From camp to camp through the foul womb of night,
               The hum of either army stilly sounds;
               That the fix'd sentinels almost receive
               The secret whispers of each other's watch.
               Fire answers fire, and through their paly flames
               Each battle sees the other's umber'd face;
               Steed threatens steed, in high and boastful neighs
               Piercing the night's dull ear; and from the tents
               The armourers, accomplishing the knights
               With busy hammers closing rivets up,
               Give dreadful note of preparation.

CAMERA TRACKS IN to the French Camp.

               Proud of their numbers and secure in soul,
               The confident and over-lusty French,
               Do the low-rated English play at dice;
               And chide the cripple tardy-gaited night,
               Who, like a foul and ugly witch, doth limp
               So tediously away.

FANFARE.

DISSOLVE TO:

C.S. The Constable's Armour inside the French Duke's Tent.

MUSIC STOPS.

CAMERA PANS R. on to the Constable seated at a Dining table.

CONSTABLE: Tut! I have the best armour of the world,

CAMERA TRACKS BACK to include Orleans and Bourbon.

                Would it were day!

ORLEANS: You have an excellent armour; but let
               my horse have his due.

CONSTABLE: It is the best horse of Europe.

BOURBON: Will it never be morning?

Dauphin enters.

DAUPHIN: My lord Orleans, my lord high
               Constable, you talk of horse and
               armour?

The Dukes rise.

ORLEANS: You are as well provided of both as
               any prince in the world.

Dauphin motions them to sit down and they do so.

DAUPHIN: What a long night is that!
               I will not change my horse with any
               that treads on four hooves;
               Ca, ha! He bounds from the earth.

CAMERA TRACKS IN to centre the Dauphin and Constable.

DAUPHIN: When I bestride him, I soar, I am a
               hawk: he trots the air: the earth sings
               when he touches it: he is of the
               colour of nutmeg. And of the heat of
               the ginger. He is pure air and fire;
               and all other jades you may call beasts.

CONSTABLE: It is indeed, my lord, a most absolute
               and excellent horse.

DAUPHIN: It is the prince of palfreys.

He walks R. behind Orleans and Bourbon, CAMERA PANS with him.

                His neigh is like the bidding of a

DAUPHIN (Cont'd)

>monarch, and his countenance enforces
>homage.

BOURBON: No more, cousin.

DAUPHIN: Nay, cousin, the man hath no wit that
cannot, from the rising of the lark
to the lodging of the lamb, vary
deserved praise on my palfrey:

The Dauphin has walked round to the front of the table and the CAMERA HAS TRACKED BACK to include the whole group.

>I once writ a sonnet in his praise,
>it began thus, 'Wonder of nature' --

BOURBON: I have heard a sonnet begin so to one's
mistress

DAUPHIN: Then did they imitate that which I
compos'd to my courser, for my horse
is my mistress.

CONSTABLE: Methought yesterday your mistress
shrewdly shook your back.

ORLEANS: My lord Constable, the armour that I see
in your tent tonight, are those stars
or suns upon it?

CONSTABLE: Stars, my lord.

DAUPHIN: Some of them will fall tomorrow, I hope.

CONSTABLE: That may be.

DAUPHIN: (looking out of the tent)
Will it never be day?

He turns round and the CAMERA TRACKS IN a short distance.

DAUPHIN: I will trot tomorrow a mile, and my
way shall be paved with English faces.
Who'll go hazard with me for twenty
prisoners?

FANFARE.

BOURBON: 'Tis midnight.

DAUPHIN: I'll go arm myself.

He goes out.

ORLEANS: Ha! The Dauphin longs for morning.

M.C.S. Orleans and Bourbon. Bourbon gets up from the table and walks left to the tent opening, CAMERA TRACKS BACK to include the Constable.

BOURBON: He longs to eat the English.

CONSTABLE: I think he will eat all he kills.

ORLEANS: He never did harm, that I heard of.

CONSTABLE: Nor will do none tomorrow: He'll
              keep that good name still.

ORLEANS: I know him to be valiant.

CONSTABLE: I was told that, by one that knew him
              better than you.

ORLEANS: What's he?

CONSTABLE: Marry, he told me so himself,

Orleans laughs.

              and he said he car'd not who knew it.

Messenger enters left. He bows down to the Constable.

MESSENGER: My lord high constable.

C.U. Messenger and Constable.

MESSENGER: (contd).
              the English lie within fifteen
              hundred paces of your tents.

CONSTABLE: Who hath measur'd the ground?

MESSENGER: The Lord Granpre.

CONSTABLE: A valiant and most expert gentleman.

M.C.S. The Group -- the Messenger withdraws left.

CONSTABLE: (he gets up) Would it were day!

He turns left to the tent opening.

                              FANFARE.

CONSTABLE: (walking out of the tent)
              Alas, poor Harry of England. He longs
              not for the dawning as we do.

M.S. OUTSIDE THE FRENCH TENT at night.
The Constable, Bourbon and Orleans come out and stand overlooking the
English Camp in the far b.g.

                              FANFARE

ORLEANS: What a wretched and peevish fellow is this
              King of England, to mope with his fat-
              brain'd followers so far out of his knowledge.

CONSTABLE: If the English had any apprehension they'd
              run away.

ORLEANS: That they lack; for if their heads had any
              intellectual armour, they could never wear
              such heavy headpieces.

BOURBON: That island of England breeds very valiant
              creatures; their mastiffs are of unmatchable
              courage.

ORLEANS: Foolish curs, that run winking into the mouth
              of a Russian bear, and have their heads
              crush'd like rotten apples! You may as
              well say, that's a valiant flea, that dare
              eat his breakfast on the lip of a lion.

CONSTABLE: Just, just; and the men are like the mastiffs,
              give them great meals of beef, and iron and
              steel, they'll eat like wolves, and fight
              like devils.

ORLEANS: Ah, but these English are shrewdly out of beef.

BOURBON: Then shall we find tomorrow, they've only
              stomachs to eat, and none to fight.

FANFARE

CONSTABLE: Now it is time to arm; come, shall we about
               it?

They turn and go back into the tent.

ORLEANS: It is now two o'clock; but, let me see, by
               ten we shall have each a hundred Englishmen.

Orleans drops the tent flap.

FADE OUT.

FADE IN.
L.S. The French Camp at night. CAMERA PANS SLOWLY LEFT in the direction
of the English Camp.

MUSIC.

CHORUS: (off) The country cocks do crow, the clocks do toll;
               And the third hour of drowsy morning name.
                    The poor condemned English,
               Like sacrifices, by their watchful fires
               Sit patiently, and inly ruminate
               The morning's danger; and their gesture sad,
               Investing lank-lean cheeks, and war-worn coats,
               Presenteth them unto the gazing moon
               So many horrid ghosts.

The CAMERA is now centred on English Camp and TRACKS IN.

                    O now, who will behold
               The royal captain of this ruin'd band
               Walking from watch to watch, from tent to tent;
               Let him cry 'Praise and glory on his head'.

DISSOLVE TO:

M.S. THE ENGLISH CAMP. The CAMERA TRACKS IN SLOWLY to centre an English
Soldier warming himself by a brazier.

CHORUS: (off) For forth he goes, and visits all his host
               Bids them good morrow with a modest smile,
               And calls them brothers, friends and countrymen.
               A largess universal, like the sun,
               His liberal eye doth give to everyone,
               Thawing cold fear, that men and gentle all . . .

CHORUS (Cont'd)
>Behold, as many unworthiness define,
>A little touch of Harry in the night.

A shadow falls across the soldier and the CAMERA PANS UP as Henry, Gloucester, Salisbury and Guard walk on away from Camera.

MUSIC STOPS.

HENRY: Gloucester . . .

M.S. Henry and his Knights.

HENRY: 。 。 。 'tis true that we are in great danger,
The greater therefore should our courage be.

Erpingham comes up from b.g.

>Good morrow, old Sir Thomas Erpingham:
>A good soft pillow for that good white head
>Were better than a churlish turf of France.

ERPINGHAM: Not so, my liege: this lodging suits me better,
Since I may say 'Now lie I like a king!'

They laugh.

HENRY: Lend me thy cloak, Sir Thomas.
I and my bosom must debate a while,
And then I would no other company.

Henry takes Erpingham's cloak and puts it on.

ERPINGHAM: The Lord in heaven bless thee, noble Harry!

The Knights move out left.

HENRY: God-a-mercy, old heart!

He turns and walks away from Camera. CAMERA TRACKS FORWARD and centres tent's flap on L. from which Pistol emerges.

PISTOL: Qui va là?

M.S. Henry. He swings round.

HENRY: A friend.

M.S. Pistol. He draws his sword.

PISTOL: Discuss unto me, art thou officer,
             Or art thou base, common and popular.

HENRY: (off) I am a gentleman of a company.

PISTOL: Trail'st thou the puissant pike?

HENRY: (off) Even so: what are you?

PISTOL: Huh! As good a gentleman as the emperor.

HENRY: (off) Then you are better than the King.

PISTOL: Ah! The King's a bawcock, and a heart of gold,
             A lad of life, an imp of fame,
             Of parents good, of fist most valiant:
             I kiss his dirty shoe, and from heartstring
             I love the lovely bully.

Pistol comes closer and peers into the CAMERA.

PISTOL: What is thy name?

HENRY: (off) Henry Le Roy.

PISTOL: Le Roy? A Cornish name: are thou of
             Cornish crew?

HENRY: (off) No, I'm a Welshman.

PISTOL: Know'st thou Fluellen?

HENRY: (off) Yes.

PISTOL: Art thou his friend?

HENRY: (off) I am his kinsman too.

PISTOL: Well, tell him, I'll knock his leek about his head
             Upon Saint Davy's day.

HENRY: (off) Do not wear your dagger in your cap that day,
             Lest he knock that about yours.

PISTOL: A figo for thee, then!

Pistol runs back.

HENRY: (off) I thank you: God be with you!

PISTOL: My name is Pistol call'd.

HENRY: (off) It sorts well with your fierceness . . .

Pistol goes out R.

M.C.S. Henry. He laughs and walks R. CAMERA TRACKS WITH him. He suddenly stops.

M.C.S. A man is scrabbling in the undergrowth. CAMERA TRACKS LEFT with him, and STOPS as the Man (Fluellen) stands up and jumps down to a trench.

GOWER: (off) Captain Fluellen!

CAMERA PANS LEFT to show Gower. He walks right CAMERA PANS with him.

GOWER: Captain Fluellen!

Fluellen jumps up beside him.

FLUELLEN: Sh! Sh! In the name of Beezlebub
                speak lower. It you would take the pains
                but to examine the wars of Pompey the
                Great, you shall find, I warrant you,
                there is no tiddle taddle nor pibble
                pabble in Pompey's camp; I warrant
                you, you shall find the ceremonies
                of the wars, and the cares of it, and
                the forms of it, to be otherwise.

GOWER: Why, the enemy is loud, you can hear
                him all night.

FLUELLEN: If the enemy is an ass and a fool, and
                a prating coxcomb; is it meet, think
                you, that we should also, look you,
                be an ass and a fool, and a prating
                coxcomb in your own conscience, now?

GOWER: I will speak lower.

FLUELLEN: I pray you, and do beseech you, that you will.

They move off.

HENRY: (off) Though it appear a little out of fashion
               There is much care and valour in this Welshman.

CAMERA TRACKS L. and centres on Court, Bates and Williams, seated round
a camp fire.

COURT: Brother John Bates, is not that the
               morning which breaks yonder?

BATES: I think it be: But we have no great
               cause to desire the approach of day.

CAMERA TRACKS LEFT.

WILLIAMS: We see yonde- .ne beginning of the day,
               but I think we shall never see the end
               of it.

He looks up.

               Who goes there?

M.L.S. Henry.

HENRY: A friend.

Williams comes into L. f.g.

WILLIAMS: Under what captain serve you?

HENRY: Under Sir Thomas Erpingham.

Williams and Henry join Court and Bates at the camp fire, and sit down
with them.

WILLIAMS: A good old commander, and a most kind gentleman:
               I pray you, what thinks he of our estate?

HENRY: Even as men wreck'd upon a sand that
               look to be wash'd off the next tide.

BATES: He hath not told his thought to the
               king?

HENRY: No; nor it is not meet he should.
               For, I think the king is but a man,

HENRY (Cont'd)
   as I am: the violet smells to him as
   it doth to me; his ceremonies laid by,
   in his nakedness he appears but a man;
   therefore, when he sees reason of fears,
   as we do, his fears without doubt, be
   of the same relish as ours are; yet,
   no man should find in him any
   appearance of fear; lest he, by showing it, should dishearten his army.

WILLIAMS: He may show what outward courage he
   will; but I believe, as cold a night
   as 'tis, he wish himself in Thames
   up to the neck; so I would he were,
   and I by him, at all adventures, so
   we were quit here.

C.U. Henry.

HENRY: By my troth, I will speak my conscience
   of the king. I think he would not
   wish himself anywhere, but where he is.

C.U. Bates.

BATES: Then I would he were here alone; so
   should he be sure to be ransomed, and
   a many poor man's lives saved.

C.U. Henry.

HENRY: Methinks, I would not die anywhere
   so contented, as in the king's company;
   his cause being just, and his quarrel
   honourable.

M.C.S. Bates and Williams.

WILLIAMS: That's more than we know.

BATES: Ay, or more than we should seek after;
   for we know enough, if we know we are
   the king's subjects; if his cause be
   wrong, our obedience to the king wipes
   the crime of it out of us.

COURT: (off) But if the cause be no good . . .

C.U. Court.

COURT (Cont'd). . . the king himself hath a heavy
reckoning to make, when all those legs,
and arms, and heads, chopp'd off in a
battle, shall join together at the
latter day, and cry all "We died at
such a place" some swearing, some
crying for a surgeon, some upon their
wives left poor behind them; some
upon the debts they owe, some upon
their children rawly left. I'm afraid
there are few die well that die in a
battle; for how can they charitably
dispose of anything, when blood is
their argument? Now if these men do
not die well, it will be a black
matter for the king, that led them to
it.

WILLIAMS: (off) Ay!

M.S. The Group.

BATES: Ay!

HENRY: So, if a son that is by his father sent
about merchandise do sinfully miscarry
upon the sea, the imputation of his
wickedness, by your rule, should be
imposed upon his father that sent him:
but this is not so: the king is not
bound to answer for the particular
endings of his soldiers, nor the father
of his son, for they purpose their
services. Every subject's duty is the
king's but every subject's soul is his
own.

WILLIAMS: Ay, 'tis certain, every man that dies ill,
ills on his own head, the king's not to
answer for it.

BATES: I do not desire he should answer for
me, and yet I determine to fight
lustily for him.

HENRY: I myself heard the king say he would
not be ransom'd.

WILLIAMS: He said so, to make us fight cheerfully:
                 but when our throats are cut, he may
                 be ransom'd, and we ne'er the wiser.

HENRY: If ever I live to see it, I'll never
                 trust his word after.

C.U. Williams. He laughs, turning L. then R.

WILLIAMS: That's a perilous shot out of a pop-
                 gun, that a poor and a private displeasure
                 can do against a monarch!

He moves R. Closes up to Henry, CAMERA PANS WITH HIM.

                 You may as well go about to turn the sun
                 to ice, with fanning in his face with a
                 peacock's feather. You'll never trust
                 his word after! Come, 'tis a foolish
                 saying.

HENRY: Your reproof is something too round,
                 I should be angry with you, if the
                 time were convenient.
                                        FANFARE.
WILLIAMS: Let it be a quarrel between us then
                 if you live.

BATES: Be . . .

C.U. Bates.

BATES: . . . friends, you English fools . . .

He grabs Williams by the arm and they walk away from camera, which
TRACKS BACK to leave Henry sitting alone with the sleeping Court.

BATES: . . . be friends, we have French
                 quarrels enough if you could tell how
                 to reckon.

C.U. Henry.

HENRY: (off)
                 Upon the king! Let us our lives, our souls,
                 Our debts, our careful wives
                 Our children, and our sins, lay on the king!
                 We must bear all. What infinite heart's ease
                 Must kings forego, that private men enjoy!

HENRY (Cont'd)
>   And what have kings, that privates have not too,
>   Save ceremony.
>   And what art thou, thou idol ceremony?
>   . . . That suffer'st more
>   Of mortal griefs than do thy worshippers?

The CAMERA IS TRACKING SLOWLY IN to BIG C.U.

HENRY:
>   What drink'st thou oft, instead of homage sweet,
>   But poison'd flattery? O, be sick, great greatness,
>   And bid thy ceremony give thee cure!
>   Canst thou, when thou command'st the beggar's knee,
>   Command the health of it? No, thou proud dream,
>   That play'st so subtly with a king's repose;
>   I am a king that find thee:

Henry looks R.

>   . . . and I know,
>   'Tis not the orb and sceptre, crown imperial,
>   The throne he sits on; not the tide of pomp
>   The beats upon the high shore of this world;
>   Not all these, laid in bed majestical,
>   Can sleep so soundly as the wretched slave;

Henry looks down and CAMERA TRACKS BACK to show Court asleep at his feet.

>   Who with body fill'd, and vacant mind,
>   Gets him to rest, crammed with distressful bread,
>   Never sees horrid night,

The CAMERA IS STILL SLOWLY TRACKING BACK as Henry looks at the sunrise in the b.g.

>   . . . the child of hell;
>   But like a lackey, from the rise to set,
>   Sweats in the eye of Phoebus; and all night
>   Sleeps in Elysium; next day after dawn,
>   Doth rise and help Hyperion to his horse,
>   And follows so the ever-running year
>   With profitable labour to his grave:
>   And, but for ceremony, such a wretch,
>   Winding up days with toil, and nights with sleep,
>   Had the fore-hand and vantage of a king.

Henry sits back against a tree.

C.S. Henry. A knight comes round behind him.

ERPINGHAM: (off) My lord, . . .

Henry looks up.

C.U. Erpingham.

ERPINGHAM: (contd)
                . . . your nobles, jealous of your absence,
                Seek through your camp to find you.

Henry standing up, comes into picture on L.

HENRY: Good old knight.

Henry turns L. and walks on to the camp followed by Erpingham.   CAMERA
TRACKS WITH THEM.
                              CHANTED PRAYERS ARE HEARD.
Henry hears them and walks to a tent.

C.U. Henry pulls back the tent flap and sees a service in progress.
The chanting has stopped and prayers are being read. Henry walks on L.
CAMERA TRACKS WITH HIM an 'AMEN' is chanted and more prayers are spoken
from a second tent. Henry stops and turns to Erpingham . . .

HENRY: Collect them all together at my tent;
                I'll be before thee.

Erpingham goes out left.
Henry walks on alone, CAMERA PANS WITH HIM.

                              FANFARE.

Henry turns round to CAMERA and kneels down.

HENRY: O God of battles, steel my soldiers' hearts,
                Possess them not with fear; take from them now
                The sense of reckoning lest the opposed numbers
                Pluck their hearts from them.

GLOUCESTER: (off)
                My lord!

M.S. Gloucester comes down the hillside to Henry.

GLOUCESTER: (contd).
                . . . My lord, the army stays upon your presence.

                              FANFARE.

HENRY: I know thy errand, I will go with thee,

                              FANFARE.

        The day, my friends, and all things stay for me.

                              FANFARE.

Henry takes Gloucester's shoulder and they walk away up the hill.

                              FADE OUT:

FADE IN.
M.S. FLEUR DE LIS TENT FLAP is swept aside to show French Dukes arming
themselves.

                              MUSIC STARTS

BOURBON: The sun doth gild our armour!
                Up, my lords!

DAUPHIN: Montez a cheval! My Horse! Varlet!
                Lacquais! Ha!

ORLEANS: O brave spirit.

DAUPHIN: Via! Les eaux et la terre.

ORLEANS: Rien puis? L'air et le feu.

DAUPHIN: Ciel, cousin Orleans.

Constable enters right.

CONSTABLE: Hark, how our steeds for present
                service neigh.

DAUPHIN: Mount them, and make incision in their hides,
                That their hot blood may spin in English eyes,
                And quench them with superior courage, ha!

Messenger comes in left.

MESSENGER: The English are embattled, you French
                peers.

He exits left.

CONSTABLE: A very little little let us do,
                 And all is done: then let the trumpets sound
                 The tucket sonance, and the note to mount;

He walks down and goes out left, CAMERA PANS L. with him.

                 Come, come away!
                 The sun is high, and we outwear the day:

M.L.S. FRENCH CAMP.
Constable enters R. and is escorted to his horse, CAMERA PANS L.
Bourbon and Orleans follow, finally the Dauphin is escorted to his
horse.

                                        DISSOLVE TO:

C.S. THE CROSS OF ST. GEORGE, CAMERA PANS R. with it to reveal in
M.L.S. the Standard Bearer and Group of English Knights. Gloucester
enters L. in the English Camp.

GLOUCESTER: Where is the King?

SALISBURY: The King himself is rode to view their
                 battle.

WESTMORELAND: Of fighting men they have full three
                 score hundred.

EXETER: There's five to one, besides they are
                 all flesh.

GLOUCESTER: God's arm strike with us, 'tis a
                 fearful odds.

Salisbury shakes hands with his fellow Knights.

SALISBURY: Well, God with you, princes all; I'll to my charge:
                 If we no more meet, till we meet in heaven,
                 Then joyfully, my noble Westmoreland,
                 My dear Lord Gloucester, my good Lord Exeter,
                 And my kind kinsman, warriors all adieu!

WESTMORELAND: Farewell, good Salisbury.

GLOUCESTER: And good luck go with thee!

EXETER: Farewell, kind lord.

Salisbury goes out R.

WESTMORELAND: O that we now had here
                But one ten thousand of those men in England
                That do not work today!

HENRY: (off) What's he that wishes so?

                                                MUSIC STOPS

M.S. Henry.

HENRY: My cousin Westmoreland? No, my fair cousin:

He walks L. to the group of Knights, CAMERA PANS with him.

                If we are mark'd to die, we are enough
                To do our country loss: and if to live,
                The fewer men, the greater share of honour.
                God's will, I pray thee wish not one man more.
                Rather proclaim it, Westmoreland, through my host,

He walks L. and away from camera, CAMERA PANS with him.

                That he which hath no stomach to his feast,
                Let him depart, his passport shall be drawn
                And crowns for convoy put into his purse:

He turns round to face camera:

                We would not die in that man's company
                That fears his fellowship to die with us.

He walks down to camera.

                This day is call'd the feast of Crispian:
                He that outlives this day, and comes safe home,
                Will stand a tip-toe when this day is named,
                And rouse him at the name of Crispian.

He walks R. still closer to camera, CAMERA PANS with him.

                He that shall live this day, and see old age,
                Will, yearly on the vigil feast his neighbours,
                And say, 'Tomorrow is Saint Crispian':
                Then will he strip his sleeve, and show his scars,
                And say 'These wounds I had on Crispian's day.'

He turns and walks L. CAMERA TRACKS L.

> Old men forget; yet all shall be forgot
> But he'll remember with advantages,
> What feats he did that day: Then shall our names
> Familiar in his mouth as household words,
> Harry the King, Bedford and Exeter,

He climbs on to a cart. CAMERA TRACKS SLOWLY BACK to L.S. to show his
Army clustered around him.

> Warwick and Talbot, Salisbury and Gloucester,
> Be in their flowing cups freshly remember'd.
> This story shall the good man teach his son;
> And Crispin Crispian shall ne'er go by,
> From this day to the ending of the world,
> But we in it shall be remembered,
> We few, we happy few, we band of brothers;
> For he today that sheds his blood with me,
> Shall be my brother be he ne'er so base.
> And gentlemen in England, now a-bed,
> Shall think themselves accurs'd they were not here;
> And hold their manhoods cheap, whiles any speaks
> That fought with us upon Saint Crispian's day.

The soldiers cheer.

M.S. Henry in Left f.g. Salisbury pushes through the soldiers from the
side of the cart.

SALISBURY: My sovereign lord, bestow yourself with speed:
                The French are bravely in their battles set,
                And will, with all expedience charge on us.

HENRY: All things are ready, if our minds be so.

Westmoreland comes round to the cart.

WESTMORELAND: Perish the man whose mind is backward now!

C.U. Henry.

HENRY: Thou dost not wish more help from England, coz ?

C.U. WESTMORELAND.

WESTMORELAND: God's will, my liege, would you and I alone,
                Without more help, could fight this . . .

C.U. Henry.

WESTMORELAND: (off) . . . battle out!

HENRY: You know your places! God be with you all!

M.L.S. Henry turns and jumps on a horse, CAMERA PANS LEFT with him.

                                        MUSIC STARTS

He rides round R. close to and then away from camera.

L.S. Men driving in stakes.

M.C.S. a Soldier helping Henry to put on his chain mail.

M.C.S. The Dauphin being lowered by pulley onto his horse.

M.L.S. The Dauphin being settled on his horse. It is led round R. and
CAMERA PANS with it.

M.S. Line of French Drummers.

M.S. Orleans, Dauphin and Bourbon being handed cups of wine on horseback.

M.S. Constable and another Knight toasting the Dauphin and company.

M.S. The Dauphin and company acknowledging the toast.

C.S. Englishmen banging in a stake.

L.S. Line of Englishmen banging in stakes.

M.S. Arrows being distributed to English archers.

M.S. Englishmen sharpening stakes.

                                        FANFARE

The man nearest camera looks ahead of him (screen R.)

L.S. Mountjoy and Standard Bearer escorted by two Heralds ride up towards camera. The Heralds stop and sound a FANFARE as Mountjoy and
Bearer ride on into the English camp, CAMERA PANS LEFT with them round
to the camp.

M.S. Mountjoy dismounts and is escorted by English Herald out of picture left.

M.S. Henry in full armour on his horse. Mountjoy and English Herald come in R. and doff their hats to the King. Henry smiles at Mountjoy.

M.C.S. Mountjoy. The head of Henry's horse in L. f.g.

MUSIC STOPS

MOUNTJOY: Once more I come to know of thee, King Harry,
              If for thy ransom thou wilt now compound,
              Before thy most assured overthrow:

The King's horse shakes its head.

M.S. Henry and Mountjoy.

HENRY: Who hath sent thee now?

MOUNTJOY: The Constable of France.

DRUM IN BACKGROUND.

HENRY: I pray thee, bear my former answer back:
              Bid them achieve me, and then sell my bones.
              Good God, why should they mock poor fellows thus?
              The man that once did sell the lion's skin
              While the beast lived was killed in hunting him,
              And many of our bodies shall no doubt,
              Find native graves: upon the which, I trust,
              Shall witness live in brass of this day's work.
              And those that leave their valiant bones in France,
              Dying like men, though buried in your dunghills,
              They shall be fam'd; for there the sun shall greet them
              And draw their honours reeking up to heaven,
              Leaving their earthly parts to choke your clime,
              The smell whereof whall breed a plague in France.
              Let me speak proudly: tell the Constable
              We are but warriors for the working day;
              Our gayness and our gilt are all besmirch'd
              With rainy marching in the painful field;
              And time hath worn us into slovenry:
              But, by the mass, our hearts are in trim;

SOLDIERS CHEER.

Come thou no more for ransom, gentle herald,

MUSIC STARTS.

> They shall have none, I swear, but these my bones;
> Which if they have as I will leave 'em them,
> Shall yield them little, tell the Constable.

Henry rides out left.

M.C.S. Mountjoy -- he flourishes his hat.

MOUNTJOY: I shall, King Harry. And so fare thee well.

He prepares to mount his horse.

M.C.S. Mountjoy -- he mounts his horse.

MOUNTJOY: Thou never shalt hear herald any more.
                                             FANFARE.
He rides out R. of screen followed by his Standard-Bearer.

Henry rides in Left b.g.

HENRY: Now, soldiers, march away.

                                        SOLDIERS CHEER.

> And how thou pleasest, God, dispose the day!

                                        DISSOLVE TO:

L.S. AERIAL VIEW OF THE BATTLEFIELD.

L.S. THE FRENCH ARMY.
                                        FANFARE.

L.S. THE ENGLISH ARMY.
                                        FANFARE.

M.S. Line of French Drummers.

L.S. French Crossbowmen moving up.

M.C.S. French drums.

L.S. French Cavalry moving up to battle position. The Constable signals with his sword and they turn left.

C.S. French Standards dip and move out of picture left.

M.S. Mire. The reflection and then the hoofs of French Cavalry cross the screen, CAMERA PANS LEFT with them.

                                        FANFARE
                                        DISSOLVE.

L.S. The French Cavalry in battle order at the walk.

M.S. A line of English Bowmen draw their bows.

M.C.S. Henry on his horse.

L.S. The French Cavalry break into a trot, then a canter then a gallop then a full tilt charge.

M.S. Line of English Archers with bows drawn.

M.C.S. Low angle shot of Henry with sword poised for signal to Archers. His glance changes from left to right.

L.S. The French Cavalry charging with English stakes in foreground.

M.C.S. Line of English Bowmen with bows drawn.

M.C.S. Henry -- he slashes down his sword.

                                        MUSIC STOPS.

M.C.S. Line of English Archers -- they fire.

M.L.S. Line of English Archers -- they fire.

L.S. The French Cavalry with stake emplacements in foreground. Arrows sizzle through the air overhead and strike home. The French Cavalry rears.

                                        MUSIC STARTS.
M.S. English Archers firing.

L.S. French Cavalry in confusion. Stakes in f.g.

M.S. French Cavalry in confusion.

M.S. French Cavalry in confusion.

M.S. French Cavalry in confusion.

M.C.S. French Charger rearing madly.

M.C.S. French Charger rearing madly.

M.S. English Archers firing.

M.S. French Cavalry in confusion.

M.S. French Cavalry in confusion.

M.C.S. French Cavalry in confusion.

C.U. Horse neighing hysterically.

C.U. Horse neighing hysterically.

M.S. English Archers run forward and prepare to fire.

M.C.S. French Charger rearing.

M.S. French Cavalry in confusion.

M.C.S. French Cavalry in confusion.

M.S. French Cavalry in confusion.

M.C.S. French Cavalry in confusion.

L.S. Second wave of Cavalry charging towards camera.

M.C.S. French Cavalry in confusion, and turning to retreat.

M.L.S. French Cavalry turning and retreating screen right.

L.S. Second Wave of French Cavalry charging screen left.

L.S. French Cavalry in full retreat.

L.S. Second Wave of French Cavalry charging.

L.S. First Wave of French Cavalry in retreat clashes with Second Wave of advancing French Cavalry. CAMERA PANS L. to R.

M.S. Advancing French Cavalry trying to make headway.

M.S. The two waves of Cavalry enmeshed.

M.L.S. English Archer firing.

M.S. French Cavalry enmeshed. CAMERA PANS R. to morass behind them.

M.S. English Archers fire and run forward.

M.L.S. French Infantry, in support of Cavalry become entangled in the morass. CAMERA PANS L. to R.

M.S. French Cavalry enmeshed.

M.L.S. French Infantry struggling in the morass. CAMERA PANS L. & TRACKS BACK TO L.S.

> DISSOLVE TO:
> MUSIC STOPS.

L.S. French Infantry bogged down in the morass.

> DISSOLVE TO:
>
> MUSIC STARTS.

L.S. The Third Wave of advancing French Cavalry appears over a hilltop. They charge towards CAMERA.

L.S. The French Cavalry charging. English Archers are firing from the fringe of a wood in f.g. but they retreat.

> DISSOLVE TO:

L.S. Top shot of French Cavalry charging through the wood, CAMERA PANS LEFT with them. An English Infantryman jumps from the branch of a tree on to a French Knight.

M.C.S. Infantryman drags Knight from his horse and goes to stab him.

M.S. Infantryman jumps from branch of the tree.

M.S. He hits the ground.

M.S. Another Infantryman jumps from the branch of the tree.

M.S. Infantryman lands on ground among French Knights.

M.S. Two more Infantrymen jump from branches.

M.L.S. English and French Infantry fighting hand to hand. Henry with Standard Bearer leads flank attack of his Knights. CAMERA PANS R. to centre the Standard.

> DISSOLVE TO:

L.S. THE BATTLEFIELD. Henry rides round from R. b.g. CAMERA PANS LEFT
with him.

HENRY: Well have we done, thrice valiant countrymen
              But all's not done, yet keep the French the field.

He has ridden to camera and on his last word slashes with his sword.

DISSOLVE TO:

C.S. The English Standard, the Cross of St. George, CAMERA PANS R. to
reveal Henry and Standard Bearer riding through the thick of the
Infantry fighting. CAMERA centres the Standard.

DISSOLVE TO:

C.S. The French Standard. CAMERA PANS R. to reveal in L.S. French
Knights and Mountjoy with Herald fleeing to a hilltop.

M.S. The French Knights on the hilltop.

DAUPHIN: O everlasting shame! Let's stab ourselves:
              Be these the wretches that we play'd at dice for?

ORLEANS: Is this the king we sent to for his ransom?

Constable rides in R. f.g.

CONSTABLE: Shame, and eternal shame, nothing but shame!
              Let's die in honour: once more back again.

M.S. Dauphin and Orleans.

ORLEANS: We are enough yet living in the field
              To smother up the English in our throngs,
              If any order might be thought upon.

Constable rides in picture left round to the f.g.

CONSTABLE: The devil take order now! I'll to the throng:
              Let life be short, else shame will

He rides out of picture left.

M.S. Bourbon and Standard Bearer. The Constable and Standard Bearer
dash across picture R. to L.

CONSTABLE: (contd) . . . be too long.

Bourbon starts to move off L.

L.S. French Knights on the hilltop. Constable and Standard Bearer ride down the hill and out L. Bourbon leads a second party of Knights who pause to wait for the remaining few but turn and ride on out of picture.

M.S. The Dauphin and Mountjoy on the hilltop looking screen L.

M.C.S. Mountjoy -- he looks R. then L.

M.C.S. The Dauphin -- he looks screen L.

DISSOLVE TO:

L.S. The English Camp. French Knights ride in from screen R.

M.S. French Knight riding into the English Camp. CAMERA PANS L. with him as he cuts down a tent and kills a boy.

C.U. The dead Boy. Another camp boy picks him up and looks at him then drops him quickly.

M.S. The second boy running hard to camera. A French Knight crosses screen L. to R.

M.C.S. A small fire on the ground. A French Knight rides in and picks up a fire brand with his sword, CAMERA PANS LEFT to reveal him in L.S. as he flings it into a tent. Another Knight rides in L. CAMERA PANS R. down to the fire, as this Knight spears a fire brand with his sword.

C.U. Fire brand on sword held aloft, CAMERA PANS R. AND DOWN to reveal this Knight in L.S. preparing to fling it into a cart. Another French Knight crosses the screen R. to L. as a boy runs towards Camera with a casket in his hand.

M.C.S. The BOY runs into picture R. and stops near a bush with a brazier along side. He looks R.

L.S. The Knight flinging the fire brand into the cart.

M.C.S. The Boy thrusts the casket under the bush and runs out L. The Knight dashes in R. and overturns the brazier.

C.U. The Bush catching fire.

MUSIC STOPS:

M.S. INSIDE TENT IN ENGLISH CAMP. The tent is on fire and a dead boy can be seen in the f.g. Through the tent opening French Knights can be seen to ride away.

DISSOLVE.
MUSIC STARTS.

L.S. THE ENGLISH CAMP ON FIRE.

M.C.S. The Dauphin looking at the camp. He surveys the scene then rides out L. Mountjoy rides in R.

L.S. The Marauding French Knights ride in L. and join Mountjoy. CAMERA PANS L. with them. In the distance the Dauphin is seen in flight.

M.C.S. Fluellen in the English Camp with a dead boy in his arms.

FLUELLEN: God's plud, Kill the boys and the
                luggage!

Gower walks in L. b.g. with a Monk. CAMERA TRACKS BACK to M.S.

                'tis expressly against the law of
                arms. 'Tis as arrant a piece of
                knavery, mark you now, as can be
                offered, in your conscience now, is
                it not?

GOWER: 'Tis certain there's not a boy left
                alive, and the cowardly rascals that
                ran from the battle ha' done this
                slaughter . . .

Henry, on foot, followed by Soldiers leading his horse enters L. b.g. with Standard Bearer on another horse.

MONK: Here comes His Majesty.

Henry walks on to the Group, CAMERA TRACKS FORWARD.

HENRY: I was not angry since I came to
                France until this instant.

He mounts his horse and rides out L.

MUSIC STARTS.

L.S. Henry riding full tilt back to the battlefield. CAMERA PANS L. to R. with him.

M.S. The Constable in the thick of the fighting.

C.U. The Constable lifts his visor and looks screen L.

L.S. Henry followed by his Standard Bearer riding up to meet the Constable.

C.U. The Constable slams down his visor.

M.C.S. Constable rears his horse and rides screen L.

M.C.S. Henry and the Constable clash swords.

L.S. The Constable positions to attack again.

L.S. Henry swings his horse round and the Constable rides in L. They exchange sword blows.

C.U. The Constable striking with his sword.

C.U. The sword crashing on Henry's helmet.

M.C.S. Constable's horse rearing.

M.S. Henry rides L. to the b.g. CAMERA PANS with him. Constable rides in L. f.g.

M.C.S. The Constable swinging his horse round L. to attack again.

M.C.S. Henry swinging his horse round L. He rides extreme R.

M.C.S. Constable riding extreme L.

M.S. Henry and the Constable. They exchange sword blows.

C.U. Henry's sword knocking the Constable's sword out of his hand.

M.L.S. Henry's horse rearing. Constable rides out L.

M.C.S. The Constable dropping his shield. He grabs his mace. Henry rides in R. The Constable knocks Henry's sword out of his hand.

C.S. The Constable's mace striking Henry's hand and Henry's sword flying out of it.

C.S. Henry's sword sticking in the ground.

C.U. Low angle shot. The Constable raises his mace.

C.U. Henry looking screen L.

C.U. The Constable about to strike.

C.U. Henry, CAMERA PANS LEFT and he strikes the Constable's chin with his fist.

M.S. Henry in L. f.g. The Constable falls from the horse CAMERA PANS R. to the ground with him.

C.U. Constable on the ground.

M.S. Two soldiers leave the circle of British Onlookers and take the Constable's horse as Henry turns and rides R. to the place where the Constable fell. He bends down to pick up Constable's sword. CAMERA PANS R. with him.

M.S. The Constable's body with Henry's sword beside it. Henry comes into picture L. and the CAMERA PANS UP R. and then L. with him as he rides out.

L.S. Henry riding down the hill as the English soldiers surge round the body of Constable. Henry rides up to the English Herald in mid-shot -- CAMERA PANS R. with him.

HENRY: Take a trumpet herald.
                Ride thou unto the horsemen on yon hill;
                If they will fight with us, bid them come down,
                Or void the field; they do offend our sight.

Henry rides out L. and the Herald rides away from camera towards French Knights on a hill in the b.g.

M.S. Group of English Knights -- Henry rides in R. Exeter points screen R.

EXETER: Here comes the herald of the French, my
                liege.

L.S. Mountjoy meets the English Herald on the hillside and they ride toward L. of screen together.

M.S. Henry and the English Knights.

SALISBURY: His eyes are humbler than they us'd to be.

HENRY: God's will, what means this, herald?
                Com'st thou again for ransom?

Mountjoy enters R. f.g. and bows.

MUSIC STOPS.

C.U. Mountjoy.

MOUNTJOY: No, great King;
                I come to thee for charitable licence.
                That we may wander o'er this bloody field,
                To look our dead, and then to bury them.
                The day is yours.

C.U. Henry.

HENRY: Praised be God, and not our strength,
                for it!

CAMERA TRACKS BACK as Henry takes off his helmet to leave Henry and Mountjoy in mid-shot with Agincourt castle in the b.g.

MUSIC STARTS.

HENRY: What is this castle call'd that stands hard
                by?

MOUNTJOY: We call it Agincourt.

HENRY: Then call we this the field of Agincourt,
                Fought on the day of Crispin Crispianus.

Mountjoy kneels and kisses Henry's hand. Standard Bearer steps forward and raises the Cross of St. George.

C.U. The Cross of St. George comes into picture, Agincourt Castle in R. b.g.

DISSOLVE:

L.S. Dead Soldiers lie in the L. f.g. of the field of Dead.

DISSOLVE:

M.S. The English Knights drinking in the English Camp. Fluellen ushers the English Herald forward, who walks L. to Henry who is surrounded by Exeter and one or two others. CAMERA TRACKS LEFT with Herald. He hands Henry a paper.

HERALD: Here is the number of slaughtered French.

HENRY: This note doth tell me of ten thousand French
                That in the field lie slain,
                Where is the number of our English dead?

The Herald hands him another paper.

                                        MUSIC STOPS.

                Edward the Duke of York, the Earl of Suffolk,
                Sir Richard Ketly, Davy Gam, esquire;
                and of all other men but five and twenty score.
                O God, thy arm was here!

EXETER: 'Tis wonderful!

HENRY: Come, go we in procession to the village;

Henry's horse is led in L.

                Let there be sung 'Non Nobis' and 'Te Deum'.

                                        SINGING STARTS.

Henry mounts his horse.

                . . . and then to Calais and to England then . . .

Henry leads the procession out of the English Camp, CAMERA PANS L. to R.

                . . . where ne'er from France arriv'd more happier men.

                                        DISSOLVE TO:

L.S. The English Army walking in procession towards Agincourt Village.

                                        DISSOLVE TO:

L.S. THE FIELD OF DEAD.

L.S. THE ENGLISH ARMY in procession.

                                        FADE OUT.
                                        SINGING STOPS.

FADE IN:

L.S. AGINCOURT VILLAGE IN THE SNOW

                                        MUSIC STARTS.

DISSOLVE TO:

M.S. THE GATE TO THE VILLAGE. CAMERA TRACKS FORWARD to reveal Pistol flirting with village women inside house. CAMERA PANS R. to show three boys singing carols, CAMERA TRACKS FORWARD again as a couple emerge from a house and goes into the Church alongside. A Man comes out of the Church and CAMERA PANS L. with him to reveal Fluellen and Gower sitting on a wall. CAMERA TRACKS to them in M.C.S.

MUSIC STOPS.

Gower laughs.

GOWER: Nay, that's right; but why wear you your leek
                today? Saint Davy's day is past.

FLUELLEN: There is occasions and causes why and where-
                fore in all things Captain Gower: I will
                tell you as my friend, Captain Gower: the
                rascally, beggarly, lousy, knave Pistol, which
                you and yourself, and all the world, know to
                be no petter than a fellow, look you, of no
                merits; he is come to me, and prings me
                pread and salt yesterday, look you, and bid
                me eat my leek:

Gower laughs.

                It was in a place where I could not breed no
                contention with him; but I will be so bold as
                to wear it in my cap till I see him once
                again, and then I will tell him a little piece
                of my desires.

GOWER: Why, 'tis a gull, a fool, a rogue, that now
                and then goes to the wars, to grace himself
                at his return into London, under the form of
                soldier, and what such of the camp can do
                among foaming bottles, and ale-washed wits, is
                wonderful to be thought on:

He laughs and points screen L.

                Here he comes . . .

M.S. Pistol walking L. to R. CAMERA PANS with him to bring him in front of Fluellen and Gower.

GOWER: (off) . . . swelling like a turkey-cock.

FLUELLEN: (off) 'Tis no matter for his swellings, nor
                his turkey-cocks.

Fluellen and Gower are now in picture.

                God pless you, Pistol! you scurvy lousy
                knave, God pless you.

PISTOL: Ha! art thou bedlam? Hence! I am qualmish
                at the smell of leek.

Fluellen jumps off the wall and confronts Pistol.

FLUELLEN: I peseech you heartily, scurvy, lousy knave,
                to eat, look you, this leek:

Fluellen snatches the leek from his cap and holds it under Pistol's
nose.

PISTOL: Not for Cadwallader and all his goats.

Pistol walks away, CAMERA PANS R. with him. Fluellen kicks Pistol's
bottom.

FLUELLEN: There is one goat for you. Will you be so good
                as eat it?

Pistol draws his sword.

PISTOL: Base Trojan, thou shalt die.

Fluellen snatches the sword from Pistol and bangs him on the head with
it. Pistol falls to his knees.

FLUELLEN: You say very true when God's will is: I will
                desire you to live in the meantime, and eat
                your victuals. Come, there is sauce for it.

He hits Pistol in the face with the leek.

                If you can mock a leek, you can eat a leek.
                Bite, I pray you.

PISTOL: Must I bite?

FLUELLEN: Out of doubt and out of question too.

PISTOL: By this leek, I will most horribly revenge.

Fluellen threatens with the sword.

              I eat. I eat. I swear.

Pistol peels the leek.

FLUELLEN: Nay, pray you, throw none away, the skin is
              good for your broken coxcomb, when you take
              occasions to see leeks hereafter, I pray you
              mock at 'em, that is all.

PISTOL: Good.

FLUELLEN: Ay, leeks is good;

M.C.S. Gower sitting on the wall. He chuckles.

              (off) Hold you,

M.S. Fluellen and Pistol.

FLUELLEN: Here is a penny to heal your hand.

PISTOL: Me, a penny?

FLUELLEN: Yes, verily, and in truth you shall take it,
              or I have another leek in my pocket, which
              you shall eat.

Pistol takes the penny. Fluellen kisses Pistol's head and goes off L.

              God b'wi' you and keep you, and heel your head.

Pistol gets up and rushes to the gate at the side of the wall. CAMERA
PANS AND TRACKS with him.

PISTOL: All hell shall stir for this.

Gower enters L.

GOWER: Go, to, you are a counterfeit, cowardly knave,
              You thought because he could not speak
              English in the native garb, he therefore could not
              handle an English cudgel; you find it
              otherwise, and henceforth let a Welsh
              correction teach you a good English condition;
              Fare you well.

CAMERA PANS L. as Gower walks away from Pistol. Gower turns and throws a coin out of screen R.

M.C.S. Pistol. Pistol takes the coin that has fallen into his helmet. He turns and walks straight into camera.

PISTOL: Doth Fortune play the strumpet with me now
                News have I that my Nell lies dead i' th' hospital
                Of the malady of France.
                And there my rendezvous is quite cut off.
                Old do I wax, and from my weary limbs
                Honour is cudgell'd. Well, bawd I'll turn,
                And something lean to cutpurse of quick hand.
                To England will I steal, and there I'll steal:
                And patches will I get unto these scars,
                And swear I got them in these present wars.

                                MUSIC STARTS.

Pistol scurries off L. and disappears in a barn. CAMERA TRACKS with him and past the barn. Pistol emerges from other side of barn with a pig under his arm and a cockerel in his hand. He runs up the hill away from camera and disappears.

                                DISSOLVE TO:

L.S. THE FRENCH PALACE.

L.S. THE GREAT HALL OF THE FRENCH PALACE. A choir is in the f.g. It is a high angle shot and the CAMERA TRACKS FORWARD and DOWN as the Duke of Burgundy and Attendants, later the French King and Court and Henry and Court take their places.

                                MUSIC STOPS.

HENRY: Peace to this meeting, wherefore we are met!
                Unto our brother France, and to our sister,
                Health and fair time of day; joy and good wishes
                To our most fair and princely cousin Katharine:
                And, as a branch and member of this royalty,
                We do salute you, Duke of Burgundy:
                And, princes French, and peers, health to you all!

M.S. King Charles and Queen Isabel surrounded by their court.

CHARLES: Right joyous are we to behold your face,
                Most worthy brother England, fairly met.
                So are you, princes English everyone.

ISABEL: So happy be the issue, brother England,
                 Of this good day, and of this gracious meeting,

M.S. Henry surrounded by his court.

ISABEL: (off) As we are now glad to behold your eyes . . .

M.S. Charles and Isabel.

ISABEL: . . . Your eyes which hitherto have borne in them
                 Against the French that met them in their bent,
                 The fatal balls of murdering basilisks.
                 The venom of such looks, we fairly hope,
                 Have lost their quality, and that this day,
                 Shall change all griefs and quarrels into love.

M.S. Henry.

HENRY: To cry amen to that, thus we appear.

He turns R.

L.S. The Duke of Burgundy. Henry in L. f.g. Charles in R.

BURGUNDY: My duty to you both, on equal love.
                 Great Kings of France and England,
                 Since that my office hath so far prevail'd
                 That face to face, and royal eye to eye,
                 You have assembled; let it not disgrace me,
                 Yet I demand before this royal view,
                 Why that naked, poor and mangled Peace,
                 Dear Nurse of arts, of plenties, and of joyful births,
                 Should not in this best garden of the world,
                 Our fertile France, put up her lovely visage?

M.C.S. Burgundy.

                                       MUSIC STARTS.

BURGUNDY: Alas, she hath from France too long been chas'd,

Burgundy turns and steps up to a window, CAMERA TRACKS with him.

                 And all her husbandry doth lie on heaps,
                 Corrupting in its own fertility.
                 Her vine, the merry cheerer of the heart

CAMERA PANS SLOWLY R. beyond the window out over the countryside.

BURGUNDY (Cont'd)

>   (off) Unpruned, dies, her hedges, even-pleach'd
>   Put forth disorder'd twigs; her fallow leas,
>   The darnel, hemlock, and rank fumitory
>   Doth root upon; while that the coulter rusts
>   That should deracinate such savagery;
>   That even mead, that erst brought sweetly forth
>   The freckled cowslip, burnet, and green clover,
>   Wanting the scythe, all uncorrected rank,
>   Conceives by idleness, and nothing teems,
>   But hateful docks, rough thistles, kecksies, burs,
>   Losing both beauty and utility;
>   Even so our houses, and ourselves, and children,

The slow CAMERA PAN pauses on two children then SLOWLY PANS UP to the French Castle.

BURGUNDY:

>   (off) Have lost, or do not learn, for want of time,
>   The sciences that should become our country;
>   But grow like savages, as soldiers will
>   That nothing do but meditate on blood,
>   To swearing, and stern looks, defus'd attire,

>   DISSOLVE TO:

M.S. Shooting from Outside the Window, Burgundy standing at it.

BURGUNDY: . . . and everything that seems unnatural.

>   MUSIC STOPS.

He turns and steps down from the window. Henry and Court can be seen in b.g. CAMERA TRACKS FORWARD.

>   Which to reduce into our former favour,
>   You are assembled . . .

HENRY: Then, Duke of Burgundy, you must gain that peace,
>   With full accord to all our just demands.

M.S. Charles and Isabel.

CHARLES: I have but with a cursory eye
>   O'erglanced the articles; pleaseth your grace
>   To appoint some of your council presently
>   To sit with us, we will suddenly
>   Pass our accept and peremptory answer.

M.C.S. Henry.

HENRY: Brother we shall.
                  Will you, fair sister,
                  Go with the princes, or stay here with us?

M.S. Charles and Isabel. Princess Katharine and Alice are in L. b.g.

ISABEL: Our gracious brother, I will go with them:
                  Haply a woman's voice may do some good,
                  When articles too nicely urg'd be stood on.

HENRY: (off) Yet leave our cousin Katharine here with us.

ISABEL: She hath good leave.

                                      MUSIC STARTS.

Isabel leads Katharine forward, CAMERA TRACKS BACK as the French Court
take their leave of Henry, to leave Henry and Katharine alone together.
Henry walks over to Katharine, CAMERA PANS L. to include Alice.

HENRY: Fair Katharine and most fair,
                  Will you vouchsafe to teach a soldier terms,
                  Such as will enter at a lady's ear,
                  And plead his love-suit to her gentle heart.

KATHARINE: Your majesty shall mock at me.
                  I cannot speak your England.

HENRY: O fair Katharine, if you will love me
                  soundly with your French heart, I will be
                  glad to hear you confess it brokenly with
                  your English tongue.

C.U. Henry.

HENRY: Do you like me Kate?

C.U. Katharine -- Alice in R. b.g.

KATHARINE: Pardonnez-moi, I cannot tell vat is 'like me'.

C.U. Henry -- he chuckles. He takes Katharine by the hand and she comes
in L. f.g. followed by Alice as CAMERA PANS R. with them and TRACKS
BACK. They are now at a window.

HENRY: An angel is like you, Kate, and you are like
                  an angel.

                                      MUSIC STOPS.

KATHARINE: Que dit-il? que je suis semblable à les anges?

ALICE: Oui, vraiment, sauf votre grace, ainsi dit-il.

KATHARINE: O bon Dieu! Les langues des hommes sont
             pleines de tromperies.

HENRY: What says she, fair one? that the tongues
             of men are full of deceits?

ALICE: Oui . . .

C.U. Alice.

ALICE: . . . dat de tongues of de mans is be full of
             deceits.

M.C.S. Henry and Katharine at the window. Henry walks over to the R.
of Katharine, CAMERA PANS with him.

HENRY: I'faith, Kate, I am glad thou canst speak
             no better English, for, if thou couldst thou
             wouldst find me such a plain king that thou
             wouldst think I had sold my farm to buy my
             crown. I know no ways to mince it in love,
             but directly to say, 'I love you'. Give me
             your answer, i' faith, do, and so clasp hands
             and a bargain: how say you lady?

C.U. Alice -- she nods encouragingly to Katharine.

M.C.S. Katharine and Henry.

KATHARINE: Sauf votre honneur, me understand vell.

HENRY: Marry, if you put me to verses, or to
             dance for your sake, Kate why you undo me.
             If I might buffet for my love, or bound
             my horse for her favours,
             I could lay on like a butcher, and
             sit like a jack-an-apes, never off.

He has stepped down from the window and CAMERA TRACKS BACK. With back
to camera in f.g. he talks to Kate in centre b.g.

             But before God, Kate I cannot look greenly,
             nor gasp out my eloquence . . .

He walks out of picture R. CAMERA TRACKS SLOWLY IN towards Katharine.

HENRY: (off) . . . nor have I no cunning in
                protestation. If thou canst love a fellow
                of this temper, Kate, that never looks in
                his glass for the love of anything he sees
                there, whose face is not worth sunburning . . .

He comes into picture L. f.g.

                . . . take me.

He steps up to the window beside Katharine.

HENRY: (contd) If not, to say to thee that I shall
                die, is true; but for thy love, by the lord,
                no!

Katharine stands up.

C.U. Alice stands up in alarm.

M.C.S. Henry and Katharine.

HENRY: Yet I love thee too.

Henry stands up and Katharine sits down.

                And while thou liv'st, dear Kate, take a
                fellow of plain constancy; for these fellows
                of infinite tongue, that can rhyme themselves
                into ladies' favours, they do always reason
                themselves out again. A speaker is but a
                prater, a rhyme is but a ballad, a straight
                back will stoop, a black beard will turn
                white, a fair face will wither, a full eye
                will wax hollow, but a good heart, Kate, is
                the sun and the moon. If thou wouldst have
                such a one, take me, and take me, take a
                soldier; take a soldier; take a king.
                And what say'st thou then to my love? speak,
                my fair, and fairly, I pray thee.

Katharine rises and walks R. alone to a window, CAMERA PANS with her.

M.C.S. Katharine at the window.

KATHARINE: Is it possible dat I sould love de enemy
                of France?

Henry steps up to the window beside her.

HENRY: No, Kate, but in loving me you should love
                the friend of France; for I love France so
                well that I will not part with a village of
                it; and Kate, when France is mine, and I am
                yours, then yours is France, and you are mine.

KATHARINE: I cannot tell vat is dat.

HENRY: No, Kate? I will tell thee in French, which
                I am sure will hang upon my tongue like a new-
                married wife about her husband's neck, hardly
                to be shook off. Je quand sur le possession
                de France, et quand vous avez le possession
                de moi donc votre est France et vous êtes
                mienne.

They both laugh.

                I shall never move thee in French, unless
                it be to laugh at me.

KATHARINE: Sauf votre honneur, le François que je vous
                parlez, il est meilleur que l'Anglois lequel
                je parle.

HENRY: No faith, is't not, Kate: thy speaking of
                my tongue, and I thine, must needs be granted
                to be much alike. But, Kate, dost thou under-
                stand thus much English? Canst thou love me?

KATHARINE: I cannot tell.

Katharine walks away from the window.

M.C.S. Henry at the window.

HENRY: Can any of your neighbours tell, Kate? I'll
                ask them.

He steps down from the window and walks past Alice over to Katharine.
CAMERA TRACKS R. to L. with him.

                Come I know thou lovest me: and at night,
                when you are come into your chamber, you
                will question this gentlewomen about me;
                and I know, Kate, you will to her dispraise

HENRY (Cont'd)

those parts in me that you love with your
heart: but, good Kate, mock me mercifully,
the rather, gentle princess, because I
love thee cruelly, what sayest thou, my fair
flower-de-luce? La plus belle Katharine du
monde, mon tres cher et devin déesse?

KATHARINE: Your majesty ave fausse French enough to
deceive de most sage demoiselle dat is en
France.

Henry laughs and comes round to screen R. of Katharine. CAMERA PANS
with him.

HENRY: Now fie upon my false French! By mine
honour in true English, I love thee, Kate;
by which honour though I dare not swear thou
lovest me, yet my blood begins to flatter me
that thou dost;

CAMERA TRACKS BACK a little.

Put off your maiden blushes, avouch the
thoughts of your heart with the looks of
an empress, take me by the hand, and say
'Harry of England I am thine'; which word
thou shalt no sooner bless mine ear withall,
but I will tell thee aloud 'England is thine,
Ireland is thine, France is thine, and Henry
Plantagenet is thine'; Therefore, queen of
all, Katharine, break thy mind to me in
broken English, wilt thou have me?

KATHARINE: Dat is as it sall please de roi mon père.

HENRY: Nay, it will please him well, Kate, it shall
please him, Kate.

KATHARINE: Den it sall also content me.

HENRY: Upon that I kiss your hand, and I call you
my queen.

Henry kisses her hand. Katharine, shocked, runs L. to a doorway. Alice
joins her, CAMERA PANS L. with Katharine.

KATHARINE: Laissez, mon seigneur, laissez, laissez: ma

KATHARINE (Cont'd)
>   foi, je ne veux point que vous abaissiez
>   votre grandeur en baisant la main d'une de votre
>   seigneurie indigne serviteur;

C.U. Henry.

KATHARINE: (off) Excusez-moi, je vous supplie, mon
              tres-puissant seigneur.

HENRY: Oh, then I will kiss your lips, Kate.

M.S. Katharine and Alice shriek, and run R. to stand behind a window.
Henry is in L. f.g. CAMERA HAS PANNED with them.

KATHARINE: Les dames et demoiselles pour être baisees
              devant leurs noces, il n'est pas la coutume
              de France.

Henry walks up to them behind the window -- CAMERA TRACKS IN to centre
Henry and Katharine. He turns L. and CAMERA PANS to centre Alice and
Henry.

HENRY: Madame, my interpreter, what says she?

ALICE: Dat it is not be de fashion pour les ladies of
              France -- I cannot tell vat is baiser en
              Anglish.

HENRY: To kiss.

C.U. Katharine.

ALICE: (off) Your majesty entendre bettre que moi.

HENRY: (off) It is not the fashion for the maids in
              France to kiss before they are married, would
              she say?

ALICE: (off) Oui, vraiment.

HENRY: (off) O Kate . . .

                                   MUSIC STARTS.

M.L.S. Henry leads Katharine from the window and walks down to Camera.
CAMERA PANS L. then TRACKS BACK to centre then finally in C.U.

HENRY: Nice customs curtsy to great kings. Dear
                Kate, you and I cannot be confin'd within
                the weak list of a country's fashion: we
                are the makers of manners, Kate: therefore
                patiently, and yielding.

He kisses her.

C.U. Henry's hand clasping Katharine's. The heraldry of England and
France can be seen on the rings of their fingers.

HENRY: (off) You have witchcraft in your lips, Kate.

CAMERA STARTS TO TRACK BACK.

BURGUNDY: (off) God save your majesty;

                                        MUSIC STOPS.

CAMERA HAS TRACKED BACK to L.S. showing the French Court assembled behind Henry and Katharine.

BURGUNDY: . . . my royal cousin, teach you our princess
                English?

The court titters.

HENRY: I would have her learn, my fair cousin,
                how perfectly I love her, and that is
                good English.

Court applauds.

                Shall Kate be my wife?

King Charles steps forward and takes the hands of Henry and Katharine.

CHARLES: Take her, fair son, that the contending kingdoms
                Of France and England, whose very shores look pale
                With envy of each other's happiness,
                May cease their hatred;
                That never war advance his bleeding
                            sword 'twixt England and fair France.

THE COURT: Amen!

                                        MUSIC STARTS.

Henry and Katharine separate, Henry to the English Attendants on the
Left and Katharine to the French on the Right. CAMERA TRACKS BACK.

L.S. A longer shot of the same scene. Henry and Katharine are crowned
and joining hands walk away from camera to two thrones in the b.g.
CAMERA TRACKS FORWARD following them.

C.U. Henry turns round on reaching the throne. He is wearing the crude
Globe Theatre make-up.

APPLAUSE IS HEARD.

CAMERA PANS R. to show a boy made-up as Katharine acknowledging applause.

M.S. Henry and the Boy as Katharine, CAMERA TRACKS BACK to reveal the
Stage of the Globe Theatre. Chorus enters L. and pulls the curtain
across.

CHORUS: Thus far, with rough and all-unable pen,
Our bending author hath pursued the story,
In little room confining mighty men,
Mangling by starts the full course of their glory.

Chorus walks towards Camera and flings out his arms.

Small time: but in that small, most greatly lived
This star of England: Fortune made his
sword: and for his sake . . .

L.S. HIGH ANGLE SHOT FROM THE TOP GALLERY. AUDIENCE in f.g.

CHORUS: In your fair minds let this acceptance . . .

M.C.S. Chorus.

CHORUS: . . . take.

He bows. Elizabethan Gallants come into picture from L. and R. and
crowd round Chorus. CAMERA TRACKS UP to the stage Balcony where the
Bishop of Ely is conducting Choir Boys. CAMERA TRACKS IN to Ely. He
looks up and nods.

M.C.S. THE ORCHESTRA GALLERY. The Leader of the Orchestra acknowledges
the signal and the Orchestra play louder. The Leader looks up and
CAMERA TRACKS UP to platform at foot of flagpole. A man is pulling
down the Playhouse flag and rolling it up. He exits through door at
back.

L.S. LONDON IN 1600. The Globe Playhouse in the f.g. CAMERA TRACKS
BACK to full shot of London. A playbill comes fluttering out of the
sky and hits the camera lens. It has the cast and credits on it.
CAMERA TRACKS DOWN THE TITLE.

THE CAST
In order of appearance.

CHORUS	LESLIE BANKS
ARCHBISHOP OF CANTERBURY	FELIX AYLMER
BISHOP OF ELY	ROBERT HELPMANN
THE ENGLISH HERALD	VERNON GREEVES
EARL OF WESTMORELAND	GERALD CASE
EARL OF SALISBURY	GRIFFITH JONES
SIR THOMAS ERPINGHAM	MORLAND GRAHAM
DUKE OF EXETER	NICHOLAS HANNEN
DUKE OF GLOUCESTER	MICHAEL WARRE
KING HENRY V OF ENGLAND	LAURENCE OLIVIER
MOUNTJOY, THE FRENCH HERALD	RALPH TRUMAN
DUKE OF BERRI, FRENCH AMBASSADOR	ERNEST THESIGER
CORPORAL NYM	FREDERICK COOPER
LIEUTENANT BARDOLPH	ROY EMERTON
ANCIENT PISTOL	ROBERT NEWTON
MISTRESS QUICKLY	FREDA JACKSON
BOY	GEORGE COLE
SIR JOHN FALSTAFF	GEORGE ROBEY
KING CHARLES VI of FRANCE	HARCOURT WILLIAMS
DUKE OF BOURBON	RUSSELL THORNDIKE
THE CONSTABLE OF FRANCE	LEO GENN
DUKE OF ORLEANS	FRANCIS LISTER
THE DAUPHIN	MAX ADRIAN
THE FRENCH MESSENGER	JONATHAN FIELD
FLUELLEN)	ESMOND KNIGHT
GOWER) Captains in the	MICHAEL SHEPLEY
JAMY) English Army	JOHN LAURIE
MACMORRIS)	NIAL MACGINNIS
THE GOVERNOR OF HARFLEUR	FRANK TICKLE
PRINCESS KATHARINE	RENEE ASCHERON
ALICE	IVY ST. HELIER
QUEEN ISABEL OF FRANCE	JANET BURNELL
COURT)	BRIAN NISSEN
BATES) Soldiers in the	ARTHUR HAMBLING
WILLIAMS) English Army	JIMMY HANLEY
A PRIEST	ERNEST HARE
DUKE OF BURGUNDY	VALENTINE DYALL

Produced and Directed
by
LAURENCE OLIVIER

In close association with -

```
The Editor ---------------------------------------- REGINALD BECK
The Art Director ---------------------------------- PAUL SHERIFF
Assisted by --------------------------------------- CARMEN DILLON
The Costume Designer ------------------------------ ROGER FURSE
Assisted by --------------------------------------- MARGARET FURSE
The Associate Producer ---------------------------- DALLAS BOWER
The Text Editor ----------------------------------- ALAN DENT
The Director of Photography ----------------------- ROBERT KRASKER
The Operating Cameraman --------------------------- JACK HILDYARD
The Sound Recorders ------------------------------- JOHN DENNIS
                                                    DESMOND DEW
Make-up ------------------------------------------- TONY SFORZINI
Hairdressing -------------------------------------- VIVIENNE WALKER
Special Effects ----------------------------------- PERCY DAY
Assistant Director -------------------------------- VINCENT PERMANE
Scenic Artist ------------------------------------- E. LINDEGAARD
Continuity ---------------------------------------- JOAN BARRY
Chief Electrician --------------------------------- W. WALL
Master of the Horse ------------------------------- JOHN WHITE m.r.c.v.s.
Production Unit ----------------------------------- ALEC HAYES
                                                    P.G. BANGS
                                                    LAURENCE EVANS

                        and
The music by -------------------------------------- WILLIAM WALTON
Conducted by -------------------------------------- MUIR MATHIESON
Played by ----------------------------------------- THE LONDON SYMPHONY
                                                       ORCHESTRA


                                                    DISSOLVE TO:


L.S. LONDON

                        T H E   E N D

FADES IN on the sky

                                                    FADE OUT

                                                    MUSIC STOPS.
```

THE BIG SLEEP

1946—A Warner Brothers First National Picture
Director   Howard Hawks
Script   William Faulkner, Leigh Brackett, Jules Furthman
Source   Raymond Chandler, *The Big Sleep* (New York: Knopf, 1939). A novel
Stars   Humphrey Bogart, Lauren Bacall

Raymond Chandler shares with Dashiell Hammett the honor of being the best of the writers of "hard-boiled" detective fiction. His hero, Philip Marlowe, is more fully realized in the several novels in which he appears than Hammett's Sam Spade. Tough, cynical, but stubbornly clinging to decency in a society permeated by evil, Marlowe became a favorite of millions of readers of detective fiction long before *The Big Sleep* was filmed.

The fine adaptation of Chandler's novel by William Faulkner and others preserves the essentials of Marlowe's character as well as the clipped, understated, often ironic quality of Chandler's dialogue. Chandler's fascination for the colors and contrasts of the Southern California setting, realized in the novel through meticulous description, is preserved in the visual imagery—the photography—of the film. Faulkner's close friend Howard Hawks, who had been involved in movies since 1918, deserves much of the credit for the film's success. He is aided by the fine performances of Humphrey Bogart and Lauren Bacall in roles that helped fix identities already well established in films like *Casablanca* (1943) and *To Have and Have Not* (1945). The result is a uniquely American classic. The fast pace of the movie, which entailed loose ends criticized by many reviewers, seems in retrospect a significant asset that anticipates the emphasis on action rather than logic and scene rather than transition evident in both *avant garde* and popular work of the sixties—*Blow-up*, for example, and the television series *Mission: Impossible*.

A study of evil that extends from the world of bums and gunsels to the apparently untroubled world of millionaires and debutantes, *The Big*

Sleep includes a good deal of violence and skirts subjects like dope addiction and nymphomania. Although its overt brutality will seem mild enough to audiences inured to technicolor slaughter and screen nudity, it shocked James Agee. In *The Nation* (August 31, 1946) Agee complained that "the picture is often brutal and sometimes sinister . . . it is a dream world and doubtless it stimulates socially undesirable appetites." Bosley Crowther attacked it in the New York *Times* (September 1, 1946) as "morbid" and "disturbing" under the review title "Violence Erupts Again." Other reviewers, praising Hawks' energetic direction and Bogart's fine action, were less disturbed. One of the most perceptive comments was by Raymond Chandler in a letter to his British publisher Hamish Hamilton: "When and if you see the film of *The Big Sleep* (the first half of it anyhow) you will realize what can be done with this sort of story by a director with the gift of atmosphere and the requisite touch of hidden sadism. Bogart, of course, is also so much better than any other tough-guy actor. As we say here, Bogart can be tough without a gun. Also he has a sense of humour that contains that grating undertone of contempt. . . . Bogart is the genuine article. . . . All he has to do to dominate a scene is to enter it." (*Raymond Chandler Speaking*, ed. Dorothy Gardiner and Katherine Walker [Boston, 1962], pp. 216–17.)

Useful background reading includes Philip Durham, *Down These Mean Streets a Man Must Walk* (Chapel Hill, 1963), a critical study of Raymond Chandler's fiction; and Joseph Blotner, "Faulkner in Hollywood," in *Man and the Movies* (New Orleans, 1967), pp. 261–303. For Hawks as a director, see Peter Bogdanovich, *The Cinema of Howard Hawks* (New York, 1962).

The Script This is a shooting script, but, unlike several shooting scripts in this collection, it has no revisions although it must have passed through several stages before reaching its present form. Like many other shooting scripts, it begins with a list of characters, each of whom is described briefly. The descriptions are intended for actors, makeup men, costume designers, and, of course, the producer and director. They are obviously also useful to the critic of film. Note that the script is divided into 195 master scenes which include considerable description of scene and action but very few directions for camera or sound. The script is thus somewhat more "literary" than the script of *Henry V*.

Credits Producer, Howard Hawks; Director, Howard Hawks; Author, Raymond Chandler; Script, William Faulkner, Leigh Brackett, Jules Furthman; Art, Carl Jules Weyl; Music, Leo Forbstein; Photography, Sid Hickox; Special Effects, E. Ray Davidson; Editor, Christian Nyby.

Cast	Marlowe:	Humphrey Bogart
	Vivian:	Lauren Bacall
	Carmen:	Martha Vickers
	Eddie Mars:	John Ridgely
	Mona Mars:	Peggy Knudsen
	Bernie Ohls:	Regis Loomey
	Gen. Sternwood:	Charles Waldron
	Norris:	Charles D. Brown
	Canino:	Bob Steele
	Harry Jones:	Elisha Cook, Jr.
	Joe Brody:	Louis Jean Jeydt
	Agnes:	Sonia Darrin
	Arthur Geiger:	Theodore Von Eltz
	Girl in Bookstore:	Dorothy Malone
	Girl Taxi Driver:	Joy Barlowe

Awards *The Big Sleep* ranked twenty-eighth on the New York Film Critics' 1946 list of the year's best pictures. *The Lost Weekend* was voted "Best Picture" of that year and *Henry V* (released in this country in 1945) was ranked seventh.

CAST OF CHARACTERS

PHILIP MARLOWE . . . .   "Doghouse Reilly" -- private
                              detective, working for the D.A.
                              husky, confident, well-dressed
                              but not flashy. 38 years old --
                              unmarried.

GENERAL STERNWOOD. . . . . .   Old -- obviously dying; only in
                              his fierce eyes seems to be
                              life. A widower; a millionaire
                              with two daughters: Carmen and
                              Vivian.

CARMEN STERNWOOD . . . . . .   About 20; sullen; always biting
                              her thumb.

VIVIAN STERNWOOD . . . . . .   Mrs. Rutledge -- spoiled,
                              exacting, smart, ruthless, with
                              a habit for getting married.
                              She is beautiful, giving the
                              impression of strong will and
                              strong emotions -- the dangerous
                              unpredictable type.

NORRIS . . . .   Sternwood butler -- thin, silver-
                              haired, gentle -- an intelligent
                              face. He writes the checks in
                              the Sternwood menage.

OWEN TAYLOR. . . . .   Sternwood chauffeur -- handsome,
                              boyish-looking -- in love with
                              Carmen; at one time wanted to
                              marry her, but was prevented
                              by Vivian and re-hired as their
                              chauffeur. He doesn't like
                              the game Geiger is playing with
                              Carmen.

SHAWN REGAN. . . . .   Ex-brigade commander of the
                              Irish-Republican Army -- at one
                              time rum-runner from Mexico.
                              A big guy -- tall and heavy --
                              an ex-bootlegger. Friend of
                              the General.

ARTHUR GWYNNE GEIGER . . . .   In his early 40's. Medium
                              height, fattish, soft all over --

a Charlie Chan moustache; his
left eye is glass.
Operator of a smut bookstore;
blackmail racket on the side.

AGNES. . . . . Hard-looking, expensive blonde,
working in Geiger's bookstore --
with a phony veneer.

JOE BRODY. . . . . Middle-aged, important-looking
incongruously furtive and
nervous in manner. His face
well-fed, haggard and lined.

PROPRIETRESS IN
SECOND BOOKSTORE . . . . . Small, dark, shrewd-faced woman.

CAROL LUNDGREN . . . . Dark, handsome kid -- Geiger's
shadow.

BERNIE OHLS. . . . . A D.A.'s man -- dapper, slightly
flashy man -- his clothes are
expensive -- but always a little
wrong. He's pleasant and
affable to all -- respects
courage -- loves no man.

EDDIE MARS . . . . Operator of the Mars Cypress
Club at Las Olindas.
Handsome, hard, horsy-looking
man, wears beautiful, expensive,
restrained clothes. He owns
the house Geiger lives in.

MONA MARS . . . . Eddie's blonde wife who
supposedly ran away with Shawn
Regan. She's tall, blonde,
strikingly beautiful -- a
woman who knows her way around,
yet shows a certain dignity
and finesse.

EDDIE MARS' THUGS. . . . . . One a bodyguard . . . young, good-
looking, pale-faced boy;
the other -- older, slim, deadpan.

WILDE . . . . District Attorney -- wears
evening clothes.

CAPTAIN CRONJAGER. . . . . .   Of the city police homicide
                               detail.
                               In plain clothes. He is a
                               cold, hatchet-faced man.

CAPTAIN GREGORY. . . . . . .   A slow, burly man who looks
                               stupid but who isn't.
                               Also in plain clothes.

ABBA . . . .   Secretary in Gregory's office;
                               a middle-aged woman.

LARRY COBB . . . .   A big, blonde expensive-looking
                               man; Vivian's escort to the
                               Casino. Drunk in the car.

HARRY JONES. . . . .   Small, hardly 5 feet -- in cheap
                               snappy "underworld" suit. In
                               his wizened, ugly face there
                               is honesty, reliability, courage
                               and dependability.
                               He comes to Marlowe with a
                               "straight" proposition.

CANINO . . . .   Mona Mars' watchdog. He does
                               the dirty jobs for Eddie Mars.

ART HUCK . . . .   Operator of the Huck garage
                               and paint shop -- the "Mars
                               hide-out". A gaunt, hard face.

GIRL TAXI-CAB DRIVER . . . .   Smart, competent girl.

LIBRARIAN. . . . .   Typical -- in Hollywood library.

          BARMAN AT MARS CASINO
          WAITERS "   "   "
          CROUPIER   "   "
          MAN AT GAMBLING TABLE -- beside Vivian
          CROWD IN CASINO
          THUG
          MOTORCYCLE COPS
          MEDICAL EXAMINER
          UNIFORMED DEPUTY
          GUARD AT PIER
          4 STRETCHER BEARERS
          2 PLAINCLOTHESMEN
          ETC.

FADE IN

1.   ESTABLISHING SCENE EXT. STERNWOOD PLACE

It is a millionaire's house, big, sprawling, California
style, with clipped lawns and gardens, on a hill above
the now abandoned oil field which was the family's
wealth. A small coupe drives up to the door and stops,
and Philip Marlowe gets out. We just have time to
establish him as he approaches the door --- a husky, self-
confident man, well-dressed but not flashy.

2.   INSERT: BRASS DOORPLATE KNOCKER WITH A BELL BENEATH
     lettered

               STERNWOOD

3.   CLOSE SHOT EXT. FRONT DOOR MARLOWE

as Norris opens the door. NORRIS is thin, silver-haired
with a gentle intelligent face.

                    NORRIS:
               (holding the door)
          Good morning, sir.

                    MARLOWE:
          I'm Philip Marlowe. General
          Sternwood sent for me.

                    NORRIS:
               (opens door, steps aside)
          Yes, Mr. Marlowe. Will you come in?

                    MARLOWE:
               (entering)
          Thanks.

4.   INT. FORMAL HALL SAME OPULENT BIG-SCALE STYLE MARLOWE --

as Norris shuts the door, takes Marlowe's hat.

                    NORRIS:
          Will you sit here? I'll tell
          the General you have come.

                    MARLOWE:
          Okay.

Norris exits. Marlowe looks about, interested and
curious, sees something, moves toward it.

5.   CLOSE SHOT MARLOWE

as he stands before a portrait, examining it with curious
interest. It is a portrait of General Sternwood, in
regimentals, beneath crossed battle-torn cavalry
pennons and a sabre. He is still staring at the portrait
when at a SOUND OFF, he turns and sees CARMEN STERNWOOD
approaching. She is about 20, in slacks, something sullen
and hot about her. She stops about 10 feet from him and
stares at him, biting the thumb of her left hand.

> MARLOWE:
> Good morning.

> CARMEN:
> (after a moment)
> You're not very tall are you?

> MARLOWE:
> I tried to be.

> CARMEN:
> Not bad looking, though -- you
> probably know it.

> MARLOWE:
> Thanks.

He goes to a chair and sits down. When he looks up, he
sees Carmen approaching, still staring at him.

> CARMEN:
> (approaching)
> What's your name?

> MARLOWE:
> Reilly -- Doghouse Reilly.

> CARMEN:
> (beside the chair now)
> That's a funny name. Are you a
> prize fighter?

> MARLOWE:
> No. I'm a shamus.

                    CARMEN:
A what?

                    MARLOWE:
A private detective.

                    CARMEN:
You're cute.

As she speaks, she sits suddenly on the arm of his chair.
As she does so, Marlowe rises, shifts the chair in doing
so, so that to her surprise, Carmen finds herself sitting
in the chair itself. She stares up, surprised and then
angrily, is about to speak again when they both see the
butler. He has just entered noiselessly, stands beside
the chair. On Norris' face there is now a curious expression of grief, sadness. Carmen glances up at him,
rises quickly as if he had reprimanded her with words,
and exits. Marlowe looks after her, thoughtful, a little
grim.

                    NORRIS:
The General will see you now.

                    MARLOWE:
             (looking after Carmen)
Who was that?

                    BUTLER:
Miss Carmen Sternwood, sir.

                    MARLOWE:
You ought to wean her. She
looks old enough.

                    BUTLER:
Yes, sir. This way, if you please.

They exit through French doors.

6.   EXT. REAR LAWN SAME WEALTHY SCALE

Garage at one side, beyond it a tremendous greenhouse.
The butler is leading Marlowe along the path toward the
greenhouse. A chauffeur is washing a car before the
garage. We establish him in passing -- a handsome,
boyish-looking man, OWEN TAYLOR. Marlowe follows the
butler on to the greenhouse, looking at the tremendous

size of it as the butler opens the door and stands
aside for Marlowe to enter.

7.   INT. GREENHOUSE CHOKED WITH ORCHID PLANTS

Marlowe, following the butler between the crowding
tendrils and branches. The place is oven-hot, damp with
sweat, green with gloom. Marlowe is already reacting
to it, is already mopping his face with his handkerchief.

> MARLOWE:
> (mopping neck, following
> butler)
> Couldn't we have gone around this?

> BUTLER:
> (over shoulder; walking on)
> The General sits in here, sir.

8.   MED. CLOSE SHOT   GENERAL STERNWOOD

in a wheelchair in center of the greenhouse, in a cleared
space about which the plants crowd and hover. The
GENERAL is the man we saw in the portrait, though older,
and obviously dying, so that only his fierce eyes seem to
have any life. Even in the terrific heat his body is
wrapped in a traveling rug and a heavy bathrobe, his
gnarled hands lying like dead gnarled twigs on the rug,
his fierce eyes following as Norris leads Marlowe in.

> NORRIS:
> (stopping)
> This is Mr. Marlowe, General.

The General does not speak, only the fierce eyes stare
at Marlowe as the butler pushes a wicker chair up
behind Marlowe's legs.

> STERNWOOD:
> Brandy, Norris.
> (to Marlowe)
> How do you like your brandy, sir?

> MARLOWE:
> (sitting down)
> Just with brandy.

Norris takes Marlowe's hat, exits.

STERNWOOD:
I used to like mine with champagne.
The champagne cold as Valley Forge
and about three ponies of brandy
under it. You may take your coat
off, sir.

MARLOWE:
Thanks.

He rises, removes his coat, takes out his handkerchief,
hangs his coat on chair.

STERNWOOD:
(watching him)
It's too hot in here for any man
who still has blood in his veins.

Marlowe sits again, mops his face and neck.

STERNWOOD:
(still watching him)
You may smoke too. I can still
enjoy the smell of it, anyway.

MARLOWE:
Thanks.

He produces a cigarette, lights it, blows smoke, Sternwood's
nostrils moving as he sniffs the smoke. Norris enters,
pushing a teawagon bearing decanter, siphon, initialled
ice-bucket.

STERNWOOD:
That man is already dead who must
indulge his own vices by proxy.

The butler wheels the wagon up, starts to prepare a
drink.

STERNWOOD:
(watching pettishly)
Come, man. Pour a decent one.

NORRIS:
(adding brandy)
Yes, General.

                    MARLOWE:
          (watching)
     But not too decent, Norris. I don't
     want to exchange places with it.

Norris adds soda, hands glass to Marlowe.

                    MARLOWE:
          (taking glass)
     Thanks.

He sits back. Norris covers the ice-bucket with a napkin,
exits. SOUND of DOOR CLOSING as Norris leaves the
greenhouse. Marlowe raises the glass, sips. Sternwood
watches him, licks his lips with longing pleasure and
enjoyment. Marlowe lowers the glass.

                    STERNWOOD:
     Tell me about yourself, Mr. Marlowe.
     I suppose I have the right to ask.

                    MARLOWE:
     There's not much to tell. I'm thirty-
     eight years old, went to college once.
     I can still speak English when there's
     any demand for it in my business. I
     worked for the District Attorney's office
     once. It was Bernie Ohls, his chief
     investigator, who sent me word you
     wanted to see me. I'm not married.

                    STERNWOOD:
     You didn't like working for Mr. Wilde?

                    MARLOWE:
     I was fired for insubordination --
     I seem to rate pretty high on that.

                    STERNWOOD:
     I always did, myself. Sir --
          (he slides one hand under
           the rug on his knees)
     What do you know about my family, Mr.
     Marlowe?

                    MARLOWE:
          (mopping)
     You're a widower, a millionaire, two

MARLOWE: (Cont.)
young daughters. One unmarried, the
other married once but it didn't take.
Both now living with and both --
    (he breaks off; the General's
    fierce eyes watch him)

STERNWOOD:
Go on.

MARLOWE:
Am I to swap you gossip for hospitality?

STERNWOOD:
    (sternly)
You are to swap me your confidence for
my own.

MARLOWE:
    (shrugs)
All right. Both pretty, and both
pretty -- wild. What did you want to
see me about?

STERNWOOD:
I'm being blackmailed again.

MARLOWE:
    (mopping)
Again?

STERNWOOD:
    (draws his hand out from
    under the rug, holding a brown
    envelope)
About a year ago I paid a man named
Joe Brody five thousand dollars to let
my younger daughter alone.

MARLOWE:
Ah.

STERNWOOD:
What does that mean?

MARLOWE:
It means 'ah.' It never went through
the D.A.'s office, or I'd have known

                    MARLOWE: (Cont.)
it. Who handled that for you?

                    STERNWOOD:
Shawn Regan did.

                    MARLOWE:
          (alternating between the
           drink, the cigarette and the
           now sodden handkerchief with
           which he mops his face and neck)
There must be some reason why Regan's
not handling this one too. Am I to
know it?

                    STERNWOOD:
Shawn has left me.

                    MARLOWE:
I thought I hadn't seen him around
lately.

                    STERNWOOD:
Yes, he left about a month ago, without
a word. That was what hurt. I had no
claim on him, since I was only his
employer. But I hoped we were more than
that and that he would have said goodbye
to me. You knew him too?

                    MARLOWE:
Yes. From the old days, when he
was running rum from Mexico and I
was on the other side, and now and then
we swapped shots between drinks -- or
drinks between shots, if you like
that better.

                    STERNWOOD:
My respects to you. Few men ever
exchange more than one shot with
Shawn Regan. He commanded a brigade
in the Irish Republican Army, you
know.

                    MARLOWE:
          (mopping)
No, I didn't. But I knew he was

                    MARLOWE: (Cont.)
            a good man at whatever he did.
            Nobody was pleased better than me
            when I heard you had taken him on
            as your -- whatever he was here.

                    STERNWOOD:
            As my friend, my son almost. Many's
            the hour he would sit here with me,
            sweating like a pig, drinking the
            brandy I could no longer drink, telling
            me stories of the Irish revolution --
            But enough of this.
                    (he holds out the
                     envelope)
            Here. And help yourself to the brandy.

        Marlowe takes the envelope, sits again, wipes his hands
        on his wet handkerchief, removes from the envelope a
        card and three clips of stiff paper.

9.   INSERT: CARD

        -- in Marlowe's hand.

                    Mr. Arthur Gwynn Geiger
                Rare Books and De Luxe Editions

        Marlowe's hand turns the card over. On the back, in
        hand-printing.

                "Dear Sir:

                In spite of the legal uncollectibility
                of the enclosed, which frankly are gambling
                debts, I assume you might wish them
                honored.
                                Respectfully,
                                A. G. Geiger."

                                        DISSOLVE TO:

10.   INSERT: THREE PROMISSORY NOTES

        filled out in ink, dated: September 3
                                   September 8
                                   September 11

"On demand I promise to pay to Arthur
Gwynne Geiger on order the sum of
One Thousand Dollars ($1,000.00)
without interest. Value Received.
Carmen Sternwood."

11.   STERNWOOD AND MARLOWE   (AS BEFORE)

Sternwood watching from wheelchair as Marlowe mixes
himself a drink at the wagon, then turns toward chair.

                    STERNWOOD:
                 (watching Marlowe)
            Well?

                    MARLOWE:
                 (Standing)
            Who's Arthur Gwynne Geiger?

                    STERNWOOD:
            I haven't the faintest idea.

                    MARLOWE:
            Have you asked your daughter?

                    STERNWOOD:
            I don't intend to. If I did she
            would suck her thumb and look coy.

                    MARLOWE:
            Yeah. I met her in the hall. She
            did that at me. Then she tried to
            sit in my lap.

Sternwood stares at him. After a moment Marlowe raises
the glass, drinks, lowers it.

                    STERNWOOD:
                 (harshly)
            Well?

                    MARLOWE:
                 (stares at him a moment)
            Am I being polite, or can I say
            what I want.

                    STERNWOOD:
            Say it.

                    MARLOWE:
Do the two girls run around
together?

                    STERNWOOD:
I think not. They are alike only
in their one corrupt blood. Vivian
is spoiled, exacting, smart, ruthless.
Carmen is still the child who likes to
pull the wings off flies. I assume they
have always had all the usual vices;
whatever new ones of their own invention --
        (again he makes the repressed
         convulsive movement, glares at
         Marlowe)
Well?

                    MARLOWE:
Pay him.

                    STERNWOOD:
Why?

                    MARLOWE:
It's cheaper. A little money against
a lot of annoyance. The money you
won't miss, and if your heart hasn't
broken long before this time, whatever's
behind these --
        (indicates the notes
         on the chair)
-- can't do it now.

                    STERNWOOD:
Not my heart. No Sternwood ever had
one. But there is my pride, which I
at least, and I believe my older
daughter still, both have.

                    MARLOWE:
Sure. A man named A. G. Geiger's just
betting himself three thousand bucks
on that pride. Who was this Joe Brody
you paid the five thousand to?

                    STERNWOOD:
I don't recall. Norris would know.
My butler. I think he called himself

STERNWOOD: (Cont.)
a gambler.
          (hopefully)
This may be an authentic gambling debt,
after all.

Marlowe looks at Sternwood for a moment. Then he half
turns, sets the glass on the wagon and takes the napkin
from around the ice bucket and mops himself with it.
Sternwood watches him.

                    MARLOWE:
Do you think it is?

                    STERNWOOD:
          (after a second)
No.

Marlowe mops himself again with the napkin, puts it back
on the wagon, takes up his glass, drinks.

                    MARLOWE:
I guess you want me to take this
Geiger off your back: that right?

                    STERNWOOD:
Yes.

                    MARLOWE:
Do you want to know anything, or do
you just want to be rid of him?

                    STERNWOOD:
Didn't you just tell me I no longer
have any heart to be broken?

                    MARLOWE:
It may cost you a little -- besides
my own twenty-five a day and expenses.

Sternwood says nothing, merely makes a faint, impatient
movement of his head or shoulders. Marlowe drains the
glass, sets it back on the wagon.

                    MARLOWE:
When do I start?

                    STERNWOOD:
At once. And now if you will excuse
me -- But another brandy before you go?

                    MARLOWE:
                (takes up papers from
                  chair, then his coat)
No thanks.

                    STERNWOOD:
                (presses bell plugged
                  into chair arm)
Then good morning. And good luck.

He lies back in the chair, closes his eyes. Marlowe
watches him a moment, then, his coat over his arm and
still mopping his neck, he turns and exits.

12.   EXT. GREENHOUSE   MARLOWE

    emerges, still carrying his coat, dripping wet, mopping
    with his sodden handkerchief, breathing the cool air,
    starts away. Before he reaches the house, Norris meets
    him, pauses two feet away, silver-haired, respectful,
    grave.

                    NORRIS:
Mrs. Rutledge, the older daughter
would like to see you before you leave,
sir. And about the money: the General
has instructed me to give you a check for
whatever you require.

                    MARLOWE:
Instructed you how?

                    NORRIS:
                (blinks, stares, then
                  smiles)
Ah, I see, sir. I forgot you are a
detective. By the way he rang the
bell.

                    MARLOWE:
You write his checks.

                    NORRIS:
I have that privilege.

                         MARLOWE:
                    (starts on)
          That ought to save you from a pauper's
          grave. I won't need any money now,
          thanks -- How did Mrs. Rutledge know
          I was here?

                         NORRIS:
          She saw you through the window. I
          was obliged to tell her who you were.

                         MARLOWE:
          I don't like that.

                         NORRIS:
          Are you attempting to tell me my
          duties, sir?

                         MARLOWE:
          No. Just having fun trying to guess
          what they are.

                         NORRIS:
          This way, sir.

13.   INT. VIVIAN'S SITTING ROOM

       The room is large, over-elaborate, feminine. VIVIAN
       reclines on a chaise-lounge, showing her legs to good
       advantage. She is beautiful, giving an impression of
       strong will and strong emotions, the dangerous unpredict-
       able type. She sips a drink, insolently at ease, watching
       Marlowe as he enters. Marlowe is still rumpled and
       sweating. He adopts her be-damned-to-you attitude, looks
       her over, and sits down unbidden, wiping his face and
       neck with his handkerchief.

                         VIVIAN:
          So you're a private detective.
          I didn't know they existed except
          in books, or else they were little
          greedy men snooping around hotels.
          My, you're a mess, aren't you?

                         MARLOWE:
          Yeah -- I'm not the orchid-bearing
          type.

VIVIAN:
This business of Dad's -- think you
can handle it for him?

MARLOWE:
(sardonically)
It doesn't look too tough.

VIVIAN:
Really. I would have thought a
case like that took a little effort.

MARLOWE:
Not too much.

VIVIAN:
Well! What will your first step be?

MARLOWE:
The usual one.

VIVIAN:
I didn't know there was a usual one.

MARLOWE:
Oh, yes. It comes complete with
diagrams on Page forty-seven of "How
to be a Detective in Ten Easy Lessons",
correspondence school textbook.

VIVIAN:
You must have read another one on how
to be a comedian. I'm quite serious, Mr.
Marlowe. My father is not well, and
I want this case handled with the least
possible worry to him.

MARLOWE:
That's the way I'm going to handle it.

VIVIAN:
I see. No professional secrets.

Marlowe doesn't answer. He's still admiring her legs.
Vivian sets her glass down, looking him over coolly,
as though he were something in a bottle.

                    VIVIAN:
How do you like Dad?

                    MARLOWE:
I liked him.

                    VIVIAN:
He liked Shawn. I suppose you
know who Shawn is?

                    MARLOWE:
Yeah, I know.

                    VIVIAN:
You don't have to play poker with me.
Dad wants to find him, doesn't he?

                    MARLOWE:
Do you?

                    VIVIAN:
Of course I do! It wasn't right for him
to go off like that. Broke Dad's heart,
although he won't say much about it.
Or did he?

                    MARLOWE:
He mentioned it.

                    VIVIAN:
I don't see what there is to be cagey
about. And I don't like your manners.

                    MARLOWE:
I'm not crazy about yours. I didn't
ask to see you. And I don't mind your
ritzing me, or drinking your lunch out
of a bottle. I don't mind your showing me
your legs. They're very swell legs and it's
a pleasure to make their acquaintance. I
don't mind if you don't like my manners.
They're pretty bad. I grieve over them
during the long winter evenings. But
don't waste your time trying to cross-
examine me.

Vivian is really angry now. She swings her legs to the
floor, and her anger is something sparkling and terrific.

                    VIVIAN:
People don't talk like that to me.

Marlowe laughs at her softly. His eyes are warm and
mocking. Vivian relaxes slowly, looking at him, and
something besides fury comes into her own face.

                    VIVIAN:
Do you always think you can handle
people like trained seals?

                    MARLOWE:
Just what is it you're afraid of?

They watch each other, and Vivian's face closes against
him like a door.

                    VIVIAN:
Dad didn't want to see you about
Shawn at all.

                    MARLOWE:
Didn't he?

                    VIVIAN:
Get out.
     (as Marlowe rises and
      turns from her)
Please . . . you could find Shawn if
Dad wanted you to.

                    MARLOWE:
     (still dead pan)
When did he go?

                    VIVIAN:
A month back. He just drove away
one afternoon without saying a word.
They found his car in some private garage.

                    MARLOWE:
They?

                    VIVIAN:
     (her manner suddenly
      different, as though she
      has won her bout with him)
Dad didn't tell you then.

                    MARLOWE:
          He told me about Regan, yes. That's
          not what he wanted to see me about.
          Is that what you've been trying to
          get me to say?

                    VIVIAN:
          I'm sure I don't care what you say.

                    MARLOWE:
               (giving her a look she
                could chin herself on)
          You might change your mind about that
          some day. So long, Mrs. Rutledge.

Vivian watches him as he goes out, with smoldering,
puzzled eyes.

14.   INT. MAIN HALL

Marlowe comes down the hall, heading for the door. Norris
appears with Marlowe's hat and hands it to him.

                    MARLOWE:
          You made a mistake. Mrs. Rutledge
          didn't want to see me.

                    NORRIS:
          I'm sorry, sir. I make many mistakes.

He opens the door. Marlowe pauses to look at the view.

15.   LONG SHOT   MARLOWE'S ANGLE

Beyond the lawns and hedges of the Sternwood estate the
ground falls away to barren fields with several old
wooden derricks, some of them still wearily pumping oil.
The derricks are at a considerable distance from the
house, but a man with binoculars could see any activity
around them clearly enough. The sky is clouded; THUNDER
SOUNDS distantly.

16.   AT THE STERNWOOD DOOR

                    MARLOWE:
          How long those wells been pumping?

                         NORRIS:
About thirty years. The General
likes to take his field glasses
sometimes and sit by the window
and watch the walking-beams. They're
like life, he says -- an endless
seesaw, forever up and down and
getting nowhere.

                         MARLOWE:
They get oil. Black stuff, with
a smell to it . . . worth dollars.

He goes out, gets into his car and drives away. The
SOUND of THUNDER follows him.

                                        DISSOLVE TO:

17.   INSERT: A BRONZE PLAQUE

                "HOLLYWOOD PUBLIC LIBRARY"

                                        DISSOLVE TO:

18.   INT. LIBRARY

The typical reading room, with the usual characters
hunched over books at the tables. Marlowe stands by the
librarian's desk. A boy comes from the door to the
stacks and hands the librarian a book. She looks at it.

                         LIBRARIAN:
Famous First Editions.
            (looking at Marlowe--
            it is obvious that
            she feels he's not
            the type to be
            reading about first
            editions)
This was the one you wanted?

                         MARLOWE:
            (blandly, as he
            takes the book)
I collect blondes, too -- in
bottles.

He walks over to a table and sits down, leaving the
woman staring after him.

19.   EXT. GEIGER'S STORE   ESTABLISHING SHOT

Sign on window: "RARE EDITIONS". etc.

Marlowe walks up and pauses to assure himself that it's
the right place. The store front is narrow. Discreet
gold lettering on the plate glass repeats the legend on
Geiger's card:

A. G. GEIGER

Rare Books and De Luxe Editions

The windows are blanked off with Chinese screens, fronted
by large Oriental urns. Marlowe puts on a pair of horn-
rimmed sun glasses, adjusts his hat to a less rakish
angle, and enters.

20.   INT. GEIGER'S STORE

The room is small, dim, expensively underfurnished with
leather chairs, smoking stands, and a small psuedo-
Oriental desk. A few sets of tooled leather binds on
narrow tables, others in glass cases.

AGNES, a hard-looking, expensive blonde in a tight black
dress, rises from behind the desk as Marlowe approaches
and moves to greet him. Her manner is professionally
distant, her accent betrays her phony veneer.

                    AGNES:
          Can I be of any assistance?

                    MARLOWE:
          Would you happen to have a Ben
          Hur 1860?

                    AGNES:
                (hanging on hard to
                 her composure, seeing
                 that she's going to
                 have trouble with
                 Marlowe)
          A first edition?

                    MARLOWE:
          No. Third -- the one with the
          erratum on page one-sixteen.

AGNES:
I'm afraid not -- at the moment.

MARLOWE:
How about a Chevalier Audubon --
the full set of course?

AGNES:
(with a frozen smile)
Uh -- not at the moment.

MARLOWE:
(politely)
You do sell books?

AGNES:
(dropping the act,
 pointing to the
 display books)
What do those look like --
grapefruit?

MARLOWE:
They look like books from here,
anyway. Maybe I'd better talk
to Mr. Geiger.

AGNES:
He's not in at the moment.

Marlowe glances up as a man enters the store; a middle-
aged, important-looking person who has an incongruously
furtive and nervous manner. He looks quickly at Marlowe,
then at Agnes, who gives him an almost imperceptible warning nod. Marlowe remains blandly unaware of the byplay,
all his attention apparently on the cigarette he's
lighting.
The man walks quickly to the rear of the store. Agnes
pushes a button on the desk. A door in the back wall
opens on a buzzer lock. The man darts through it like
a rabbit.

AGNES:
(to Marlowe)
I said Mr. Geiger is not in.

MARLOWE:
I heard you. I'll wait for him.

> AGNES:
> He won't be back until very late.

At this point the furtive man comes out of the rear
part of the store and leaves hurriedly, looking at
neither Agnes nor Marlowe. His face is lined and
haggard. Marlowe is interested.

> MARLOWE:
> (watching the man out)
> He must have got hold of the
> wrong title.
> (to Agnes)
> Well, guess I'd better blow. I'm
> already late now for my lecture
> on Argentine cera-micks.
> (mispronouncing
> the word)

> AGNES:
> (icily, correcting
> him)
> The word is cerAMics. And they
> ain't Argentine: they're Egyptian.

> MARLOWE:
> You did sell a book once, didn't
> you? Well, even the Argentine's
> a little too far for me today.
> Guess I'll just stick to the public
> library -- or I might try that
> book store across the street.

> AGNES:
> (freezing)
> Do so.

Agnes stares viciously at his back until he is out.
Then she goes to the door at the rear, knocks and goes
through.

21.   MOVING SHOT   MARLOWE

He walks across the boulevard, turns into a small
bookstore, the second-hand variety, cluttered and dingy.
Several nondescript people browse among the tables. At
the rear a small, dark, shrewd-faced woman sits reading
at a desk -- apparently she is the proprietor. Marlowe
approaches her, and she looks up blank-faced from her book.

MARLOWE:
Would you do me a very small
favor?

PROPRIETRESS:
I don't know. What is it?

MARLOWE:
You know Geiger's store across
the street?

PROPRIETRESS:
I think I may have passed it.

MARLOWE:
You know Geiger by sight?

PROPRIETRESS:
I should think it would be
easy enough to go to his store
and ask to see him.

MARLOWE:
I don't want to see him that
close, just yet.
          (as he gets no
          response)
Know anything about rare books?

PROPRIETRESS:
You could try me.

MARLOWE:
Would you have a Ben Hur, 1860,
Third Edition, with the duplicated
line on page one-sixteen?

The woman pulls a fat volume in front of her, starts
to open it.

MARLOWE:
(continued)
. . . or a Chevalier Audubon 1840 . . . ?

The woman stops, closes the book.

PROPRIETRESS:
Nobody would. There isn't one.

                    MARLOWE:
Right.
        (as the woman
         gives him a
         puzzled stare)
The girl in Geiger's store didn't
know that.

                    PROPRIETRESS:
I see. You begin to interest me --
vaguely.

                    MARLOWE:
I'm a private dick on a case.
Perhaps I ask too much.
        (leaning forward
         to hold a match
         for her cigarette)
It didn't seem much to me somehow.

                    PROPRIETRESS:
        (after a pause)
In his early forties, medium
height, fattish, soft all over,
a Charlie Chan moustache. Well
dressed, goes without a hat,
affects a knowledge of antiques
and hasn't any. Oh yes, his left
eye is glass.

                    MARLOWE:
You'd make a good cop.

                    PROPRIETRESS:
        (returning to
         her reading)
Only if he wore smoked glasses.

                    MARLOWE:
        (laughing softly
         pulling a flat
         pint from his
         hip pocket)
I shouldn't think you'd have to work
too hard to start anything smoking.

He shakes the bottle up and down, invitingly. She
looks up at him, searchingly, then smiles slowly.

PROPRIETRESS:
It's going to rain, soon.

MARLOWE:
I'd rather get wet in here.

She pulls open a drawer and stands two small glasses on
the desk. Marlowe smiles, and starts pouring. Through
the window behind him the front of Geiger's store can
be seen.

DISSOLVE TO:

22. INT. BOOKSHOP   NIGHT   (RAIN)

It is raining hard outside. The proprietress is a
little tight, quite relaxed, and slightly philosophical,
leaning against Marlowe, who sits on a stack of
Britannicas beside her, watching the window. The
proprietress picks up the bottle, which is now empty,
shakes it forlornly, and sets it down again.

PROPRIETRESS:
A couple of hours, an empty bottle,
and so long, pal. That's life.

MARLOWE:
But it was a nice two hours.

PROPRIETRESS:
(sighing)
Uh-huh.
(looking toward
 the window)
There's Geiger's car driving up.

MARLOWE:
(over above action)
Who's the other guy?

PROPRIETRESS:
Damon -- or Pythias. I don't know.
Geiger's shadow, anyway. Name's
Carol Lundgren.

Marlowe has risen, is now in a hurry to follow Geiger.

MARLOWE:
So long, pal.

> PROPRIETRESS:
> If you ever want to buy a book . . .

> MARLOWE:
> A Ben Hur eighteen-sixty . . .

> PROPRIETRESS:
> (sighing)
> With duplications. . . . So long.

DISSOLVE TO:

23.   INSERT: A STREET SIGN ON A LAMP POST   (RAIN) NIGHT

wet with rain:

LAVERNE TERRACE

DISSOLVE TO:

24.   LONG SHOT   (RAIN) NIGHT
ESTABLISHING A SECTION OF LAVERNE TERRACE

A narrow street with a high bank on one side and a
scattering of cabinlike houses built down the slope on
the other side, so that their roofs are not much above
street level. They are masked by hedges and shrubs.
Sodden trees line the dark road. The headlights of a
car appear. Geiger's coupe drives up and stops in front
of the garage of a small house almost completely hidden
by a square box hedge. Geiger gets out, opens an um-
brella, and vanishes behind the hedge. Almost immediately
Marlowe's car appears, continuing slowly past
Geiger's house. It turns, stops under a tree. The
lights go out.

DISSOLVE TO:

25.   INT. MARLOWE'S CAR   (RAIN) NIGHT

Marlowe yawns, gets a bottle out of the dash compartment, shakes it reflectively.

> MARLOWE:
> Another hour, another bottle --
> another dame?

He uncaps the bottle, salutes an unseen person wryly,
drinks, then lights a cigarette and settles down to wait.

DISSOLVE TO:

26.   EXT. LAVERNE TERRACE   RAIN NIGHT

A dark convertible stops in front of Geiger's house.
The lights go out. A small slim woman in a vagabond
hat and raincoat gets out. She pauses, looking around --
we see her face dimly. It is CARMEN STERNWOOD. She
vanishes behind the hedge. The DOORBELL RINGS faintly,
the door opens and closes.

27.   INT. MARLOWE'S CAR   RAIN NIGHT

Marlowe looks offscene after Carmen, with an unpleasant
grin.

                    MARLOWE:
          Yeah -- another dame.

His expression indicates that things may pick up
shortly. He looks at his watch -- the CAMERA MOVES IN
to feature the watch -- the hands standing at 6:35.

DISSOLVE TO:

28.   INSERT: THE WATCH   ON MARLOWE'S WRIST

The hands now indicate: 7:20.

29.   INT. MARLOWE'S CAR   RAIN NIGHT

SHOOTING obliquely across Marlowe's shoulder, showing
the street and particularly Geiger's house through
the rain-streaked windscreen. Suddenly a hard white flash
of light shoots out of Geiger's house like a flash of
lightning. Close on its heels comes a woman's thin
half-pleasurable scream. Marlowe is out of the car and
on his way.

30.   EXT. GEIGER'S HOUSE   RAIN NIGHT

Marlowe rounds the hedge on the run. There is a wooden
footbridge bridging the gap between the bank and the
front door. He covers this in two jumps and stops at
the front door. The knocker is in the shape of a lion's
head, and ring in its mouth. Marlowe puts his hand on
it, and as he does, three SHOTS SOUND from inside.
Marlowe freezes. From inside we HEAR a sighing groan and

the thud of a falling body, then footsteps going away.
Marlowe looks over the railing of the bridge, but there's
no way around to the back.
He stands still, listening. Light shows from the house,
behind draperies. From offscene at some distance, we
HEAR someone running down steps.

31.   EXT. REAR STEPS EXTREME CLOSE   RAIN NIGHT

On a man's feet, running with hysterical speed down the
wet treads. We follow them across muddy ground,
apparently a dirt road surface, to a car.

32.   LONG SHOT   ALLEY BELOW GEIGER'S HOUSE   RAIN NIGHT

As a car starts and roars away with clashing gears.
Almost before it is out of sight a second car pulls
out from under shrouding trees and follows it.

33.   EXT. GEIGER'S HOUSE   AT FRONT DOOR   RAIN   NIGHT

The SOUND of the two cars is still audible, fading into
distance. Marlowe listens to it. When everything is
quiet again he tries the front door, finds it locked.
French windows flank the door just out of reach beyond
the railing of the bridge. Marlowe swings out over the
railing, kicks in the right-hand window, and pulls himself over the sill.

34.   INT. GEIGER'S HOUSE   LIVING ROOM   NIGHT

As Marlowe comes in through the window. The room is
wide, low-beamed ceiling, brown plaster walls with
strips of Chinese embroidery and Oriental prints on them.
Low bookshelves, a desk, thick rug floor cushions, low
divans -- an exotic messy atmosphere. On a low dais at
one end of the room is a carved teakwood chair, a
massive thing in which Carmen Sternwood sits, rigidly
erect, in the pose of an Egyptian goddess. She wears a
man's large silk dressing gown -- it doesn't pretend to
fit her and gives the impression of having been thrown
hurriedly around her by someone other than herself.
Carmen's eyes have a queer fixed stare. She pays no
attention to Marlowe. She looks as if, in her mind, she
is doing something very important and doing it well. She
seems pleased about it, her lips curved to a smile. She
laughs from time to time -- softly, secretly.

Opposite her, Geiger lies on the floor in front of a
thing like a totem pole. The eye of the totem is a
camera lens; it focuses on the chair where Carmen sits.
A blackened flash bulb is clipped to the totem beside it.
Geiger is dressed in semi-oriental fashion. His em-
broidered coat is soaked with blood. He is obviously dead.

Marlowe takes all this in, sniffs the air. It is heavy
with something unpleasant. He crosses to a small lacquer
table bearing a flagon of dark liquid and two glasses.
Marlowe sniffs the flagon, makes a grimace of disgust.
Carmen's clothes are wadded up on the divan. Marlowe
picks up her coat and shoes and goes to her.

> MARLOWE:
> Hello. Remember me.

She doesn't seem to see him. The soft, secret laughter
is his only answer. He goes closer, and deliberately
slaps her face. This gets a reaction -- he slaps her
again, without emotion, but hard. Carmen comes to,
slightly, giving him a sly, mad smile.

> MARLOWE:
> You're higher than a kite. Come
> on, let's be nice. Let's get
> dressed, Carmen.

He puts her shoes on.

> CARMEN:
> (giggling)
> You tickle.

> MARLOWE:
> Yeah, you tickle me, too.

Marlowe pulls her to her feet and puts her coat on,
trying not to dislodge the dressing gown. She falls
against him, very happy about it all, apparently about
to pass out. Marlowe is not happy.

> MARLOWE:
> Let's take a walk.

> CARMEN:
> (thickly, half
> conscious)
> You're cute.

                    MARLOWE:
          Sure, sure. So's your boyfriend.
          Want to look at him?

He walks the staggering girl over to Geiger's body.
It is hard work -- and Carmen is not impressed.

                    CARMEN:
               (as before)
          He's cute.

                    MARLOWE:
          Cute. Yeah. Let's walk.

He walks her back and forth across the room a couple of
times -- LOW CAMERA FEATURING the dead man as their legs
pass in front of him. Then she passes out in his arms,
still convinced that everything is cute. He spreads
her out on the divan, unconsciously wiping his hands
on his coat as though he has touched something dirty.
Then he returns to the totem and Geiger's body. He
examines the concealed camera. The plateholder is gone.
He rolls Geiger's body over enough to see under it.
No plateholder. He frowns thoughtfully at the girl . . .
then goes into the rear of the house.

35.   INT. GEIGER'S HOUSE   REAR ROOMS   NIGHT

Marlowe passes quickly through the bath and kitchen,
pausing to try the locked kitchen door and to examine
a window which had been jimmied open. The scars show
plainly on the wood, the rain blowing in unheeded. Marlowe then goes to the bedroom, which is in keeping with
the living room. He glances briefly through the closet,
with a man's clothes in it, then picks up a keyholder
from the dressing table, where it has been placed along
with other contents of Geiger's pockets -- money, handkerchief, etc.

36.   INT. GEIGER'S HOUSE   LIVING ROOM   NIGHT

Marlowe returns and unlocks the desk. In one drawer
he finds a locked steel box, which he opens with
Geiger's keys. He takes from it a leather book.

37.   INSERT: THE BOOK   IN MARLOWE'S HANDS

He leafs through the pages slowly, showing an index

and writing in code, in the same slanted printing as
on the cards General Sternwood gave him.

38.   INT. GEIGER'S HOUSE   LIVING ROOM   NIGHT

Marlowe places the book in his pocket, wipes his fingerprints carefully from the box, replaces it and locks
the desk. He pockets the keys, turns off the lamps and
the gas logs in the fireplace, makes a wadded bundle
of Carmen's clothes, jams her hat on her head and picks
her up, holding her clothes awkwardly in one hand.
On the way out he pushes down the light switch by the
door, and kicks the door shut behind him.

39.   EXT. GEIGER'S HOUSE   RAIN   NIGHT

as Marlowe carries the sleeping girl out to her car.

                                        DISSOLVE TO:

40.   EXT. STERNWOOD HOUSE   RAIN   NIGHT

Marlowe has just rung the doorbell. In the drive behind
him stands Carmen's Packard. The door opens.

Norris appears in it, recognizes Marlowe, looks swiftly
past him and recognizes the car also. Then he looks
at Marlowe again -- the same quiet, grave face with
its expression of grief and sadness which the sight of
the car brought into it. His voice though is quiet and
calm.

                    NORRIS:
          Good evening, sir.

                    MARLOWE:
               (rapidly)
          Mrs. Rutledge in?

                    NORRIS:
          No, sir.

                    MARLOWE:
          The General?

                    NORRIS:
          He's asleep.

                    MARLOWE:
Good. Where's Mrs. Rutledge's
maid?

                    NORRIS:
Mathilda? She's here.

                    MARLOWE:
Better get her down here. This
job needs a woman's touch. Take
a look inside the car.

But Norris does not move, only his eyes go again to the
waiting car and return, his face still grave, only the
grief a little sharper behind it.

                    NORRIS:
                 (quickly)
She's all right?

                    MARLOWE:
Sure. She's okay. Just get
that maid. Mathilda can do all
right for her.

                    NORRIS:
We all try to do our best for her.
I'll call Mathilda at once.

                    MARLOWE:
                 (turning)
Then I'll leave it with you.
Goodnight.

                    NORRIS:
May I call you a cab, sir?

                    MARLOWE:
                 (pauses)
No. In fact, I'm not here. You
haven't even seen me tonight --
see?

                    NORRIS:
Yes, sir.

Marlowe turns on, fast, walking down the drive in the rain.

DISSOLVE TO:

41. INT. GEIGER'S DARK HOUSE   RAIN   NIGHT

Marlowe, a shadowy figure, enters, closes door behind
him, crosses the room to a lamp, turns the switch.
Marlowe is quite wet, indicating that he has walked back
from Sternwood's. He stands with his hand still on
the light switch, looks about the room, crosses to
another lamp, puts it on, is about to turn away when he
stops dead, reacts as he looks at the totem pole and
at the floor beneath it where Geiger's body had lain.
The body is gone. Marlowe crosses the room, wasting no
time, determined. He passes through door to bedroom,
snaps light on beyond it, after a moment the light beyond
the door snaps off and Marlowe re-enters living room.
He has not found the body. He stands for a moment,
thinking, then he goes and kneels so that he can squint
along the surface of the thick rug. He sees in the
nap the marks where Geiger's heels were dragged along it,
across the room toward the front door. He rises at
last, thoughtful, slowly takes out a cigarette and lights
it, drops match into ashtray, stops, takes up the dead
match and puts it into his pocket. The he takes out
his handkerchief, goes and wipes off the bedroom doorknob,
goes to the first lamp, turns it out and wipes it off,
leaving room in darkness and himself a shadow which can be
barely seen in the act of wiping off that button. Then
he crosses the room.

42. EXT. DOOR TO HOUSE   NIGHT

Marlowe as he closes and locks it, wipes off knob,
pockets keys, turns.

43. INT. MARLOWE'S APARTMENT   NIGHT

Marlowe, sitting at a table, the code book which he
found at Geiger's open before him, a highball at his hand
as he tries to work out the code. He cannot solve it.
His hand reaches for the highball glass.

DISSOLVE TO:

44. INT. MARLOWE'S BEDROOM   MORNING

Marlowe, in bed, wakes reluctantly as LOUD KNOCKING
on the apartment door penetrates his slumber. He

crawls out of bed, obviously the worse for a hangover,
pulls on a dressing gown as he staggers sleepily toward
the next room.

>   MARLOWE:
>   (as the KNOCKING
>   CONTINUES)
>   All right, all right. Keep your
>   pants on . . .

45.   INT. MARLOWE'S LIVING ROOM   AT FRONT DOOR

as Marlowe opens it to admit BERNIE OHLS, a dapper,
slightly flashy man, whose clothes are expensive and
always a little wrong. His face is dapper and deceiving
since it is actually the face of a man who has been in
close places in the course of his duty, has killed
several lawbreakers, at times when he was outnumbered
and they thought he was covered and helpless until too
late. He is pleasant and affable to all, respects courage,
loves no man.

>   MARLOWE:
>   Well Bernie. Don't you ever go
>   to bed?

>   OHLS:
>   (entering --
>   surveying Marlowe)
>   Boy, what a beautiful hangover!
>   Tut, tut -- man your age, out on
>   the town all night . . .

>   MARLOWE:
>   I got it right here.

>   OHLS:
>   (sitting)
>   That's even worse.

>   MARLOWE:
>   All right -- what is it?

>   OHLS:
>   Does it have to be something?

>   MARLOWE:
>   Look, Bernie, when somebody

                    MARLOWE: (Cont.)
from the Homicide Squad comes
over to help . . .

                    OHLS:
You're working for the Sternwoods,
aren't you?

                    MARLOWE:
     (warily)
Yeah.

                    OHLS:
Done anything for 'em yet?

                    MARLOWE:
How could I do anything
yesterday in all that rain?

                    OHLS:
     (laughing)
Okay -- They seem to be a family
that things happen to. A big
Buick belonging to one of them
is washing around in the surf off
Lido fish pier. Oh yea, I almost forgot.
There's a guy in it.

                    MARLOWE:
     (flatly, after a
      pause)
Regan?

                    OHLS:
Who? Oh, you mean that Irish
ex-legger old Sternwood hired
to do his drinking for him.
What would he be doing down
there?

He watches Marlowe's face narrowly -- it tells him
nothing.

                    MARLOWE:
What would anybody be doing down
there?

                    OHLS:
That's what I'm going to Lido to

                        OHLS: (Cont.)
          find out. Want to come?

                        MARLOWE:
          Thanks, Bernie. Yeah, be with
          you in ten minutes.

He starts out, already pulling off his dressing gown.
Ohls looks after him, frowning.

                                        DISSOLVE TO:

46.   INT. CAR   OHLS AND MARLOWE   MORNING

Ohls is driving. It is an official car, now and then
Ohls sounds the siren.

                        OHLS:
          It ain't Regan. I checked up.
          Regan's a big guy, tall as you
          and a shade heavier. This is a
          young kid.
               (he SOUNDS SIREN --
                the car is going fast)
          What made you think it was Regan?

                        MARLOWE:
          Who is it? Don't they know yet?

                        OHLS:
          Now, now. Behave. What made
          Regan skip out? Or ain't you inter-
          ested in that either?

                        MARLOWE:
          Why should I be?

                        OHLS:
          That wasn't what old Sternwood
          wanted you for, then?

                        MARLOWE:
          Can't a guy quit a job anymore
          without notifying the District
          Attorney?

                        OHLS:
          When an ex-bootlegger gets himself
          hired into a job where all he's

OHLS: (Cont.)
got to do is sit in a greenhouse
and drink a millionaire's brandy,
when he throws that job up --

MARLOWE:
I'm not looking for Regan.

OHLS:
Okay, keep buttoned, kid.

MARLOWE:
General Sternwood told you to send
me out to see him. But he never
told me I was to report --

OHLS:
I said, keep it buttoned, didn't I?
     (SOUNDS SIREN)
After all, you got to eat too --
even if I don't know why.

MARLOWE:
Sometimes I don't know either.

Ohls SOUNDS the SIREN AGAIN. The car speeds on.

47.   EXT. ENTRANCE TO LIDO FISH PIER   MORNING

A faded stucco arch, the sea beyond it, the pier stretching
away as Ohls' car stops before the entrance and Ohls
and Marlowe get out. Beside the arch are parked a
police car and several police motorcycles. The long
pier, railed with white two-by-fours, runs out over
the water. There are several private cars parked along
the road, a crowd of people is gathered at the far end of
the pier as a motorcycle officer, stationed beneath
the arch, is holding back another crowd as Ohls and
Marlowe come up. Ohls shows the officer his badge.

OHLS:
     (to guard)
Medical examiner come yet?

GUARD:
     (checks pass,
      waves them on)
Beat you by 15 minutes. He's
examining the guy now probably.

                    OHLS:
              (pockets his pass)
          Oh, he is, huh? Didn't you guys
          ever hear of the D.A.'s office?

                    GUARD:
          Keep your shirt on. There's a
          deputy in charge.

Ohls, followed by Marlowe, passes onto the pier.

48.   SEAWARD END OF PIER

A shattered gap in the railing at the end of the pier
shows where the car crashed through. Another crowd of
people held back by other policemen, gather along the
broken railing in b.g. Beyond them, moored to the end of
the pier, lies a flat barge with wheelhouse and derrick.
As Ohls and Marlowe approach, the police herd the crowd
back and four men come up from the barge, carrying a
sheet-covered stretcher and carry it on across the SHOT --
the crowd gaping after it. As the bearers are about to
pass, Ohls stops them.

                    OHLS:
          Wait a minute.

The bearers stop. Ohls turns the sheet back, looks at
the dead man's face.

                    OHLS:
              (over his shoulder
                to Marlowe)
          Want a look?

Marlowe looks at the face for a moment. Ohls drops the
sheet back.

                    OHLS:
              (to bearers)
          All right. Beat it.

The bearers go on. Ohls and Marlowe approach the barge,
the crowd gawking about them, after the stretcher, the
policemen shoving among them.

                  A POLICEMAN:
              (to crowd)
          That's all now. Go on.

49.   DECK OF BARGE   MOORED TO THE END OF THE PIER

On it sits the car which has been lifted from the water.
It is the same black sedan which Marlowe saw the
chauffeur washing yesterday in Sternwood's garage --
bent and stained with water. In front of the car are
gathered Ohls, Marlowe, a uniformed deputy, two plain-
clothesmen and the Medical Examiner who has just finished
repacking his small black bag.

                    OHLS:
               (to deputy)
          What's the story?

                    DEPUTY:
          You can see most of it from here.
          Went through the rail yonder. Must
          have hit it pretty hard. The rain
          stopped down here about nine P.M.
          The broken ends of the rails are
          dry inside. That would put it
          about nine-thirty last night.

                    OHLS:
          Drunk, huh?

                    PLAINCLOTHESMAN:
          Then he must have been that guy you
          hear about that always drives better
          drunk. He plowed an awful straight
          furrow down that pier, right to the
          end of it. Then he hit the railing
          right square head-on -- hard and clean --
          or he wouldn't have gone through it.

                    OHLS:
          All right. Suicide then.

                    DEPUTY:
          The hand-throttle was set half-way
          down. Something had hit him a pretty
          hard lick across the left temple.

                    OHLS:
               (to Medical Examiner)
          All right, Doc. Let's have it.

                    MEDICAL EXAMINER:
          His neck was broken.

                         OHLS:
What made the bruise? Steering-wheel?

                    MEDICAL EXAMINER:
It was made by something covered.
The wound had already bled under the
skin while he was still alive.

                       MARLOWE:
A blackjack?

They all turn and glance at Marlowe.

                         OHLS:
                    (after a moment)
I'd forgotten about you. Let's go
back to town.

50.   EXT. PIER   MARLOWE AND OHLS

They are walking back toward their car. A few people
still hang around, staring at the barge.

                         OHLS:
So you recognized him.

                       MARLOWE:
Yeah. Sternwood's chauffeur. I saw
him washing that same car yesterday.

                         OHLS:
So that was what old Sternwood wanted
with you.

                       MARLOWE:
Look, I don't even know his name --

                         OHLS:
I do. His name's Owen Taylor. About a
year or so back he run Sternwood's
daughter, the hotcha one, off to Yuma.
The older sister run after them and
brought the girl back and had Taylor
thrown into the icebox. Then the
next day she comes down and begs the
kid off -- said the kid meant to
marry the sister, only the sister can't
see it. So they let the kid go, and

OHLS: (Cont.)
darned if the Sternwoods don't have
him come back to work, same as if nothing
had happened.

MARLOWE:
And now somebody'll have to go see them
about this.

OHLS:
Yep. That's me, probably.

MARLOWE:
Leave the old man out of it, if you
can. He's got enough troubles already
besides being sick.

OHLS:
Regan, huh?

MARLOWE:
I don't know anything about Regan.
I told you that.

OHLS:
Then what are you doing in this?

MARLOWE:
I'm not looking for Regan. I can
tell you that much.

OHLS:
(drily)
Yeah. I heard you the first time.

DISSOLVE TO:

51.   INT. GEIGER'S STORE

Marlowe enters, wearing the dark glasses as before, and
as before, Agnes rises from behind the desk. She is
not happy to see Marlowe.

MARLOWE:
(cheerily)
Hello -- I'm back again. Mr. Geiger in?

AGNES:
I'm afraid not. No.

Marlowe glances around to make sure they're alone, then removes the glasses and moves close to Agnes.

> MARLOWE:
> It was just a stall about those first
> editions. I got something to sell.
> Something Geiger's wanted for a long time.

> AGNES:
> Oh -- I see. Well -- you might come
> back tomorrow. I think. . . .

> MARLOWE:
> Drop the veil, sister. I'm in the
> business too.

Agnes stares at him, scared stiff, not knowing how to get rid of him.

> MARLOWE:
> (impatiently)
> I haven't got forever. Is he sick?
> I could go up to the house.

> AGNES:
> (frantically)
> No, that wouldn't do any good --
> he's out of town. Couldn't you --
> tomorrow -- ?

Marlowe glances up sharply as Carol Lundgren, the dark handsome boy in the leather jacket, opens the door in the rear wall. Behind him, through the open door, we see the back room, littered with the papers and boxes of hurried packing, and a gaunt, hard-looking man with a certain animal attractiveness in the midst of it, cramming folios and stacks of large-sized envelopes into the packing boxes. Carol is obviously strained and under tension, looking as though he has not slept.

> CAROL:
> (desperately)
> Agnes, you've got to --

He becomes aware of Marlowe, shuts up abruptly, and slams the door. From the partition his voice rises, sharp but unintelligible, answered by a heavier, man's voice -- no words come through, but the implica-

tion is clearly that Carol shall shut up and get out.
A door slams violently, then there is silence. Marlowe,
ignoring this byplay, and the stricken look on Agnes'
face, puts on his glasses and touches his hat.

> MARLOWE:
> Tomorrow, then. Early.

> AGNES:
> Yes, early.

Before Marlowe has quite left the shop she darts back
through the rear door.

52.   EXT. GEIGER'S STORE   MOVING SHOT   MARLOWE

As he walks rapidly along the Boulevard to a taxi standing
at the curb. A smart, competent-appearing girl sits
reading a pulp magazine behind the wheel.

53.   INT. CAB

Marlowe sticks his head in, does a take, and relaxes.

> MARLOWE:
> (disgustedly)
> I would have to pick a girl at
> this point.

> CABBY:
> (giving him a cold
> stare)
> Anything you want, bud, I can give you.

> MARLOWE:
> (grinning)
> And with both fists, too, I'll bet.
> Tail job?

> CABBY:
> Cop?

> MARLOWE:
> Private.

> CABBY:
> (laying aside the
> magazine)
> Hop in.

Marlowe looks down at the magazine.

54.   INSERT   THE MAGAZINE ON THE SEAT

It is a copy of TWO-GUN DETECTIVE TALES, with a lurid
cover of gunmen and a gory corpse.

55.   INT. CAB   THE SHOT AS BEFORE   MARLOWE AND CABBY

                    MARLOWE:
                (grinning)
            Okay, kid. Take it.

He gets in quickly.

                    CABBY:
                (slapping down the
                  flag)
            I got it.

56.   EXT. HOLLYWOOD STREET   CAB IN F.G.

A light panel pickup job comes out of an alley and turns
down the street. The gaunt, hard-looking man is driving.
Marlowe leans forward and gives the cabby the high sign.
The cab pulls out to follow.
                                    DISSOLVE TO:

57.   INSERT   STREET SIGN

                    RANDALL PLACE
                                    DISSOLVE TO:

58.   LONG SHOT   ESTABLISHING

A section of Randall Place, featuring an apartment
building with a basement garage. An awning stretches
out over the sidewalk -- lettering along the awning's
side reads, RANDALL ARMS. The panel truck drives past
the entrance and turns into the basement garage. Some
distance behind it we see the cab pull into the curb.
Marlowe gets out and walks toward the RANDALL ARMS.

59.   INT. RANDALL ARMS   THE ENTRY

The door stands open onto a small foyer, without desk
or switchboard. A panel of gilt mailboxes is let into
one wall of the entrance. Marlowe, after a glance

inside, examines the names under the mail drops. One
in particular catches his eye.

60.   INSERT   THE CARD ON THE MAILBOX

The name JOE BRODY is typewritten on the card.

61.   INT. RANDALL ARMS   THE ENTRY AS BEFORE

Marlowe taps the card, then gives the foyer one more
meaning look, turns.

62.   EXT. RANDALL PLACE   AT THE CAB

As Marlowe returns to it. He speaks to the girl, who
nods and drives away with him.

                                            DISSOLVE TO:

63.   EXT. HOLLYWOOD STREET

as the cab pulls into the curb in front of a nondescript office building. Marlowe gets out and leans
in to pay the driver.

64.   INT. CAB

                         MARLOWE:
                   (handing her a bill)
                Nice going, kid. Buy yourself an
                orchid.

                          CABBY:
                Thanks. You can take my number
                in case you have any more jobs
                you want done right.
                     (indicating the
                        serial number on
                        her driver's cap)
                I mean <u>this</u> number.

                         MARLOWE:
                What number did you think I
                thought you meant?

The Cabby flustered clashes the gears savagely, shoots
the cab away. Marlowe tips his hat to her and enters
the building as she drives away.

65.   INT. BUILDING HALLWAY AT MARLOWE'S OFFICE DOOR

Marlowe opens the door, which has Philip Marlowe in
glit letters on the upper glass.

66.   INT. MARLOWE'S OFFICE   THE-WAITING ROOM

A small room, cheaply furnished, with a closed door in
one wall. Vivian sits waiting for him, beautifully
but simply dressed, quite at ease. She seems in a
better humor this morning, smiling at the surprised
Marlowe.

                    VIVIAN:
          Well, you do exist, after all.
          I'd begun to think I dreamed you
          out of a bottle of bad gin.

                    VIVIAN: (Cont.)
                 (with underlying hint
                  of seriousness)
          I've been trying to get you on the
          phone all morning.

                    MARLOWE:
          You can insult me just as well face
          to face. I don't bite -- much.

                    VIVIAN:
                 (apologetically)
          I was rather rude.

                    MARLOWE:
                 (smiling)
          An apology from a Sternwood?
                 (unlocking the
                  connecting door,
                  holding it for her)
          Come into my boudoir.

67.   INT. MARLOWE'S OFFICE

Like the waiting room, it's shabby and not large. The
usual desk, chairs, and filing cabinets.

                    VIVIAN:
                 (sitting)
          You don't put on much of a front.

MARLOWE:
You can't make much money at this
trade, if you're honest. If you
have a front, you're making money --
or expect to.

VIVIAN:
Oh -- are you honest?

MARLOWE:
Painfully.

VIVIAN:
(taking out a
cigarette)
How did you get into this slimy
business, then?

MARLOWE:
(giving her a look as he
lights it for her)
Because people like you pay good
money to have the slime cleaned up.

She looks away from him, angry but not able to say
anything. Marlowe sits down behind the desk.

MARLOWE:
What did you want to see me about?
Taylor?

VIVIAN:
(softly)
Poor Owen. So you know about that.

MARLOWE:
A D.A.'s man took me down to Lido.
Turned out he knew more about it
than I did. He knew Owen Taylor
wanted to marry your sister -- once.

VIVIAN:
(quietly)
Perhaps it wouldn't have been a bad
idea. He was in love with her. We
don't find much of that in our circle. . . .
(changing her tone)
But I didn't come to see you about

                    VIVIAN: (Cont.)
          Owen. Do you feel yet that you can
          tell me what my father wants you to do?

                    MARLOWE:
          Not without his permission.

                    VIVIAN:
          Was it about Carmen?

                    MARLOWE:
          I can't even say that.

Vivian watches him for a moment, then gives in. She
takes a thick white envelope from her bag and tosses
it on the desk.

                    VIVIAN:
          You'd better look at this anyway.

Marlowe examines the envelope.

                    VIVIAN:
          A messenger brought it this morning.

                    MARLOWE:
          Eight-thirty-five it says --
          for you or your father.

He opens the envelope, takes out a medium-sized
photograph. We do not see the subject of the picture,
but Marlowe's reaction is significant. He whistles
softly.

                    MARLOWE:
          So that's what Carmen looks like!
               (to Vivian)
          How much do they want for this?

                    VIVIAN:
          Five thousand -- for the negative and
          the rest of the prints. The deal has
          to be closed tonight, or they give
          the picture to some scandal sheet.

                    MARLOWE:
          The demand came how?

                    VIVIAN:
A woman telephoned me, shortly after
this thing was delivered.

                    MARLOWE:
There's nothing in the scandal sheet
angle. Juries convict on that racket
without leaving the box. What else
is there?

                    VIVIAN:
Does there have to be something else?

Marlowe nods -- his face is uncompromising.

                    VIVIAN:
         (giving in again)
The woman said there was a police
jam connected with it, and I'd
better lay it on the line fast or
I'd be talking to my little sister
through a wire screen.

                    MARLOWE:
         (deadpan, nodding)
What kind of a jam?

                    VIVIAN:
I don't know.

                    MARLOWE:
Where's Carmen now?

                    VIVIAN:
She's at home -- still in bed, I
think. She was sick last night.

                    MARLOWE:
She go out at all?

                    VIVIAN:
The servants say she didn't. I
was up at Las Olindas across the
State line playing roulette at
Eddie Mars' Cypress Club. I lost
my shirt.
         (taking another cigarette --
           laughing wryly)

                    MARLOWE:
              (getting up to
               hold the match
               for her)
So you like roulette. You would.

                    VIVIAN:
Yes, the Sternwoods all like
losing games. The Sternwoods can
afford to. The Sternwoods have
money.
         (bitterly)
All it's bought them is a raincheck.

                    MARLOWE:
What was Owen doing with your car
last night?

                    VIVIAN:
Nobody knows. He took it without
permission. Do you think. . . . ?

                    MARLOWE:
He knew about this photo?
         (shrugging)
I don't rule him out. . . . Can you
get five thousand in cash right
away?

                    VIVIAN:
I can borrow it -- probably
from Eddie Mars.
         (sardonically)
There's a bond between us, you
see. Shawn Regan ran away with
Eddie's blonde wife.

                    MARLOWE:
              (turning away --
               leaving a pause)
You may need the money in a
hurry.

                    VIVIAN:
How about telling the police?

                    MARLOWE:
You know better than that. The
police might turn up something

MARLOWE: (Cont.)
they couldn't sit on -- and then
where would the Sternwoods be?
     (after a pause)
How was it left?

VIVIAN:
The woman said she'd call me back
with instructions at five.

MARLOWE:
Okay -- call me here as soon as
you've heard from her.

VIVIAN:
Can you do anything?

MARLOWE:
I think so. But I can't tell you
how -- or why.

VIVIAN:
I like you. You believe in miracles.

MARLOWE:
     (laughing)
I believe in people believing
they're smarter than they are --
if that's a miracle. Have a drink?

He reaches down into the desk drawer.

VIVIAN:
I'll have two drinks.

Marlowe grins at her. He comes up with a bottle and
two glasses, fills them, and takes one to her. They
salute, start to drink and find that their eyes have
met over the glass rims and refuse to come apart.
Vivian breaks it, not because she is shy or coy, but
because suddenly there is a sadness in her face. Her
gaze drops briefly, then returns to Marlowe, clear,
steady, and sad.

VIVIAN:
You're a lot like Shawn Regan.

Marlowe looks at her, almost with tenderness and
understanding.

                    MARLOWE:
        You want to tell me now or later?

                    VIVIAN:
        What?

                    MARLOWE:
        What you're so anxious to find out.

                    VIVIAN:
        It couldn't be -- you.

                    MARLOWE:
        Let's do one thing at a time.

                    VIVIAN:
                (rising)
        I think we've done enough for
        one day. . . .

                    MARLOWE:
                (gently)
        Want that other drink?

                    VIVIAN:
                (going toward door)
        No. . . .

Marlowe sets his glass down on the desk and picks up
the envelope.

                    MARLOWE:
        You forgot this . . .

She turns by the door as he approaches, holding out her
hand for the envelope. Marlowe gives it to her, but
doesn't let go of it.

They are not thinking about the envelope. Slowly he
bends to her -- she leans back against the wall, her
lips parted, her eyes soft, misted with tears.
Marlowe's mouth covers hers. Presently they break --
Vivian puts her hand on Marlowe's cheek.

                    VIVIAN:
                (softly)
        Your face is like Shawn's too --

                          VIVIAN: (Cont.)
          clean and thin, with hard bones
          under it. . . .

     She turns, neither slowly nor fast, away from him, opens
     the door, and goes out.

                                        DISSOLVE TO:

68.   EXT. LAVERNE TERRACE   AT MARLOWE'S CAR   DAY

       Parked unobtrusively under some trees a reasonable distance
       from Geiger's house. Marlowe sits patiently, waiting,
       his hat pushed to the back of his head, his collar
       loosened, smoking quietly. Presently, in b.g. in front
       of Geiger's house, Carmen Sternwood appears furtively
       around the far end of the hedge, and goes quickly in
       through the gap leading to the front door. Marlowe
       reacts, then gets out, to follow her.

69.   MED. CLOSE SHOT   CARMEN

       standing in an attitude of terror, her back pressed
       against the wall beside the front door to Geiger's
       house, staring at Marlowe as he enters. She raises
       one hand and clenches her teeth on her thumb, staring
       at him. The terror fades a little as she recognizes
       him. She wears coat, hat, veil, etc.

                          MARLOWE:
              Remember me now, don't you? Dog-
              house Reilly, the man that didn't
              grow very tall. Remember?

                          CARMEN:
                     (making an effort
                      to seem natural)
              Is this your doghouse?

                          MARLOWE:
              Sure. Let's go inside, huh?

                          CARMEN:
                     (shrinking, cringing)
              Inside?

                          MARLOWE:
              You wanted to get in, didn't you?

He pushes her away, unlocks the door, pushes it inward.

MARLOWE:
In with you.

He shoves Carmen in ahead of him, follows.

70.   INT. GEIGER'S LIVING ROOM   CARMEN AND MARLOWE

Carmen standing, looking about the room, as Marlowe
shuts the door and stands looking at Carmen. She
feels him watching her, smiles at him. He doesn't
answer it. The smile fades. Marlowe takes out pack of
cigarettes, offers it. She shakes her head dumbly,
staring at him. He lights a cigarette.

MARLOWE:
How much do you remember about
last night?

CARMEN:
Remember what? I was sick last
night. I was home.

MARLOWE:
Sure you were. I mean, before you
went home. In that chair yonder --
on that orange shawl while they were
taking pictures. Quit stalling.
(staring at him, she
starts to put her
thumb in her mouth
again)
And stop biting your thumb too.

CARMEN:
You -- were the one?

MARLOWE:
Me. How much do you remember?

CARMEN:
Are you the police?

MARLOWE:
No. I'm a friend of your father's.
(a moment)
Who killed him?

                    CARMEN:
        (faintly)
Who else . . . knows?

                    MARLOWE:
About Geiger? Not the police, or
they'd be camping here.
        (a moment)
Maybe Joe Brody.

                    CARMEN:
Joe Brody? Who's he?

                    MARLOWE:
Sure. Not Steve Brody: Joe
Brody. Did Joe kill him?

                    CARMEN:
Kill who?

                    MARLOWE:
Look sister. I don't know how much
trouble you are accustomed to, but
I hope you've had plenty of practice
dodging it.

                    CARMEN:
        (nods her head)
Yes. Joe did it.

                    MARLOWE:
Why?
        (she watches him out
         of the corners of her
         eyes, biting her thumb;
         he draws on cigarette,
         expels)
Seen much of him lately?

                    CARMEN:
No! I hate him!

                    MARLOWE:
So you're all ready to tell the
cops he did it, huh?
        (quickly, as she
         stares at him)
That is, if we can just get rid

                    MARLOWE: (Cont.)
of that photograph Geiger made
last night.

          CARMEN:
Photograph? What photograph?

          MARLOWE:
     (drags at cigarette,
      expels smoke)
Just like last night. What a scream
we are. Sternwood and Reilly, two
stooges in search of a comedian.

          CARMEN:
Your name isn't Reilly. It's Marlowe.
Vivian told me.

          MARLOWE:
So you are beginning to remember.
And you came back to look for the
photograph, but you couldn't get
into the house.
     (she stares at him)
The photo's gone. I looked for it
last night. Brody took it with him.

          CARMEN:
I've got to go home now.

          MARLOWE:
Sure. But I wouldn't tell the police
about Brody yet. Don't even tell a
soul you were ever here -- either last
night, or today. Not even Vivian.
Leave it to Doghouse Reilly. Where's
your car?

          CARMEN:
On the back street, where nobody
would see it.

She turns to go out as he turns to follow.

          MARLOWE:
You're not going to tell anybody
we were here, are you?

> CARMEN:
> (gives him a swoon-
> ing look)
> It depends. I never tell on people
> who are nice to me.

She gives him a languishing, swooning, inviting look,
so that her attitude is a caricature of what her more
brilliant and vivid sister's might be. Marlowe grasps
her arm almost savagely, turns her toward the door.

> MARLOWE:
> Come on. Get out of here --

He stops; they both react as FEET SOUND beyond the door,
approaching, they pause dead as the BELL RINGS. While
they stand staring at each other, Carmen drooling almost
with terror, the BELL RINGS AGAIN, ceases, then SOUND
of KEY at the lock and a moment later the door opens
and EDDIE MARS enters quickly and then stops dead, staring
at them. He is a handsome, hard, horsy-looking man in
beautiful, restrained, expensive clothes, who stands
staring at them with complete composure for a moment.
Then he looks at Carmen, shuts the door, takes his hat off.

> MARS:
> Excuse the casual entrance. The bell
> didn't answer. Is Mr. Geiger around?

> MARLOWE:
> No. We don't know just where he is.
> We found the door open and stepped in.

> MARS:
> I see. Friends of his?

> MARLOWE:
> Just business. We dropped in for a book.

Mars stares hard at Marlowe, who stares just as hard
back.

> MARLOWE:
> But we missed him.
> (takes Carmen's arm,
> pushes her toward
> door to pass Mars)
> So we'll trot along.

As Marlowe is about to shoulder Mars aside to pass,
Mars himself steps aside until Carmen has passed him,
then he moves in between Marlowe and the door.

> MARS:
> The girl can go. But I'd like
> to talk to you a little.

Marlowe stares at him, then makes a slight motion
toward the gun inside his coat.

> MARS:
> Don't try it. I've got two boys out-
> side in the car.

He turns, opens the door, Carmen scuttles through it.
Mars shuts the door behind her, looks about the room.

> MARS:
> (puts hat back on)
> There's something wrong around here.
> I intend to find out what it is. If
> you want to pick lead out of yourself,
> go ahead.

> MARLOWE:
> A tough guy.

Mars makes no answer. He walks on into the room, looking
around. Marlowe watches him.

> MARLOWE:
> I suppose it's all right if I smoke.

Mars does not answer. He looks about, sees the totem
pole, is astonished, approaches it, stops suddenly as
he moves the small rug over the bloodstain with his foot,
then kneels swiftly out of sight for an instant beyond
the desk. When he rises, he is facing Marlowe and his
hand is just emerging from inside his coat, holding a
Luger postol.

> MARS:
> Blood. On the floor there, under
> the rug. Quite a lot of blood.

> MARLOWE:
> (in interested tone)
> Is that so?

Mars slides into the chair behind the desk, still watching
Marlowe, hooks the telephone toward him with the
pistol-barrel, then shifts the pistol to his left hand and
puts his right hand on the phone but without raising it.

                     MARS:
        I think we'll have some law.

Marlowe approaches while Mars watches him, and looks
down at the stain, pretends to have seen it for the
first time.

                  MARLOWE:
        That's old blood. Dried.

                     MARS:
        Just the same, we'll have some law.

                  MARLOWE:
        Why not?

                     MARS:
        Just who are you anyway?

                  MARLOWE:
        Marlowe's the name. I'm a private
        detective.

                     MARS:
        Who's the girl.

                  MARLOWE:
        A client. Geiger was trying to
        throw a loop on her. We came to
        talk it over. He wasn't here.

                     MARS:
        Convenient -- the door being
        open, when you didn't have a key.

                  MARLOWE:
        Wasn't it? By the way, how'd you
        happen to have one?

                     MARS:
        Is that any of your business?

                  MARLOWE:
        I could make it my business.

                    MARS:
               (smiles tightly)
          And I could make your business mine.

                    MARLOWE:
          You wouldn't like it. The pay's
          too small.

                    MARS:
          I won this house. Geiger is my
          tenant. Now what do you think of it?

                    MARLOWE:
          You know some nice people.

                    MARS:
          I take them as they come.
               (he glances down
                 at the pistol,
                 shrugs, puts it
                 back inside coat)
          Got any ideas, detective?

                    MARLOWE:
          One or two. Somebody gunned Geiger.
          Somebody got gunned by Geiger, who
          ran away. Or Geiger was running a
          cult and made blood sacrifices in
          front of that barber pole there. Or
          he had meat for dinner and does his
          butchering in the front parlor.
               (Mars scowls at him)
          All right. I'll give up, then. Call
          your friends downtown.

                    MARS:
          I don't get it. I still don't
          get your game here.

                    MARLOWE:
          Don't you, Mr. Mars?

     Mars stares at Marlowe, who meets his stare steadily.
     Mars' face is now hard.

                    MARS:
          You seem to be telling me Geiger
          was in a racket of some sort.
          What racket?

                    MARLOWE:
          I don't know. I'm not his land-
          lord. And I'll tell you something
          else you missed. Somebody cleaned
          out whatever was in that back room
          in his bookshop today.

Mars stares at Marlowe a long moment. Marlowe takes out
a cigarette deliberately, is starting to light it.

                    MARS:
          You talk too much.

While Marlowe stands, the cigarette in his mouth, the
match-box arrested in his hands, Mars suddenly whips
out the pistol again, holds it on Marlowe, and whistles
shrilly. SOUND of car door SLAMMING OFF, then RUNNING
FEET.

                    MARS:
          Open the door.

                    MARLOWE:
          Open it yourself. I've already got
          a client.

Mars rises, still holding the pistol on Marlowe, crosses
toward the door as the SOUND OF FEET reaches the door
and the knob is rattled from outside. Mars reaches the
door, opens it. Two men plunge into the room, already
reaching inside their coats. One is a young hoodlum,
good-looking, pale-faced boy, the other is older, slim,
deadpan.

                    MARS:
               (jerks his head
                at Marlowe)
          Look him over. . . .

The slim man flicks out a short pistol, covers Marlowe.
The boy approaches, searches Marlowe, who turns, helping
the boy search him with the burlesqued air of a bored
beauty modelling a gown in a shop.

                    BOY:
          Okay. No iron.

                    MARS:
          Find who he is.

The boy draws Marlowe's wallet from his breast pocket,
flips it open, studies the contents.

                    BOY:
          A shamus.

He strikes. Marlowe, moving faster, catches his wrist,
wrenches it suddenly and sharply, so that in the next
instant the wallet is in Marlowe's hand. The boy
reacts angrily, but Mars stops it.

                    MARS:
                (sharply)
          That'll do. Beat it.

The boy stops sullenly, glaring at Marlowe.

                    MARS:
                (coldly vicious)
          I said, outside.

The two guards withdraw, exit.

                    MARS:
          All right. Talk.

Marlowe deliberately finishes lighting the cigarette,
inhales.

                    MARLOWE:
          Not to you. I told you I've already
          got a client.

                    MARS:
          Who was it cleaned out the back of
          Geiger's store?

                    MARLOWE:
          Quite a shower yesterday. Did it
          rain up there at Las Olindas?

                    MARS:
                (slaps the pistol
                 angrily down on
                 the desk)
          I might even make it worth your
          while to talk to me.

                    MARLOWE:
That's the spirit. Leave the gun
out of it. I can always hear money.
How much of it are you clinking at me?

                    MARS:
          (slams the desk
           again with the
           flat pistol)
I ask you a question, and you ask
me another. My guess is, you need
some help yourself. So cough up.

                    MARLOWE:
Not me. It's Geiger's kinfolks that
need help -- provided a man like
Geiger had anybody who loved him and
will care who bumped him off. So
I'd better give what I know to the
Law. Which puts it in the public
domain and don't leave me anything
to sell. So I guess I'll drift.

Marlowe makes a move to lift the gun, but does not.

                    MARLOWE:
          (easily)
By the way, how's Mrs. Mars these days?

Mars' hand jerks at the gun, almost lifts it, pauses.
He glares at Marlowe.

                    MARS:
          (almost whispers:
           raging inside)
Beat it. Get out of here.

Marlowe moves easily and unhurriedly toward the door.

71.   EXT. STREET   BEFORE GEIGER'S HOUSE

as Marlowe gets into his car. A short distance behind
it Mars' car is parked, the two guards in it. Marlowe
drives away. He expects a shot perhaps. As he drives
away he burlesques it: holds his hand out the window as
if he were testing the air for rain. He drives on.

DISSOLVE TO:

72.   INT. MARLOWE'S OFFICE   MARLOWE   EVENING

sitting at his desk, the phone pulled up in front of
him. He smokes nervously -- he seems to have been
waiting some time -- and glances at his wristwatch. The
PHONE RINGS. He grabs it.

>   MARLOWE:
>   Yeah . . . What's the news? . . . Nothing!
>   -- you mean they haven't called you?
>   (smiling sardonically)
>   Mrs. Rutledge. . . . You are <u>not</u> a very
>   good liar. I thought you were going
>   to trust me . . .
>   (jerking the phone
>   away from his ear
>   with exaggerated
>   haste)
>   Why, <u>Mrs</u>. Rutledge!

The PHONE CLICKS LOUDLY as the other end is slammed
down on the hook. Marlowe replaces his instrument
slowly. He is not clowning now. He speaks softly to
the telephone as though to Vivian herself, half in
admiration, half in anger.

>   MARLOWE:
>   You crazy darn fool. . . .

He picks up his hat and goes out.

73.   EXT. RANDALL PLACE   NIGHT

on Marlowe, parked a few doors from the Randall Arms,
obviously waiting for something.

74.   EXT. RANDALL PLACE   AT THE RANDALL ARMS   NIGHT

as Vivian drives up, parks, and enters the apartment.

75.   EXT. RANDALL PLACE   NIGHT

Marlowe gets out of his car and walks toward the Randall
Arms.

76.   INT. UPPER HALLWAY   AT STAIRHEAD   NIGHT

as Marlowe climbs the last steps. He walks down the
hall to 405 and presses the bell. In one of the other
apartments a radio plays softly. Presently the door of
405 opens noiselessly, just wide enough to show the man
who stands behind it -- JOE BRODY, whom we have seen
before, in the back room of Geiger's store and later
driving the panel truck. He looks steadily at Marlowe
and does not speak. His right hand holds the door. A
cigarette smolders in the corner of his mouth.

> MARLOWE:
>
> Geiger?

> BRODY:
> (after a pause, deadpan)
> You said what?

> MARLOWE:
>
> Geiger. Arthur Gwynne Geiger. The
> guy with the blackmail racket.

Brody's right hand drops slowly out of sight -- we get
the impression he's reaching for a gun.

> BRODY:
> Don't know anybody by that name.

Marlowe gives him a hard smile. Brody doesn't like the
smile.

> MARLOWE:
>
> You're Joe Brody?

> BRODY:
>
> So what?

> MARLOWE:
>
> So you're Joe Brody -- and you don't
> know anybody named Geiger. That's
> very funny.

> BRODY:
>
> Yeah? You got a funny sense of humor,
> maybe. Take it away and play it
> somewhere else.

Marlowe leans against the door and gives him a dreamy
smile.

                        MARLOWE:
            You got Geiger's stuff, Joe. I
            got his sucker list. We ought to
            talk things over.

                        BRODY:
                  (glancing sideways
                   into the room, then
                   back to Marlowe)
            There's plenty of time to talk.
            Make it tomorrow, bud.

He starts to close the door. Marlowe bares his teeth
and shoves the door in against Brody, viciously.

                        MARLOWE:
                  (pleasantly)
            We'll make it now.

77.   INT. BRODY'S APARTMENT   NIGHT

A pleasant room, nicely furnished. French windows open
onto a balcony; near the windows a closed door, and near
the entrance another door with a heavy curtain drawn
across it. Marlowe closes the entrance door behind him,
not taking his eyes from Brody. Brody stands still,
his hand frozen underneath his coat, his eyes wolfish.
Presently he breaks, letting his hand drop.

                        BRODY:
                  (shrugging --
                   turning away)
            Why not, if you think you got
            something.

Marlowe smiles, glancing at the curtained doorway. A
woman's shoes show below the edge.

                        MARLOWE:
            You alone, Joe?

                        BRODY:
                  (meaningfully)
            Yeah.

Marlowe lifts the curtain, high enough to show a very
spiffy leg -- Vivian's, in fact. He admires it.

                    MARLOWE:
          I could be alone with that almost
          any time.

He drops the curtain again, goes to the davenport, and
sits down, tossing his hat beside him. Brody picks up
a box of cigars from a nearby table, walks to an easy
chair opposite Marlowe, and sits.

                    BRODY:
          Well, I'm listening.

He drops his cigarette stub into a tray and puts a cigar
between his lips.

                    BRODY:
          Cigar?

He tosses one to Marlowe through the air. As Marlowe
reaches out to catch it Brody takes a Police Special
out of the cigar box and covers Marlowe, who relaxes
slowly, like a steel spring.

                    BRODY:
          Okay, stand up. Slow.

                    MARLOWE:
             (not moving, smiling
              sardonically)
          My, my -- such a lot of guns around
          town, and so few brains. You're the
          second guy I've met today who seems
          to think a gat in the hand means the
          world by the tail.
             (derisively)
          Put it down, Joe.
             (as Joe doesn't
              move, only looks
              nastier)
          The other guy's name is Eddie Mars.
          Ever hear of him?

                    BRODY:
          No.

                    MARLOWE:
          If he ever gets wise to where you

                    MARLOWE: (Cont.)
were last night in the rain -- you'll
hear of him.

                    BRODY:
     (deadpan, but
       lowering the gun)
What would I be to Eddie Mars?

                    MARLOWE:
Not even a memory.

                    BRODY:
Don't get me wrong. I'm not a tough
guy -- just careful.

                    MARLOWE:
You're not careful enough. That play
with Geiger's stuff was terrible. I
saw it, you know. I don't think
Geiger's boy friend liked it.

                    BRODY:
Carol Lundgren? That punk.

                    MARLOWE:
Yeah. Punk burns, sometimes.
       (raises his
         voice to the
         curtain door)
You might as well come out, Vivian.
Brody decided not to shoot me just yet.
       (as the curtain
         parts slightly to
         show Vivian, undecided)
Oh, yeah, and bring the blonde with you.

Vivian comes out, followed by Agnes. Vivian looks
strained, angry, indomitable. Agnes looks merely vicious.

                    MARLOWE:
     (to Agnes)
Hello, sugar.

                    AGNES:
     (sourly)
Hello -- trouble!

Agnes flounces down on the arm of an overstuffed chair.
Brody watches, his eyes hard and narrow, expressionless.
Vivian stands looking down at Marlowe. She is definitely
not glad to see him.

                    MARLOWE:
So you don't really believe in
miracles -- or me.

                    VIVIAN:
I've learned not to believe in any-
thing. I don't need you, Marlowe.
I don't know how you got here, but
I don't want you. Will you get out?

                    MARLOWE:
But darling, the man with the gun
won't let me. Look -- he's all
bothered and curious, wondering
about stuff.

                    BRODY:
                 (menacingly)
Yeah -- you bet I'm wondering.
                 (looking sharply from
                  Vivian to Marlowe,
                  then to Agnes)
Agnes -- put some more light on so
I can see to shoot if I have to.
                 (to Vivian, as
                  Agnes switches
                  on a floor lamp)
You -- sit down, and keep quiet.

                    VIVIAN:
Joe, I swear I didn't have anything
to do . . .

                    MARLOWE:
                 (attempting to
                  draw her down
                  beside him)
Don't argue with the man. Here . . .
                 (taking Vivian's handbag,
                  hefting it to assure
                  himself the wad of bills
                  is still inside, and grinning
                  with satisfaction, placing

                    MARLOWE: (Cont.)
               bag on couch)
          Sit on this, baby . . . . Go ahead. You
          won't need it.

                    VIVIAN:
          Marlowe, you're ruining everything.

                    MARLOWE:
               (finally losing
                patience, yanking
                her down bodily)
          Sit down!

Vivian struggles with him angrily. Marlowe puts his arm
around her and smiles mockingly at Brody, who raises his
gun slightly, with unpleasant significance.

                    BRODY:
          Okay, fella. Give out.

                    MARLOWE:
               (shaking his head)
          Uh-uh, Joe -- you're doing the giving.

                    BRODY:
               (leaning forward,
                menacingly)
          Listen. . . .

                    MARLOWE:
          Sure, sure -- You're the hard boy
          with the gun. Okay -- go ahead,
          blow holes in me. That won't take
          the cops off your neck.

                    BRODY:
          What cops?

                    MARLOWE:
          The cops that are going to find out
          where all that lead in Geiger came from.

He rises, pacing with nervous catlike energy as he talks,
his sheer ease and conviction holding Brody motionless.

                    MARLOWE:
               (continuing)
          You shot Geiger, last night in the

MARLOWE: (Cont.)
rain. The trouble is he wasn't alone
when you whiffed him. Either you
didn't notice that -- and I think you
did -- or you got scared and ran.
But you had nerve enough to take the
plate out of his camera, and you had
nerve enough to come back later and
hide his corpse, so you could clean
out his store before the law knew it
had a murder to investigate.

BRODY:
(dangerously quiet)
It's kind of lucky for you I didn't
kill Geiger.

MARLOWE:
You can hold your breath for it, just
the same.

BRODY:
You think you got me framed.

MARLOWE:
Don't go simple on me, Joe. I told
you there was a witness.

BRODY:
(suddenly seeing
the light)
Carmen! That little. . . . She would --
just that!

Vivian reacts to this - Marlowe puts his hand strongly
on her shoulder, holding her quiet!

MARLOWE:
(laughing)
I thought you had that picture of her.

For a moment nobody moves. There is a feeling of preda-
tory animals; caged and waiting. Vivian looks slowly up
into Marlowe's face. Then Brody puts his gun down on an
end table by his chair.

BRODY:
Let's all calm down here. Let's all
just sit quiet a minute and think.

                          BRODY: (Cont.)
                     (to Marlowe)
               Who are you? And what do you get
               out of this?

                          MARLOWE:
               I'm just a guy paid to do other
               people's laundry. And all I get
               out of it is those pictures of Carmen.

                          BRODY:
               What pictures?

                          MARLOWE:
                     (as to a child)
               Oh, Joe!

He sits down beside Vivian again, talks to her as though
Brody were not present.

                          MARLOWE:
               How do you like that? He drops the
               whole thing in my lap, and then he
               says "What pictures"?
                     (to Agnes)
               Poor Aggie. I hate to think of you
               standing outside the gas chamber
               watching him while he chokes.

                          AGNES:
                     (to Brody)
               Joe. . . .

                          BRODY:
               Shut up.
                     (to Marlowe)
               How did you get to me?

                          MARLOWE:
               I never saw so many streets leading
               to one place in my life. Every-
               where I turn I fall over Joe
               Brody -- and I been doing a lot of
               turning.

                          BRODY:
               So Carmen says I gunned him.

MARLOWE:
With the photos in hand, I might be
able to convince her she was wrong.

BRODY:
  (after a pause,
  scowling)
I'm not saying I have or haven't
got the photos. I'm only saying
I'm broke. Agnes and I are down to
nickels, and we got to move on for
a while till this Geiger thing cools off.

MARLOWE:
No dough from my client.

BRODY:
  (to Vivian -- with
  cold fury)
So you did go to somebody after all.
  (rising)
All right! I don't need your five
grand. I can take you off my back,
Marlowe, and I can get the cops taken
off. I got a connection, see? I got
a handle on something big enough to
turn this town upside down --

MARLOWE:
Why haven't you pulled it?

BRODY:
I'm going to. And what I get out of
it will make your five grand look like
a roll of nickels.

AGNES:
Joe -- you're not gonna do it. You
can't go up against Eddie Mars, he'll --

BRODY:
  (furiously)
Shut up! You have to let that big
mouth run off in front of -- ?

He is interrupted by the sudden RINGING of the DOORBELL.
They hold it, all of them apprehensive of who may be on
the other side of the door, while the RINGING STOPS and

becomes an insistent rapping. Brody jerks open a desk
drawer and draws out a bone-handled automatic, which he
hands out to Agnes. She takes it, shaking nervously.
Brody indicates Marlowe.

> BRODY:
> (to Agnes)
> If he gets funny, use your own
> judgment -- and the dame, too.

Agnes sits on the arm of the davenport beside Marlowe,
the gun out of sight against him. Marlowe, observing
her shaking hand, is not happy. Brody puts his own gun
in his pocket, leaving his hand on it, and opens the
door. Carmen Sternwood pushes him back in the room,
using a tiny revolver which she pushes against his hips.
Carmen kicks the door shut behind her; Agnes leaps up,
standing out of Marlowe's reach, her gun wavering between
him and Carmen. She remains oblivious of the other
people in the room. Vivian reacts to her entrance, but
says nothing. Marlowe sits still, automatically stroking
the sleepy cat.

> CARMEN:
> (to Brody, with
> quiet viciousness)
> I want my pictures, Joe.

Brody is scared, playing it very easy, backing up as she
follows him.

> BRODY:
> Take it easy, Carmen.

> MARLOWE:
> (sharply, eyeing Agnes)
> Carmen. . . .

> AGNES:
> (to Carmen)
> Get away from him, you.

Vivian rises sharply, also getting out of Marlowe's
reach; she whips a small automatic out of her coat pocket.

> VIVIAN:
> (to Agnes, trying
> to watch her and

```
                    VIVIAN: (Cont.)
                Brody at the same
                time)
          Let her alone.
                (to Brody, moving
                toward him)
          Joe, if you dare to hurt her. . . .

                    MARLOWE:
          This is cute.  Hasn't anybody else
          got a gun? -- We can play ring
          around the roses.

                    CARMEN:
                (ignoring them
                all -- to Brody)
          You shot Arthur Geiger.  I saw you.
          I want my pictures.

                    MARLOWE:
          For Pete's sake, all of you -- relax!
```

No one hears him. The three women continue to behave
like nervous cats -- the lead may start flying at anybody, any minute. Brody still has his hand in his
pocket; he may blast Carmen -- and Marlowe, gunless,
sits in the middle of the possible crossfire. Vivian is
closer to him than Agnes, having moved beyond the hampering
arm of the couch. Marlowe moves abruptly. Grabbing the
couch cushion which Vivian has just vacated, he slings
it at Agnes, knocking her off balance and down.

Almost as a continuation of the same movement Marlowe
makes a dive for Vivian's legs. She falls on top of
him, they struggle for the gun, and Vivian bites Marlowe's
wrist. He whacks her across the side of the head with
his free hand, wreches the gun free and stands up. Carmen's
attention has been distracted slightly by this dust-up,
and Brody strikes at her gun hand. The gun goes off,
making a small sharp crack, shattering a pane of glass
in the French windows, then skitters out of Carmen's hand
and across the floor. Agnes lets go a frightened bleat and
collects herself, about to fire at Carmen. Marlowe makes
a quick rush, kicks the gun out of her hand, and puts his
foot on Carmen's gun just as Carmen gets there, her hands
and knees, reaching. She puts her hand on Marlowe's foot,
and then looks up at him, sidewise, and giggles. He
bends over and pats her on the back.

                    MARLOWE:
          Get up, angel. You look like a
          Pekinese.

She draws back and rises as Marlowe scoops up her gun
with his left hand and drops it in his pocket. The gun
he has taken from Vivian still dominates the room.

                    MARLOWE:
          Everybody -- stand still.

They do, and he walks over and picks up Agnes' gun,
sticking that on in his hip pocket. Brody is wiping
the nervous sweat off his face -- Agnes and Vivian still
crouch half stunned on the floor. Marlowe laughs.

                    MARLOWE:
          My, don't we have fun! You can get
          up now, kiddies.
                    (walking over
                     to Brody)
          All right, Joe. Give.

Brody goes sullenly to the desk, opens a secret compartment, and pulls out a fat envelope, hands it to Marlowe.
Marlowe glances at the contents.

                    MARLOWE:
          Sure this is all of it?

                    BRODY:
          Yeah. Now will you dust, so I can
          air out the room?

Marlowe turns as the Sternwood girls approach him. Carmen
gives him a languishing smile and holds out her hand for
the envelope.

                    CARMEN:
          Can I have them now?

                    MARLOWE:
          I'll take care of them for you.

He hands the envelope to Vivian, who thanks him with her
eyes.

                    MARLOWE:
            (to Carmen and Vivian)
        You'd better go on home now.

Carmen continues to look at him, sidelong, biting her
thumb.

                    CARMEN:
        You'll take care of Carmen, won't you?

                    MARLOWE:
        Check.

                    CARMEN:
        Could I have my gun back?

                    MARLOWE:
        Later.

                    CARMEN:
        You're awfully cute.

                    MARLOWE:
        Yeah.
            (stopping Vivian
            as she passes him,
            heading toward the
            door)
        Countess -- you forgot something.

He picks up her bag off the davenport and hands it to
her -- the scene is almost a repetition of the one in
Marlowe's office, with Marlowe still holding the handbag.

                    MARLOWE:
        Did I hurt your head much?

                    VIVIAN:
            (softly)
        You -- and every other man I ever met.

She goes out. Carmen follows her, but at the door she
turns impulsively, flings her arms around Marlowe's neck
and kisses him.

                    CARMEN:
        I like you.

She runs off down the hall. Marlowe looks at her, puzzled
by her unusual attitude. He closes the door and turns
again to Brody and Agnes. Agnes, considerably scratched
up, gives him a snakely glare as she pats her wounds
with a handkerchief.

                    BRODY:
          I got enough of you, chum.

                    MARLOWE:
          Yeah, but there's still some unfinished
          business. What's this handle you got
          on Eddie Mars that's big enough to
          turn the town upside down?

                    BRODY:
          Listen -- you got your pictures --
          you got nothing more on me. Get
          outa here.

                    MARLOWE:
          Sure, I can go. You can go, too.
          Up to Quentin, to the big chair in
          the little room with the window.
          They stand outside, Joe, with stop-
          watches. They clock you in seconds,
          but from where you sit the centuries
          stink of cyanide, and they wrap around
          your throat, and a lot of people say
          it's easier than hanging -- I don't
          know.

                    BRODY:
          What are you trying to do?

                    MARLOWE:
          Keep your neck out of a noose -- in
          return for some information. Got an
          alibi for last night?

                    BRODY:
          I was right here with Agnes.

                    MARLOWE:
               (picking up his hat)
          Okay, Joe. You can only die once,
          even for a couple of murders.

Brody stares at him as he turns to leave. Agnes is
scared -- she puts her hand on Brody's shoulder.

> BRODY:
> Wait a minute. What do you mean --
> a couple of murders?

> MARLOWE:
> But then, you don't have to worry,
> do you? You got a connection.

> BRODY:
> Sit down.

> MARLOWE:
> (laughs, sits down
>   on table edge)
> Where were you about seven-thirty
> last night?

> BRODY:
> (sullenly)
> Watching Geiger's place, to see if
> he has any friends too big for me
> to kick out of the way when I take
> over his business. It's raining
> hard, I'm shut up in my car, and
> I don't see anything except another
> car parked in the alley below
> Geiger's. I look at it -- it's a
> Buick, registered to Mrs. Rutledge.
> That's all. Nothing happened, and
> I got tired waiting and went home.

> MARLOWE:
> Know where that Buick is now?

> BRODY:
> How would I?

> MARLOWE:
> In the Sheriff's garage. It was
> fished out of twelve feet of water
> off Lido pier this morning.
> There was a dead man in it, Owen
> Taylor, the Sternwood's chauffeur --
> the guy you got the pictures
> from. He'd been sapped and the

                    MARLOWE: (Cont.)
car pointed out the pier and the
hand throttle pulled down.

Brody gives Marlowe a stricken look. Agnes tightens her
grip on him.

                    AGNES:
Joe, you didn't. . . .

                    BRODY:
Shut up.
     (to Marlowe)
You can't hang that one on me.

                    MARLOWE:
I can make a good try -- unless
you talk and talk straight.

                    BRODY:
All right, all right! Yeah, I
heard the shots. I see this guy
come slamming down the back steps
with something in his hand. He
shoots off in the Buick, and I
follow him, and out of the highway he skids off the road and has
to stop, so I stop too, and play
cop. His nerve is bad, and I sap
him down -- and I figure the film
might be worth something, so I take
it. That's the last I see of him.

                    MARLOWE:
Uh-huh -- so Taylor gave Geiger the
works, and all for the love of little
Carmen. Agh! The sap! . . . How'd you
know it was Geiger he shot?

                    BRODY:
Seemed like a good guess. When I
saw what was on the film I was sure,
and when Geiger didn't show at the
store this morning, Agnes and I figured it was a good time to do ourselves some business.

                    MARLOWE:
Yeah, you figured, all right. You

                    MARLOWE: (Cont.)
          businessed yourself right into a
          hot box.

                    BRODY:
          Yeah -- yeah, I guess I did.

                    MARLOWE:
          I got connections too, you know,
          with the D.A.'s office. If I know
          about Eddie Mars I might be able to
          cool you down some.

                    AGNES:
            (as Brody hesitates)
          Go on, Joe -- tell him!

                    BRODY:
          Okay. It's kind of a funny story.
          It ain't about Eddie Mars, really --
          it's about his wife. I. . . .

The DOORBELL starts to RING. Brody stands up, with
Agnes beside him. Marlowe stays put.

                    BRODY:
          So she's back again.

                    MARLOWE:
          If she is, she doesn't have her
          gun. Don't you have any other
          friends?

                    BRODY
            (crossing to
             the table, picking
             up the Colt)
          Just about one.
            (going angrily
             to the door)
          I got enough of this.

He opens the door about a foot, with his left hand,
holding the Colt ready by his thigh. It is impossible
to see who stands in the hall. Almost instantly two
shots sound, close together. Brody doubles up, falls
forward against the door, slamming it shut. Agnes reacts,
but does not scream. Marlowe leaps up, hauls Brody
away from the door -- Brody is quite dead. Marlowe runs out.

78.   INT. HALLWAY   THE RANDALL ARMS   NIGHT

as Marlowe runs toward the stairs. A frightened woman
peers out of a doorway, pointing to the stairs. The
SOUND of RUNNING FEET comes from the treads below.
Marlowe races to the stairway and down.

79.   INT. FOYER   THE RANDALL ARMS   NIGHT

The front door is closing itself quietly as Marlowe
races down the last flight of steps. He goes through
the door, catching it before it closes.

80.   EXT. RANDALL PLACE   THE RANDALL ARMS   NIGHT

as Marlowe comes out, pauses to get his bearings.

81.   EXT. RANDALL PLACE   LUNDGREN   NIGHT

He runs between two parked cars diagonally across the
street, whirls to fire.

82.   EXT. RANDALL ARMS   MARLOWE   NIGHT

As two shots sound -- we see the impact of the bullets on
the wall beside Marlowe, too close for comfort.

83.   EXT. RANDALL PLACE   LONG SHOT   LUNDGREN   NIGHT
       (MARLOWE'S ANGLE)

as Lundgren vanishes behind parked cars, in the dense
tree shadows, running hard.

84.   EXT. RANDALL PLACE   NIGHT

as Marlowe gets in his car and heads down the street,
following Lundgren.

                                        DISSOLVE TO:

85.   EXT. HOLLYWOOD STREET   NIGHT

a quiet residential street, with trees growing heavy
along the parkway. Marlowe's car pulls in to park.
Marlowe gets out into the street, crouching low, and pulls
Carmen's little gun from his pocket. He walks back the
way he has come, crouching for shelter behind the line of
parked cars. Aside from him the street is deserted.

86.   EXT. HOLLYWOOD STREET   LONG SHOT   MARLOWE'S ANGLE
                                                     NIGHT

as Carol Lundgren walks unconcernedly along, approaching
Marlowe. He seems to feel that he's in the clear, even
whistles softly as he walks.

87.   EXT. HOLLYWOOD STREET   MARLOWE   NIGHT

As Lundgren draws abreast of him, Marlowe steps from
between the parked cars, holding the gun at his side. An
unlighted cigarette droops from his lips.

                    MARLOWE:
          Got a match, bud?

Lundgren stands still, taken by surprise, not sure what
to do. His hand rises instinctively to his leather
jacket, but not inside. A siren wails off, going toward
the Randall Arms -- Lundgren turns his head instinctively
toward the sound, and Marlowe steps in against him,
the little gun jammed into Lundgren's midriff.

                    MARLOWE:
          Me, or the cops?

                    LUNDGREN:
          Get away from me.

                    MARLOWE:
          This is a small gun, kid. I can give
          it to you through the belly, and in
          three months you'll be well enough
          to walk the last mile up at Quentin.

Lundgren holds it, glaring at Marlowe, then relaxes.

                    LUNDGREN:
          What do you want?

                    MARLOWE:
             (turning -- indicating car)
          Get into my car, kid.
             (as Lundgren obeys --
              slowly)
          Under the wheel. You drive.

88.   INT. MARLOWE'S CAR   NIGHT

As Lundgren slides under the wheel, from the curb side,
and Marlowe gets in beside him, keeping him covered.

              MARLOWE:
         Let's go to Laverne Terrace --
         Geiger's house.
              (pleasantly -- as
              Lundgren starts the car)
         And by the way, Carol -- if you shot
         Brody for friendship's sake, you shot
         the wrong guy.

Lundgren gives him a hard, nasty look and laughs.

              MARLOWE:
              (softly)
         Not all friendship, was it? Yeah,
         money talks, all right. It talks,
         and it's breath smells of blood. . . .
              (laughing to himself)
         I told Brody that sometimes punk burns. . . .

89.   EXT. GEIGER'S HOUSE   AT FRONT DOOR   NIGHT

Marlowe and Lundgren stand on the footbridge. Marlowe
still carries the toy gun. He pulls the keys out of his
pocket with his left hand and gives them to Lundgren.

              MARLOWE:
         You open it.

Lundgren starts to take the keys, then slams Marlowe a
quick, hard punch on the jaw. Marlowe rocks back, but
doesn't fall -- he smiles and throws the gun down at
Lundgren's feet.

              MARLOWE
         Maybe you need this.

Lundgren goes for the gun. As he bends down Marlowe
steps in fast, bringing his knee up into Lundgren's face.
The force of the blow straightens Lundgren up, and Marlowe uncorks a terrific left. Lundgren falls heavily.
Marlowe, unperturbed, unlocks the door, puts the gun back
in his pocket, and starts to drag Lundgren inside.

                                      DISSOLVE TO:

90.   INT. GEIGER'S HOUSE   LIVING ROOM   MARLOWE AND LUNDGREN

Lundgren is stretched out on the couch, his hands bound
behind him, under his back. A single lamp shines down
into his face. He has bled somewhat from the nose. Marlowe sits on the couch, twisted sideway, so that Lundgren's
head is strained back over his knee. Marlowe
helps the straining by having his left hand wound in
Lundgren's hair. His manner is gentle, almost friendly.

> MARLOWE:
> (softly)
> You're going to cop a plea, brother --
> don't ever think you're not. And when
> you talk, you're going to say just
> what I want you to say, and nothing
> else. You hear me, sweetheart?

Lundgren makes no reply, staring stonily into the light.

> MARLOWE:
> (almost caressingly)
> It's your face, Carol. You can do
> what you want with it.

He jerks Lundgren's head back harder and raises his free
hand, bringing it down.

> DISSOLVE TO:

91.   INT. GEIGER'S HOUSE   LIVING ROOM   NIGHT

Marlowe stands at the telephone, speaking into the instrument. His face is beaded with sweat, his collar open.
He smokes jerkily -- we get the impression he hasn't
enjoyed slapping Lundgren around. In b.g. Lundgren lies
on the couch, both hands over his face.

> MARLOWE:
> (into phone)
> Hello, Bernie? -- Yeah, Marlowe. How
> you fixed for red points, Bernie . . . ?
> Well, come on up to 7244 Laverne
> Terrace -- I got some cold meat set
> out . . . might interest you.

> DISSOLVE TO:

92.   INT. GEIGER'S BEDROOM   MARLOWE AND OHLS   NIGHT

They stand by the bed, looking down. Geiger is laid out
on the bed. Two strips of Chinese embroidery cover the
wounds on his breast, in the shape of a cross, his hands
folded over them. The only light in the room comes from
two black candles burning on either side of the bed.

                    OHLS:
          Nice gesture of friendship. Lundgren?

                    MARLOWE:
          Yeah.

Ohls bends over, lifts up the Chinese embroidery, studies
Geiger's chest, then straightens up.

                    OHLS:
          So that's where the three slugs went
          out of Owen Taylor's gun. Well, I
          can understand that.
                    (making a gesture
                     of distaste)
          Let's get out of here.

93.   INT. GEIGER'S SITTING ROOM   CAROL

sprawled sideways on the couch, leaning his head against
the wall, showing signs of his recent battle with Marlowe. Marlowe sits in b.g., easily, smoking. Ohls stands
over Carol. Ohls is annoyed with Marlowe, shows it in
succeeding scenes.

                    OHLS:
                    (to Carol)
          Do you admit shooting Brody?

                    CAROL:
                    (not moving -- not
                     opening his eyes)
          Take a jump, Jack.

                    MARLOWE:
                    (through smoke)
          He doesn't have to admit it. I've
          got the gun.

                    OHLS:
                    (he rouses himself)
          I've called Wilde. Come on. We'll
          deliver this punk to him.

He leans down, grasps Carol's arm.

                    OHLS:
          Get up.
               (Carol flings his hand off --
                rises sullenly -- Ohls
                moves in beside him)
          Come on, Marlowe. The D.A. will
          want to see the man that solves
          singlehanded what we make busts on.
          And on the way to him, you and I
          will talk a little too.

Marlowe rises, follows as Ohls takes Carol out, snapping
off the lights as he passes them and all exit.

94.   INSERT: (ESTABLISHING SHOT) DOOR

       lettered:
                    "DISTRICT ATTORNEY"

                                   DISSOLVE THRU TO:

95.   INT. SUMPTUOUS DISTRICT ATTORNEY OFFICE

indicating a city of some size, wealth, etc. The D.A.
sits behind his desk. He wears a dinner jacket, has been
called hastily from a party obviously. At corner of the
desk sits Captain Cronjager of the city police homicide
detail, in plain clothes. He is a cold, hatchet-faced
man obviously displeased with the way things have happened.
Ohls enters, followed by Marlowe.

                    OHLS:
               (to Wilde)
          Evening, Chief. Evening, Cronjager.
               (he pulls up a
                chair to sit down)
          Meet Sherlock Holmes, gentlemen.
               (to Marlowe)
          Grab yourself a chair -- unless you'd
          rather be on your feet while Cronjager
          gives you a going-over.

                    WILDE:
          Sit down, Marlowe. We'll try to
          handle Captain Cronjager. But I
          think you'll admit you were going a
          little fast, won't you?

                    MARLOWE:
          Thanks.

He sits down, takes out a cigarette, holds it unlighted
in his hand. Ohls and Cronjager stare at him.

                    OHLS:
          Fast is right. But just wait and
          watch him go when his foot finally
          does slip.
              (to Cronjager)
          Maybe you'd better tell Sherlock
          Holmes here what else you got on
          the Randall Place killing.

                    CRONJAGER:
          A blonde. Down on the street, trying
          to start a car that didn't belong to
          her. Hers was right next to it, the
          same model. She acted rattled, so
          the boys brought her in and she
          spilled. Claims she didn't see the
          killer.

                    OHLS:
              (still riding Marlowe)
          He's in the back office now -- hand-
          cuffed. Here's the gun.

He takes Carol's gun from his pocket, drops it on the
desk. Cronjager looks at the gun, but without touching
it. After a moment Wilde chuckles, enjoying Cronjager's
discomfiture and Ohls' annoyance. ..

                    OHLS:
          But that's just one of them.
              (he stares at Marlowe while
              he addresses Cronjager)
          You heard about a car being lifted
          out of the surf at Lido pier this
          morning with a dead guy in it?

                    MARLOWE:
              (mildly)
          Do you have to be coy about it?

                    OHLS:
              (staring at Marlowe --

                    OHLS: (Cont.)
                addressing Cronjager
                with malicious sarcasm)
Sure. The guy they found drowned in
the car shot another guy last night
in your territory; a guy named Geiger
who ran a racket in the back room of
a bookstore on the boulevard. The
punk I got in the back office worked
for Geiger.
                    (to Marlowe)
You're on the air. Let's have it.

                    MARLOWE:
That's all. When I finally located
the lad that moved the packing case
out of Geiger's back room, Geiger's
blonde secretary was with him. It was
Brody. While I was trying to persuade
Brody to tell what became of the packing
case, the doorbell rang again and
Brody opened the door and somebody
shot him twice. You know the rest of it.
                (he lights his cigarette)

                    OHLS:
Except what was in the packing case -- yes.

                    MARLOWE:
                (smoking)
Brody didn't tell me.

                    OHLS:
                (staring at Marlowe)
You see, Cronjager? Even as smart as
he is, he's got to guess sometimes, too.

                    MARLOWE:
My guess is the same as yours. Black-
mailing stuff. Geiger's customers must
have been wearing a path across that
rug, coming in to knock on that locked
door and pay their monthly installments.

                    OHLS:
                (staring at Marlowe)
That's right, Cronjager. Maybe Sherlock's
even going to show us his evidence for
guessing that.

                    MARLOWE:
Do you folks still guess when you have
evidence?

                    WILDE:
      (sharply)
That's enough of this.
      (to Marlowe)
So Taylor killed Geiger because he was
in love with the Sternwood girl. And
Brody followed Taylor, sapped him and
took the photograph and pushed Taylor
into the ocean. And the punk killed
Brody because the punk thought he should
have inherited Geiger's business and
Brody was throwing him out.

                    MARLOWE:
That's how I figure it.

                    WILDE:
      (extends his hand)
Let's see your evidence.

                    OHLS:
Give, pal. Hiding murders. Spending
a whole day foxing around so that this
punk of Geiger's can have plenty of
time to commit another one.

Marlowe takes from his coat and puts on the desk before
Wilde the three notes and Geiger's card to General Stern-
wood, and the notebook with its code list of names.
Wilde looks at them, lights a cigar. Ohls and Cronjager
rise and look at the articles over Wilde's shoulders.
Marlowe smokes quietly.

                    WILDE:
      (after a time)
These notes. If General Sternwood
paid them, it would be because he
was afraid of something else. Do
you know what he was afraid of?

                    MARLOWE:
No.

Wilde stares at Marlowe.

> WILDE:
> (after a moment)
> Have you told your story complete?

> MARLOWE:
> I left out some personal matters.
> (they stare at each other)
> I intend to keep on leaving them out.

> WILDE:
> Why?

> MARLOWE:
> I've still got a client. You recom-
> mended me to him through Bernie. My
> first duty is to him.

Wilde, Ohls and Cronjager all stare at Marlowe. He
smokes quietly. Wilde, staring at Marlowe, makes a
slight signal with his hand.

> OHLS:
> (to D.A.)
> Okay. But you're wasting time.
> If you'd let me handle Sherlock. . . .

> WILDE:
> That'll do, Bernie.

> OHLS:
> (to Cronjager)
> I want to surrender a prisoner to
> you. Come on.
> (he goes toward door --
> Cronjager following. As
> Ohls opens the door
> he pauses and looks back
> at Marlowe. To Marlowe)
> I like you. Better and better. Some
> day I'm going to like you so well I
> won't be able to bear having you out
> of my sight.

He and Cronjager exit, close the door. Wilde puffs his
cigar, staring at Marlowe. Marlowe smokes quietly.

                        WILDE:
          (after a time)
Do you know why I'm not tearing your
ear off?

                      MARLOWE:
I expected to lose both of them.

                        WILDE:
          (smoking -- watching
           him steadily -- after
           a time)
What are you getting for all this?

                      MARLOWE:
Twenty-five a day and expenses.

                        WILDE:
And for that money you're willing to
get yourself in dutch with the law
enforcement of this county, maybe lose
your license.

                      MARLOWE:
          (quietly)
I've still got a client.

                        WILDE:
Is he still just a client?
          (Marlowe doesn't
           answer -- smoking)
Listen to me, son. My father was a
close friend of old General Sternwood. I like him as well as you do.
I've done all my office permits --
maybe a good deal more -- to save him
from grief. But in the long run,
nothing can save him except dying.

                      MARLOWE:
Yeah -- the big sleep. That'll cure
his grief.

                        WILDE:
It cures all the grief. . . . You really
don't know yet what General Sternwood
wants with you?

MARLOWE:
Yes. To settle this business with
Geiger.

WILDE:
He's afraid that ex-bootlegger, Regan,
that he took up about a year ago, is
mixed up in this somewhere. What he
really wants is for you to find out
that Regan isn't.

MARLOWE:
Regan's no blackmailer. I knew him.

Wilde shrugs slightly.

WILDE:
Maybe you'd better find him and prove it.

MARLOWE:
Maybe I had.

Marlowe rises. He indicates the objects on the desk.

MARLOWE:
Can I have these?

Wilde looks again at the objects, then he takes up the
notebook containing the code names and addresses, opens
the desk drawer, drops the book in and shuts it, pushes
the other things across the desk toward Marlowe.

WILDE:
Take them.

DISSOLVE TO:

96.   EXT. HOBART ARMS APARTMENT   MARLOWE   NIGHT

as he unlocks the entrance, enters.

97.   INT. LOBBY   MARLOWE

as he enters, is shutting the door when a man, the only
occupant, sitting with a newspaper in a lobby chair,
lowers the paper. It is the young hoodlum who was with
Mars at Geiger's house this morning. He rises, flicks

his cigarette stub into a potted palm and thrusts the tip
of his right hand into the V of his coat-opening.

> BODYGUARD:
> (jovially)
> Well, well, if it ain't Hawkshaw
> himself. The boss wants to talk
> to you.

> MARLOWE:
> What about?

> BODYGUARD:
> What do you care, Hawkshaw? Just keep
> your nose clean. Let the boss do all
> the thinking and ask the questions.

> MARLOWE:
> (drops hand into
>   side pocket)
> I'm too tired to talk. Too tired to
> think too. But if you think I'm too
> tired to refuse to take orders from
> Eddie Mars -- try getting your gat out
> before I shoot that good ear off.
> (bodyguard stares at
>   him -- undecided)

> BODYGUARD:
> A comedian, huh?

> MARLOWE:
> Yeah. I'm going to die laughing in
> just about a minute.

> BODYGUARD:
> (baffled)
> You ain't got no gun. Have you forgot
> about this morning?

> MARLOWE:
> That was this morning. I'm not always
> barefooted.

The bodyguard stares at Marlowe a while longer. Then he
waves his left hand airily.

                         BODYGUARD:
          Okay, hot shot! You win. But don't
          let it go to your head, see?
                    (moves toward the door)
          You'll hear from us.

                         MARLOWE:
          Too late will be too soon.

The bodyguard crosses to the street door, exits. Then
Marlowe follows to the door, sees it is locked, turns, his
lip twisted in contempt, and crosses toward elevator.

98.   **INT. MARLOWE'S APARTMENT   MARLOWE**

      as he enters, snaps on light, tosses his hat onto the bed,
      takes Carmen Sternwood's little pistol from his pocket,
      tosses it onto table beneath the lamp, crosses to book-
      case on which a bottle of whiskey sits, takes up the
      bottle and goes on to the kitchen, exits.

      OVER SOUND OF REFRIGERATOR DOOR, CLINK OF GLASS, etc.

                                        LAP DISSOLVE TO:

99.   CLOSE SHOT   MARLOWE

      at table beneath the lamp, half-emptied highball beside
      him, as he finishes cleaning Carmen's pistol. He closes
      the pistol, and holding it in his left hand, he gathers
      up the remaining tiny shells he had removed from it,
      examines them, shrugs sardonically, tosses them into desk
      drawer, closes drawer and is folding a greased rag about
      the pistol when the telephone rings. He puts the pistol
      on the desk and turns.

100. CLOSE SHOT   MARLOWE   AT TELEPHONE

      He holds the receiver lowered somewhat, so that Mars'
      harsh voice comes clearly from it.

                         MARS' VOICE:
          So you're tough tonight.

                         MARLOWE:
          Sleepy, too. What can I do for you,
          Mister Mars?

                    MARS' VOICE:
Cops over there -- you know where.
Did you keep me out of it?

                    MARLOWE:
What do you think?

                    MARS' VOICE:
Listen, soldier. I'm nice to be nice to.

                    MARLOWE:
You listen. Maybe you'll hear my
teeth chattering.

                    MARS' VOICE:
    (laughs shortly)
Did you -- or did you?

                    MARLOWE:
I did. I don't know why, but I did.

                    MARS' VOICE:
Thanks, soldier. Who gunned him?

                    MARLOWE:
Somebody you never heard of. Let it
go at that.

                    MARS' VOICE:
If that's on the level, someday I may
be able to do you a favor.

                    MARLOWE:
You can now. Hang up and let me go
to bed.

                    MARS' VOICE:
    (laughs again)
You're looking for Shawn Regan,
aren't you?

                    MARLOWE:
Everybody I meet seems to think I am.
But I'm not.

                    MARS' VOICE:
If you were, I could give you an idea.
Drive up to the club and see me. Any
time.

                    MARLOWE:
Thanks.

                    MARS' VOICE:
Be seeing you then.

The other receiver clicks. Marlowe puts his receiver
down slowly, sits a moment, thoughtful. He seems to be
waiting for something. He takes out a cigarette, has
just struck the match when the phone rings. Without moving
he blows out the match and wedges the paper stem into
the telephone bell, muffling it, so that it now merely
buzzes, steadily as whoever it is continues to ring.
Then he strikes another match, lights the cigarette, rises
and begins to unknot his tie as he walks out of SHOT.
The muffled telephone buzzes, the light snaps off, leaving
the room in darkness. The muffled phone continues to
buzz as whoever it is keeps on ringing.

                                    FADE OUT.

FADE IN

101.   ESTABLISHING SHOT   DOOR

       lettered:
                    Bureau of Missing Persons

                                    DISSOLVE THRU TO:

102.   INT. OFFICE MARLOWE   DAY

Marlowe seated, facing across the desk Captain Gregory,
a slow, burly man who looks dull and stupid but is not.
Gregory in plain clothes looks at Marlowe's credentials,
looks up.

                    GREGORY:
Private, eh? What can I do for you?

                    MARLOWE:
I'm working for General Guy Sternwood.
The D.A. knows him.

                    GREGORY:
I know who he is too. Did the D.A.
send you here?

                    MARLOWE:
Isn't your information available to
anybody, unless it's a homicide
matter?

                    GREGORY:
Did the D.A. send you here?

                    MARLOWE:
No.

                    GREGORY:
Did he know you were coming?

                    MARLOWE:
        (after a moment -- takes
          out cigarettes)
Mind if I smoke?

                    GREGORY:
Go ahead.

                    MARLOWE:
        (lights up)
Thanks.

                    GREGORY:
What do you want?

                    MARLOWE:
I want to know what became of a man
named Shawn Regan, who used to work
for General Sternwood.

                    GREGORY:
I don't know where he is. He scrammed --
pulled down the curtain, and that's that.

                    MARLOWE:
Will you give me what you have got on him?

Gregory rings a bell on desk-edge. The door opens, a
middle-aged woman secretary enters.

                    GREGORY:
Get me the file on Shawn Regan, Abba.

The woman exits. Marlowe smokes. Gregory takes up a

charred pipe, digs tobacco dottle deliberately from it,
is about to fill it when the woman enters, lays an
official file on the desk, exits. Gregory puts down the
pipe, puts on glasses, opens the file.

> GREGORY:
> He blew on the sixteenth of September.
> No one reported it. We got into it by
> finding the car. It was the chauffeur's
> day off, so nobody at Sternwood's saw
> Regan take his car out of the garage.
> We found the car four days later in a
> garage belonging to a ritzy bungalow
> court on Sunset. The garage man
> reported it to the stolen car detail;
> said it didn't belong there. We
> couldn't find who it belonged to.

> MARLOWE:
> And of course Eddie Mars' wife couldn't
> tell you, because she had disappeared too.

> GREGORY:
> (stares at Marlowe a moment)
> If you knew so much already, why did
> you come to me?

> MARLOWE:
> Sorry. Go ahead.

> GREGORY:
> So you have been talking to some
> Sternwood about Regan.

> MARLOWE:
> Why not? You just said nobody has
> accused anybody of any crime yet.

> GREGORY:
> Yes, Mrs. Mars was gone too, dis-
> appeared within two days of the day
> Regan's car was left in the garage.

> MARLOWE:
> What are the angles?

> GREGORY:
> Mrs. Mars lived in the apartment the

GREGORY: (Cont.)
garage belonged to. Regan was known
to carry a roll, fifteen grand, in his
clothes all the time --

MARLOWE:
Yes. I had heard that.

GREGORY:
It don't seem to have been any secret
to anybody that Regan was sweet on
Mars' wife.

MARLOWE:
So it looks like they went off
together.

GREGORY:
Regan had fifteen grand in cash with
him. Mrs. Mars had some rocks, and
a car of her own -- making two cars
available. Everything disappeared
but one of the cars.

MARLOWE:
What did she look like? Have you
got a photograph?

GREGORY:
No. . . . A blonde. She won't be
now though.

MARLOWE:
What was she before she married Mars?

GREGORY:
A torcher.

MARLOWE:
Maybe she isn't anything now.
Maybe neither of them are.

GREGORY:
You're thinking of Eddie Mars.
You're wrong. Mars is a business man,
and a good one. Jealousy's a luxury --
murdering for it, at least -- that a
man like Eddie Mars knows he can't afford.

MARLOWE:
So, as far as you're concerned, Mars
is out.

GREGORY:
Mars is out. And, until something
more turns up, we are too.

MARLOWE:
(rising)
And so am I, it looks like. There's
no law on my book either against a
man with fifteen grand going away
with the woman he loves.
(turning)
Thanks.

GREGORY:
(closing the file)
Not at all.
(Marlowe moving toward
the door)
Give my best to the D.A.

MARLOWE:
(half halts --
being slyly kidded)
I will.

He exits.

103. EXT. STREET MARLOWE

gets into his car, drives away. As he does so, a coupe
starts up behind him, following him.

104. INT. MARLOWE'S CAR MOVING MARLOWE

is aware that the other car is following him, is sardonic,
is careful to let the other car keep in sight of him.

105. INT. MARLOWE'S OFFICE ANTEROOM MARLOWE

entering, finds Norris waiting for him.

MARLOWE:
(closing door)
Good morning, Norris.

                    NORRIS:
              (rises)
          Good morning, Mr. Marlowe.

                    MARLOWE:
          How's the General this morning?

                    NORRIS:
          Not so well, sir. I -- ah --

                    MARLOWE:
          Yeah? What's on your mind?

                    NORRIS:
              (in sort of a rush)
          I read the papers to him this
          morning. From -- ah -- certain
          items we assume that your investi-
          gation is now complete.

                    MARLOWE:
          Yes, as regards Geiger. I didn't
          shoot him, though.

                    NORRIS:
          Quite so, sir.

                    MARLOWE:
          I guess you've called for the debris.

                    NORRIS:
          The debris, sir?

                    MARLOWE:
              (crossing to other door)
          This way.

    Norris follows him.

106.   INT. MARLOWE'S OFFICE   MARLOWE

    at desk takes out papers, evens them, puts them into
    envelope.

                    MARLOWE:
          There you are. Three notes, and
          the card.

                    NORRIS:
          (steadily)
Thank you, sir. Mrs. Rutledge
tried several times to telephone
you last night --

                    MARLOWE:
I know. I was busy getting tight.

                    NORRIS:
          (puts hand inside coat)
Quite so, sir.
          (he draws out check,
           hands it to Marlowe)
The General instructed me to hand
you this. Will it be satisfactory?

                    MARLOWE:
          (takes check, glances
           at it, folds it)
Five hundred. Quite.

                    NORRIS:
          (curiously insistent)
And we may now consider the entire
incident closed?

                    MARLOWE:
          (gets the overtone but
           covers completely, easily)
Sure. Tight as a vault with a
busted time lock.

                    NORRIS:
Thank you, sir. We all appreciate
it. When the General is feeling
better, he will thank you himself.

                    MARLOWE:
Fine. I'll come out and drink some
more of your brandy. Maybe with
champagne.

                    NORRIS:
          (departing)
I'll see that some is properly
iced, sir.

He exits, closes the door. Marlowe's air changes now.
He opens the check slowly, looks at it, speculatively.

                    MARLOWE:
                (musing: aloud)
            Completely closed . . . completely closed.

He rouses, puts the check into his wallet, goes to
phone, dials, speaks into phone.

                    MARLOWE:
            Hello. . . . Let me speak to Eddie. . . .
            Sure, Eddie . . . Phil Marlowe.
                (holding phone between head
                and shoulder, he takes out
                cigarette, is about to light
                it, speaks into phone, still
                holding cigarette and burning
                match in both hands)
            Hello, Eddie. I want to see you.
            I'll drive up tonight. . . . Check.

                                    DISSOLVE TO:

107.   ESTABLISHING SHOT   INSERT   SIGNBOARD

            Stateline, Nevada

                                    DISSOLVE THRU TO:

108.   INT. LAS OLINDAS CLUB ENTRANCE   NIGHT   MARLOWE

checking his hat and coat at counter. The slim,
pasty-faced bodyguard who had been with Mars and the
other guard at Geiger's house enters, approaches.

                    MARLOWE:
            Hello. How's the pistol-packing
            business up here?

                    BODYGUARD:
                (blandly)
            Better. We don't have so many
            amateurs around.

                    MARLOWE:
            Not amateurs -- just suckers, huh?

                              BODYGUARD:
                         (turning)
                    This way.

Marlowe follows him.

109.   INT. MARS' PRIVATE OFFICE   MARS AND MARLOWE

The office is suave, restrained, well-furnished, shows
money. A wall safe in one wall, radio, liquor cabinet,
comfortable chairs, etc. Mars wears a well-cut,
expensive dinner suit. He shakes hands with Marlowe as
the bodyguard withdraws, shuts the door.

                              MARS:
                         (shaking hands)
                    Took you a long time to get here,
                    didn't it?

                              MARLOWE:
                    I wouldn't be here now if you hadn't
                    hinted you had something for me.

                              MARS:
                         (turns to liquor cabinet,
                          opens it, starts to fix drinks)
                    What did you change your mind about?
                    About what you are after, or just
                    about admitting it?

Marlowe, lighting a cigarette, doesn't answer. Mars
prepares the highballs, approaches, hands one to Marlowe.

                              MARLOWE:
                         (taking drink)
                    Thanks.

Mars leans against the desk, elegant, holding his drink.

                              MARS:
                    A friend of yours is outside playing
                    the wheels. I hear she's doing well.
                    Mrs. Rutledge --
                         (Marlowe says nothing,
                          drinks)
                    I liked the way you handled that
                    yesterday. You made me sore at
                    first. But I see now you knew what

                    MARS: (Cont.)
you were doing. You and I ought
to get along.
        (Marlowe says nothing,
         drinks, smokes. Mars
         watches him)
But I like to pay my checks as I go
along. How much do I owe you?

                MARLOWE:
For what?

                  MARS:
Still cagey, huh?

                MARLOWE:
All right. How much have you got
that I can use?

                  MARS:
        (waves hand, easy)
Oh, that. I heard you had all
the information already.

                MARLOWE:
I don't know. You didn't bump
Regan off, did you?

                  MARS:
No. Do you think I did?

                MARLOWE:
I came up here to ask you.

                  MARS:
        (stares at Marlowe)
You're kidding.

                MARLOWE:
Yes, I'm kidding. I used to know
Regan. You haven't got the men
for that work. And while I think
of it, don't send me any more gun
punks. I might get nervous and
shoot one of them.

Mars stares at Marlowe, lifts glass and drinks, staring
at Marlowe across the glass, lowers the glass.

MARS:
You talk a good game, but I still
think we can get along. Are you
looking for Regan, or not?

MARLOWE:
Geiger was trying to blackmail
General Sternwood. I finally
figured out that at least half the
General's trouble was being afraid
Regan might be behind it.

MARS:
I see. Well, Sternwood can turn
over now and go back to sleep.
It was Geiger's own racket. I like
to know who rents anything from me,
so I did some inquiring today myself.
So if it was just Geiger you were
after, whoever gunned him washed you
and Sternwood both up.

MARLOWE:
        (sets glass down, rises)
I guess that's what the General
thinks too since he paid me off
today.
        (Mars takes up Marlowe's
          empty glass)
No thanks. No more.

MARS:
Another won't hurt you.

MARLOWE:
No thanks.

MARS:
        (sets glass down)
I'm sorry about that. I wish Sternwood would hire you on a straight
salary to keep these girls of his
home at least a few nights a week.
        (he drains his glass, sets
          it down, wipes his mouth)
They're plain trouble. The older
one's a pain in the neck around here.
If she loses, she plunges, and I end

                    MARS: (Cont.)
up with a fist full of paper not even
worth the ink on it. If she wins,
she takes my money home with her.

                    MARLOWE:
Don't you get it back the next night?

                    MARS:
She's spent it by then.

                    MARLOWE:
And is back on the cuff, huh?
Mind if I look the joint over?

                    MARS:
Go ahead.
      (indicates small door)
That comes out behind the tables.

                    MARLOWE:
Thanks. I'll go in with the
other suckers.

                    MARS:
As you please. We're friends,
aren't we?

                    MARLOWE:
Sure.

They shake hands.

                    MARS:
Maybe I can do you a real favor
some day.

                    MARLOWE:
Maybe! There's just one thing
puzzling me, Eddie. You don't
seem in much of a rush to find
your wife. From what I hear she's
not the kind of a wife a guy <u>wants</u>
to lose. Could it be you know
where she is -- with Regan?

                    MARS:
      (deadly quiet)
Look, soldier. . . . What's between

MARS: (Cont.)
me and my wife is between us.

MARLOWE:
Okay. Sorry.
        (he goes to door, turns)
You don't have anybody watching me,
tailing me around in a gray Plymouth
coupe, do you?

MARS:
        (sharply, surprised,
        actually innocent of it)
No. A gray Plymouth? When?

MARLOWE:
Then it don't matter. If it's not
you, it's just an enemy. I can
take care of him.

He exits. Mars stares after him.

110.   INT. CASINO   MARLOWE

leans against small, swank bar, looking into the gambling
room, which is big, spacious, various small lay-outs
along the wall. At the end of the big room are three
roulette wheels. The two outside ones are deserted;
even the croupiers have been drawn into the crowd
which is packed densely about the middle one. In the
center of the crowd VIVIAN'S HEAD can be seen as she
plays her winning streak. Marlowe is watching her. On
the fringe of the crowd the waiters stand also, watching.
All this is a build-up to show a phenomenal run which
Vivian is making. The barman leans on the bar behind
Marlowe.

BARMAN:
She's sure picking them tonight.
She comes here a lot, and from the way
it's been running for her, she's due
to pick them. But it's been a long
time since this place seen anything
like that.

Two men emerge from the crowd about the wheel and
approach the bar, excitedly. The barman moves to
them, waits.

                    FIRST MAN:
              (to Barman)
         Scotch and soda.
              (the barman starts
               the drinks. The
               speaker mops his face)
         Boy, I never saw such a run. Eight
         wins and two stand-offs in a row on
         that red. Betting a grand at a
         crack too.

                    BARMAN:
              (serves the two drinks)
         A grand at a crack, huh? I saw an
         old horse-face in Havana once --

Marlowe moves away as the two men take up their drinks.

111.   GROUP AT WHEEL   MARLOWE

as he reaches the crowd. The play has stopped. The
croupiers of all three wheels are now facing Vivian
across the table. A mass of bills, chips, etc.,
before Vivian.

                    CROUPIER:
         If you will just be patient a moment,
         Madame. The table cannot cover your
         bet. Mr. Mars will be here in a
         moment.

                    VIVIAN:
              (looks about, cool,
               insolent, though her
               face shows excitement)
         What kind of a cheap outfit is this?
         Get busy and spin the wheel. I want
         one more play and I'm playing table
         stakes. You take it away fast enough,
         I notice. But when it comes to dishing
         it out, you begin to whine.

                    CROUPIER:
         The table cannot cover your bet, Madame.
              (indicates her pile)
         You have over sixteen thousand
         dollars there.

                    VIVIAN:
It's your money. Don't you want it back?

                    A MAN:
              (beside her, much more
               excited than she is)
Look, lady --

                    VIVIAN:
              (turns on him,
               vicious, cutting)
Do you want another sixteen
thousand of it?

The man falls back, discomfited. A door opens in the
wall behind the table. The crowd falls silent, turns,
as Mars comes out the door, smiling, indifferent,
immaculate, hands in his jacket pockets as he strolls
to the table.

                    MARS:
Something the matter, Mrs. Rutledge?
              (she is about to speak
               when he continues,
               easily, courteous)
If you're not playing any more, you
must let me send someone home with you.

                    VIVIAN:
One more play, Eddie. All of it on
the red. I like red. It's the
color of blood.

Mars stares at her a second, smiles faintly, takes from
his inner breast pocket a large pinseal wallet with
gold corners, very elegant, and tosses it carelessly to
the croupier without opening it.

                    MARS:
Cover her bet in even thousands.
              (to the gaping crowd)
If no one objects to this turn of
the wheel being for the lady alone.

The crowd remains breathless. Vivian leans down and
shoves the whole mass of her winnings savagely onto
the RED diamond of the layout, stands back. The
croupier leans without haste and rapidly and skillfully

counts the money, stacks it, places all but a few
scattered chips and bills, rakes these into a neat pile
and pushes it off the layout with his rake, leaving the
bet on the RED. Then he opens Mars' wallet with the
same detached deliberate swiftness, draws out two flat
packets of thousand-dollar bills. He breaks the tape
around one, counts off six bills, adds them to the
unbroken packet, puts the four other bills back into
Mars' wallet and lays the wallet aside as carelessly as
if it were a packet of paper matches. Mars does not
touch the wallet. He stands as before, elegant,
detached, courteous. The croupier spins the wheel with
one hand, snaps the ball into it with the other, draws
back and folds his arms.

112.   CLOSE SHOT   VIVIAN'S FACE

as she watches the spinning wheel.

113.   CLOSE SHOT   WHEEL

as it spins, slows, stops.

114.   GROUP AROUND TABLE

CROUPIER:
Red. Odd. Second dozen.

Vivian laughs, triumphant, for the first time her excite-
ment seems to come through as she lets go for the
moment. Then she stops, watches the croupier add the
bills to her bet, then with the rake shove the whole
thing across to her. Mars smiles faintly, expressionless
still, takes up the wallet, puts it back into his pocket,
goes back to the door and exits.

115.   INT. ENTRANCE LAS OLINDAS CLUB   MARLOWE

at the checkroom, gets his hat and coat, drops a coin
into plate, goes toward the door, putting on coat.

116.   EXT. ENTRANCE LAS OLINDAS   NIGHT   MARLOWE

buttoning his coat, comes out, walks on.

117.   EXT. SHRUBBERY-BORDERED PATH   NIGHT   MARLOWE

as he enters, stops, looks about. His face is intent,

watchful. He listens, puts his hand into his pocket,
draws out a pipe, looks at it, tosses it slightly, con-
temptuously, regretful, shrugs, thrusts pipe into his
side-pocket, his hand still clutching it, goes on moving
quietly and stealthily now, pauses, listens again, is
about to go on when SOUND OF A SLIGHT COUGH comes from
ahead. Marlowe steps quickly and soundlessly into the
shrubbery.

118.   CLOSE SHOT   MARLOWE

hidden behind a shrub, peering out. Ten feet away
another man crouches behind a shrub beside the path,
watching the path. He turns his head; we see that he
wears a mask. He watches the path again, reacts as
FAINT SOUND OF FEET begins. Vivian enters, walking
rapidly along the path, clutching her handbag to her.
As she passes the shrub, the man steps quickly out.
Vivian stops but makes no sound.

> THUG:
> (quickly; low-tone)
> This is a gun, lady. Gentle now.
> Just hand me the bag.

For a moment Vivian does not move. Then she draws a
deep breath as if to scream, still clutching the handbag.

> THUG:
> Yell, and I'll cut you in half.
> (he opens the bag,
> thrusts his hand inside)
> It better be here --

> MARLOWE:
> (quietly, from behind him)
> Hi, pal.
> (the thug stops dead.
> After a second his empty
> hand starts to steal upward)
> Easy now.

As Marlowe and the thug stare it out tensely, two
shadowy figures emerge from the shrubbery. One of them
slugs Marlowe from behind. As he falls, the other grabs
for Vivian, apparently about to do the same for her.
She lets out a wild scream and starts shooting from the
pocket. One of the thugs cries out in mingled pain and

anger -- in the distance people begin to shout -- the
noise has attracted attention.

                    THUG:
          You clumsy yap . . .

                    SECOND THUG:
          Let's get outa here.

They run, vanishing into the dark shrubbery. Vivian
crouches beside Marlowe, helping as he tries to sit up.

                    MARLOWE:
               (in pain, holding his head)
          Agh -- good thing I got a thick skull --

People from the club, parking attendants, etc., run up.
Flashlights play on them.

                    CROWD:
               (ad lib)
          What's the matter? . . . What happened? . . .
          The guy's hurt. . . .

                    MARLOWE:
               (rising groggily)
          It's okay. Just a slight holdup --
          the lady flashes too much dough around.
               (to Vivian)
          You all right?

                    VIVIAN:
          Yes -- are you?

                    MARLOWE:
          Let's go. I don't like crowds.

They get away from the curious onlookers, walking down
a dark path toward the parking lot.

                    MARLOWE:
          You got a car with you?

                    VIVIAN:
          I came with a man. He's dead drunk.
          Forget him. What are you doing here,
          besides playing bodyguard?

                    MARLOWE:
We both seem to have been doing
a bit of that -- Eddie Mars wanted
to see me.

                    VIVIAN:
What for?

                    MARLOWE:
He changed his mind. He never did
tell me.

                    VIVIAN:
You lie.

                    MARLOWE:
All right. I'm lying.

They walk on.

                                    DISSOLVE TO:

119.   EXT. PARKING LOT   MARLOWE AND VIVIAN

enter, cross to Marlowe's coupe.

                    MARLOWE:
               (pauses)
What are trembling for? Tell
me you're scared, because I won't
believe that.

                    VIVIAN:
               (draws him on)
I wasn't used to being high-jacked.
Give me a little time.

                    MARLOWE:
High-jacked. That's -- all it was?

                    VIVIAN:
What else?

                    MARLOWE:
               (studying the holes
                in her coat)
You always go heeled?

                    VIVIAN:
          I feel safer, around the heels
          I go with.

                    MARLOWE:
               (laughing)
          You're terrific.

120.   CLOSE SHOT   MARLOWE'S COUPE   MARLOWE AND VIVIAN

     He helps her in, gets in, shuts door, starts engine.

                                        LAP DISSOLVE TO:

121.   INT. MOVING CAR   DESERT NIGHT   MARLOWE AND VIVIAN

     The car is going pretty fast, Marlowe intent on the road.
     Vivian seems nervous, is looking about, smoking.

                    VIVIAN:
               (smoking nervously)
          So Eddie had you come all the way
          up here and then wouldn't tell
          you what he wanted?

                    MARLOWE:
               (drily)
          That's right. I'm still lying.

     Suddenly she flings the cigarette out the window.

                    VIVIAN:
          Have you got a drink?

                    MARLOWE:
          Sure.
               (still driving, watching
                the road, he leans, takes a
                flask from dashboard com-
                partment, hands it to her)

                    VIVIAN:
               (takes flask)
          I can't drink like this. Stop
          the car.

     Marlowe stops the car.

VIVIAN:
(puts flask unopened back
   into compartment, slams
   it shut)
I don't want a drink. Let's talk.

MARLOWE:
Do we need to? The General paid me
off today -- I'm all washed up.

VIVIAN:
Are you?

MARLOWE:
All right. What's Eddie Mars got
on you?

VIVIAN:
(easily; lifts the hand-
   bag, slaps it)
This, for instance. And tonight's
not the first time.

MARLOWE:
Which would make Eddie Mars sore.
So we'll pass that and start over.
What's he got on you?

VIVIAN:
Wittier, please, Marlowe. Wittier.

MARLOWE:
I can't. I'm too old to learn now.

VIVIAN:
But not old enough to outgrow
some of your other habits.

MARLOWE:
For instance?

VIVIAN:
Killing people.
   (she stares at him,
   secretive, while he tries
   to follow her, catch up
   with what's going on)
So you're a killer.

                    MARLOWE:
Does that mean Geiger, or Brody --
or maybe both of them?

                    VIVIAN:
Why not?
        (she looks at him. Sud-
        denly her manner changes;
        she speaks with a quiet
        and complete sincerity)
I wish I was sure you had done it.
Then I could thank you -- in my grand-
father's name. He still has pride,
at least.

                    MARLOWE:
And you and your sister haven't.

                    VIVIAN:
    (with bitter contempt)
Carmen and me. . . .
        (rapidly)
We're his blood. That's where the
hurt is. That Father might die
despising his own blood. It was
always wild, but it wasn't always
rotten.
        (she pulls herself together,
        takes out a cigarette,
        slumps back in the seat as
        Marlowe strikes a match.
        But when he holds the match
        to her, he sees her lying back
        in the seat, the cigarette in
        her mouth, looking at him with
        lazy and inviting challenge.
        When he brings the match near,
        without moving she blows it out.
        When she speaks it is almost
        a whisper)
Move closer.

Marlowe stares at her. After a moment he flings the
dead match deliberately away, puts his arm around her,
approaches his face to hers. Suddenly Vivian flings the
unlighted cigarette over her shoulder toward the window,
clasps him in her arms.

                    VIVIAN:
          Hold me close!

They kiss, a long kiss. Marlowe raises his head at last.

                    VIVIAN:
          Where do you live?

                    MARLOWE:
          Hobart Arms.

                    VIVIAN:
          I've never seen it.

                    MARLOWE:
          Would you like to?

                    VIVIAN:
          Yes.

                    MARLOWE:
          What's Eddie Mars got on you?

She is motionless in his arms for a second. Then she
flings him back with one arm, sits violently up.

                    VIVIAN:
          So that's the way it is.

                    MARLOWE:
          That's the way it is.

                    VIVIAN:
               (controls herself; takes out
                a wisp of handkerchief and
                scrubs her lips savagely with it)
          Men have been shot for less than this,
          Marlowe.

                    MARLOWE:
          Men have been shot for less than nothing.
          The first time we met I told you I was a
          detective. Get it through your lovely
          head. I work at it, lady. I don't play
          at it.

                    VIVIAN:
          What makes you think Eddie Mars has

VIVIAN: (Cont.)
anything on me?

MARLOWE:
He lets you win a lot of money, then he
has a gunpoke meet you in the back yard
and take it all away from you. And
you're not even surprised. You don't
even thank me for saving it for you.

VIVIAN:
Do I need to tell you what I think
of you, Mister Detective?

MARLOWE:
You don't owe me anything. Your father
paid me. I owe you something for the kiss.

VIVIAN:
Let me congratulate you on keeping your head.

MARLOWE:
Maybe I didn't.

VIVIAN:
Take me home.

Marlowe starts the car again, drives on.

DISSOLVE TO:

122.   INT. MARLOWE'S APARTMENT   NIGHT

As Marlowe enters, closing the door behind him. The
only light in the room filters in from a streetlamp
outside. Marlowe flings his hat carelessly toward
a chair, evidently out of long habit, and starts
across the room toward the kitchen, in search of a
drink and in too much of a hurry to bother turning
on lights.

123.   INT. MARLOWE'S APARTMENT   REVERSE ANGLE FROM KITCHEN
                                             NIGHT

As Marlowe approaches, his body filling the f.g. As
he reaches the kitchen door a lamp goes on suddenly
behind him. He freezes, his body blocking the view

of what is behind him. Then, as he turns slowly, we
see past him -- Carmen Sternwood sits in an armchair,
the one, in fact, into which Marlowe has pitched his
hat. Carmen holds it up, smiling. She wears an
evening gown, more or less covered by a light wrap.

                    CARMEN:
                  (coyly)
          What does the hatcheck girl get for
          a tip?

                    MARLOWE:
                  (grimly)
          I'm trying to think of something
          appropriate -- How did you get in here?

                    CARMEN:
          Bet you can't guess.

                    MARLOWE:
                  (bleakly, lighting a
                   cigarette)
          Bet I can. You came in through
          the keyhole, like Peter Pan.

                    CARMEN:
          Who's he?

                    MARLOWE:
          Guy I used to know around the
          poolroom.

                    CARMEN:
          You're cute.

                    MARLOWE:
          And getting cuter every minute.
          How did you get in?

                    CARMEN:
          I showed your manager your card.
          I stole it from Vivian. I told
          him you told me to come here and
          wait for you.

                    MARLOWE:
          Fine. Now tell me how you're going
          to get out.

                    CARMEN:
               (slipping off her wrap)
          I'm not going.

She looks at him -- a surprisingly honest, steady
look. This is a different Carmen -- a puzzled, half-
frightened girl who seems to be waking from a dream --
not sure she wants to, but unable to help herself.
Marlowe looks back at her, nastily. But he senses a
difference, and his voice is surprisingly gentle
when he speaks.

                    MARLOWE:
          Listen, Carmen. I'm tired. I've
          had a hard day's work. I like you,
          I'm your friend, and any other time I'd
          be tickled to death to see you. But
          not now. Will you please go home?

                    CARMEN:
               (quietly, hungrily)
          Are you really my friend, Phil?

                    MARLOWE:
          Sure . . .

                    CARMEN:
          I need a friend, Phil . . . someone to --

She stops, apparently confused, groping for words.

                    MARLOWE:
          Someone to what, Carmen?

                    CARMEN:
          I don't know.

She looks up at him again, searching his face. As
though Marlowe is a magnet, she is drawn to her feet,
still looking at him. She comes close, but does not
touch him.

                    CARMEN:
               (almost to herself)
          What is it in you? . . . I'm afraid of
          you, and yet . . . there's something
          straight and hard . . . Phil, I wish
          I'd met you before -- a long time ago . . .

MARLOWE:
    (trying to josh
    her out of it)
Hey, hey. . . . What's all this?

CARMEN:
I don't know.
    (angrily)
Why did you have to come? I was
all right. I was fine.

MARLOWE:
And now?

CARMEN:
    (almost weeping)
I don't know.

MARLOWE:
Look -- you and I want to go on
being friends -- and you shouldn't
be here.
    (holding her wrap for her)
Be a good girl.

During this speech, Carmen seems to take the wrap.
But the wrap falls on to the floor, revealing the
fact that Carmen is holding Marlowe's hand.

CARMEN:
Do you think I can be a good girl?

MARLOWE:
It doesn't matter what I think.

Carmen kisses his hand.

CARMEN:
But don't you want me to try?

MARLOWE:
    (trying to free his
    hand now)
I just want you to get out of here.

CARMEN:
    (clinging to his hand)
You've got funny thumbs. Can I
bite it?

Before he can answer, she raises his hand, starts to
put his thumb into her mouth. With a sharp violent
motion he flings her hand away.

>   MARLOWE:
>   Stick to your own thumb. Hasn't it
>   carried you all right all your life?

>   CARMEN:
>   (obediently)
>   All right.

She puts her thumb in her mouth, or her hand to her
face in such a way as to appear to be sucking her
thumb as usual. Marlowe takes up the fallen wrap
and approaches with it.

>   MARLOWE:
>   Okay. Take your thumb now and
>   get out of here.

>   CARMEN:
>   (giggling)
>   It's not my thumb. See?

She removes the object from her mouth and holds it
up for him to see. It is the white queen from his
set of chessmen. Marlowe stares at her for a moment,
then he slaps her terrifically across the face, rocking
her back. The chessman falls from her hand and she
stares at Marlowe, frightened now, as he walks toward her.

>   CARMEN:
>   Do that again.

>   MARLOWE:
>   (seething with repressed
>   rage; almost whispering)
>   Get out.

>   CARMEN:
>   Maybe if people had done that to me
>   more often, I would have been good
>   now.

Marlowe reaches her, grasps her arm, hurries her across
to the door, jerks the door open, almost hurls her
through it, flings the wrap after her, slams the door,

turns the bolt as she rattles the knob, then begins
to hammer on the door. He turns and crosses the room
rapidly to the bath while she still beats on the door,
and washes his hand savagely with soap and water, his
face now actually beaded with sweat. The KNOCKING
CONTINUES. He examines his hand, is still not satisfied, jerks open shaving cabinet, looks at the inocuous
bottles of mouthwash, etc., when what he needs is
carbolic acid, goes to the kitchen while the knocking
still continues, jerks savagely from the shelf his
last bottle of whiskey. It is about half full. He
jerks the stopper out, flings it away and pours about
a dollar's worth of expensive Scotch over his hand,
flings the bottle away, returns to the living room,
and while the KNOCKING STILL CONTINUES, he kneels at
the hearth, lays the delicate chess piece on it and
with a heavy fire-dog hammers the chess-piece into
dust, still beating even after the piece has vanished,
his blows at last drowning out the SOUND of the knocking
on the door.

                                    FADE OUT.

124.   FADE IN

INT. MARLOWE'S BEDROOM   TELEPHONE   ON BEDSIDE TABLE

ringing. Marlowe wakes, rises onto elbow and takes
the phone. He holds it loosely, so that we can HEAR
OHLS' rasping VOICE from the other end.

                    MARLOWE:
            Yeah?

                    OHLS' VOICE:
            Marlowe? Come down here. I want
            to see you.

                    MARLOWE:
            I'm not up yet. I haven't had breakfast.

                    OHLS:
            Never mind the breakfast. If you're
            not in my office in thirty minutes,
            you'll be eating it on the county.

Ohls' telephone clicks shut. Marlowe puts his down,
throws covers back to get up.

LAP DISSOLVE TO:

125.   INT. OHLS' OFFICE   OHLS AND MARLOWE

                    OHLS:
          Lay off.

                    MARLOWE:
          Lay off what?

                    OHLS:
          If you don't know what, it ought
          to be easy not to do it.

They stare at each other. Ohls takes up a box of
cigarettes from the desk, offers it.

                    OHLS:
          Smoke?

                    MARLOWE:
             (not moving)
          I haven't had breakfast yet. Who
          says for me to lay off?

                    OHLS:
          The D.A. does.

                    MARLOWE:
          And beyond him?

                    OHLS:
          So you want to know. Okay it came from
          your client. That satisfy you?

                    MARLOWE:
          I haven't got a client. General Sternwood
          paid me off yesterday. I'm through.

                    OHLS:
          Well, apparently he don't think so. And
          he's a friend of the D.A. and the D.A. is
          the chief crime prosecutor of this county,
          and I'm the D.A.'s head man Friday, and
          all three of us tell you to lay off.

                    MARLOWE:
          Will you tell me one more thing: Why
          General Sternwood thinks I haven't laid off?

                    OHLS:
No. But I'll tell you what he might be
thinking. That you are trying to uncover
enough stuff about his family affairs
to put the squeeze on him yourself.

                    MARLOWE:
That's a lie. General Sternwood never
told the D.A. nor you nor anybody else
that. I don't think the message even
came from General Sternwood. It was --
        (he stops, but Ohls
        has already broken in)

                    OHLS:
Never you mind what you think. You
just lay off. You get it?

                    MARLOWE:
        (quietly)
I get it. Or else I lose
my license and take my pick and
shovel out of the mothballs.

Thoughtful, he reaches out and takes a cigarette from
the box.

                    OHLS:
        (watching him)
Changed your mind, huh?

                    MARLOWE:
        (recovers, sees the cigarette in his
        hand, drops it back into the box)
No. I haven't changed it.

                                    DISSOLVE TO:

126. INT. MARLOWE'S OFFICE   LATER   MARLOWE

The TELEPHONE IS RINGING. Marlowe takes it up.

                    MARLOWE:
        Yes, speaking --

127. INT. STERNWOOD HOME   VIVIAN STERNWOOD AT TELEPHONE

She wears hat and coat as if about to depart.

                              VIVIAN:
                         (rapidly)
               I've found Shawn. I'm leaving at
               once to meet him. We'll send you
               a picture postal from Mexico
               perhaps. So you can call off the
               bloodhounds, and many thanks.
                         (she hangs up)

128.   CLOSE SHOT   MARLOWE   AT PHONE

as the click of Vivian's phone comes through it.

                                        LAP DISSOLVE TO:

129.   EXT. STERNWOOD HOUSE   AT FRONT DOOR   MARLOWE   (RAIN)

facing Norris, who has answered the bell. Norris
stands holding the door half open, as if barring
Marlowe from entering.

                              NORRIS:
                         (courteous, inscrutable)
               No, sir. She left no address.
               We don't expect to hear until she
               and Mr. Regan reach Mexico City
               perhaps.

                              MARLOWE:
               So she found him.

                              NORRIS:
                         (inscrutable)
               Yes, sir. We are all most happy.
               -- Was there anything else?

                              MARLOWE:
               The General . . .

                              NORRIS:
               Is resting. I won't disturb him now.

                              MARLOWE:
               Thanks.

Norris watches him, still barring him from entering.
He turns. Norris closes the door. Marlowe walks on.

DISSOLVE TO:

130.   CLOSE SHOT   PLYMOUTH COUPE   PARKED AT CURB   DAY   (RAIN)

the same car which was following Marlowe yesterday. Marlowe passing, recognizes it, pauses, thoughtful, walks on.

131.   EXT. HOLLYWOOD STREET   MOVING SHOT   MARLOWE

as he passes the mouth of a narrow alley two men step out quickly. One of them saps Marlowe expertly -- they drag him out of sight.

132.   EXT. ALLEY   A DEEP DOORWAY   (RAIN)

Marlowe is dazed, but not out. He fights, but the two boys give him an expert going-over, very quickly and efficiently. Marlowe goes down onto the wet bricks. One of the men leans over him.

>   THUG:
>   (gently)
>   This is just our way of saying --
>   lay off. Get it, Marlowe? Lay off.

He boots Marlowe in the stomach -- the pair of them depart while Marlowe is getting rid of his breakfast. Presently, while Marlowe is trying unsuccessfully to stand up, HARRY JONES comes up to him. Harry is small, hardly five feet, in a cheap snappy 'underworld' suit. Yet in his wizened ugly face there is independence, honesty, reliability, courage. He helps Marlowe to his feet, steadies him, hands him a handkerchief.

>   MARLOWE:
>   (still groggy --
>   wiping his face)
>   You're the guy that's been tailing me.

>   JONES:
>   Yeah. The name's Jones. Harry
>   Jones. I want to see you.

>   MARLOWE:
>   That's swell. Did you want to see
>   those two guys jump me?

> JONES:
> I didn't care one way or the other.

> MARLOWE:
> You could have yelled for help.

> JONES:
> A guy's playing a hand, I let him
> play it. I'm no kibitzer.

> MARLOWE:
> (grinning)
> You got brains. Come on up to
> the office.

DISSOLVE TO:

133. INT. MARLOWE'S OFFICE   MARLOWE AND JONES

Marlowe removes his coat and hat, hangs them up. Jones
watches him. Marlowe is reasonably steady now, gradually
getting his wind back.

> MARLOWE:
> Might as well take yours off too.
> We may be here a good while, unless
> I get another case.

He goes to the desk, sits down, lights a cigarette,
pours a stiff shot from the office bottle, then starts
to riffle through a small stack of mail on his desk.
Jones watches him. He opens top letter, reads it.

> JONES:
> I been around too. Used to run a
> little liquor. Rode the scout car
> with a tommy gun in my lap.
> A tough racket.

> MARLOWE:
> (reading, squinting
> through smoke)
> Terrible.

He tosses the letter into wastebasket, takes up the
next, opens it, sees Jones still standing.

                    MARLOWE:
Sit down. You make me nervous
standing there.

Jones sits on edge of a chair; Marlowe opens and rapidly
reads the next letter, tosses it in wastebasket, opens
the next one. Jones watches him.

                    JONES:
Maybe you don't believe me.

                    MARLOWE:
            (throws letter
             into wastebasket)
What do you want?

                    JONES:
            (approvingly, man to
             man fashion)
That's better. I got something to
sell -- cheap, for a couple of C's.

                    MARLOWE:
            (opens next letter)
Then don't let me stop you.

                    JONES:
            (baffled)
Don't you even want to know who
I am.

                    MARLOWE:
            (rapidly reading letter)
I already know. You're not a cop.
You don't belong to Eddie Mars,
because I asked him.
                (throws last letter into
                 wastebasket, sits back
                 and looks at Jones)
So Agnes is loose again, huh?

                    JONES:
            (taken aback)
How'd you know?

                    MARLOWE:
Well -- she's a blonde.

                    JONES:
She's a nice girl. We're talking
of getting married.

                    MARLOWE:
She's too big for you. She'll
roll on you and smother you.

                    JONES:
       (injured)
That's a dirty crack, brother.

                    MARLOWE:
You're right. I've been running
around with the wrong people lately.
Let's cut out the babble. What do
you want?

                    JONES:
You're looking for something.
Will you pay for it?

                    MARLOWE:
If it does what?

                    JONES:
Helps you find Regan.

                    MARLOWE:
Is that what you want the two C's
for -- for telling me I'm looking
for Regan? People have been
telling me that for two days now.
I don't even give cigars for
it anymore.

                    JONES:
       (patiently)
Do you want to know what I got,
or don't you?

                    MARLOWE:
I don't know. Two C's buys a lot
of information in my circle.

                    JONES:
Would you pay two hundred dollars to
know where Eddie Mars' wife is?

                    JONES: (Cont.)
Would you pay two hundred bucks for
that, shamus?

                    MARLOWE:
          (leans forward and
           rubs out cigarette)
I think I would. Where?

                    JONES:
Agnes found her. She'll tell you --
when she has the money in her hand.

                    MARLOWE:
You might tell the coppers for
nothing.

                    JONES:
          (quietly)
I ain't so brittle.

                    MARLOWE:
          (speculatively)
Agnes must have something I didn't
notice.

                    JONES:
          (quietly, with
           dignity even)
I ain't tried to pull anything.
I come here with a straight proposi-
tion -- take it or leave it; one
right guy to another. Then you
start waving cops at me. You
ought to be ashamed of yourself.

                    MARLOWE:
          (quietly too)
I am. -- Okay. Two hundred it is.
I'll have to go to the bank.

                    JONES:
          (rises)
Okay. After dark'll be better, anyway.
You know Puss Walgreen's office --
Fulwider building -- four-twenty-eight
at the back?

                    MARLOWE:
          I can find it.

                    JONES:
          I'll meet you there at seven o'clock
          tonight. You bring the money, and
          I'll take you to Agnes. Okay?

                    MARLOWE:
          Okay.

                    JONES:
               (going out)
          So long then.

     He exits.

                                    DISSOLVE TO:

134. EXT. FULWIDER BUILDING   ESTABLISHING SHOT   MARLOWE
                                          RAIN   EVENING

      enters.

135. INT. FULWIDER BUILDING   LOBBY   MARLOWE

      It is deserted. Marlowe pauses at elevator, the door
      is open, a shabby old man is asleep on the stool.
      Marlowe goes on.

136. CLOSE SHOT   MARLOWE   AT FIRE DOOR

      pushes the door open, enters stairs, door closes behind him.

137. INT. CORRIDOR   (DIM)   MARLOWE

      standing flattened against the wall beside a door lettered:

               "L. D. WALGREEN -- INSURANCE"

      The transom above it is open, light shines through.

                    JONES' VOICE:
               (beyond transom)
          Canino? Yeah, I've seen you
          around. Sure.

CANINO'S VOICE:
(purring)
I thought you'd remember.

Marlowe steals quietly back along the wall, reaches
another door, pushes it quietly. It is locked.
He takes out his wallet, removes his driver's license
from its celluloid, takes the envelope and slips back
the door-lock, opens the door carefully and quietly,
enters, shuts the door.

138. INT. OFFICE (DIM) MARLOWE

as he stands beside an inner door which is slightly
open, a light burning beyond it. Through the crack
in the door Harry Jones can be seen, sitting behind a
shabby desk. The other man, CANINO, is not in sight
at this angle. Jones is sweating; he cannot help that.
But there is no fear in his voice and he is not
trembling either.

CANINO'S VOICE:
So you go to see this peeper, this
Marlowe. That was your mistake.
Eddie don't like it. And what
Eddie don't like ain't healthy.

JONES:
You know why I went to the peeper.
Account of Joe Brody's girl. She's
got to blow. That takes dough.
She figured the peeper could get
it for her.

CANINO'S VOICE:
Dough for what?

JONES:
You know about the night the kid
bumped Brody? Well, the young
Sternwood girl was there. She not
only dropped in, she took a shot
at Brody. Only the peeper didn't
tell the cops that. So Agnes figures
it's railroad fare for her as soon as
she can get hold of the peeper.
You get it?

                    CANINO'S VOICE:
        Sure thing. Where's this Agnes?

                    JONES:
        What do you care? All she wants is
        to touch the peeper and blow --

His voice stops. He sits back, staring at Canino off,
shows terror now despite himself, but still no fear.

                    CANINO'S VOICE:
                    (purring)
        That's right. Look at it. You'll
        tell me, little man. Where's Agnes?

                    JONES:
        Listen --

                    CANINO'S VOICE:
        You want me to count three or some-
        thing, like a movie? Where's Agnes?

                    JONES:
                    (gives in, collapses)
        You win. She's in an apartment at
        28 Court. Apartment 501. I guess
        I'm yellow, all right.

                    CANINO'S VOICE:
        You just got good sense. I ain't
        going to hurt her. If everything's
        like you say, I'll tell Eddie it's all
        jakeloo. We'll even dip the bill on it.

As Canino's hand comes into sight setting a whiskey
bottle on the desk, Marlowe steps quickly back.

                    CANINO'S VOICE:
        Got a glass?

                    JONES:
                    (stares at the bottle,
                    hopeless now, sweating
                    but still bravely)
        There at the cooler.

As Canino enters, Marlowe steps quickly out. Canino
crosses the open door. We now SEE HIM; a stocky,

vicious man in brown: a killer.

139.   ANOTHER ANGLE   MARLOWE   FLATTENED AGAINST THE WALL

beside the door. Jones cannot be seen now, only Canino
as he takes the glass from water cooler and crosses the
door again. Now he too is not visible. Marlowe follows
him by SOUND ALONE as he returns to the table, clinks the
bottle against the glass as he pours the drink.

> CANINO'S VOICE:
> (purring, falsely
> hearty)
> There you are. Drink her down.
> Mud in your eye.

Jones' breathing can be heard as he pants. When
Canino speaks next, his voice is a little sharper.

> CANINO'S VOICE:
> Drink it. What do you think it
> is -- poison? I bet that Agnes
> of yours wouldn't turn it down.

> JONES:
> No.
> (SOUND of his movement
> as he takes the glass)
> Success.

> CANINO'S VOICE:
> Lots of it.

SOUND as Jones drinks, dies, the glass CLINKS as he
drops it, his body thuds as he falls forward, gasps,
chokes. Marlowe starts forward, catches himself.
The other room goes dark. SOUND as Canino leaves it:
his feet, the other door opens, closes again.

140.   GLASS DOOR   MARLOWE'S ANGLE

The door opens on the corridor. With the light gone,
the glass in the door is faintly luminous, lettering
in reverse, Canino's shadow crosses it. SOUND of his
feet dies away. Marlowe moves swiftly toward the
inner door.

141.   INT. OTHER OFFICE   MARLOWE

his hand on the switch as he turns on the light, looks
for an instant at Jones sprawled dead across the desk,
the whiskey bottle and overturned glass beside him.
Marlowe pauses only a second. He looks about, sees
what he wants, crosses to telephone, takes it up,
dials hurriedly.

> MARLOWE:
> (into phone)
> Information, can you give me the
> phone number of Apartment 301,
> 28 Court Street?
> > (he lowers phone,
> > waits, raises phone
> > quickly again,
> > listens attentively)
> Thanks.
> > (puts phone down,
> > takes it up
> > again, dials)
> Is Agnes in?

The VOICE that answers is a MAN'S VOICE, burly and
loud, so that it can be heard over the phone.

> VOICE:
> No Agnes here, buddy. What
> number you want?

> MARLOWE:
> Wentworth two-five-two-eight.

> VOICE:
> Right number, wrong gal. Ain't
> it a shame!

> MARLOWE:
> Yeah. Can you put me back on
> to the switchboard?

> VOICE:
> Here you go.
> > (phone clicks,
> > whirrs)

> MARLOWE:
> Hello, Manager? This is Wallis,
> Police Identification Bureau,

>   MARLOWE: (Cont.)
> is there a girl named Agnes
> Lozelle registered at your place? . . .
> Well, have you got a tall blonde
> with green eyes, either alone, or
> with a little chap that weighs
> about a hundred pounds, green
> hat, gray overcoat. . . . Yeah, must
> have been the wrong address. Thanks.

He puts the phone down, turns, looks at Jones.

>   MARLOWE:
>   (musing aloud,
>   with admiration)
> Well, you died like a poisoned rat.
> But you drank your poison like a
> man before you split on your girl,
> didn't you?

He approaches, gingerly and carefully shifts Jones
enough to reach inside his coat, is about to search
Jones, the telephone rings. Marlowe pauses, thinks,
makes decision, takes up phone.

>   MARLOWE:
>   (into phone)
> Yeah? . . . Hello, Agnes . . . Marlowe,
> the guy you want to see. No, he's
> not here. He's gone, beat it. But
> I've got the money. Where are you? . . .
> I don't know where he went. Do you
> want the two C's or don't you? . . .
> In half an hour. Right.

He puts the phone down, takes out his handkerchief and
wipes his fingerprints off of it, crosses to the light
switch, wipes it off too, turns it with the handkerchief,
goes to the door, through which he came, exits.

142.   INT. CORRIDOR   DOOR HE ENTERED BY   MARLOWE

as he wipes off the knob with his handkerchief.

                              DISSOLVE TO:

143.   INT. AGNES' CAR   MARLOWE AND AGNES   RAIN   NIGHT

as Marlowe gets into the car -- the gray Plymouth.   Beyond
the rain-streaked windows a Los Angeles street is visible;
lighted store windows, etc.

          AGNES:
I thought you were never coming. . . .
Give me the money.

Marlowe hands her folded bills.   She counts them
rapidly by the dash light, then puts them in her
handbag.

          AGNES:
This is a getaway stake, copper.
I'm on my way. What happened to
Harry?

          MARLOWE:
I told you he ran away. Canino got
wise to him somehow. Forget Harry.
I've paid for information and I want it.

          AGNES:
You'll get it. Joe and I were out
riding Foothill Boulevard a couple
weeks ago. We passed a brown coupe,
and I saw the girl who was driving.
She was Eddie Mars' wife. There
was a guy with her -- the watchdog,
Canino. They're people you don't
forget, even if you only saw them
once. So we got curious, and Joe
tailed them. About a mile east of
Realito there's a side road, and
nothing around it but brush and
hills. Just off the highway there's
a two-bit garage and paintshop run
by a guy named Art Huck -- hot car
drop, likely -- and a frame house
behind it. That's where Eddie Mars'
wife is holed up.

          MARLOWE:
     (studying her coldly)
You're sure of that?

          AGNES:
Why should I lie? . . . Well, goodbye,

AGNES: (Cont.)
copper -- wish me luck. I got a raw deal.

MARLOWE:
Yeah. Your kind always does.

He turns and opens the door to get out.

DISSOLVE TO:

144.	INSERT:	A HIGHWAY MARKER	RAIN	NIGHT

illuminated by the spotlight of a car. Above a black
arrow the sign says:

"REALITO -- 7 MILES"

DISSOLVE TO:

145.	EXT. HIGHWAY	LONG SHOT	RAIN	NIGHT

Marlowe's car spinning along at high speed. The highway runs between miles of orange groves, with mountains
in the b.g.

146.	RAPID MONTAGE	NIGHT

Orange groves -- a neon sign: "WELCOME TO REALITO" --
small lighted store fronts -- a bar -- a theatre --
then dark, barren fields.

DISSOLVE THRU TO:

147.	EXT. HIGHWAY	LONG SHOT	RAIN	NIGHT

Marlowe's car rushing along the wet highway, which now
runs through barren country close to the foothills.
The car takes an S curve, skidding dangerously.

148.	CLOSER SHOT	ON MARLOWE'S CAR

as it swings into another curve, a sharp one, and
deliberately skids off the shoulder, jarring finally
to a stop in the ditch.

149.	CLOSE SHOT	MARLOWE

as he climbs out and bends to inspect the tires. It

is raining heavily.

150.   CLOSE SHOT   MARLOWE   RAIN   NIGHT

as he lets the air out of the two right-hand tires.

151.   CLOSE SHOT   MARLOWE

as he straightens up and looks ahead.

152.   EXT. HUCK'S GARAGE   LONG SHOT   MARLOWE'S ANGLE

A SMALL DINGY GARAGE, with a frame house behind it.
Lights show dimly through shaded windows.

153.   CLOSE SHOT   MARLOWE

as he nods, satisfied, then gets back into the car.

154.   INT. MARLOWE'S CAR   RAIN   NIGHT

Marlowe takes the license holder from the steering post
and puts it in his pocket, then leans lower behind the
wheel.

155.   EXTREME CLOSE   FRONT OF THE CAR SEAT   NIGHT

as Marlowe's hand pushes open a weighted flap, disclosing
a secret compartment with two guns in it. He weighs them,
selects the heavier of the two, and draws it out.   The
flap swings shut.

156.   EXT. HIGHWAY   AT HUCK'S GARAGE   RAIN   NIGHT

Marlowe approaches the garage.   There is a sign on the
blank side wall -- Marlowe holds a flashlight on it,
and we SEE the lettering of the sign:

A R T   H U C K

AUTO REPAIRS -- PAINTING

Marlowe goes round to the front.   The big doors are
closed, but a streak of light shows through the crack.
Marlowe hesitates, then walks past them to glance at
the house.

157.   EXT. FRAME HOUSE   MARLOWE'S ANGLE   RAIN   NIGHT

The only signs of life are the light from the shaded
windows and Canino's brown coupe parked in front by
a row of stunted trees.

158.   EXT. HUCK'S GARAGE   RAIN   NIGHT

At the door, as Marlowe goes up and hammers on it with
the butt of his heavy flashlight. There is a moment of
silence. Then the inside light goes off. Marlowe
centers his flash in a white circle of light on the doors.

> HUCK:
> (speaking through
> the door)
> Whaddaya want?

> MARLOWE:
> Open up, I got two flats back on
> the highway and only one spare.

> HUCK:
> Sorry, mister. We're closed up.
> Better try Realito.

Marlowe doesn't appreciate this. He kicks the door, hard,
and keeps on kicking it, until a second voice -- Canino's
voice -- speaks from close inside. Then he stops to
listen.

> CANINO'S VOICE:
> Okay, Art -- open up for the wise guy.

A BOLT SQUEALS, and half the door opens inward. Marlowe's
flash outlines a gaunt hard face, Huck's face. Then
Huck swings a gun down across the flash, knocking it out
of Marlowe's hand, still burning.

> HUCK:
> Kill that spot, bud.

Marlowe picks up the flash, turning it off. Light goes
on inside the garage, revealing HUCK, a tall man in
dirty coveralls. He backs away from the door, keeping
Marlowe covered.

> HUCK:
> Come inside and shut the door.

159. INT. HUCK'S GARAGE   NIGHT

as Marlowe closes the door behind him. There is the
usual paraphernalia of a garage, and two cars. One is
being painted, a spray-gun lying on the fender, the
other is Carmen Sternwood's Packard convertible.
Canino lounges easily in the shadows by the bench.
The RAIN BEATS on the tin roof.

                    MARLOWE:
               (indicating Huck's gun)
          You could scare off a lot of
          trade that way.

                    HUCK:
          I'm too far out of town to take
          chances.
               (pointedly)
          You can get yourself hurt, kicking
          on doors.

                    CANINO:
               (softly)
          Cut it out, Art. You run a garage,
          don't you?

                    MARLOWE:
               (not looking at Canino)
          Thanks.
               (to Huck)
          I suppose you <u>can</u> fix flats.

                    HUCK:
               (putting the gun
                in his pocket)
          As good as you can make 'em, bud.
          But right now I'm busy.

                    CANINO:
               (pleasantly)
          Art -- you got time to fix his
          tires.

                    MARLOWE:
          You can use my spare -- that'll
          help some.

                    HUCK:
Listen, I told you I'm busy with
a spray job. . . .

                    CANINO:
It's too damp for a good spray job,
Art. Get moving -- and take two
jacks.

                    HUCK:
Now wait a minute. . . .

Canino looks at Huck with a soft quiet-eyed stare, then
away again, not saying anything. Huck wilts and
moves away, pulling on a raincoat and banging out with
a socket wrench, a hand jack, and wheeling a dolly.
Canino closes the door behind him and returns to the
workbench. Marlowe watches silently, lighting a cigarette.

                    CANINO:
Bet you could use a drink. Wet
the inside, and even up.

                    MARLOWE:
Thanks.

Canino produces a bottle and two glasses from under the
bench, pours two shots, and hands one to Marlowe. They
salute -- Canino drinks, and Marlowe, remembering Harry
Jones and the cyanide cocktail, hesitates, then drinks also.

                    CANINO:
               (casually)
Live around here?

                    MARLOWE:
No. Just got in from Reno and
Carson City.

                    CANINO:
The long way round, huh?
Business trip?

                    MARLOWE:
Partly. And in a hurry.

                    CANINO:
Too bad -- you may have a long wait.

                        CANINO: (Cont.)
                     (reaching for Marlowe's
                         empty glass)
          How about another, to pass the time.

                                           DISSOLVE TO:

160.   EXTREME CLOSE   A WHEEL   NIGHT

    -- the tire already on a spreader and loose from the rim.
    A man's hands and feet working at the job viciously.
    The CAMERA PULLS BACK to show Art Huck as he rips out
    the tube. Marlowe and Canino stand almost as before,
    by the workbench.

                        HUCK:
                     (grumbling over
                       above action)
          I don't have enough to do -- guys have
          to get flats in the middle of a
          cloudburst.

                        CANINO:
                     (laughing)
          Don't crab so much. You can use
          an extra bath.
                     (taking a roll of coins
                       out of his pocket,
                       tossing them idly
                       in the palm of his hand)
          Just get busy.

    Huck carries the tube to an airhose and starts to fill it.

                        HUCK:
          I am busy, brother. Plenty busy.

    He starts to place the tube in the galvanized tub
    under the hose, then turns swiftly, lifting the tube
    high, and brings it down over Marlowe's head and
    shoulders, a perfect ringer. Marlowe, unable to
    reach the gun in his pocket, bends forward, trying to
    throw Huck over his back. Canino steps in lightly,
    like a dancer, his hand closed hard over the roll of
    coins, and hangs one with delicate precision on
    Marlowe's jaw. Marlowe's tough -- he goes on fighting,
    although he's already out on his feet. Huck pulls him
    head back by the hair as Canino clips him again with

the weighted fist. Marlowe tries, but it's no use.
He goes down and stays that way.

161.   INT. MARS' HIDEOUT   LIVING ROOM   NIGHT

A small room, in keeping with the exterior -- furnished
comfortably but not luxuriously. The only light comes
from a floor lamp beside the davenport where Marlowe
lies. His hands are cuffed behind him, his feet roped
to the leg of the davenport. He is still out, his face
considerably the worse for wear. Vivian sits beside
him on a straight chair, holding a half empty glass in
her hand. She seems to have forgotten about it. She
seems to have forgotten everything but Marlowe --
who begins to come out of it. He opens his eyes
presently and looks at Vivian -- he doesn't seem surprised. He winces and shuts his eyes again.

                    MARLOWE:
                (thickly)
            Move the light, honey. . . .

Vivian rises and turns the light away from his face.
He looks up at her again.

                    MARLOWE:
                (still groggy)
            That's better -- where are the
            boys -- out digging a grave?

                    VIVIAN:
                (desperately)
            Phil, why did you have to go on
            with this?

                    MARLOWE:
            Why did you?

Vivian turns away from him -- she's obviously keyed up,
scared, desperate.

                    VIVIAN:
            I've only known one fool as big as
            you. . . .

                    MARLOWE:
                (after a pause)
            You might spare me a little of that

                     MARLOWE: (Cont.)
          drink you're not using.

Vivian goes to him, sits down, and holds the glass to
Marlowe's lips, then touches his battered face with
her fingertips.

                     VIVIAN:
               (shakily)
          Your face looks like a collision
          met. . . .

                     MARLOWE:
          It won't last long, even this good.
               (after a pause, looking
                up at Vivian softly)
          I'll give it back to you -- I've
          only known one fool as big as you.

They hold it, a twisted uncomfortable moment, and then
MONA MARS enters. She is tall, blonde, strikingly
beautiful -- a woman who knows her way around, yet
having a certain dignity and fineness.

                     MARLOWE:
          You would be Mrs. Eddie Mars . . . the
          blond that Shawn Regan <u>didn't</u> run
          away with.

                     MONA:
          Why did you have to make trouble?
          Eddie wasn't doing you any harm.
          I was never in love with Shawn --
          we were just good friends. But
          you know perfectly well that if
          I hadn't hid out here when Shawn
          disappeared, the police would have
          been certain Eddie killed him.

                     MARLOWE:
               (quietly)
          But he did kill him.

                     MONA:
               (after a pause,
                with quiet dignity)
          Eddie's not that sort of man.

                    MARLOWE:
You mean Eddie never kills people.

                    MONA:
No.

                    MARLOWE:
You really believe that, don't you?
And in a way, I suppose you're right. . . .

                    MONA:
    (sincerely)
I'm married to Eddie Mars. I love
him. I know what's inside of him.

                    MARLOWE:
Well, if Eddie's such a nice guy,
I'd like to talk to him without
Canino around. You know what Canino
will do -- beat my teeth out and then
kick me in the stomach for mumbling.

                    VIVIAN:
You'll get your talk, Phil. Canino's
gone for Eddie.

                    MARLOWE:
Leaving Art Huck within call, I
suppose. Well, I suppose nobody's
luck holds forever.
    (to Vivian)
You could really have gone to Mexico,
you know. You'd have liked it better.
Blood doesn't spatter that far.

                    MONA:
Oh, stop talking that way!

Vivian and Marlowe are no longer conscious of her
presence, having retired into a private world of their
own.

                    MARLOWE:
But then you couldn't go, could you.
The border police would have checked
you through alone, and too many people
might have seen you -- without Shawn
Regan. Much safer to come down here

                         MARLOWE: (Cont.)
          with Mona. Much safer -- especially
          for Eddie Mars.

                         VIVIAN:
          I did it as much for you. . . . Why wouldn't
          you believe me? Why wouldn't you stop?

                         MARLOWE:
          Too many people tried to make me. And
          besides I knew Shawn Regan -- and I
          know you.

They look at each other -- and Mona Mars takes herself
quietly out of the room.

                         VIVIAN:
          Why did I have to meet you? Why
          out of all the men in the city, did
          my father have to call you in?

                         MARLOWE:
          Things happen that way, sometimes. . . .
          Light me a cigarette. . . .

She takes one from a table, lights it, and bends over
to place it between Marlowe's lips. Marlowe's eyes
hold her as though his hands were on her shoulders;
she sits down.

                         MARLOWE:
                    (softly)
          You know what they're going to do,
          don't you? You know the only thing
          they can do.

Vivian's hands grip the shoulders of his coat. She
shuts her eyes and drops her head, holding herself
rigid.

                         MARLOWE:
                    (still softly)
          It's not pretty, is it -- even from a
          distance. And when you're right on top
          of it, it isn't pretty at all.

                         VIVIAN:
                    (rising abruptly)
          Oh, stop it, Phil. Stop it!

> VIVIAN: (Cont.)
> Nothing's going to happen. . . .

> MARLOWE:
> Mona's in love with Eddie Mars, but
> you're not. Are you going through
> with it?

Vivian moves away, as far from him as she can get, and
stands with her back to him, rigid, staring at the curtained window as though she could see through it. Marlowe studies her, then laughs, a quiet sardonic chuckle
and relaxes, leaning back on the cushion.

> MARLOWE:
> Pride is a great thing, isn't it?
> And courage -- and honor -- and
> love. All the things you read about
> in the copybooks -- only in the copy-
> books nothing ever gets tangled. The
> road always lies so straight, and clear,
> and the signs say to love and honor and
> be brave. . . . Take this thing out of my
> mouth, will you, honey? It's burning me.

Vivian comes slowly to him and takes the cigarette stub
from his lips. She hesitates, then goes down onto the
couch, dropping the cigarette on the floor. Her arms
go around Marlowe, her mouth crushed to his. When she
breaks for air, putting her cheek against his, she is
almost crying. Marlowe is far from unmoved himself,
turning his head against hers, hard.

> MARLOWE:
> (after a pause,
> whispering)
> Get a knife, and cut this rope off me. . . .

Vivian rises, runs out of the room. The SOUND of a
kitchen drawer being opened comes OVER from o.s., then
the RATTLE of CUTLERY. Vivian returns almost at once
with a knife and slashes the rope from Marlowe's feet.
Dropping the knife, she helps him get up -- he's not too
steady on his legs. They cross the room together,
Vivian with her arm around Marlowe. The handcuffs
glittering on Marlowe's wrists. From outside comes
the SOUND of a car skidding to a stop. Mona Mars appears

294 The Big Sleep

in the doorway, holding a gun.

                    MONA:
          (quietly, without menace)
     Eddie is here -- I think you'd
     better wait.

162.   EXTREME CLOSE   CANINO'S HAND

opening, playing idly with the roll of coins. The
CAMERA PULLS BACK -- we are still in the living room.
Marlowe is sitting on the couch, Vivian beside him --
his hands are still cuffed behind him, but his feet
are free. Canino leans unobtrusively against the
wall -- near Marlowe. Eddie Mars holds center stage,
moving like a lion keyed up for the kill. Mona Mars,
the gun forgotten in her hand, sits in the b.g., watching.
Her face is still, intent.

                    VIVIAN:
          (quietly)
     Eddie -- this is where I get off.

                    MARS:
     You bought a ticket for the whole
     run, Countess -- destination unknown.
     Keep your mouth out of this.
          (to Marlowe)
     You're making it tough for me,
     soldier.

                    MARLOWE:
     Not me, Eddie. Murder. Murder can
     make things tough for anybody. You
     keep tripping over it, all the time.

                    MARS:
          (contemptuously)
     Murder! I haven't killed anybody.

                    MARLOWE:
     Not personally, maybe -- but your
     hand is behind Canino's, aiming the
     gun -- or pouring the cyanide into
     Harry Jones' glass.
          (as Mars gives him a
            startled look)
     Yeah -- I was there, in the next

                    MARLOWE: (Cont.)
room. Canino had a gun and I
didn't, so all I could do was
watch . . . I kind of liked Harry
Jones.

                    MARS:
You kind of like too many people,
soldier.

                    MONA:
Eddie -- what does he mean? What's
happened? Who was Harry Jones?

                    MARS:
He's just talking. Maybe you better
get out, Mona. We may have to push
him around a little before we get
through.

                    MARLOWE:
          (to Mona)
Yeah -- push me a little, right
over the edge. Eddie won't spoil
his manicure to do it -- but
Canino won't mind. He's used to
having his hands dirty.

Canino leans over and slaps Marlowe hard across the
face. Vivian springs up, toward Canino -- Eddie Mars
grabs her, looking toward Mona. Mona has never seen
that look on Eddie's face before.

                    MARS:
          (quietly)
Get out, Mona.

                    MONA:
Eddie. . . .

                    MARS:
Get out.

Mona studies him -- it seems that she is looking at a
stranger, a stranger who frightens her, someone evil
and beyond the pale. She seems to grow in stature and
dignity, even as her heart realizes how far down the
wrong road it has travelled. She turns, then, slowly,

and goes out. After she has gone, Vivian wrenches
free from Mars' grip. There is something rather wonderful
about her now -- a blazing, catlike courage. She
faces Eddie Mars.

> VIVIAN:
> You don't dare go through with this,
> Eddie.

> MARS:
> You think I can't get away with it?

> VIVIAN:
> You think I'm going to let you
> get away with it?

Mars studies her, then Marlowe -- realizes what the
score is, and smiles sardonically.

> MARS:
> You women kill me. You'll spend
> years and wreck lives to get
> something you want, and then
> throw it all away in a minute
> because some guy has a new way
> of putting his mouth on yours.
> (sitting down,
>   easily, smiling)
> All right, Countess. While we're
> doing all this thinking . . . do you
> think you're going to have a chance
> <u>not</u> to let me get away with it?

Silence as this sinks in. Vivian sits down quietly
beside Marlowe, who looks at both her and Mars with
a cold, cynical smile.

> MARLOWE:
> (laughing softly)
> It's amazing how fast a beautiful
> friendship breaks when a dead body
> falls on top of it. . . . Which one
> of you killed Regan? If he was
> shot in the back, I'll bet on you,
> Eddie, because that's the only way
> <u>you</u> could have got to him. But if
> he took it from the front --
> (looking at Vivian)

MARLOWE: (Cont.)
I can see how you both would have
been jealous of Mona.

Vivian stares at him, a hard, shocked look as though
Marlowe is something not human. Marlowe gives it back
to her -- then almost at once Canino steps forward and
places his hand on Marlowe's head, bending it back,
his fingers and thumb biting cruelly into Marlowe's
temples. Canino smiles, as though he is very fond of
Marlowe.

CANINO:
(gently amused)
Ever see a dick with such a one-track
mind? He's sitting right on the edge
of a hole in the ground, but he still
cares who killed Regan. Want to tell
him, Eddie? Want to send him to bed
happy?

Mars makes an annoyed gesture and starts to get up,
then freezes as Mona speaks from the doorway.

MONA:
(very quietly)
Eddie. . . .

Everyone turns to look at her -- there is a quality of
fate in her voice. She leans almost negligently
against the door jamb, wearing a heavy coat, holding
a big felt hat in her hands.

MONA:
I've been a good wife to you, Eddie --
as good a wife as you'd let me be.
I believed in you, and there wasn't
anything I wouldn't have done for you --
anything but this.

MARS:
Don't be a fool, Mona. Can't you see. . . .

MONA:
(slowly)
I can only see one thing. I've been
married to a killer, and I've helped
him kill.

She turns and goes out. Mars rises, looking after her.

                    MARS:
                (to Canino)
            Hold the fort, Canino. I'll be back.

He goes out after Mona, not even waiting for Canino's
nod of assent. Canino goes to a window and peers
through the crack of the blind, still keeping Marlowe
covered. We HEAR a car start outside and drive off.

                    CANINO:
                (sardonically)
            He made it. And he can talk about
            love!

He turns back into the room. Vivian has risen, she
stands by a table lighting a cigarette with a wooden
match from a box which she retains in her left hand.

163.   INSERT   THE MATCH BOX   IN VIVIAN'S HANDS

An ordinary small box of matches. The cover has been
pushed almost shut, leaving the hand of one match
protruding. Vivian holds the flaming match with which
she has just lighted her cigarette to the uncovered
match hand, igniting it.

164.   INT. MARS HIDEOUT   THE LIVING ROOM

As Vivian blows out the first match and drops it
casually into an ash tray, shielding the box in her
hand from Canino's view. Canino strolls back, looking
Marlowe over with sadistic humor.

                    CANINO:
            I don't really mind the boss leaving.
            I can have a lot more fun alone.

165.   INSERT   THE MATCH BOX   IN VIVIAN'S HAND

The match has burned back, charring the paper cover.
Smoke rises from the box.

166.   INT. MARS HIDEOUT   THE LIVING ROOM

                    VIVIAN:
            Canino --

CANINO:
(looking around, grinning)
Save your breath, baby --

The match box burst into flame. Vivian hurls it into
Canino's face, then turns aside, clutching her scorched
fingers.

VIVIAN:
(over above action)
Phil!

Marlowe throws himself forward into Canino's legs -- they
roll, struggling.

167.   CLOSE SHOT MARLOWE AND CANINO

as Canino comes out on top of Marlowe, at an angle, and
whips his pistol down at Marlowe's head. Marlowe
wrenches aside -- the gun barrel misses by a fraction,
smacking hard on the carpet. Marlowe doubles his knees
into his chest and lets go with his feet, getting both
heels under Canino's jaw. Canino goes backward and
down, dropping his gun, but he's not clear out -- the
blow was glancing. He grabs Vivian as she tries to get
by him, pulling her down. Marlowe manages to get the
gun in his shackled hands. Canino pulls another, fires
at him, misses, tangled up with Vivian. Marlowe makes
it out the door.

168.   EXT. MARS HIDEOUT AT THE FRONT DOOR   (RAIN) NIGHT

As Marlowe comes out and runs down the steps toward
Canino's car. Over by the garage Art Huck stands,
scared but undecided. Marlowe snaps a shot at him.
Huck makes up his mind in a hurry. He vanishes -- a
second later we HEAR a car start and race off down
the highway, o.s. Marlowe, working fast but awkwardly
because of the handcuffs, opens the door of Canino's
car, backs in.

169.   INT. CANINO'S CAR MARLOWE   (RAIN) NIGHT

fumbling for the ignition key and starter button, behind
him. He starts the motor, then slides out again,
quickly, hugging the ground by the rear wheels, offside.

170.   EXT. MARS HIDEOUT MARLOWE'S ANGLE   (RAIN) NIGHT

As a darkened window goes up. THREE SHOTS are fired
from it. We HEAR the whine of the bullets, their impact
on the coupe. Marlowe cries out as though hit. Then
again there is silence, except for the beating rain and
the purring motor. Presently the house door opens --
there is no light behind it. Vivian appears,
walking stiffly, and behind her is Canino, shielded
from possible fire. They walk slowly toward Marlowe
and the car.

>   CANINO:
>   Can you see anything?

>   VIVIAN:
>   (tonelessly)
>   Nothing. The windows are all
>   misted.

They come steadily closer to the dark car. Suddenly
Vivian stops, rigid, and lets go a thin, tearing scream.

>   VIVIAN:
>   Behind the wheel!
>   (as though pleading
>   with Marlowe not to fire)
>   Phil!

Canino shoves her roughly aside, dropping to one knee,
and pours three SHOTS through the car window. His gun
is now empty. No shots answer him -- he is satisfied
that Marlowe is dead. He rises, moving to open the car
door, as Marlowe emerges from behind the car.

>   MARLOWE:
>   Finished?

Canino whirls around, and Marlowe, the gun pressed
awkwardly against his side, puts four bullets in him.
He collapses into the mud and stays there.

>   MARLOWE:
>   (to Vivian)
>   Get the keys, honey.

Vivian, white-faced and silent, gets the keys from
Canino's pocket and unlocks the handcuffs. Marlowe
rubs his wrists -- they look at each other, both tired
and drained of emotion -- there seems to be nothing to
say.

                    MARLOWE:
               (quietly)
          You played that hand all right,
          Countess.

                    VIVIAN:
               (dully)
          I don't know why I cared. . . .

She turns and walks away from him toward the garage
and her car, not looking back. Presently Marlowe
goes back into the house.

                                        FADE OUT.

FADE IN

171.   INT. STERNWOOD HALL   NORRIS AND MARLOWE   MORNING

As Norris stands in the open door, in the act of
admitting Marlowe.

                    MARLOWE:
          The General sent for me. . . .

                    NORRIS:
          Yes, sir. He's waiting, in the
          orchid house.

Marlowe enters, walking along the hall toward the rear
with Norris. Subtly, Norris has the air of a guard.
Marlowe looks tired and sombre, the marks of last
night's encounter still plain on his face. He has
obviously not been home; he wears the same rumpled suit,
no tie, and he has not shaved. Vivian comes out of an
adjoining room, as though she has been waiting, and
stops them.

                    VIVIAN:
          I'd like to see you, Mr. Marlowe.

She gives Norris the nod -- he goes away, and Marlowe
follows Vivian into the room, closing the door.

172.   INT. SMALL SITTING ROOM   MARLOWE AND VIVIAN

lavishly furnished. Vivian also looks exhausted, stony,
but giving an impression of submerged but volcanic
emotion. She does not look at Marlowe.

                    VIVIAN:
Well?

                    MARLOWE:
I kept you out of it. I told a
straight story, and Canino left his
thumbprint on Harry Jones' door to
back me up. I don't know whether
they believed me, but there's nothing
they can do about it. I'm clear --
self defense. And all Eddie Mars has
to say is that Canino was roughing me
on his own time.

                    VIVIAN:
        (looking at him now,
         forced to admire him)
It wasn't as easy as you make it sound.

                    MARLOWE:
        (shrugging)
My neck is usually stuck out, one
way or another. It's a little tougher
than the General's, that's all.

                    VIVIAN:
        (after an uncomfortable
         pause)
It's too bad Father can't know what
you've done for him. I'm afraid
he's . . . angry with you.

                    MARLOWE:
Why not? Everybody else is.

                    VIVIAN:
You -- won't say anything to him?

                    MARLOWE:
Of course not.

                    VIVIAN:
Phil. . . .

                    MARLOWE:
        (brutally)
Listen . . . I'm tired. I killed a man
last night. I stink of cops, and I've

                    MARLOWE: (Cont.)
        still got a rotten taste in my mouth.
        I want a hot bath with strong soap,
        and I can't have it until I've seen
        your father. Do you mind if I go now?

                    VIVIAN:
                (going close to him)
        Phil -- I didn't kill Shawn Regan.

                    MARLOWE:
                (cold, deadpan)
        Is he dead?

Vivian stares at him, getting a slow, deadly look in
her eyes.

                    VIVIAN:
                (very calmly)
        It's quite possible. He's been
        gone a long time, and he's not a
        peaceful man.
                (turning away)
        I'll send you my personal check in
        the morning, Mr. Marlowe.

                    MARLOWE:
        Your personal check?

                    VIVIAN:
        I'm sure my father would wish you
        to be repaid for your . . . extra
        services, last night.

                    MARLOWE:
                (quietly, after pause)
        I'm sure your father would know
        better . . . and I know you do. --
        What about Eddie Mars?

                    VIVIAN:
        What about him?

                    MARLOWE:
        You think he's going to forget
        all this?

                    VIVIAN:
        I'm tired, too. Get out, Marlowe.

Marlowe shrugs, goes toward the door. He speaks over his shoulder with an air of casual politeness.

> MARLOWE:
> How's Carmen?

Vivian, her back to him, takes the question just a little too easily.

> VIVIAN:
> She's fine. She went up to
> Santa Barbara last night.

> MARLOWE:
> That ought to be nice for her.

> VIVIAN:
> Yes.

There seems to be nothing more to say. Marlowe exits.

> DISSOLVE TO:

173. EXT. STERNWOOD REAR GARDEN   MARLOWE AND NORRIS   DAY

as they walk down the path toward the orchid house. Marlowe glances around, apparently looking for something he doesn't see. Norris opens the door, permitting Marlowe to pass him into the greenhouse.

174. INT. ORCHID HOUSE   MARLOWE

As he follows the path between the banks of orchid to the place where General Sternwood sits, as before -- in the wheelchair, wrapped in robe and blanket -- only his eyes are alive, proud and piercing.

> STERNWOOD:
> Sit down, Mr. Marlowe.

Marlowe pulls up a chair, already beginning to suffer with the heat. He starts to remove his coat, then something in Sternwood's attitude makes him change his mind.

> STERNWOOD:
> I didn't ask you to look for
> Shawn Regan.

MARLOWE:
You wanted me to, though.

STERNWOOD:
You assume a great deal. I usually
ask for what I want.
     (as Marlowe does
        not answer)
The money I paid you is of no
consequence. I merely feel that you
have, no doubt unintentionally,
betrayed a trust.

MARLOWE:
Is that all you wanted to see me about?

STERNWOOD:
You're angry at that remark.

MARLOWE:
You have an advantage over me, General.
It's an advantage I wouldn't want to
take away from you. You can say anything you like to me, and I wouldn't
think of getting angry. I'd like to
offer you your money back. It may mean
nothing to you. It might mean something
to me.

STERNWOOD:
What does it mean to you?

MARLOWE:
It means I've refused payment for an
unsatisfactory job. That's all.

STERNWOOD:
     (after a pause)
Why did you go to Captain Gregory?

MARLOWE:
I suppose I played a hunch. I
was convinced you put those Geiger
notes up to me chiefly as a test, and
that you were a little afraid Regan
might somehow be involved in an
attempt to blackmail you. Besides,
as I said -- I knew Regan. It meant

                    MARLOWE: (Cont.)
something to me to find out, too.

                    STERNWOOD:
And you allowed Captain Gregory to
think I had employed you to find Shawn?

                    MARLOWE:
Yeah, I guess I did -- when I was sure
he had the case.

                    STERNWOOD:
And do you consider that ethical?

                    MARLOWE:
Yes, I do.

                    STERNWOOD:
Perhaps I don't understand.

                    MARLOWE:
Maybe you don't. When you hire a
boy in my line of work it isn't
like hiring a window-washer and showing
him eight windows and saying:
"Wash those windows and you're through".
You don't know what I have to go
through or over or under to do your
job for you. I do it my way. I do my
best to protect you, and I may have
to break a few rules, but I break them
in your favor -- After all, you didn't
tell me <u>not</u> to go to Captain Gregory.

                    STERNWOOD:
          (with a faint smile)
That would have been rather difficult.

                    MARLOWE:
Well, what have I done wrong? Your man
Norris, seemed to think the case was over
when Geiger was eliminated. I don't see
it that way. I'm not Sherlock Holmes. I
don't expect to go over ground the police
have covered and pick up a broken penpoint
and build a case from it. If you think
there's anybody in the detective business
making a living doing that sort of thing,

MARLOWE: (Cont.)

you don't know much about cops. If they
overlook anything, it's something much
looser and vaguer, like a man of Geiger's
type sending you his evidence of debt
and asking you to pay like a gentleman.
That isn't normal. Why did he do that?
Because he wanted to find out if there
was anything putting pressure on you. If
there was, you'd pay him. If not, you'd
ignore him and wait. But something <u>was</u>
putting pressure on you. Regan. You
were afraid he'd stayed around and been
nice to you just long enough to find out
how to play games with your bank account.
> (interrupting Sternwood,
> as he starts to speak)

Even at that, it wasn't your money you
cared about. It wasn't even your daughters.
You've more or less written them off.
It's that you're still too proud to be
played for a sucker -- and you really liked
Shawn Regan.

STERNWOOD:
> (quietly, after a pause)

You think entirely too much, Marlowe --
Are you still trying to solve that
puzzle?

MARLOWE:

No. I've been warned to quit. The
boys at the City Hall think I play too
rough. That's why I thought I should
give you your money back -- because it
isn't a completed job by my standards.

STERNWOOD:
> (smiling)

Quit, nothing. I'll pay you another
thousand to find Shawn Regan. He doesn't
have to come back. I don't even have
to know where he is. A man has a right
to live his own life. And he must have
had his reasons for running off like that.
I only want to know that he's all right.
I want to know it from him directly, and
if he should happen to need money, I

> STERNWOOD: (Cont.)
> should want him to have that also. Am
> I clear?

> MARLOWE:
> Yes, General.

Sternwood leans back in the chair, his eyes closed
wearily.

> STERNWOOD:
> (trying to smile)
> I guess I'm a sentimental old goat,
> and no soldier at all. Find him for
> me, Marlowe. Just find him.

> MARLOWE:
> (rising)
> I'll try. You'd better rest now.
> I've talked your arm off.

He starts away. Sternwood's voice stops him.

> STERNWOOD:
> (quietly)
> You have a lot that Shawn had.
> Strength -- and a steady eye.

Marlowe stands a moment, remembering Vivian's words.
Then he turns quietly and goes away.

175. EXT. GREENHOUSE DOOR   MARLOWE

as he emerges, mopping again, finds Norris waiting for
him, already holding Marlowe's hat for him. Marlowe,
surprised at this, is still further surprised when he
looks up and sees his car, which he left in front of
the house, now in the drive not far away and already
turned so that it is headed back toward town.

> NORRIS:
> I took the liberty of turning it
> around for you, sir. Since you were
> in the greenhouse, I brought it on
> around here at the same time.

> MARLOWE:
> (ironically)
> So that now I won't lose hardly any

                    MARLOWE: (Cont.)
time getting back to work, huh?

                    NORRIS:
          (impenetrable)
You will always be welcome here, sir,
if only to receive our gratitude.

                    MARLOWE:
          (stuffs handkerchief
           into pocket, takes his
           hat, turns)
Thanks.

He walks toward the car. But still Norris walks beside
him. Marlowe already realizing that he is being practically
frog-walked off the place. They reach the car. Norris
steps ahead, opens the door, holds it open for Marlowe
to get in.

                    MARLOWE:
You don't even need a gun, do you?

                    NORRIS:
I've never had occasion for one, sir.
I don't think I ever will.

                    MARLOWE:
Neither do I.
          (nods toward
           greenhouse)
What do you think of him this
morning?

                    NORRIS:
He's stronger than he looks. As
you would see for yourself if
occasion arose -- which, thanks to
you, it will not now.

                    MARLOWE:
Yeah -- What did Regan have that got
to the General so?

                    NORRIS:
Youth, sir. And the soldier's eye.

                    MARLOWE:
Like yours.

                         NORRIS:
          Thank you, sir. And yours.

                         MARLOWE:
          Thanks.
               (he starts to get
                into the car, Norris
                still holding the door)
          So Miss Carmen went to Santa Barbara.

                         NORRIS:
          Yes. This morning.

                         MARLOWE:
               (getting into car, stops)
          Mrs. Rutledge told me she went
          last night.

                         NORRIS:
               (smoothly)
          It was near midnight, sir. I
          thought it was later. I was
          probably wrong.

                         MARLOWE:
          I see.

     He gets in. Norris shuts the door. Marlowe starts
     the engine, puts car in gear.

                         MARLOWE:
          If the General has any more trouble,
          you know how to call.

                         NORRIS:
          And whom to call. Thank you
          again.

     Marlowe drives on. In the mirror he can see Norris
     standing in the drive still watching him, guarding the
     house which Marlowe realizes he is not to enter again.

                                        DISSOLVE TO:

176.   INT. MARLOWE'S APARTMENT   LIVING ROOM

     Marlowe has just entered. He kicks the door shut,
     crosses the living room, shedding his hat and suit

coat on the floor as he passes.

177.   INT. MARLOWE APARTMENT   BEDROOM

as Marlowe continues on his way to the bath, still peeling.
He vanishes into the bath -- we HEAR the shower turned
on. In the bedroom the PHONE RINGS. Marlowe returns,
picks up the phone.

                    MARLOWE:
            Yeah?

The voice of Eddie Mars comes clearly from the
instrument.

                    MARS' VOICE:
            Hello, soldier.

                    MARLOWE:
            Hello, Eddie. I been waiting to
            hear from you.

                    MARS' VOICE:
            Got a little news for you, soldier.
            I'm skipping the manicures, till I
            finish up this job.

                    MARLOWE:
            Yeah, I kind of thought you would.
            I got a T.L. for you, too, Eddie.
            Sternwood offered me a thousand
            bucks to find Shawn Regan. I took it.

                    MARS' VOICE:
                (softly, after a
                 pause)
            Maybe I can help you earn that grand.
            You remember that stuff that Joe Brody
            moved out of Geiger's back room?

                    MARLOWE:
            Yeah.

                    MARS' VOICE:
            Well, I tracked it down where Joe
            stashed it, and moved it back up to
            Geiger's place after the cops got
            through. You might take a look at it.

> MARLOWE:
> Yeah -- I might.

> MARS' VOICE:
> (laughing softly)
> After last night I'm beginning to think
> you're as tough as you look. I told
> you we could do business together.
> So long, soldier.

> MARLOWE:
> Be seeing you.

The receiver clicks. Marlowe sets his instrument down
slowly, looks at it a moment, then returns to the
shower, dropping his shirt in the doorway.

> DISSOLVE TO:

178.   INT. MARLOWE APARTMENT   BEDROOM

as Marlowe comes out of the bath, buttoning his pajama
coat. He is freshly shaved, his hair still damp and
rumpled from the shower. He pulls down the shades,
putting out the daylight, and collapses into the bed.
Just as he is comfortably settled, already half asleep,
the doorbell RINGS. It rings insistently, with a quality
of nervous urgency. Marlowe finally gets up to answer
it, pulling on a dressing gown.

179.   INT. MARLOWE APARTMENT   LIVING ROOM

as Marlowe admits Vivian. She is obviously in a fine
state of nerves. She enters quickly -- he shuts the door.

> VIVIAN:
> Phil. . . .

> MARLOWE:
> All right, now what?

> VIVIAN:
> Eddie Mars just called me. He's
> out to get you.

> MARLOWE:
> We knew that a long time ago.

              VIVIAN:
But now you must believe it. You
must get out of town -- now.

             MARLOWE:
You better sit down, baby, and
catch your breath.

He sits down on the davenport.

              VIVIAN:
Phil, how do you feel about me?

             MARLOWE:
Just like I feel about a stick of
dynamite. Smooth on the outside -- but
it makes a mess when it goes off.

              VIVIAN:
I got a diffirent idea last night.
Or maybe you're not a man except
when two or three people are trying
to murder you.

They kiss -- one of those kisses. Vivian frees herself.

              VIVIAN:
Now go. At once. I'll give you money -- a
a thousand -- five thousand if you'll
get out of town now -- today. . . .

             MARLOWE:
That would be stage money. I like
to earn my money. I can't earn that
much at one time, but what I do earn
doesn't smell bad to me.

              VIVIAN:
Would you get out of town if you
knew Shawn Regan was dead?

             MARLOWE:
Is Shawn Regan dead?

              VIVIAN:
Would you?

             MARLOWE:
How did he die?

                    VIVIAN:
Kiss me.

                    MARLOWE:
Later -- maybe. How did Shawn die?

                    VIVIAN:
I killed him. By accident. He was
teaching me to shoot and the gun went off.

                    MARLOWE:
And that's what Eddie Mars has got
on you. And so he sent you here,
to buy me off with you.

Vivian stares at him, slaps him viciously across the
face. Marlowe takes it.

                    MARLOWE:
Will you have the kiss now, too?

She slaps him again. He takes it.

                    MARLOWE:
You're good, you're very good, but
you can't do it, baby. It won't wash.

                    VIVIAN:
You fool, I killed him, I tell you.
Just as you're going to be dead if
you don't get out of town. Don't
you see Eddie Mars can't let you
stay alive now?

                    MARLOWE:
Eddie never developed that trouble
this morning. Now I'll ask you one.
What's your game with me?

                    VIVIAN:
There's no game -- with you.

                    MARLOWE:
You've been playing spin the bottle
with me ever since I met you. It's
'please, Phil' one minute, and 'get
out, Marlowe' the next. You haven't

                    MARLOWE: (Cont.)
      told me a straight truth since the
      first day. . . .

                    VIVIAN:
      That's a lie. I'm trying to play
      straight now. You fool, don't you
      realize you're going to die if you
      stay here?

                    MARLOWE:
      No. All you've told me is that you
      want me out of town at any price --
      and that you still believe I can
      be bought if you can just find the
      right currency. Sure I'm a fool.
      I try to do my job and keep my nose
      clean. I risk my whole future, the
      hatred of the cops and Eddie Mars'
      gang. I dodge bullets and eat saps.
      But I'm not supposed to feel anything
      about it either way, because anybody
      can buy my immortal soul with a few
      bucks -- or maybe just a kiss. Sure,
      I'm a fool.

She stares at him, her eyes blazing. Suddenly she
raises her hand, but before she can slap him, he speaks
and she pauses.

                    MARLOWE:
      That's right. Have another. I
      throw them in free to old clients.

She stops, stares at him, suddenly takes his face
between her hands, stares at him.

                    VIVIAN:
      You're going to find Shawn Regan?

                    MARLOWE:
      Yeah.

                    VIVIAN:
      No matter who gets hurt?

                    MARLOWE:
      No matter who gets hurt.

                         VIVIAN:
                    (letting her hands
                     drop to his shoulders)
                 All right, Phil. It's funny -- I
                 think I really like you now, for
                 the first time.

She turns to the door, her head high, her voice very
cool and steady. Only her eyes, hidden from Marlowe,
tell how she feels.

                         VIVIAN:
                 Goodbye, Phil.

She goes out.

                                        DISSOLVE TO:

180.   EXT. HOBART ARMS AT FRONT ENTRANCE   NIGHT

       as Marlowe comes out, wearing a hat and trench-coat
       against the rain which has begun to fall. He gets into
       his car and drives off. As he does so, a second car,
       a dark convertible seen indistinctly in the shadowy
       street, swings around the corner behind him, slows,
       falters, then picks up speed, following Marlowe.

181.   EXT. LAVERNE TERRACE   RAIN   NIGHT

       as Marlowe drives slowly, cautiously toward Geiger's
       house. The street is dark, deserted. Marlowe drives
       without lights. He stops in the tree-shadows by the
       angle of Geiger's hedge and slides quietly out of the
       car, keeping close to the hedge. His gun gleams faintly
       in his hand.

182.   EXT. LAVERNE TERRACE   RAIN   NIGHT

       A section of the road over which Marlowe has just come.
       The dark convertible creeps along in the shadows, also
       without lights. It is still impossible to see who is
       driving.

183.   EXT. GEIGER'S PLACE   RAIN

       as Marlowe makes his way like a stalking cat through
       the garden, toward the front door. Nothing stirs. There
       is no sound but the rain. Marlowe crosses the exposed

bridge at a crouching run. Nothing happens. He pauses
in the shadows by the front door, then tries the knob.
Silently the door swings open. He waits, then darts
swiftly inside.

184. EXT. LAVERNE TERRACE

The dark convertible, still shrouded in the heavy shadows
of the trees, parks quietly behind Marlowe's car across
the road.

185. INT. GEIGER'S HOUSE   LIVING ROOM

Marlowe stands beside the door, which he has closed,
listening. He is only a shadow among shadows. The
house is utterly still. Marlowe, still cautious,
crosses into the rear part of the house, then returns.

                    MARLOWE:
                 (laughing softly)
             Okay, Eddie. I get it -- on the
             way out.

He draws the heavy curtains quickly across the windows,
turns on the lights and sheds his hat and coat. The
packing box from Geiger's back room stands on the hearth-
rug. Marlowe bends over to look inside.

186. INSERT: THE PACKING BOX

filled with manila filing envelopes, ledgers, etc. On
the top of the stack is a folder labelled "Sternwood".
It has obviously been placed there on purpose.

187. INT. GEIGER'S HOUSE LIVING ROOM

Marlowe picks up the folder -- a KNOCK SOUNDS on the
front door. Marlowe reacts, dropping the folder, and
raises his gun. He moves quickly to turn out the lights,
then stands beside the door, flat against the wall.

                    MARLOWE:
             Yeah?

                    CARMEN'S VOICE:
             Phil -- let me in.

MARLOWE:
(after a pause, unlocking
the door)
Come in fast and shut the door
behind you.

He retains his wary position while Carmen obeys. When
he is sure she's alone, he sighs, relocks the door and
turns on the lights. His face is beaded with sweat,
his hand shaking slightly. Carmen is lightly clad,
without hat or coat. Apparently she has left home in
a hurry.

CARMEN:
Did I scare you?

MARLOWE:
(drily)
No -- I was expecting visitors. . . .
I thought you were in Santa
Barbara.

CARMEN:
They had me locked in my room.
They even had my clothes locked
up. But I climbed down the drain
pipe. I had to see you again.

MARLOWE:
Why did you come here?

CARMEN:
You were just driving away when I
got to your place. I followed.

She is obviously wrought up, in a highly emotional state.

MARLOWE:
It must have been important.

CARMEN:
It was. Phil, I -- I'm sorry about
the other night.

MARLOWE:
Forget it.

CARMEN:
I can't. Phil, you . . . I don't know

CARMEN: (Cont.)
quite how to say this . . . have you
ever seen something, perhaps in a
dream? Something perfect and beautiful,
a long way off, and you try to reach
it but there are too many things in
your way?

MARLOWE:
Yeah. I know what you mean.

CARMEN:
Maybe if everything had been different --
if I hadn't been born a Sternwood, if
my mother had lived -- if I'd known a
man like you before. . . . Oh, Phil, is
there ever any way back?

MARLOWE:
That depends.

CARMEN:
(softly, intensely
serious)
You could help me find the way.

He looks at her, saying nothing. She comes closer to
him, childlike, pleading.

CARMEN:
Phil, you've got to help me. I'm
getting lost. I don't know where
I'm going any more, and I'm scared.

MARLOWE:
Why me, Carmen?

CARMEN:
Because. . . . Just because you came
into the house, and I saw you. Just
a little thing like that. Don't you
understand, Phil? You've got something I need, something I've got to
have. Strength, maybe. I don't
know. But I've got to have it, or --
I don't know what's going to happen
to me.

She puts her hands on his chest, looking up into his
face. For once she's completely honest.

>   MARLOWE:
>   (quietly)
>   Was that what you wanted from
>   Shawn Regan?

She draws away from him, very slowly, her eyes changing,
hardening, becoming wary.

>   CARMEN:
>   Perhaps . . . Phil . . .

>   MARLOWE:
>   (gently)
>   I'm sorry, Carmen. That's how it
>   goes. People have to find their
>   own way -- wherever they're going.
>   You can, if you really want to.

He turns away, to let Carmen have that moment to herself.

>   MARLOWE:
>   (after a pause)
>   Before you go . . . I have something
>   that belongs to you.

>   CARMEN:
>   (dully)
>   What?

>   MARLOWE:
>   Your gun. I've been carrying it
>   around, thinking I'd see you.

He hands her the little gun, out of his coat pocket.

>   MARLOWE:
>   Careful of it, now. It's cleaned
>   and loaded in all five.

>   CARMEN:
>   (taking the gun)
>   Thanks.

Marlowe moves past her, as though to open the door.

                    CARMEN:
          Turn around.

He does so -- she has the gun levelled, and there's no
doubt what she's going to do with it.

                    MARLOWE:
          Carmen!

                    CARMEN:
          It's Vivian, isn't it?

                    MARLOWE:
          That has nothing to do . . .

                    CARMEN:
          It was Vivian with Shawn, too. It's
          always Vivian.

She fires point blank as Marlowe takes a step toward her,
continues to fire, four shots in all. Then she waits
until he has almost reached her and thrusts the pistol
almost into his face. He catches her wrist just before
she fires, pushes her hand aside as the shot goes off.
She snatches her hand free, steps back, hurls the
pistol at his chest. It falls to the ground. He stoops
and picks it up.

                    MARLOWE:
          So that's the way it was with
          Shawn.

                    CARMEN:
               (dazedly)
          But he died . . . why didn't you?

                    MARLOWE:
          I blanked the shells.

                    CARMEN:
               (still stunned,
                breathless)
          You knew I -- You knew --

                    MARLOWE:
          I sort of figured it that way. And
          I'd like it better if Shawn had taken
          it in the back after all, from Eddie

                    MARLOWE: (Cont.)
Mars. -- He was teaching you to shoot,
wasn't he? That's what he thought he
was doing. Only you didn't fire at
the target.

                    CARMEN:
           (with half-dreamy
            vindictiveness)
No -- they put him in the sump --
down where the old wells are.

                    MARLOWE:
Couldn't you have found a cleaner place?

                    CARMEN:
He didn't mind.

                    MARLOWE:
No. I suppose oil and water are
the same as wind and air when you're
dead . . . So Vivian paid Eddie Mars,
and covered up for you.

                    CARMEN:
Yes. You'd like to do something
about it, wouldn't you? But you
can't. I'm always safe.

                    MARLOWE:
How do you figure that?

                    CARMEN:
Because Vivian won't let you. And
you won't do it, anyhow. You like
my father, just as Shawn did. You
know what would happen if you took
me into court. Pictures, and long
columns in the newspapers, and the
Sternwood name all over the head-
lines. You know what that would
do to father.

A pause. She is looking at him like a wicked changeling.

                    CARMEN:
           (continuing)
And Vivian's in on this, too. Way

                       CARMEN: (Cont.)
      in. You wouldn't want to see her
      go to prison.

                       MARLOWE:
      No. I wouldn't want that. And
      the old man. I wouldn't want to
      kill him -- for you.

His attitude is one of defeat. Carmen is pleased,
triumphant. Marlowe turns away dejectedly, picks up
his hat and coat.

                       MARLOWE:
        (not looking at her)
      Better take these, Carmen, it's
      raining.

                       CARMEN:
    Thanks.

She puts them on quickly, then stands looking at Marlowe.

                       CARMEN:
      I think I'm glad I didn't kill
      you. This is going to eat you.
      You're going to lie awake nights,
      thinking about it. And every so
      often you'll see me somewhere, and
      I'll laugh at you. . . . Goodbye, Phil.

She turns quickly toward door. Marlowe steps quickly
to the light switch. As she opens the door and steps
through it, he snaps off the light. There is a brief
pause -- then gun fire.

188.   EXT. GEIGER'S HOUSE AT FRONT DOOR

    as Carmen crumples silently onto the doorstep. There is
silence. The door swings open. Presently from the
dark shrubbery Eddie Mars comes, walking slowly toward
the silent shape. His gun is in his hand. He crosses
the footbridge and moves the dead head with his foot.

Marlowe snaps the switch inside the door; light floods
suddenly out over Mars. Marlowe stands in the door,
facing Mars across Carmen's body as Mars reacts.

                          MARLOWE:
             You were a little too quick on the
             trigger that time, too, Eddie.

His voice seems to break the spell. Mars goes for his
gun, starts to raise it, but Marlowe fires first. Mars
drops beside Carmen. As Mars falls, the SOUND of a man
running away through the garden comes OVER. Marlowe
whirls, snaps a shot toward the running man, takes a few
quick steps, but stops as the SOUND of a car starting
and roaring frantically away comes OVER. Marlowe turns
toward the door.

189.   INT. HOUSE   CLOSE SHOT   MARLOWE

     as he gathers up the Sternwood folder out of the box of
     blackmail stuff, puts it in his pocket as he turns.

190.   INT. TELEPHONE PAY STATION   CLOSE SHOT   MARLOWE

     as he speaks into phone.

                          MARLOWE:
             Bernie? It's me, Marlowe. I've
             got a couple of dead people up
             here at Geiger's. . . . Yeah . . .
             Carmen Sternwood and Eddie Mars. . . .
             No, I didn't shoot -- but one of them . . .
             Yeah, I hear you. And you hear me, too.
             I'll be at Sternwood's. I can talk
             just as well there.

He starts to put the phone down. As he does so, Ohls'
angry voice comes OVER.

                          OHLS' VOICE:
                Marlowe -- !

Marlowe puts the phone down, turns to leave the booth.

191.   INT. STERNWOOD HOUSE   MARLOWE

     -- as Norris opens the front door, admits him. Norris
     stares at Marlowe, divines the truth by intuition.

                          NORRIS:
                It -- has happened?

                    MARLOWE:
          So you knew, too, did you? But
          of course you did: she would have
          needed somebody just to keep the
          nightmares off. Where is she now --
          Mrs. Rutledge --

As he speaks, Vivian enters. She stares at him as
Norris had done, divining the truth too.

                    VIVIAN:
          Phil --

                    MARLOWE:
          It's all right. I was just telling
          Norris. It's all all right.
                    (Vivian sways)
          Catch her, Norris!

Norris catches Vivian, supports her as Marlowe moves in,
puts his arm around Vivian.

                    MARLOWE:
          We've got a few minutes until the
          police get here.

                    NORRIS:
          In here, sir.

They half carry Vivian out.

192.   INT. ALCOVE   VIVIAN, MARLOWE AND NORRIS IN B.G.

Vivian has recovered control now.

                    VIVIAN:
          Poor Carmen. Even after that --
          that -- Tell me it was quick.

                    MARLOWE:
          It was quick. She didn't even know,
          probably. Eddie did. He had a good
          half second to watch his coming.

                    NORRIS:
                    (to Vivian)
          She was in the darkness, and Mr.
          Marlowe turned the light on for

                              NORRIS: (Cont.)
                   her -- don't you see?

                              VIVIAN:
                   I know. Would you really have sent
                   her to -- to the --

                              MARLOWE:
                        (quietly)
                   Yes. You don't kill people for free,
                   you know.

                              VIVIAN:
                   Yes, I know.

                              MARLOWE:
                   So you gave Eddie Mars Shawn's
                   fifteen thousand dollars to put him
                   into the sump.

                              VIVIAN:
                   Only it was my fifteen thousand. I
                   pawned the jewels mother left me. I
                   still have Shawn's money, hoping to
                   find his relatives -- if he had rela-
                   tives. Not that it matters. I know
                   what you must think of me.

                              MARLOWE:
                   Do you? -- There's one thing bothering
                   me. It's not the sump. Shawn wouldn't
                   care about that now. But he was a
                   Catholic --

                              VIVIAN:
                   I had prayers said for him in the
                   Cathedral. And I brought the Father
                   out here, too. I couldn't lie to him.
                   He stood beside the sump and blessed
                   Shawn. I prayed too -- for me, at least.

Marlowe puts his hand under her chin, tilting her head
back.

                              MARLOWE:
                   You're okay, soldier. A little
                   dumber than I am, but okay.
                        (straightening up)
                   I'm going to see your father now.

> VIVIAN:
> (rising)
> Yes. We must tell father --

> MARLOWE:
> Not we, unless you mean Norris and
> me. You wait here. You may have
> to keep Bernie Ohls from throwing
> me into his basement dungeon before
> I open my mouth.

193.   INT. CONSERVATORY   STERNWOOD

-- watching as Marlowe and Norris approach him. He, too,
seems to read something by instinct.

> STERNWOOD:
> Come, come, what's happened to my
> daughter now? Didn't you tell me
> days ago that I no longer have a
> heart to break?

> NORRIS:
> It's Miss Carmen, sir --

> STERNWOOD:
> Yes? Tell me.

> MARLOWE:
> She's dead, sir.

Sternwood closes his eyes, otherwise he doesn't move.
Norris moves quickly and anxiously toward him, but he
opens his eyes again, as black and fierce as ever.

> STERNWOOD:
> Well? Am I to know how?

Norris hesitates in dread, but Marlowe speaks smoothly.

> MARLOWE:
> It was a car crash, sir. She was on
> her way back from Santa Barbara. It
> was instantaneous. I don't think she
> suffered at all.

> STERNWOOD:
> And will no more -- since it was
> a car crash.

> MARLOWE:
> And there's one more thing. I
> found Shawn Regan. He's all right.
> Take my word for it.

Again Sternwood's eyes shut, then open fierce and black
again.

> STERNWOOD:
> But he will not return.

> MARLOWE:
> No. He sends you his affection
> and respect, but he won't come
> back.

> STERNWOOD:
> Norris --

> MARLOWE:
> (interrupts)
> We'll forget the pay on this. I
> didn't do anything. It was dropped
> in my lap --

They all react as Vivian enters.

> VIVIAN:
> Phil -- they're here.

> STERNWOOD:
> The police?

> MARLOWE:
> What would the police be doing here,
> sir?

> STERNWOOD:
> Yes. What would the police be doing
> here. Go to your friends, sir. I
> am a little tired and will ask to be
> excused. Goodnight, and thank you
> for everything.

> MARLOWE:
> Goodnight, sir.

He and Vivian walk away, Norris following.

194.   INT. STERNWOOD HALL

as Marlowe, Vivian and Norris come out of the conservatory.
Norris draws ahead, then pauses.

> NORRIS:
> (to Marlowe)
> May I add my own thanks, sir?

> MARLOWE:
> You're welcome, soldier.

Norris inclines his head, then goes off down the hall.
Marlowe and Vivian give each other one of those looks,
and Marlowe takes her hand, drawing her close to him.
They follow Norris.

195.   AT THE FRONT DOOR   GROUP SHOT   OHLS ACCOMPANIED
       BY POLICE

As Marlowe and Vivian approach.

> OHLS:
> All right, Marlowe. I'm waiting
> to see how you're going to talk
> yourself out of this one.

> MARLOWE:
> (laughing)
> For once I'm going to tell the
> truth.

> OHLS:
> It had better be good.

> MARLOWE:
> (turning to Vivian)
> It'll be good, Bernie. It'll be
> very good. Because you won't have
> to hold me here. I've decided
> already myself to stay.

> FADE OUT.

T H E   E N D.

***
*

A STREETCAR NAMED DESIRE

1951—A Charles K. Feldman Production;
released by Warner Brothers Pictures
Director Elia Kazan
Script Screenplay by Tennessee Williams;
adaptation by Oscar Saul
Source Tennessee Williams, *A Streetcar Named Desire*
(New York: New Directions, 1947)
Stars Marlon Brando, Vivien Leigh, Kim Hunter

In the opinion of many, Tennessee Williams is the finest American drama-tist since Eugene O'Neill. Employing a technique that is sometimes repre-sentational and sometimes expressionistic, he electrified and occasionally mystified American audiences of the forties and fifties with a series of plays deep in the American grain. What remains consistent throughout his dramas is his fine ear for dialogue, his ability to catch the flavor of Ameri-can, especially southern, English. Underlying the dialogue is a lyricism that elevates the language of his characters in moments of crisis to the level of poetry. The language both objectifies and sustains his vivid characteriza-tions and instinct for effective plotting.

Williams has been served well by Hollywood. Elements of caricature and comedy in his work, which gave it at times a Dickensian grotesqueness, tend to be lost in Broadway productions. On stage, the characters in his serious dramas become slightly stylized; the tragic element is projected while the comic is suppressed. Film, on the other hand, seems to bring the comic and the grotesque into sharp relief. This result is partly a by-product of movie technique, especially the closeup and the sudden cut. In other words, the camera supplies equivalences for the surrealistically detailed descriptions that give a Dickens novel its unique quality. An ex-pression that would seem intensely serious when viewed from the sixth row of a Broadway theater can become faintly ludicrous when the camera

Cautionary Notice: This photoplay in its printed form is designed for the reading public only. All dramatic rights in it are fully protected by copyright, and no public or private performance—professional or amateur—may be given.

is inches away from the actor. The effect is familiar from silent films, which are often unconsciously funny, a kind of self-parody, because of the camera's relentless fidelity. In *A Streetcar Named Desire* the same effect is entirely appropriate. It brings out a powerful undercurrent of irony, which is part of Williams' dramatic vision of reality and becomes overt in his comedies. Perhaps the best comment on this effect is Swift's description of the Brobdingnagians, who seem awesome to Gulliver from a distance but who become either ludicrous or repulsive when a closeup view reveals their huge pores, moles, and follicles, their dandruff and sweat.

The first Williams play to reach the screen was *The Glass Menagerie* (1950). A nostalgic, meditative examination of the character of a young woman passing into spinsterhood, the film was generally praised but remained somewhat theatrical because of its emphasis on dialogue and Broadway-style acting and its lack of comic irony. *A Streetcar Named Desire* followed in 1951, to be succeeded by *The Rose Tattoo* (1954) and *Baby Doll* (1956)—both comedies—and *Suddenly Last Summer* (1960) and *The Night of the Iguana* (1966)—serious dramas with the ironic element that is so prominent in *Streetcar*.

In retrospect, *A Streetcar Named Desire* is the most successful of the Williams films. Williams handles the southern setting and characters with the authority born of the love-hate relationship that seems inevitable between a southern writer and his region. The expressionistic technique and the dazzlingly abrupt alternations between the tragic and comic modes are well-suited to motion pictures. They can be expressed better on film than on stage. Here Kazan effectively brings them out through his sets and direction of camera positions. The method acting of Brando, however, is probably the major explanation for the movie's success. As intrepreted by Brando, method acting verges on caricature: emotions are exaggerated; intensity becomes superhuman; realism moves in the direction of surrealism. Many reviewers were critical of these qualities. They accused Brando of becoming a parody of himself. While they were correct about the self-parody, they were surely wrong to criticize it; for it objectifies brilliantly a quality that is intrinsic to Williams' play and to his conception of his characters.

For Bosley Crowther (the New York *Times*, September 20, 1951), the film was a "triumph." Kazan, he felt, had "wreathed" the play "with the techniques of the screen" so that it became "as fine, if not finer than the play." *Cahiers du Cinéma* (May, 1952) was puzzled by the anomaly of a Hollywood film striving for highbrow effects. The reviewer, Renard de Laborderie, observed that as "a praiseworthy effort toward quality . . . it has by no means been meant for the average American spectator whose mental age, according to statistics, is about twelve years. The play from which it is derived was destined for the exclusive and 'sophisticated' public of Broadway which, by subscribing to the *New Yorker,* seeks some cultural involvement, and shows some interest in dramatic productions called *avant garde*." The film's appeal to the happy few who read the *New Yorker* was not, however, quite enough to earn Laborderie's unqualified praise.

The Script Although this is a shooting script, divided into the master scenes typical of this form of script, its origin as a play remains evident. Its few camera directions (Kazan and his cameraman deserve credit for the photography) are supplemented by a good deal of the description of action, setting, and character of the sort normally found in a dramatic script. The dating of various pages of the shooting script indicates, nevertheless, that there were at least ten revisions of various episodes between August 8 and November 2, 1950. Note the additional revisions written into the script, presumably during shooting. The new material is underlined with dashes; deleted material, indicated in the text by asterisks, is given in the footnotes.

Credits Producer, Charles K. Feldman; Director, Elia Kazan; Author, Tennessee Williams; Adaptation, Oscar Saul; Music, Ray Heindorf; Art, Richard Day; Photography, Harry Stradling; Editor, David Weisbart.

Cast

Blanche Dubois:	Vivien Leigh
Stanley Kowalski:	Marlon Brando
Stella:	Kim Hunter
Mitch:	Karl Malden
Steve:	Rudy Bond
Pablo:	Nick Dennis
Eunice:	Peg Hillias
A Collector:	Wright King
A Doctor:	Richard Garrick
Matron:	Ann Dere
Mexican Woman:	Edna Thomas

Awards *Streetcar* was first in the "Ten Best Pictures" list of 1951; the New York Film Critics voted Kazan "Best Director" of the year and Vivien Leigh "Best Female Performer." Academy Awards went to Vivien Leigh as "Best Actress," to Karl Malden as "Best Supporting Actor," and to Richard Day for "Best Art Supervision."

FADE IN

1. RAILROAD STATION   SPACE BETWEEN TWO TRAINS
                       (To be shot in New Orleans)

The space between two trains is filled with blowing steam and
smoke. Passengers go down the lane between the trains, and a
party in Carnival costumes are seeing someone off. Passengers
from the arriving train come toward the CAMERA. Blanche's figure advances exhaustedly through the nightmarish tunnel of the
station. Everything is in misty focus. The effect is sugges-
tive of Eurydice advancing up the black, windy avenue of Hell
behind some invisible Orpheus. The flickering light from the
train windows falls with shuttle-like effect on her face and her
figure in its mothlike garments. The soft focus clears to a
thin mist, like the vapor of a steam engine. The opposing crowd
through which she struggles to move must be created non-realis-
tically. The figures are not even quite identifiable as human --
perhaps more like rocks in a torrent against which she is fighting her way to some source of light and liberation. The clatter
of the baggage trucks and the noises of the train are also filtered into a sonic abstraction. The exhausted traveler leans
for a moment against a pillar, then realizing it is sooty, she
draws away from it. Standing nearby is a very, very young sail-
or, waiting for someone -- the sort that looks like one of the
seraphic population in his snowy white uniform. The exhausted
woman's face is suddenly touched by light, the ghost of a tender
smile appearing on it. She sets down her hatbox and, lifting a
hand to the artificial violets on her lapel, speaks to him.

                        * * *

                        SAILOR:
Could I help you, Miss?

                        BLANCHE:
They told me to take a streetcar named Desire, transfer to
one named Cemetery and get off
at Elysian Field.

---

1.   [BLANCHE
                     (laughs breathlessly)
              Oh, I would rather not take that!

                        SAILOR
                      (grinning)
              The other is the streetcar named
              Desire!

> SAILOR:
> That's your streetcar right
> there, Miss.

Blanche turns and picks up her suitcase.

> SAILOR:
> Let me help you with that.

> BLANCHE:
> (kindly)
> Why, how very nice of you --
> thanks.

2.   MOVING SHOT

She moves behind him, stumbling a little in the confusing crowd.
The night is windy, and the moon three-quarters full and the
clouds are low and filmy like the torn garments of witches.
Blanche looks up at this beautiful and ominous sky as she
crosses the street.

3.   SHOT OF STREETCAR NAMED DESIRE

advancing to the corner. Blanche and the Sailor come into the
scene as he hustles her forward and assists her onto the car

---

1. (*Cont'd*)

> BLANCHE
> That is the one I prefer!

> SAILOR
> (beginning to regard
> her a bit curiously)
> Yeah. Yeah, take that one. And
> get off at a street called Elysian
> Fields.

> BLANCHE
> Elysian Fields. Thank you.
> Thank you so much.

> SAILOR
> (lifting her hatbox)
> Le'me help you with that.

> BLANCHE
> Why, how very kind of you! Now I feel
> as if I'd been met at the train.
> You lead the way and I'll follow.]

platform with her hatbox. Then he stands looking, still curiously, up at her. CAMERA MOVES UP TO CLOSE SHOT of her exhausted face, at a lighted window of the car. As her eyes fall shut:

DISSOLVE TO:

4.   EXT. NEW ORLEANS STREET

The street car is stopped. Blanche descends from it with her hatbox and it pulls away revealing in the b.g. a corner of the cemetery. A little old Mexican street vendor comes up to her suddenly. She is nearly blind. In her dark shawl she is barely visible in the dark street. She is carrying bunches of those gaudy tin flowers that lower class Mexicans display at funerals.

> MEXICAN WOMAN:
> Flowers. . . . Flowers. . . . Flowers for
> the dead. . . . Flowers?

Blanche hurries by her. The music of the Varsouviana is heard, an eerie, far-away polka. She stops, puts her hands to her head, pressing her head as if trying to drive the tune out. A shot is heard -- unreal, as if from the distant reaches of her own mind. The music stops instantly. She hurries on, crossing the street away from the cemetery.

> A STREET VENDOR:
> Red hot! Red hot!

5.   EXT. NEW ORLEANS STREET   NIGHT

The street is in a poor section of the city and has a raffish charm, not generally found in such sections in other American cities. The houses are mostly white frame, weathered gray, with rickety outside stairs and galleries and quaintly ornamented gables. The street is alive with passersby -- negro and white -- who move casually along not so much to be going anywhere as to be enjoying the life of the street. In this setting, Blanche is an incongruous figure, and people turn to look at her curiously. She hurries by them apprehensively and ill-at-ease. At the doorway of a bar, The Four Deuces, hot beating music and a burst of loud laughter pour out at her and the light falls on her face with sudden garishness. She turns away, quickly consulting her little slip of paper, searching for the number of the adjoining

house. It is separated from The Four Deuces by a narrow alley,
so that its side-windows face the side-windows of the bar.
Along the street side it shows only two long French windows, and
to find the house number she has to look up the far side, where
steps from a small court lead up to a veranda and the front
door. From the veranda a long flight of stairs leads to an upstairs gallery, and the entrance to the second-floor flat.

6.   MED. SHOT   CORNER OF HOUSE AND COURTYARD

as Blanche stops before it. On the steps, EUNICE, about thirty,
fullblown but not blowsy, is sandpapering her legs and taking
the air. A Negro Woman has stopped to chat with her and is
fanning her baby who sleeps in his cart. The two women are unaware of her for a moment.

                    EUNICE:
          . . . and he was so drunk, he ran
          halfway down the street before
          he knew he was naked. * * * And so when
          he got home she was waiting for him --
          now I'm telling you. . . . You never heard
          nothing like it.

The two women laugh. Then their attention is attracted to
Blanche. There is a silence for a moment as the two women and
Blanche regard each other.

                    EUNICE:
                    (finally)
          You lost, honey?

                    BLANCHE:
          I'm looking for Elysian Fields . . .

                    EUNICE:
          This here is Elysian Fields.

Blanche looks about incredulously.

                    EUNICE:
          What number are you looking for?

                    BLANCHE:
                    (refers to slip of paper)
          Six thirty-two.

EUNICE:
You don't have to look no further.

BLANCHE:
(uncomprehendingly)
I'm looking for my sister, Stella
DuBois. I mean -- Mrs. Stanley
Kowalski.

EUNICE:
That's the party.

BLANCHE:
(completely bewildered)
This. . . . Can this be -- her home?

EUNICE:
She's got the downstairs here,
and I got the up. She's not in
right now, though.

BLANCHE:
Oh, she's out --

EUNICE:
* * * Did you notice that bowling alley
up the street?

BLANCHE:
I'm not sure I did.

As Blanche looks up the street CAMERA MOVES RAPIDLY up the
street to a huge marquee with the word "Bowling" printed across
it in flashing neon.

EUNICE:
She's watchin' her husband bowl.
You want to leave your suitcase
here and go find her?

BLANCHE:
(uncertainly)
Well, I. . . .

---

6.   [You see]

>   EUNICE:
>   Or you could just go in and make
>   yourself at home until they get
>   back.
>
>   BLANCHE:
>   How could I do that?

Eunice goes to the door of Stella's flat, smacks it with the
palm of her hand, and it swings open. She precedes Blanche into
the flat. As they go --

>   NEGRO WOMAN:
>   (gently)
>   G'night, now.

She wheels the baby off.

7.   INT. KITCHEN   STELLA'S FLAT   FULL SHOT   NIGHT

as they enter. This is a kitchen-dining room, so common in low
rent flats. It also contains a folding bed to be used by
Blanche. People who live here happily, or who do not look upon
the place as a retreat from better circumstances will not notice
that the furniture is ill assorted and offers barely enough
comfort. They will not even have considered the matter of style.
This is not to say that no style exists. Some of the raffish
charm of the street is in the house. But Blanche is looking
about with distaste, drawing in upon herself as though the place
would contaminate her.

>   EUNICE:
>   (defensively -- noticing
>   Blanche's look)
>   It's kinda messed up right now,
>   but when it's clean it's real sweet.
>
>   BLANCHE:
>   Is it?
>
>   EUNICE:
>   Uh-huh, I think so.
>   (she sits comfortably)
>   So you're Stella's sister.
>
>   BLANCHE:
>   Yes.

BLANCHE: (Cont.)
(wanting to get rid
of her)
Thanks for letting me in.

EUNICE:
Por nada, as the Mexicans say.
Por nada. And you're from
Mississippi, huh?

BLANCHE:
Yes.

EUNICE:
She showed me a picture of your
home-place, the plantation.

BLANCHE:
Belle Reve?

EUNICE:
A great big place with white columns.

BLANCHE:
Yes.

EUNICE:
Sure must be a job to keep up, a
place like that.

BLANCHE:
If you will excuse me, I'm just
about to drop.

EUNICE:
Sure, honey. Why don't you sit down?

BLANCHE:
What I meant was, I'd like to be
left alone.

EUNICE:
(offended -- rises to go)
Well, I don't need a wall of bricks
to fall on me.

BLANCHE:
I didn't mean to be rude -- I. . . .

> EUNICE:
> That's all right, honey. Next
> time I'll just wait to be asked
> before I sit down.

Eunice exits. Blanche stands there, her hands tightly clutching her purse. After a while she begins to look around slowly.
Suddenly she notices something in a half-opened closet. She
pours a half tumbler of whiskey and tosses it down. She starts
toward bedroom, which is separated by drapes on a drawstring
from the kitchen.

8.   INT. BEDROOM   FULL SHOT

Blanche enters. Her surprise and distaste grow as she looks
around. She sees a narrow door at end of room and crossing,
opens it and looks in. Through the door we see an old-fashioned
porcelain bathtub on spindly legs. From a drying rack over the
tub hang several men's T shirts, women's stockings, some white
handkerchiefs. Now from o.s. there is an instant sudden shout
of anger. She looks at the window on the alley.

> BLANCHE:
> I've got to get hold of myself.

A burst of laughter and the blue piano crash in from the alley.
She flinches, then hearing a woman's voice outside, she hurries
to the front door and opens it. CAMERA MOVING WITH HER.

> * * * (Off stage in street)
> Get out of here. I wouldn't do that for
> the world.

> BLANCHE:
> Stella -- Stella?

9.   EXT. CORNER OF STELLA'S HOUSE

She hurries down the steps and up the street toward the bowling
alley.

10.   EXT. ENTRANCE TO BOWLING ALLEY   FULL SHOT

Blanche approaches and goes in.

11. INT. BOWLING ALLEY   FULL SHOT   NIGHT

as Blanche enters. The lanes are in full play, and the dull
clatter of the balls scattering the pins reverberates through
the place. At some distance back of the starting lines, a
glass partition separates a bar from the bowling alley proper.
Blanche looks about, trying to find her sister among the groups
that cluster back of each lane. Her dress is in sharp contrast
to the pedal-pushers and jeans and cottons that the women are
wearing. Suddenly:

                    STELLA'S VOICE:
               (o.s. -- joyfully)
          Blanche! Blanche!

Blanche looks toward the voice and sees her sister.

                    BLANCHE:
               (a wild cry)
          Stella!

12. WIDER ANGLE

as they move swiftly toward each other.

                    BLANCHE:
          Oh, Stella, Stella for Star!
          Oh, my baby sister. Now then
          let me look at you. But don't you
          look at me, Stella, no, no, no. I
          won't be looked at in this merciless glare. . . .

She clutches her sister, sobbing with relief.

                    STELLA:
          Did you find our place?

                    BLANCHE:
               (throws up her gloved
               hands in horror)
          Stella, what are you doing in a place
          like that? Why didn't you write me, honey?
          Why didn't you let me know? Never, never,
          never in my worst dreams could I picture --
          Only Poe -- Only Mr. Edgar Allan Poe could
          do justice to it! What am I saying? I didn't

BLANCHE: (Cont.)
mean to say that. I meant to be nice
about it and say -- oh, what a convenient
location and such -- ! Precious lamb,
you haven't said a word to me.

STELLA:
You haven't given me a chance to,
honey. . . . Come say hello to Stanley.

BLANCHE:
Not now.

STELLA:
Just say hello --

CAMERA PANS with them as they cross alley.

BLANCHE:
Which is he? Which one is he?

13.   FULL SHOT   BLANCHE'S VIEWPOINT

Stanley is in f.g., surrounded by other players, including
Steve, Mitch. Stanley's back is somewhat to us; his T-shirt is
dark with sweat and adheres to his skin, giving him the look of
a dark, sinewy seal.

STANLEY:
(bellowing at captain
of another team)
-- and don't tell me this is your
alley. We started our game here
and we're going to finish it here!

He grabs jacket a member of other team has draped over the
bench, and throws it at him viciously.

STEVE:
Take it easy, Stan . . .

STANLEY:
Yeah? I'm takin' it easy. I'm
takin' it easy right here.

The members of the other team, cowed, drift off. Blanche and
Stella come into scene.

BLANCHE:
He's the one that's -- ?

STELLA:
The one that's makin' the rhubarb!
Isn't he wonderful looking?

BLANCHE:
Stella! I can't meet him now.
Not until I've bathed and
rested.

STELLA:
Would you like a cold drink, honey?

BLANCHE:
Bless you for that lovely inspiration!

14.   COCKTAIL LOUNGE   BOOTH

They laugh and cross to an arched door under a neon cocktail
sign. Stella starts for a bright booth. Blanche pulls her to
a dark one.

WAITER:
Would you like a lemonade?

BLANCHE:
Honey! A lemonade! Not with my nerves
tonight! Scotch * * * _for me._

STELLA:
* * * _I'll have some grape._ . . .
(a pause)

BLANCHE:
You haven't asked me how I happened
to get away from school -- before
the spring term ended. . . .

STELLA:
Well I thought you'd volunteer
that information, if you wanted to
tell me.

---

14.   [if you please.]
             [Just a lemonade for me. . . .]

BLANCHE:
You thought I'd been fired.

STELLA:
No, I thought you might have
resigned. . . .

BLANCHE:
I was so exhausted by all that I'd
been through -- my nerves just broke.
So Mr. Graves -- Mr. Graves is the
High School superintendent -- he
suggested I take a leave of absence.
I couldn't put all these details in
my wire.

The waiter enters with the drinks.

BLANCHE:
Oh, this buzzes right through
me and feels so good! . . . You haven't
said a word about my appearance!

STELLA:
You look just fine.

BLANCHE:
God love you for a liar!
Daylight never exposed so total
a ruin! But you, you've put on
some weight. Yes, you're just
as plump as a little partridge!
And it's so becoming to you!

STELLA:
Now, Blanche --

BLANCHE:
Yes it is! It is or I wouldn't
say it. You just have to
watch around the hips a little.
I want you to look at my figure.
You know I haven't put on one
ounce in ten years, Stella! I
weigh what I weighed the summer
you left Belle Reve -- the summer
Dad died and you left us. . . .

          STELLA:
It's just incredible, Blanche,
how well you're looking.

Blanche glances at Stella. Stella looks away embarrassed by
Blanche's naked shaken state.

          STELLA:
Would you like another?

          BLANCHE:
No, one's my limit!

          STELLA:
Sure?

          BLANCHE:
Well, maybe I'll just take one
tiny little nip more . . . just to put the
stopper on, so to speak. Now don't get
worried -- your sister hasn't turned into
a drunkard! She's just all shaken up and
hot and dirty and tired. . . .

She laughs. Stella tries to laugh. She's frightened. . . .
Blanche calls the waiter.

          DISSOLVE TO:

15.   INT. STELLA'S FLAT

A bath is being run. . . .

          STELLA:
You want it hot?

          BLANCHE:
       (o.s.)
Scalding.
      (suddenly)
Stella!!

Stella comes out of the bathroom. . . . We pick up Blanche.

          STELLA:
What is it, honey?

          BLANCHE:
There are only two rooms --

BLANCHE: (Cont.)
I don't know where you're
going to put me.

STELLA:
(indicating the bed)
We're going to put you right
here. . . .

BLANCHE:
What kind of a bed is this . . .
one of those collapsible things. . . .

STELLA:
Does it feel alright?

BLANCHE:
Wonderful, honey. I don't like
a bed that gives much. But . . .
there's no door between the two
rooms, and Stanley . . . will it be decent?

STELLA:
Oh, Stanley's Polish, you know. . . .

BLANCHE:
Oh, yes, that's something like
Irish isn't it?

STELLA:
Well. . . .

They both laugh a little.

BLANCHE:
I brought some nice clothes
to meet all your lovely friends.

STELLA:
I'm afraid you won't think they're
lovely.

BLANCHE:
Well, anyhow -- I brought some nice
clothes and I'll wear them. I guess
you're hoping I'll say I'll put up at
a hotel, but I'm not going to put up

                     BLANCHE: (Cont.)
at a hotel. I want to be near you,
Stella; I've got to be with people. I
can't be alone! Because as you must
have noticed -- I'm not very well. . . .

                     STELLA:
You do seem a little . . .

                     BLANCHE:
          (cutting in)
Will Stanley like me, or will
I just be. . . .

                     STELLA:
          (looks toward a
          photograph of Stanley)
You'll get along fine together
if you just. . . .

                     BLANCHE:
          (she has picked up
          the photograph)
Oh, he was an officer!

                     STELLA:
He was a master sergeant in
the Engineers Corps. He was
decorated four times.

                     BLANCHE:
He had those on when you met him.

                     STELLA:
I assure you I wasn't just blinded
by all the brass.

                     BLANCHE:
That's not what I. . . .

                     STELLA:
But of course there were things
to adjust myself to later on. . . .

                     BLANCHE:
Such as his civilian background. . . .
How did he take it when you said I
was coming. . . .

STELLA:
Oh he's on the road a good deal . . .
and --

BLANCHE:
Oh. He travels? Good! I mean
isn't it. . . .

STELLA:
I can hardly stand it when he's
away for a night.

BLANCHE:
Why Stella.

STELLA:
When he's away for a week, I
nearly go wild.

BLANCHE:
Gracious.

STELLA:
And when he comes back, I cry on
his lap like a baby.

BLANCHE:
I guess that is what is meant by
being in love.
(she walks, turns)
Stella . . . I haven't asked you the
things you probably thought I was
going to ask you, and so I expect
you to be understanding about what
I hate to tell you. . . .

STELLA:
What Blanche?

BLANCHE:
Well, Stella -- you're going to
reproach me -- I know you're bound
to reproach me, but before you do --
take into consideration -- you left!
I stayed and struggled! You came
to New Orleans and looked after
yourself. I stayed at Belle Reve
and tried to hold it together! I'm

BLANCHE: (Cont.)
not meaning this in any reproachful
way, but all the burden descended on
my shoulders. . . .

STELLA:
The best I could do was make
my own living.

BLANCHE:
I know, I know, but you're the
one that abandoned Belle Reve, not
I. I stayed and fought for it,
bled for it, almost died for it. . . .

STELLA:
Stop this hysterical outburst and
tell me what happened?

BLANCHE:
I knew it, I knew you would take
this attitude.

STELLA:
About what . . . please?

BLANCHE:
The loss . . . the loss.

STELLA:
Belle Reve? Lost is it?

TRAIN SOUND . . . APPROACHING.

STELLA:
But how did it go? What happened. . . .

BLANCHE:
You're a fine one to ask me how it
went. . . .

STELLA:
Blanche!

BLANCHE:
You're a fine one to stand there
accusing me of it. . . .

                    STELLA:
          Blanche.

                    BLANCHE:
          I won't stay here! I won't! I'd
          rather sleep in the street

THE TRAIN IS NOW JUST BEHIND THE HOUSE . . . SHE RUNS OUT
CLUTCHING HER HAT BOX . . . STELLA FOLLOWS.

16.   EXT. COURTYARD AND CORNER OF STREET   BY STELLA'S FLAT

Stella catches up to Blanche.

                         BLANCHE:
                    I took the blows on my
                    face and my body. All those deaths . . .
                    the long parade to the graveyard --
                    Father, Mother, Margaret -- that dread-
                    ful way. You just came home in time
                    for the funerals. Stella -- and
                    compared to deaths funerals are pretty . . .
                    unless you were there at the
                    bed you would never suspect there was
                    this struggle for breath and bleeding.
                    You didn't dream, but I saw . . . saw . . .
                    and you stand there telling me with your
                    eyes . . . I let the place go. . . . How do
                    you think all that sickness and
                    dying was paid for? Death is expen-
                    sive -- Miss Stella -- and I with my
                    pitiful salary at the school. Yes.
                    Accuse me, stand there and stare at
                    me thinking I let the place go . . .
                    I let the place go! Where were
                    you? In there with your Polack! --

                         STELLA:
                    Blanche! You be still! That's enough!

She goes into the house. Blanche follows uncertainly.

17.   INT. KITCHEN

as Blanche follows Stella in.

> BLANCHE:
> Oh, Stella, Stella, you're crying!

> STELLA:
> Does that surprise you?

She runs out of the kitchen into the bedroom and we hear the bathroom door slam. Suddenly there is a loud shout from outside.

> STANLEY:
> (offscene)
> Hey, Mitch! You bring the beer tomorrow!

Blanche runs from the front room to the bedroom, and stops out of sight of the front room. O.S. Stanley and Steve laugh.

> EUNICE:
> (offscene)
> Break it up down there!

18.   EUNICE AT HEAD OF STAIRS   EXT.   NIGHT

Stanley and Steve below.

> EUNICE:
> I made the spaghetti dish and I ate it myself!

> STEVE:
> (climbing the stairs)
> I told you and phoned you that we was playing Jax Beer. I told you at breakfast, I phoned you at lunch.

> EUNICE:
> * * * Well, never mind. Why don't you get yourself home once in awhile.

                                        CUT TO:

19.   INT. BEDROOM   BLANCHE LISTENING
                     ENTRANCE DOOR SEEN BEHIND HER

STEVE:
(o.s. -- yelling as he
pounds up the stairs)
Do you want it in the newspapers?

Stanley enters, goes to icebox. Music from Three Deuces.
Drums. Blanche finally makes up her mind to face him, goes
into the kitchen.

BLANCHE:
(at last speaking)
You must be Stanley. I'm Blanche.

STANLEY:
Stella's sister?

BLANCHE:
Yes. . . .

STANLEY:
H'lo. . . . Where's the little woman?

BLANCHE:
In the bathroom.

STANLEY:
Well! Where you from, Blanche?

BLANCHE:
Why, I -- live in Auriol.

STANLEY:
In Auriol, huh? Oh, yeah. Yeah, in
Auriol, that's right. Not in my
territory.

He crosses to the closet and removes the whiskey bottle. He
then holds the bottle to the light to observe its depletion.

STANLEY:
Liquor sure goes fast in hot
weather. Have a shot?

BLANCHE:
No, I -- rarely touch it.

STANLEY:
Some people rarely touch it, but it

STANLEY: (Cont.)
touches them often.

BLANCHE:
(faintly)
Ha-ha.

STANLEY:
My shirt's stickin' to me. Do you
mind if I make myself comfortable?
(he starts to remove his shirt)

BLANCHE:
Please, please do.

STANLEY:
Be comfortable, that's my motto, up
where I come from.

BLANCHE:
It's mine, too. . . . It's hard to stay
looking fresh in hot weather. Why,
I haven't washed or even powdered --
and here you are!

STANLEY:
(as he gets the
shirt over his head)
You know, you can catch cold sitting
around in damp things . . . especially
when you've been exercising hard like
bowling is. You're a teacher, aren't you?

BLANCHE:
Yes.

STANLEY:
What do you teach?

BLANCHE:
English.

STANLEY:
I was never a very good English student.
How long you here for, Blanche?

BLANCHE:
I -- don't know yet.

> STANLEY:
> You going to shack up here?

> BLANCHE:
> I thought I would if it's not incon-
> venient to you all. . . .

> STANLEY:
> Good.

> BLANCHE:
> Travelling wears me out.

> STANLEY:
> Well, take it easy.

A cat screeches near the window. Blanche springs up.

> BLANCHE:
> What's that?

> STANLEY:
> Cats.
> > (he growls in imitation of
> > a cat and laughs -- then walks
> > into the bedroom)
> Hey, Stella, what did you do, fall
> asleep in there?
> > (he grins at Blanche. She
> > tries unsuccessfully to smile
> > back. He gets a clean T-
> > shirt from a cabinet)
> I'm afraid I'm going to strike you as
> the unrefined type.

Blanche dabs at her forehead with cologne, goes to the front
door, opens it.

> STANLEY:
> Stella's spoke of you a good deal.
> You were married once, weren't you?

Blanche puts her hands to her head. She seems to be listening
to something. She goes to the verandah.

20.   EXT. VERANDAH   AS BLANCHE COMES OUT

                              BLANCHE:
                        (her back to the house
                         behind her)
                   Yes, when I was quite young.

The music of the <u>Varsouviana</u> has crept up from nothing until it
is quite plain.

                                                    CUT TO:

21.   MED. SHOT   STANLEY   IN KITCHEN

                              STANLEY:
                   What happened?

And there is silence around him.

                                                    CUT TO:

22.   BLANCHE   ON THE VERANDAH

And the polka is heard again, and a sort of echo: "What
happened? What happened?"

                              BLANCHE:
                   The boy -- the boy died.

The polka music rises to a frenetic pitch and tempo. Blanche
presses her hands over her ears as though she could shut it out.

Again the far-away shot, and the music stops. Blanche stands
swaying.

                              BLANCHE:
                   I'm afraid I'm going to be sick.

                              STANLEY:
                        (offscene)
                   How about it, Stella?

                                                    FADE OUT.

FADE IN

23.   STREET   IN FRONT OF STELLA'S HOUSE

A car drives up and stops. Stanley driving, Steve beside him on the front seat. They suggest a chauffeur and a footman. Roped into the luggage compartment of the car is Blanche's wardrobe trunk. The men get out and begin untying it. A NEGRO PEDDLER goes by, pushing a handcart and chanting loudly the variety of fish he has for sale. O.S. the bell of a church chimes pleasantly. The men sweat.

>   STEVE:
> Looks like she's fixin to stay
> a while.

Stanley grunts.

They get the trunk up the steps, have trouble negotiating the door.

>   STEVE:
> Hey, we playing tonight?

>   STANLEY:
>   (bridling)
> Sure we're playing.

>   STEVE:
>   (indicating the apartment)
> I figure maybe . . .

24.   INT. KITCHEN   STELLA'S FLAT   AS STEVE AND STANLEY ENTER

>   STANLEY:
> Don't figure no maybes! We're playing.

They thump the trunk down. Stella runs in from bedroom, partly dressed.

>   STELLA:
> Oh, Stanley!
>   (sees Steve -- pulls back)

>   STEVE:
> See you later.

He goes. Stella comes back, goes to Stanley, kisses him.

>   STELLA:
> Thanks, Stanley.
>   (kisses him)

                BLANCHE'S VOICE:
           (o.s.)
    Stella! Was that Stanley back
    with my trunk?

                STELLA:
           (still with Stanley)
    Yes, dear.

                BLANCHE:
           (o.s. -- or cut to)
    Honey would you get my chiffon print
    out for me.

                STELLA:
           (she and Stanley look
            at each other)
    All right, Blanche.

                BLANCHE:
           (o.s.)
    It was so good of Stanley to call
    for my trunk.

                STELLA:
    Stanley was glad to do it!
           (she grins at Stanley --
            then in a low voice, as
            she gets the trunk key)
    I'm taking Blanche to Galatoire's
    for supper and then to a picture show
    because it's your poker night.

                STANLEY:
    How about my supper, huh? I'm not
    going to no Galatoire's for supper.

                STELLA:
    I put a cold plate on ice. I'm
    going to try to keep Blanche out
    until the party breaks up, because
    I don't know how she would take it.

                STANLEY:
           (who has found the
            "cold plate")
    Isn't that just dandy!

STELLA:
So you'd better give me some money.
          (she searches his pocket --
          extracts some bills)

STANLEY:
What's she doing now?

STELLA:
She's soaking in a hot tub to quiet
her nerves. She's terribly upset.

STANLEY:
Over what?

STELLA:
Stan, we've lost Belle Reve.

STANLEY:
* * * What_do you mean? The place in
the country?

STELLA:
Yes.

STANLEY:
How?

STELLA:
Oh, it had to be sacrificed or something.
          (Blanche is heard singing
          from the bathroom)
When she comes out, be sure to mention
something about her appearance. And --
Oh! Don't mention the baby. I'm
waiting until she gets in a quieter
condition.

STANLEY:
          (ominously)
So?

STELLA:
And try to understand her and be nice to
her, Stan. She wasn't expecting to find
us in such a small place. You see I'd
tried to gloss things over in my letters --

STANLEY:
So?

STELLA:
And admire her dress and tell her she's
looking wonderful. It's important with
Blanche, her little weakness.

STANLEY:
Yeah, I get the idea. . . . Now let's
skip back a little to where you said
the country place was disposed of.

STELLA:
Oh! Yes. . . .

STANLEY:
How about that? Let's have a few
more details on that subject.

STELLA:
(thru the following she is
searching Blanche's trunk for
the dress, the accessory box,
the earrings, which she brings
out)
It's best not to talk much about it
until she's calmed down.

STANLEY:
So that's the deal, huh? Sister
Blanche cannot be annoyed with
business details right now!

STELLA:
You saw how she was last night.

STANLEY:
Yeah . . . I saw how she was. Now let's
have a gander at the bill of sale.

STELLA:
I haven't seen any.

STANLEY:
She didn't show you no papers, no
deed of sale or nothing like that?

STELLA:
It seems like it wasn't sold.

STANLEY:
Well, what was it then, give away?
To charity?

STELLA:
Shhh! She'll hear you.

STANLEY:
I don't care if she hears me.
Let's see the papers!

STELLA:
There weren't any papers, she didn't
show any papers, I don't care about
papers.

STANLEY:
Listen, did you ever hear of the
Napoleonic code?

STELLA:
No, Stanley, I haven't heard of the
Napoleonic code and if I have --

STANLEY:
Let me enlighten you on a point
or two.

STELLA:
Yes?

STANLEY:
In the state of Louisiana we have what
is known as the Napoleonic code, according to which what belongs to the wife
belongs to the husband also and vice
versa. For instance if I had a piece
of property, or you had a piece of property --

STELLA:
My head is swimming!

STANLEY:
All right! I'll wait till she gets
through soaking in a hot tub and then
I'll inquire if she is acquainted with

STANLEY: (Cont.)
the Napoleonic code. It looks to me
like you been swindled, baby, and when
you get swindled under the Napoleonic
code I get swindled too. And I don't
like to be swindled.
    (Blanche is heard singing)

STELLA:
You don't know how ridiculous you are
being when you suggest that my sister
or I or anyone of our family could have
perpetrated a swindle.

STANLEY:
Then where's the money, if the place
was sold?

STELLA:
Not sold -- lost, lost!

He turns to the open trunk, jerks out an armful of dresses.

STELLA:
Stanley!

STANLEY:
Open your eyes to this stuff!
You think she got them out of a
teacher's pay?

STELLA:
Hush!

STANLEY:
Look at these feathers and furs that
she come here to preen herself in!
What's this here? A solid-gold dress,
I believe! And this one! What is
these here? Fox-pieces!
    (he blows on them)
Genuine fox fur-pieces, a half a mile
long! Where are your fox-pieces,
Stella? Bushy snow white ones, no
less.

STELLA:
Those are inexpensive summer furs
that Blanche has had for a long time.

STANLEY:
I got an acquaintance who deals in
this sort of merchandise. I'll
have him in here to appraise it.

STELLA:
Don't be such an idiot, Stanley.

STANLEY:
I'm willing to bet you there's thousands of dollars invested in this
stuff here.

He hurls the furs to the day bed. He turns to the open box of
costume jewelry.

STANLEY:
And what have we here? The treasure
chest of a pirate?

STELLA:
Oh, Stanley!

STANLEY:
Pearls! Ropes of them! What is
this sister of yours, a deep-sea
diver? Bracelets of solid gold, too.
Where are your pearls and gold
bracelets?

STELLA:
Shhh! Be still, Stanley.

STANLEY:
And diamonds! A crown for an Empress!

STELLA:
A rhinestone tiara she wore to a
costume ball.

STANLEY:
What's rhinestone?

STELLA:
Next door to glass.

STANLEY:
Are you kidding? I have an ac-

STANLEY: (Cont.)
quaintance that works in a jewelry
store. I'll have him in here to
make an appraisal of this. Here's
your plantation, or what was left
of it, here!

STELLA:
You have no idea how stupid and
horrid you're being! Now leave
that trunk alone before she comes
out of the bathroom.

He kicks the trunk partly closed.

STANLEY:
The Kowalskis and the DuBois have
different notions.

STELLA:
(angrily)
Indeed they have, thank heaven!
I'm going outside.

Stella snatches up her hat and gloves and starts for the outside
door.

STELLA:
You come out with me while Blanche
is getting dressed.

STANLEY:
Since when do you give me orders?

STELLA:
Are you going to stay here and
insult her?

STANLEY:
You bet your life I'm going to
stay here.

Stella exits. Stanley turns at the sound of the bathroom door
opening o.s.

25.   FULL SHOT   BLANCHE

She comes out of the bathroom in a satin robe.

                    BLANCHE:
          (airily -- as she
          approaches him)
     Hello, Stanley. Here I am, all
     freshly bathed and scented and feel-
     ing like a brand new human being.

                    STANLEY:
          (lighting a cigarette)
     That's good.

                    BLANCHE:
     Excuse me while I slip on my pretty
     new dress!

                    STANLEY:
     Go right ahead, Blanche.

But he makes no move to go. Blanche waits for him to leave. He
moves sullenly into the bedroom. She draws the drapes, then
reacts as she sees the open, disordered trunk.

                    BLANCHE:
     I understand there's to be a little
     card party to which we ladies are
     cordially not invited.

                    STANLEY:
     That's right.

                    BLANCHE:
     Where is Stella?

                    STANLEY:
     Out on the porch.

                    BLANCHE:
     I'm going to ask a favor of you
     in a moment.

                    STANLEY:
     What could that be I wonder?

                    BLANCHE:
     Some buttons in back! You may enter.

She opens the drapes and Stanley enters the kitchen.

                    BLANCHE:
How do I look?

                    STANLEY:
You look okay.

                    BLANCHE:
Many thanks.   Now the buttons.

                    STANLEY:
          (tries briefly, then)
I can't do nothing with them.

                    BLANCHE:
You men with your big clumsy
fingers! May I have a drag on
your cig?

                    STANLEY:
          (taking one from
           behind his ear)
Have one for yourself.

She takes it, waits for a light. He strikes a match for her
and lights her cigarette.

                    BLANCHE:
Thanks! It looks like my trunk
has exploded.

                    STANLEY:
Me and Stella were helping you unpack.

                    BLANCHE:
          (correcting some of
           the disorder)
You certainly did a fast and thorough
job of it.

                    STANLEY:
It looks like you raided some
stylish shops in Paris.

                    BLANCHE:
Clothes are my passion.

                    STANLEY:
What does it cost for a string of

STANLEY: (Cont.)
fur-pieces like that?

BLANCHE:
Why, those were a tribute from an
admirer of mine!

STANLEY:
He must have had a lot of -- admiration!

BLANCHE:
Oh, in my youth I excited some admiration. But look at me now.
     (she smiles at him radiantly)
Would you think it possible that I
was ever considered to be attractive?

STANLEY:
Your looks are okay.

BLANCHE:
I was fishing for a compliment,
Stanley.

STANLEY:
I don't go in for that stuff.

BLANCHE:
What -- stuff?

STANLEY:
Compliments to women about their looks.
I never met a woman who didn't know if
she was good-looking or not without being
told, and some of them give themselves
credit for more than they've got. I
once went out with a dame who said to me,
"I am the glamorous type, I am the
glamorous type." I said, "So what?"

BLANCHE:
And what did she say then?

STANLEY:
She didn't say nothing. That shut her
up like a clam.

BLANCHE:
Did it end the romance?

STANLEY:
It ended the conversation -- that was
all. Some men are took in by this
Hollywood glamor stuff and some men
are not.

BLANCHE:
I'm sure you belong in the second
category.

STANLEY:
That's right.

BLANCHE:
I can't imagine any witch of a woman
casting a spell over you.

STANLEY:
That's right.

BLANCHE:
You're simple, straightforward and
honest, a little bit on the primitive
side I should think.
To interest you a woman would
have to --
        (she pauses with an
        indefinite gesture)

STANLEY:
Lay her cards on the table.

BLANCHE:
Well, I never cared for wishy-washy
people. That was why, when you walked
in here last night, I said to myself --
"my sister has married a man." -- Of
course that was all I could tell about
you at the moment.

STANLEY:
All right how about cutting the re-bop!

STELLA'S VOICE O.S.:
Stanley!

They both turn as Stella opens the door.

> STELLA:
> (entering the kitchen)
> Stanley, you come out with me and
> let Blanche finish dressing.

> BLANCHE:
> I've finished dressing, honey.

> STELLA:
> Well, you come out, then.

> STANLEY:
> Your sister and I are having a
> little talk.

> BLANCHE:
> (lightly -- as she takes
> Stella's arm and leads her
> to the door)
> Honey, do me a favor. Run to the
> drugstore and get me a lemonade
> with plenty of chipped ice in it. --
> Will you do that for me, Sweetie?-Please?
> Please?

> STELLA:
> (uncertainly)
> Yes.

She exits.

> BLANCHE:
> (turning back to Stanley)
> The poor little thing was out there
> listening to us, and I have an idea
> she doesn't understand you as well
> as I do. All right; now, Mr.
> Kowalski, I'm ready to answer all
> questions. What is it?

> STANLEY:
> In the State of Louisiana there is
> such a thing as the Napoleonic code,
> according to which whatever belongs
> to the wife belongs to the husband --
> and vice versa.

                    BLANCHE:
My but you have an impressive
judicial air!

She sprays herself with her atomizer, then playfully sprays him
with it. He seizes the atomizer and slams it down on the
dresser. She throws back her head and laughs.

                    STANLEY:
If I didn't know you was my wife's
sister I'd get ideas about you.

                    BLANCHE:
Such as what?

                    STANLEY:
Don't play so dumb. You know what!

                    BLANCHE:
All right. Cards on the table. I know
I fib a good deal. After all, a woman's
charm is fifty percent illusion, but when
a thing is important I tell the truth,
and I never cheated my sister or you or
anyone else * * * on_earth as long as I have
lived.

                    STANLEY:
Where are the papers? In the trunk?

                    BLANCHE:
Everything that I own is in that trunk. . . .

Without a word he crosses to the trunk and begins to go through
the compartments.

                    BLANCHE:
What in heaven's name are you thinking
of? What's in back of that little
boy's mind of yours? Here, let me
do that, it will be faster and simpler.
          (she crosses to the
          trunk, pushes him
          aside and takes out
          a metal box)
I keep my papers mostly in this tin
box.

STANLEY:
What's them underneath?

BLANCHE:
Those are love letters, yellowing
with antiquity, all from one boy.

Stanley snatches them and begins to pull of the ribbon with
which they are bound.

BLANCHE:
(with surprising
and hysterical
violence)
Give those back to me.

STANLEY:
I'll have a look at them first.

BLANCHE:
The touch of your hands insults
them. . . .

STANLEY:
Don't pull that stuff.

Blanche snatches them from him and they cascade to the floor.
She falls to her knees and begins to pick them up.

BLANCHE:
Now that you've touched them I'll
burn them!

STANLEY:
What are they?

Blanche is on her knees gathering them up. The Varsouviana is
heard. The words spurt out in little spasms like oaths.

BLANCHE:
Poems. A dead boy wrote. I hurt
him the way you would like to
hurt me, but you can't.
I'm not young and vulnerable any
more! But my young husband was . . .
and . . . I -- never mind about that . . .
(he's got some of the
letters in his hand)

                    BLANCHE: (Cont.)
          Give them back to me.

He reaches them across to her.

                    STANLEY:
          What do you mean you'll have to
          burn them?

                    BLANCHE:
          I'm sorry. I must have lost my
          head for a moment. Everyone has
          something he won't let others touch
          because of their -- intimate nature.

She puts the letters into her purse, clicks it sharply shut.
The music stops. Blanche now seems faint with exhaustion. She
puts on a pair of glasses and goes methodically through a large
stack of papers in the strong box.

                    BLANCHE:
          Ambler & Ambler . . .

                    STANLEY:
          What is Ambler & Ambler?

                    BLANCHE:
          A firm that made loans on the place.

                    STANLEY:
          Then it was lost on a mortgage?

                    BLANCHE:
          That must've been what happened.

                    STANLEY:
          I don't want no ifs, ands or buts!
          What's all the rest of them papers?

She hands him the entire box. He carries it to the table and
starts to examine the papers. Blanche picks up a large envelope
containing more papers, takes them out in heaps, pours them on
the table before Stanley.

                    BLANCHE:
          (pouring papers and
          ancient documents out
          of a large beat-up
          manila folder)

BLANCHE: (Cont.)
There are thousands of papers stretching back over hundreds of years, af-
fecting Belle Reve.
As piece by piece our improvident
grandfathers exchanged the land for
their epic debauches --
      (another mess of papers)
Till finally all that was left -- was
the house itself and about twenty
acres of ground including a graveyard,
to which now all but Stella and I have
retreated.
      (the table is covered)
Here they all are, all papers.
      (she seems glad to be
      rid of them)
I hereby endow you with them! Take
them. Peruse them - commit them to
memory, even! I think it's wonder-
fully fitting that Belle Reve should
finally be this bunch of old papers
in your big capable hands.
      (she leans back and
      closes her eyes)
I wonder if Stella has come back with
my lemonade. . . .

STANLEY:
I have a lawyer acquaintance who will
study these out.

BLANCHE:
Present them to him with a box of
aspirins.

STANLEY:
      (a little sheepish)
You see, under the Napoleonic code
-- a man has to take an interest in
his wife's affairs - especially now
that she's going to have a baby.

BLANCHE: (arrested)
Stella? Stella's going to have a
baby? I didn't know she was going
to have a baby.

Stella is standing in the door looking at Stanley. Blanche
hurries to her and takes her out on the verandah.

26.   VERANDAH   EVENING

                          BLANCHE:
                  Stella, Stella for star! How lovely
                  to have a baby. It's all right.
                  Everything is all right. I feel
                  a bit shaky, but I think I handled
                  it nicely. I laughed and treated it
                  all as a joke.

Steve and Pablo come by, carrying a case of beer into the house,
tipping their hats to the ladies who walk into and then along

27.   EXT. THE STREET   EVENING
       CAMERA FOLLOWING BLANCHE AND STELLA

                          BLANCHE:
                  I laughed .and called him a little
                  boy and flirted. Yes, I was flirting
                  with your husband, Stella.

Pablo and Steve appear with a case of beer.

                          BLANCHE: (Cont.)
                  The guests are gathering for the
                  poker party.

                          STELLA:
                  I'm sorry he did that to you.

                          BLANCHE:
                  I guess he's just not the sort that
                  goes for jasmine perfume. But maybe
                  he's what we need to mix with our
                  blood now that we've lost Belle Reve
                  and have to go on without Belle Reve
                  to protect us.
                          (she stops, looks
                          at the sky)
                  How pretty the sky is! I ought to
                  go there in a rocket and never come
                  down!

                              * * *

                         BLANCHE:
Which way do we go now, Stella. . . . This
way?

                         STELLA:
No, honey, this way.

                         BLANCHE:
The blind are leading the blind --

They go down the street.

28.   FADE IN

        INT. EUNICE'S BEDROOM   NIGHT
        FULL SHOT   EUNICE IN BED

        She has been sleeping for hours apparently. But now she stirs
        uneasily, wakes, reaches for the alarm clock on the bed table
        and takes a somnambulistic look at it. Then she lies back on
        the pillow and with half-closed eyes she lets her arm trail
        over the side of the bed until it touches a soft-soled bedroom
        slipper. She grabs it by the toe, raises it, and proceeds to
        hammer away on the floor.

29.   INT. KITCHEN   STELLA'S FLAT   NIGHT
        FULL SHOT   STANLEY, STEVE, MITCH AND PABLO

        playing poker. The room is in disorder. Cigarette butts and
        fruit rinds litter the table, bottles stand about on the floor.
        O.S. we hear the hammering of Eunice's shoe. The men are look-
        ing at the ceiling.

                         STANLEY:
                        (to Steve)
                You going to go up there and tell
                her to cut it out?

                         STEVE:
                If I go up I won't come down. For-
                get it. . . .

---

27.   [Stella embraces her. They go down the street.]

                    PABLO:
          Remember the night she poured boil-
          ing water through them cracks in
          the floor?

They look up.

30.   INT. EUNICE'S KITCHEN   NIGHT

Eunice is lighting the gas under a kettle of water.

31.   INT. KITCHEN   STELLA'S FLAT   NIGHT

                         MITCH:
          I got to go home pretty soon.

                         STANLEY:
          Come on, how many?

                         MITCH:
          I'm out.

                         STANLEY:
          Sure, you're out like Stout!
          Whenever you win a big pot!

                         MITCH:
          I got a sick mother. She don't
          go to sleep until I get in at night.
          I'm gonna wash up.

He crosses into the bathroom.

                         EUNICE: (o.s.)
          Stella!

32.   VERANDAH AND STAIRS   NIGHT
        BLANCHE AND STELLA RETURNING

As they come to the door.

                         STELLA:
          Yes, Eunice?

33.   EUNICE ABOVE ON GALLERY

EUNICE:
Tell those men the kettle is on
the stove.

34.   VERANDAH

STELLA:
I'm going to break up the game.

BLANCHE:
How do I look? Wait till I powder.
Do I look done in?

STELLA:
You look fresh as a daisy.

BLANCHE:
Yes, one that's been picked a few days.

The girls start into the flat.

35.   THE KITCHEN   STELLA'S FLAT   AS THEY ENTER.

PABLO:
Why don't somebody go down to the
Chinaman's and bring back a load
of chop suey?

STANLEY:
When I'm losing, you want to eat.

STELLA:
Well, well, well, I see you boys are
still at it.

STANLEY:
Where you been?

STELLA:
Blanche and I took in a show.
Blanche, this is Mr. Gonzales and
Mr. Hubbell.

BLANCHE:
How do you do?
          (no one moves)

          BLANCHE: (Cont.)
Please don't get up.
        (Steve starts to
        get up)

          STANLEY:
Nobody's getting up, so don't be
worried. Why don't you women go
up to Eunice's?

          STELLA:
How much longer is this game going
to continue?

          STANLEY:
Till we get ready to quit.

          BLANCHE:
Poker is so fascinating. Could I
kibitz?

She reaches for a card, Stanley leaps up, shoves her hand away.

          STANLEY:
You could not.

          BLANCHE:
Excuse me.
        (exits)

          STANLEY:
Why don't you women go up to Eunice's.

          STELLA:
How much longer is this game going to
continue?

          STANLEY:
Till we get ready to quit.

          STELLA:
I wish you'd call it quits after
one more hand.
        (she hands Pablo's coat
        to him across the table.
        Stanley whips it out of
        her hand, throws it on
        the floor)

PABLO:
Hey! My coat!

Stella is leaning over day bed to take cover off. Stanley leans towards her, whacks her resoundingly.

STELLA: (sharply)
That's not fun, Stanley.

Stella exits into the bedroom.

36.   INT. BEDROOM   AS STELLA ENTERS

as draws the curtains.

STELLA:
It makes me so mad when he does
that in front of people.

BLANCHE:
I think I will bathe.

STELLA:
Again?

BLANCHE:
My nerves are in knots.

Blanche goes to the bathroom door. It opens and Mitch comes out. He is dabbing at his face with a towel.

BLANCHE:
Oh -- good evening.

MITCH: (staring at her)
Hello.

STELLA:
Blanche. This is Harold Mitchell.
My sister, Blanche DuBois.

MITCH:
(with awkward courtesy)
How do you do Miss DuBois. . . .

STELLA:
How is your mother, Mitch?

MITCH:
About the same, thanks. She appreciated your sending over that
custard. Excuse me please.

He crosses slowly back into the kitchen, glancing back at
Blanche, and coughing a little shyly. He realizes he still has
the towel in his hands and with an embarrassed laugh hands it
to Stella, then exits.

       BLANCHE:
       (looking after him)
That one seems -- superior to the
others.

       STELLA:
Does he?

       BLANCHE:
       (starts to undress)
I thought he had a sort of sensitive look.

       STELLA:
His mother is sick.

       BLANCHE:
Is he married?

       STELLA:
No.

       BLANCHE:
Is he a wolf?

       STELLA:
Why Blanche!
       (Blanche laughs)
I don't think he would be.

       BLANCHE:
What does he do?

       STELLA:
He's on the precision bench in the
spare parts department. At the
plant Stanley travels for.

>   BLANCHE:
> Is that something much?

>   STELLA:
> No. Stanley's the only one of
> his crowd that's likely to get
> anywhere.

Blanche has taken off her blouse and is stealing a look through
the curtains.

>   STELLA:
> Blanche, you're standing in
> the light.

>   BLANCHE:
> Oh, am I? Gracious!

>   STELLA:
> You ought to see their wives.

>   BLANCHE:
> I can imagine.

>   STELLA:
> You know that one upstairs?
>   (they giggle)
> Well, one night the plaster cracked.

She giggles and moves out of the light. Stella giggles.

>   STANLEY'S VOICE:
>   (o.s.)
> Hey, you hens!

37.   INT. KITCHEN

O.S. Stella and Blanche laugh together.

>   STANLEY:
> Cut out that cackle in there.

>   STELLA'S VOICE:
>   (o.s.)
> You can't hear us.

>   STANLEY:
> Well, you can hear me and I

                    STANLEY: (Cont.)
          said to hush up.

Stella appears at the curtain.

                    STELLA:
          This is my house and I'll talk
          as much as I want to.

She turns back to the bedroom.

38.   INT. BEDROOM

Blanche comes up behind Stella.

                    BLANCHE:
          Stella, don't start a row.

                    STELLA:
          He's half drunk!
                    (she takes the
                    night clothes
                    she will change
                    into and starts
                    for the bathroom)
          I'll be out in a minute.

Blanche goes to a small white radio and turns it on. Then she
moves toward the streak of light, raises her arms and stretches,
then moves indolently back to the chair, remaining in the light.

39.   KITCHEN

                    STANLEY:
          All right, Mitch, you in?

                    MITCH:
                    (looking through drapes)
          What? Oh, no, I'm not.

                    STANLEY:
          Who turned that on in there?

40.   INT. BEDROOM

                    BLANCHE:
          I did. Do you mind?

> STANLEY:
> (o.s.)
> Turn it off!

Blanche remains calmly where she is.

> STEVE:
> (o.s.)
> Aw, let the girls have their
> music.

> PABLO:
> (o.s.)
> Sure, that's good, leave it on!

O.S. we hear sound of a chair scraping, then falling.

41.   INT. KITCHEN

Stanley leaps to his feet and lurches across the room to the
bedroom.

42.   INT. BEDROOM

Stanley rips the curtain aside then enters. Blanche is standing there in her slip. He turns the radio off. Then turns to
her -- points a finger at her as if in warning, then he exits.
Blanche goes for her dressing gown.

43.   INT. KITCHEN

Stanley enters.

> STEVE:
> (to Pablo, hotly)
> I didn't hear you name it.

> PABLO:
> Didn't I name it, Mitch?

> MITCH:
> I wasn't listenin'.

> PABLO:
> What were you doing then?

> STANLEY:
> He was looking through them drapes.

He jumps up and jerks roughly at the curtains to close them.

> STANLEY:
> Now deal the hand over again
> and let's play cards or quit.

Mitch rises.

> MITCH:
> Deal me out.

Stanley deals. Mitch walks to the portieres.

44.   THE BEDROOM

> STANLEY'S VOICE:
> (o.s.)
> This game is "Spit in the Ocean!"

Mitch appears at the portieres. He knocks, walks in and makes
a sign towards the wash room.

> MITCH:
> Excuse me!

> BLANCHE:
> (softly)
> The little boys' room is occupied
> right now.

She smiles a little at him. He is embarrassed. DROPS his eyes.
There is a little awkward pause.

> BLANCHE:
> Have you got any cigs?

> MITCH:
> (getting his
> cigarette case)
> Oh, sure.

> BLANCHE:
> What a pretty case. Silver?

MITCH:
Yes. Read the inscription.

BLANCHE:
Oh, is there an inscription? I
can't make it out.

He strikes a match and moves closer.

BLANCHE:
Oh.
(she takes his hand
under pretense of
moving it so that the
match light will serve
to best advantage, then
reads with feigned
difficulty)
"And if God choose,
I shall love thee better -- after -- death"
Why, that's from my favorite sonnet
by Mrs. Browning.

MITCH:
You know it?

BLANCHE:
Certainly I do.

She releases his hand, pretending embarrassment.

MITCH:
(after a pause)
There's a story connected with
that inscription.

BLANCHE:
It sounds like a romance.

MITCH:
A pretty sad one. The girl
is dead now.

BLANCHE:
Oh!

MITCH:
She knew she was dying when she

MITCH: (Cont.)
give me this. A very strange
girl, very sweet -- very.

BLANCHE:
Sick people have such deep,
sincere attachments.

MITCH:
That's right, they certainly do.

BLANCHE:
Sorrow makes for sincerity, I
think.

MITCH:
It sure brings it out in people.

BLANCHE:
The little there is belongs to people
who have experienced some sorrow.

MITCH:
I believe you are right about that.

BLANCHE:
I'm positive that I am. Show me a
person who hasn't known any sorrow
and I'll show you a shuperficial --
listen to me! My tongue is a little-
thick. You boys are responsible for
it. The show let out at eleven and
we couldn't come home on account of
the poker game so we had to go somewhere and drink. I'm not accustomed
to having more than one drink. Two
is the limit -- and <u>three</u>!
     (she laughs)
Tonight I had three.

STANLEY'S VOICE:
     (o.s.)
Mitch!

MITCH:
     (at the curtains)
Deal me out. I'm talking to Miss --

                    BLANCHE:
DuBois.

                    MITCH:
Miss DuBois?

                    BLANCHE:
It's a French name. It means woods
and Blanche means white, so the two
together mean white woods. Like an
orchard in spring. You can remember
it by that -- if you care to.

                    MITCH:
You are Stella's sister, are you not?

                    BLANCHE:
Yes, Stella is my precious little
sister. . . . I call her little in
spite of the fact she's somewhat
older than I.

                    MITCH:
Oh!

                    BLANCHE:
Just slightly. Less than a year.
Will you do something for me

                    MITCH:
Sure. Yes. What?

She gets the parcel she brought in.

                    BLANCHE:
I bought this adorable little
colored paper lantern at a Chinese
shop on Bourbon Street. Put it over
the light bulb. Will you, please?

                    MITCH:
Be glad to.

He takes the lantern and starts fixing it over the bulb.

                    BLANCHE:
I can't stand a naked light bulb
any more than I can a rude remark

       BLANCHE: (Cont.)
or a vulgar action.

       MITCH:
I guess we strike you as being
a pretty rough bunch.

       BLANCHE:
Oh, I'm very adaptable to circumstances.

       MITCH:
Well, that's a good thing to be.
You're not -- ?

       BLANCHE:
Married? No, no. I'm an old
maid school teacher.

       MITCH:
You may teach school but you're
certainly not an old maid.

       BLANCHE:
Thank you, sir! I appreciate
your gallantry.

       MITCH:
       (looking at her)
So you are in the teaching pro-
fession?

       BLANCHE:
Yes. Ah, yes. . . .

       MITCH:
Grade school or high -- ?

                  CUT TO:

45.   KITCHEN   MEDIUM SHOT STANLEY

on his feet bellowing:

       STANLEY:

MITCH!

                  CUT TO:

46.   BEDROOM

MITCH:
(bellowing back)
COMING!

BLANCHE:
Gracious, what lung-power! I
teach high school.

MITCH:
What subject do you teach?

BLANCHE:
You guess!

MITCH:
I bet you teach art or music?

BLANCHE:
(laughing delicately)
No. . . .

MITCH:
You might teach arithmetic.

BLANCHE:
Never arithmetic. Sir, never
arithmetic. I don't even know my
multiplication tables. No, I have
the misfortune to be an English
instructor. I attempt to instill
a bunch of bobby-soxers and drug-
store Romeos with a reverence for
Hawthorne and Whitman and Poe!

MITCH:
I guess that some of them are more
interested in other things.

BLANCHE:
How very right you are! Their literary
heritage is not what they prize above
all else! But they're sweet things!
And in the spring, it's touching to
notice them making their first discovery of love. As if nobody had ever
known it before.

They laugh together. Blanche puts her hand on Mitch's. Mitch mutters "Excuse me", and steps back just as Stella opens the bathroom door. He turns around rather foolishly, nearly bumping into Stella, then almost backing into Blanche, who rises and looks at the lantern.

> BLANCHE:
> Oh, have you finished?

> MITCH:
> Hm? . . . Oh, yes!

He starts to switch on the light.

> BLANCHE:
> No. Wait!

She crosses to the radio and turns it on.

> BLANCHE:
> Turn on the light above. Now.

Mitch snaps on the light. The radio plays: "Wien, Wien, nur du allein."

> BLANCHE:
> Look! We've made enchantment.

Blanche waltzes to the music. Stella applauds, Mitch sings and sways.

47.   KITCHEN

> STANLEY:
> (slamming down a hand)
> Three bullets!

> PABLO:
> Straight! I got you! I got you!
> (laughs uproariously)

Pablo collects, still laughing. Stanley leaps to his feet and stalks fiercely thru the portieres.

48.   BEDROOM

Stanley rushes to the radio, pulling the cord out of the socket --

> BLANCHE:
>
> Stella!

> STELLA:
>
> Stanley! What are you doing?

He picks it up, shoving her out of the way, carries it to the window and throws it out.

> STELLA:
>
> Drunk -- drunk -- animal thing -- you!

She runs into the kitchen.

49.   KITCHEN

Stella rushes in, shoving at Steve, pushing Pablo.

> STEVE:
>
> Take it easy, Stella!

> STELLA:
>
> All of you -- please go home! If you have one spark of decency in you --

With an hysterical sweep of her arm, she dumps cards, money, liquor off the table.

> BLANCHE'S VOICE:
>
> (o.s.)
>
> Stella, watch out, he's -- !

Stanley lurches into the shot, charging at her. She retreats.

> STEVE:
>
> Take it easy, fellow --

> STELLA:
>
> You lay your hands on me and I'll --

Pushing Steve out of the way. Stanley goes after her. We either see or hear a blow struck. Stella cries out. Blanche screams.

> BLANCHE:
>
> (shrilly)
>
> My sister is going to have a baby!

MITCH:
This is terrible!

BLANCHE:
Lunacy, absolute lunacy!

MITCH:
Get him in here, men.

Stanley is forced back onto the couch by Steve and Pablo.

STELLA:
I want to go away, I want to
go away.

MITCH:
Poker should not be played in a
house with women.

Eunice comes in at the verandah door in her wrapper, takes it
all in.

BLANCHE:
My sister's clothes. . . .

MITCH:
Where is the clothes?
        (he goes to the bedroom)

BLANCHE:
I've got them!

EUNICE:
        (a motherly arm
        around Stella)
Up to my place. Up to my place.

BLANCHE:
        (mothering from the
        other side, competitively)
Stella, precious; Dear, dear, little
baby sister, don't be afraid! Did
he hurt you?

The two women lead Stella out. Mitch follows them to the door.

STANLEY:
        (struggling at the
        couch, dully)

STANLEY: (Cont.)
What happened?

MITCH:
You just blew your top. That's
what happened.

PABLO:
(holding Stanley up)
He's okay now.

MITCH:
Put him under the shower!

The men pull the struggling Stanley towards the bathroom.

PABLO:
Coffee do him more good, now.

MITCH:
He shouldn't live with nice women!
Put him under the shower!

50.   BATHROOM   JAMMED FULL WITH THE STRUGGLING MEN

STEVE:
Get his clothes off.

MITCH:
Never mind his clothes.

The water strikes with blinding force, catching everybody.
Struggle. Cries. Oaths. Suddenly Stanley strikes back, catching them off guard. One by one he hurls them out.

51.   BEDROOM   AS THE MEN ARE HURLED OUT OF THE BATHROOM

and continue on their way, beating it fast.

MITCH:
Poker should not be played
in a house with women.

He exits. Pause. Then Stanley emerges slowly, dripping, mopping his face with a towel which he drops on the floor. He
looks about the dim room.

> STANLEY:
>
> Stella. . . .

He continues mumbling toward the kitchen, searching for Stella.

.52.   KITCHEN   AS STANLEY COMES IN

> STANLEY:
> Stella. . . . Stella. . . .
> (he is crying drunk
> but like a penitent
> boy)
> My baby doll. . . .
> (he goes to phone)
> Stella. . . . Stella. . . . Baby. . . .
> (he begins to dial)

53.   INT. EUNICE'S FLAT   KITCHEN

Blanche beside Stella. Eunice is fussing with a daybed.

> EUNICE:
> She can sleep right here. And you
> can use Steve's bed. He won't show
> up tonight, if he knows what's good
> for him.

The phone rings.

> BLANCHE:
> Stella, stop crying and listen
> to me, Stella. We've got to
> get away from here!

Eunice answers. We hear loud but undecipherable sounds.

> STELLA:
> Stanley?

> EUNICE:
> (nods)
> No, she ain't goin' to talk to
> you and she ain't comin' down-
> stairs neither! So you might
> as well not call her!

Slams the phone down.

54.   INT. STELLA'S APARTMENT

Stanley slams the phone down and goes out.

55.   STANLEY

goes to the foot of the step and yells:

                STANLEY:
      STELLA!

56.   GALLERY AND STAIRS   EUNICE ABOVE   STANLEY BELOW

                EUNICE:
              (shouting down)
You quit that howling down
there and go back to bed.

                STANLEY:
Eunice! I want my girl down here!

                EUNICE:
She ain't comin' down, so you
quit or you'll git the law on
you!

                STANLEY:
Stel-lah!

                EUNICE:
You can't beat a woman and then
call her back! She won't come,
and her goin' to have a baby!

                STANLEY:
Eunice!

                EUNICE:
I hope they haul you in and turn
the fire hose on you the same as
last time!

                STANLEY:
Eunice, I want my girl down here
with me!

EUNICE:

You stinker!

She goes in and slams the door.

57.   CLOSE SHOT   STANLEY

STANLEY:
(with heaven-splitting
violence)

STEL-LAH!   STEL --

58.   EUNICE'S FLAT

Stella moves to the door as though hypnotized, and goes out.

BLANCHE:

Stella!   Stella!

EUNICE:

I wouldn't mix in this.

Blanche stares at Eunice, horrified.

59.   STAIRS FROM EUNICE'S FLAT

Stanley is at the foot of them. Stella slowly comes down. The
low-toned clarinet from The Four Deuces moans. Stella reaches
the foot of the stairs. Stanley falls to his knees and presses
his face into her belly. He weeps. He rises and takes her in
his arms, turning into the house. Her feet are off the ground.

STANLEY:
(as Stella kisses
him passionately)

Don't ever leave me -- Don't ever
leave me. . . . Sweetheart . . . baby. . . .

The house is dark. He carries her into it. Blanche runs down
the stairs, to the door, stops on the threshold, catches her
breath as if struck.

60.   INT. STELLA'S FLAT   KITCHEN VERY DARK   BLANCHE'S VIEWPOINT

Stella and Stanley cling to each other, kissing, murmuring in-coherent words of love-making.

61.   VERANDAH   BLANCHE

She shuts the door, recoiling from what she sees, desolation and disbelief in her eyes.

> EUNICE'S VOICE O.S.:
> Blanche! Come back up here!

With a dazed look, Blanche goes down the steps toward the empty street. Music from The Four Deuces. Mitch turns the corner.

> MITCH:
> Miss DuBois?

> BLANCHE:
> Oh! . . .

> MITCH:
> All quiet on the Potomac now?

> BLANCHE:
> She went back in there with him!

> MITCH:
> Sure she did.

> BLANCHE:
> I'm terrified!

> MITCH:
> There's nothing to be scared of.
> They're crazy about each other.

> BLANCHE:
> I'm not used to such --

> MITCH:
> It's a shame this had to happen.

> BLANCHE:
> Violence is so --

> MITCH:
> Sit down on the steps and have

                    MITCH: (Cont.)
a cigarette with me.

                    BLANCHE:
I'm not properly dressed.

                    MITCH:
That don't make no difference in
the Quarter.

They sit on the steps.

                    BLANCHE:
Such a pretty silver case.

                    MITCH:
I showed you the inscription,
didn't I?

                    BLANCHE:
Yes.
        (she looks at him)
There's so much confusion in
the world. Thank you for being
so kind. I need kindness now.

                                        FADE OUT.

FADE IN

62.   INT. STELLA'S FLAT   SUNDAY MORNING

Stella is lying in bed eating a plum and very contented. Her
eyes and lips have that narcotized tranquility that is in the
faces of Eastern idols. Street cries are heard, and some
vendors pass the window. These are traditional cries: A man --
"Young fryers!" -- 2nd Man -- "Blackberries! 10¢ a quart." 1st
Woman -- "Nice fresh roas'n ears." 3rd Man -- "Watermelons!"
4th Man -- "Irish potatoes!" -- 2nd Woman -- "Tender young snap
beans!" 5th Man -- "Fresh country eggs!"

                    BLANCHE'S VOICE O.S.:
                (panicky with fear)
        Stella!

                    STELLA:
                (stirring lazily)
        Hmmmm?

Blanche runs into the room with a moaning cry and embraces
Stella in a rush of hysterical tenderness.

> BLANCHE:
> Baby, my baby sister!

> STELLA:
> Blanche, what is the matter
> with you?
> >   (she draws away)

> BLANCHE:
> He left?

> STELLA:
> Stan? Yes.

> BLANCHE:
> Will he be back?

> STELLA:
> He went to get the car greased.
> Why?

> BLANCHE:
> Why! I've been half crazy, Stella.
> How could you come back in this
> place last night?

> STELLA:
> Please, Blanche. He was as good
> as a lamb when I came back, and
> he's really very, very ashamed
> of himself.

She goes into the kitchen.

63.   KITCHEN

> BLANCHE:
> >   (following her)
> And that makes it all right?

> STELLA:
> No, but Stanley's always smashed
> things. Why on our wedding night
> soon as we came in here he snatched

STELLA: (Cont.)
off one of my slippers and rushed
about the place smashing the light
bulbs with it.

BLANCHE:
He did what?

STELLA:
He smashed all the light bulbs with
the heel of my slipper.

BLANCHE:
And you let him? You didn't run,
didn't scream?

STELLA:
I was sort of thrilled by it. Eunice
and you have breakfast?

BLANCHE:
You suppose I wanted any breakfast?
You're so matter of fact about it.

STELLA:
What other can I be? Oh, he's taken
the radio to get it fixed. It didn't
land on the pavement so only one tube
was smashed.

BLANCHE:
And you're standing there smiling?

STELLA:
What do you want me to do?

BLANCHE:
Pull yourself together and face the facts.

STELLA:
What are they in your opinion?

BLANCHE:
In my opinion you are married to a
mad man.

STELLA:
No.

BLANCHE:
Yes you are. Your fix is worse than
mine is but you can get out.

STELLA:
I'm not in anything I want to get out
of. Look at the mess in this room --
and those empty beer bottles. They
went through two cases last night. He
promised this morning he was going to
quit having these poker parties, but
you know how long such a promise is
going to keep. Oh, well, it's his
pleasure like mine is bridge and movies.
People have got to tolerate each other's
habits, I guess.

BLANCHE:
I don't understand you. · I don't
understand your indifference. Is
this some Chinese philosophy you've
cultivated?

STELLA:
Is what what?

BLANCHE:
This shuffling about and mumbling --
one tube smashed -- beer bottles --
mess in the kitchen, as if nothing out
of the ordinary had happened. Are you
deliberately shaking that thing in my
face?

STELLA:
No!

BLANCHE:
Well, put it down. I won't have you
cleaning up after him.

STELLA:
Then who's going to do it? Are you?

BLANCHE:
I? . . . I? . . .

STELLA:
No, I didn't think so.

BLANCHE:
Let me think. If only my mind would
function. We've got to get hold of
some money -- that's the way out.

STELLA:
I guess money's always nice to get
hold of.

BLANCHE:
Listen to me. I have an idea of some
kind. Do you remember Shep Huntleigh?

STELLA:
No.

BLANCHE:
Of course you remember Shep Huntleigh.
I went out with him my last year at
college. Well I ran into him last
winter, you know I went to Miami for
the Christmas holidays?

STELLA:
No.

BLANCHE:
Well, I did. I took the trip as an
investment, thinking I'd meet someone
with a million dollars.

STELLA:
Did you?

BLANCHE:
Yes, I ran into Shep Huntleigh --
I ran into him on Biscayne
Boulevard on Christmas Eve just
about dusk -- getting into his
car -- Lincoln convertible, must
have been a block long!

STELLA:
I should think it would have
been inconvenient in traffic.

BLANCHE:
You've heard of oil wells?
Well, he has them. Texas is

        BLANCHE: (Cont.)
literally spouting gold in his
pocket.

        STELLA:

My, my.

        BLANCHE:

You know how indifferent I am
to money. I think of money
only in terms of what it does
for you. But he could do it,
he could certainly do it!

        STELLA:
Do what, Blanche?

        BLANCHE:
Why -- set us up in a shop!

        STELLA:
What kind of a shop?

        BLANCHE:
Oh, a -- shop of some kind.
He could do it with half of
what his wife throws away at
the races.

        STELLA:
Oh, he's married?

        BLANCHE:
Honey, would I be here if the
man weren't married?
     (Stella laughs)
Oh. Don't laugh at me, Stella!
Please, please, don't laugh at me --
     (picks up her
     purse)
I want you to look at the contents
of my purse! Here's what's in it.
     (takes out
     coins)
Sixty-five measly cents in coin
of the realm!
     (she throws them
     out of the window)

64.   SUNNY DAY   THE ALLEY ALONGSIDE THE HOUSE

as the coins fall in, Stanley, returning from his errands, sees
them fall. He is greasy from assisting with the car job, and
he carries the radio, now repaired. He stoops and slowly picks
up coins. He gives no sign of hearing the voices which continue
without a break.

> STELLA O.S.:
> Blanche, after you've rested
> a little --

> BLANCHE O.S.:
> I can't live with him! I have
> a plan to get us both out of here.

> STELLA O.S.:
> I wish you'd stop taking it for
> granted I'm in something I want
> to get out of.

> BLANCHE O.S.:
> I take it for granted that you
> still have a sufficient memory
> of Belle Reve to find this place
> and these poker players impossible
> to live with.

> STELLA O.S.:
> Well, you're taking entirely too
> much for granted.

65.   THE STREET

Stanley moves on slowly, rounding the corner. A passerby hails
him.

> PASSERBY:
> Hi-yuh, Stanley!

> STANLEY:
> Al!

The voices come to him again, from the window on the street:

> BLANCHE O.S.:
> Stella, a man like that is some-

                    BLANCHE: (Cont.)
one to go out with once -- twice --
three times when the devil is
in you. But live with? Have
a child by?

                    STELLA O.S.:
I have told you I love him.

                    BLANCHE O.S.:
Then I tremble for you! I just
tremble for you.

                    STELLA O.S.:
I can't help your trembling
if you insist on trembling.

                    ANOTHER PASSERBY:
You bowlin' tonight?

                    STANLEY:
E-yah --

                    BLANCHE O.S.:
If you'll forgive me -- he's
common!

                    STELLA O.S.:
Why, yes, I suppose he is.

Stanley's face darkens. He leans against the side of the house.

66.   KITCHEN

                    BLANCHE:
You're hating me for saying
this, aren't you?

                    STELLA:
                    (coldly)
Go on and say it all,
Blanche.

                    BLANCHE:
He acts like an animal! Has
an animal's habits. There's
even something -- something

BLANCHE: (Cont.)
ape-like about him! Thousands
and thousands of years have
passed him right by, and there
he is -- Stanley Kowalski --
Survivor of the Stone Age.
Bearing the raw meat home from
the jungle! And you -- you here,
here waiting for him!. . . . Night
falls, and the other apes gather --
There in the front of the cave --
his poker night you call it --
this party of apes! Somebody
growls - some creature snatches
at something -- the fight is
on! Maybe we are a long way
from being made in God's image,
but Stella, my sister -- there
has been some progress since
then -- Such things as art --
as poetry and music -- In some
kinds of people some tenderer
feelings have had some little
beginning! That we have to
make grow and cling to. In
this dark march toward whatever
it is we're approaching . . . don't --
don't hang back with the brutes!

The door slams. Stanley has entered. He sets the radio down.

STANLEY:
Stella. . . . Hiyuh, Blanche.
(he grins
at Blanche)

STELLA:
Looks like -- you got under the
car.

STANLEY:
Them darn mechanics at Fritz's
don't know their axle grease
from third base!

Slowly Stella moves past Blanche, then with a quick little run
she is in his arms.

                          STANLEY:
                          (as Stella throws
                          herself fiercely
                          at him)
              Hey!
                          (he swings her
                          up with his body)

67.   CLOSEUP   BLANCHE'S FACE

alarmed, left out.

                                              DISSOLVE TO:

68.   CLOSE SHOT   STELLA ON BLANCHE'S COT

It has been freshly covered and provided with new pillows. In
fact the entire corner of the room has been transformed into a
little personal corner for Blanche. Stella is lying there,
propped up, looking pregnant, sewing. There is a laugh O.S.

                          STELLA:
              What are you laughing at honey?

69.   THE OTHER SIDE OF THE ROOM

Blanche is writing at a table. This side of the room also has
been redecorated in a style definitely not Stanley's.

                          BLANCHE:
              Myself for being such a liar. I'm
              writing a letter to Shep. "Darling
              Shep, I'm spending the summer on the
              wing, making flying visits here and
              there. And who knows -- perhaps I
              shall take a sudden notion to sweep
              down on Dallas! How would you feel
              about that?
                          (laughs -- as if she
                          were actually talking
                          to Shep)
              Forewarned is forearmed, as they
              say!" How does that sound?

                          STELLA:
              Huh, huh.

BLANCHE:
"Most of my sister's friends go
north in the summer."

They are interrupted by a disturbance from above.

EUNICE'S VOICE:
I been on to you for a long time.
You and that blonde.

STEVE'S VOICE:
That's a lie. . . .

The girls look up. . . .

69A.   DOOR TO EUNICE'S FLAT

We are shooting through the screen door that is open.

STEVE:
Don't you throw that at me.

Suddenly the door to the apartment is thrown open and Steve
jumps out clad in his pajamas. As he closes the door a pot of
metal hits it. He leaps back into the room. There is the OS
sound of a blow, and immediately Eunice appears rubbing the
side of her upper leg!

EUNICE:
Call the police. I'm going to
call the police. . . .

STEVE'S VOICE:
Eunice you come back here.

EUNICE:
I'm going to call the police. . . .

Having reached the bottom of the stairs, she is crossing towards the gate of the courtyard. We see at this moment,
Stanley getting out of a station wagon. He slams the door,
saying, "Thanks, Mac," and walks towards us. . . .

EUNICE:
(as she goes by
Stanley)
He hit me. I'm going to call the
police.

Stanley pays her little mind. He has something on his mind and continues towards his flat. . . .

69B.   STELLA'S FLAT

The girls are laughing together. . . .

> STELLA:
> Some of your sister's friends have
> stayed in the city. . . .

The girls laugh again. At this moment Stanley appears in the doorway. The laughter suddenly dies out. Blanche takes off her glasses. Stella, trying to "cover" says:

> STELLA:
> Is Eunice getting the police?

> STANLEY:
> Nah, she's getting a drink at the
> Four Deuces!

> STELLA:
> That's much more practical.

Stanley has been taking in the newly redone room, and the disorder of feminine frillery. Now he starts on his way through the room.

> STELLA:
> Blanche is going to make new cur-
> tains too, Stanley.

Behind Stanley there is a rush at the door . . . he turns. . . .
Steve appears . . . now fully dressed.

> STEVE:
> She here. . . ?

69C.   CLOSE SHOT   STANLEY   (STEVE'S VIEWPOINT)

> STANLEY:
> At the Four Deuces.

Steve exits with an oath not heard. Stanley goes into the bedroom. He begins to fling things around and make a racket. We get the girls' reactions.

> STANLEY'S VOICE:
> Stella, I can't find my other shoes.

Stella hurries into the bedroom.

> STELLA'S VOICE:
> We cleaned in there -- I'll find
> them.

> STANLEY:
> (coming to the opening
> between the two rooms)
> I can't find anything anymore. . . .

He looks straight at Blanche.

70.   BLANCHE

> BLANCHE:
> What sign were you born under?

> STANLEY:
> Sign?

> BLANCHE:
> I bet you were born under Aries.
> Aries people dote on noise. They
> love to bang things around.

> STELLA'S VOICE:
> (from inside)
> Stanley was born just five minutes
> after Christmas.

> BLANCHE:
> Capricorn, the goat!

From inside we hear Stella laugh. Stanley does not laugh.
Stanley comes close to Blanche.

> STANLEY:
> Say, do you happen to know somebody
> named Shaw?
> (her face shows
> faint shock)

BLANCHE:
Why, everybody knows somebody
named Shaw.

STANLEY:
(leaning over the
table)
Well, this somebody named Shaw
is under the impression he met
you in Auriol but I figure he
must have got you mixed up with
some other party, because this
other party is someone he met at
a hotel called The Flamingo.
(he puts on his
tie)

BLANCHE:
(laughing breath-
lessly)
The Hotel Flamingo is not the
sort of place I would dare to be
seen in!
(she dabs cologne
on her temples)

STANLEY:
You know it?

BLANCHE:
I've seen it and smelled it.

STANLEY:
You must've got pretty close if
you could smell it.

BLANCHE:
The odor of cheap perfume is pene-
trating.

STANLEY:
That stuff you use is expensive?
(he takes her hand-
kerchief, smells
it, tosses it back)

BLANCHE:
Twelve dollars an ounce! That's

                    BLANCHE: (Cont.)
          just a hint, in case you want to
          remember my birthday.
                    (she speaks lightly,
                    but there is a note of
                    fear in her voice)

                    STANLEY:
          I figure he must have got you mixed
          up -- but he goes in and out of
          Auriol all the time so he can check
          on it.
                    (calls to Stella)
          I'll see you at the Four Deuces!

                    STELLA:
          Hey! Don't I rate a kiss?

                    STANLEY:
          Not in front of your sister.
                    (he goes out)

71.   ON THE VERANDA   STEVE AND EUNICE PASS HIM

Steve's arm is around Eunice and she is sobbing luxuriously
and he is cooing love words.

                    STEVE:
          I only do that with other girls
          because I love you, Baby.

As they go upstairs, a big clap of thunder.

72.   INT. STELLA'S FLAT   BEDROOM

Blanche running to Stella.

                    BLANCHE:
          Stella!

                    STELLA:
          Blanche, are you still frightened
          of thunder?

                    BLANCHE:
          Stella, what have people been
          telling you about me?

STELLA:
Telling?

BLANCHE:
Honey, there was quite a lot of
talk in Auriol.

STELLA:
People talk. Who cares?

BLANCHE:
I haven't been so good the last
year or so. Since Belle Reve
started to slip through my fingers.
I never was hard or self-sufficient
enough. Soft people, soft people have
got to court the favor of hard ones,
have got to shimmer and glow, put on
soft colors, the colors of butterfly
wings, and put a paper lantern over
the light just to create a little
temporary magic, to pay for protection.
That's why I haven't been so awfully
good lately. I've run for protection,
Stella, but I'm scared now, awfully
scared.

LIGHTNING. She clings to her sister.

BLANCHE:
I don't know how much longer I can
turn the trick. It isn't enough to
be soft -- you've got to be soft and
attractive -- and I'm fading now.

Stella goes to the icebox. She is frightened.

BLANCHE:
Have you been listening to me?

STELLA:
I never listen to you when you're
being morbid.

BLANCHE:
Is that coke for me?

STELLA:
Not for anyone else!

BLANCHE:
Why you precious lamb, you! Is
it just coke?

STELLA:
You mean you want a shot in it?

BLANCHE:
Well, honey, a shot never did a coke
any harm. Let me! You mustn't
wait on me.

STELLA:
I like to wait on you, Blanche.
It makes it seem more like home.

BLANCHE:
I have to admit I love to be
waited on. . . .

Suddenly, overwhelmed by an emotion, she runs into the bedroom.
Stella finishes pouring whiskey into the coke and follows
Blanche.

73.   BEDROOM

STELLA:
Blanche --

BLANCHE:
I know. You hate me to talk senti-
mental! But, believe me, honey, I
feel more than I tell you! I won't
stay long. I won't, I promise.
I'll go.

STELLA:
Blanche. . . .

BLANCHE:
        (hysterically)
I'll go soon! I won't hang around
until he -- throws me out. . . .

STELLA:
Now will you stop talking foolish. . . .

BLANCHE:
Yes, baby, yes! Watch how you pour

> BLANCHE: (Cont.)
> -- That fizzy stuff spills over.

Stella pours coke -- it overflows. Blanche gives a piercing
cry.

> STELLA:
> (shocked by the cry)
> Heavens!

> BLANCHE:
> Right on my pretty white skirt.

> STELLA:
> Oh. . . . Use my hanky. Blot it
> gently, gently.

> BLANCHE:
> I know . . . gently -- gently --

> STELLA:
> Did it stain?

> BLANCHE:
> Not a bit. Ha-ha! Isn't that lucky?

> STELLA:
> Why did you scream like that --

> BLANCHE:
> I don't know why I screamed . . . Mitch . . .
> Mitch is coming at seven. I guess I
> am a little nervous about our relations.
> He hasn't gotten anything more than a
> good night kiss. I want his respect,
> Stella, and men don't want anything
> they get too easy. But on the other
> hand men lose interest quickly, especially
> when a girl is over thirty.
> (she laughs)
> Whenever I mentioned marriage -- they
> forgot my telephone number. They didn't
> even remember where I lived. So you see,
> I haven't informed him of my real age. . . .

> STELLA:
> Why are you so sensitive about your age?

> BLANCHE:
> Because of hard knocks my vanity's been
> given. What I mean is -- he thinks I'm
> sort of prim and proper. You know . . .
> I want to deceive him just enough to
> make him want me.

> STELLA:
> Blanche, do you want him?

> BLANCHE:
> I want to rest. I want to breathe
> quietly again. Yes -- I <u>want</u> Mitch
> very badly! Just think! <u>If</u> it happens!
> I can go away from here and not be
> anyone's problem.

> STANLEY:
> (o.s.)
> Hey, Steve . . . Hey, Eunice. Hey,
> Stella!

There are joyous calls from Steve and Eunice o.s.

> STELLA:
> It <u>will</u> happen.

> BLANCHE:
> It will. . . ?

> STELLA:
> It will! It will, honey, it will.
> (she kisses Blanche's head)
> But don't take another drink.

Stella goes to meet her husband.

74.   EXT. THE VERANDA AND FOOT OF THE STAIRS   LATE AFTERNOON

As Stella comes out, Eunice shrieks with laughter and runs
down the stairs. Steve bounds after her with goat-like cries.
Stanley looks at Stella and laughs. Then he puts his arm
around her waist. She pulls away and follows after Eunice and
Steve. Stanley follows.

75.   INSIDE FLAT   BLANCHE

sitting on the floor, fanning herself. We HEAR church bells.
Evening is coming. Suddenly Blanche gives a great stretch of
loneliness and hunger of love.

                    BLANCHE:
          Ah me, ah me, ah me. . . !

At this moment of longing, the doorbell rings. . . . She
crosses and looks, and there in the doorway is a handsome young
man of twenty. He might very well look like her husband.

                    COLLECTOR:
          Good evening, ma'am.

                    BLANCHE:
          Well, well! What can I do for you?

                    COLLECTOR:
          I'm collecting for the Evening Star.

                    BLANCHE:
          I didn't know that stars took up
          collections.

                    COLLECTOR:
          It's the paper, ma'am.

                    BLANCHE:
          I know -- I was joking -- feebly.
          Will you -- have a drink?

                    COLLECTOR:
          No, ma'am. No thank you. I can't
          drink on the job.

                    BLANCHE:
               (taking her purse)
          Oh, well, now let me see. No. I
          haven't got a dime. I'm not the
          lady of the house. I'm her sister
          from Mississippi. I'm one of those
          poor relations you've heard tell about.

                    COLLECTOR:
          That's all right, ma'am -- I'll drop
          by later.
               (he starts out)

                    BLANCHE:
Hey!

The young man turns.

                    BLANCHE:
Have you got a light?

                    COLLECTOR:
Sure.
        (produces a lighter)
This doesn't always work.

                    BLANCHE:
It's temperamental?
        (lighter flares)
Ah, thank you.

                    COLLECTOR:
        (moving away)
Thank you!

                    BLANCHE:
Hey!
        (he pauses)
What time is it?

                    COLLECTOR:
Fifteen of seven, ma'am.

                    BLANCHE:
So late? Don't you just love
these long rainy afternoons in
New Orleans when an hour isn't just
an hour -- but a little piece of
Eternity dropped in your hands --
and who knows what to do with it?
        (touching his shoulders)
You -- uh -- didn't get caught in
the rain?

                    COLLECTOR:
No, ma'am. I stepped inside.

                    BLANCHE:
In a drug store? And had a soda?

                    COLLECTOR:
Uh-huh.

BLANCHE:
Chocolate?

COLLECTOR:
No, ma'am. Cherry.

BLANCHE:
(laughs)
Cherry!

COLLECTOR:
A cherry soda.

BLANCHE:
You make my mouth water.
(she goes to the trunk)

COLLECTOR:
(starting out)
Well, I'd better be going --

BLANCHE:
(stopping him)
Young man!
(she takes a large
gossamer scarf
from the trunk)
Young, young, young, young -- man!
Did anyone ever tell you that you
look like a young prince out of
the Arabian Nights?

COLLECTOR:
No, ma'am.

BLANCHE:
Well, you do, honey lamb. Come
here! Come on over here like
I told you!

She drapes herself in the scarf; gripping his arms, looking
into his face, her expression one of almost ineffable sweetness.

BLANCHE:
I want to kiss you -- just once --
softly and sweetly on your mouth. . . .
(she does)
Run along now quickly. It would

BLANCHE: (Cont.)
be nice to keep you, but I've got
to be good and keep my hands off
children.
>   (he goes, rather
>   dazed, to the door)
Adios!

76.   THE VERANDA

>   COLLECTOR:
>   (looking back)
Huh?

>   BLANCHE:
>   (gaily -- from
>   the doorway)
Why look who's here!   My Rosen-
kavalier!

Mitch enters, carrying a tight little bunch of flowers which he
offers.

>   BLANCHE:
No.   Bow to me first!

He is embarrassed. Shakes his head. She is adamant. He looks
around to see if anyone is watching, then ducks a quick little
bow, the flowers extended to Blanche.

>   BLANCHE:
And now present them!
>   (he does. She
>   curtseys low)
Ahhhh! Merciiiii!

>   FADE OUT.

77.   AN OPEN PAVILLION ON LAKE PONTCHARTRAIN

Couples are waiting between dances. The Music begins. They
couple. Blanche and Mitch are seen coming towards us. The
impression is that they are not ideal dancing partners. They
look rather guiltily at each other. We PULL BACK with them,
revealing a piece of the railing along the edge of the
Pavillion.

MITCH:
I'm afraid that you haven't
gotten much fun out of this
evening, Blanche.

BLANCHE:
I spoiled it for you.

MITCH:
No you didn't. . . .

BLANCHE:
I don't think I've ever tried
so hard to be gay and made such
a dismal mess of it. I get ten
points for trying. I did try.

MITCH:
Why did you try if you didn't
feel like it, Blanche?

BLANCHE:
I was just obeying the law of
nature.

MITCH:
Which law is that?

BLANCHE:
The law that says the lady must
entertain the gentleman or no
dice.
        (she looks up. They're
        at the rail)
Hello Moon. . . . I am looking for the
Pleides. The seven sisters -- but
those girls are not out tonight.
Oh yes, they are! There they are --
God bless them -- all in a bunch,
going home from their little
bridge party. . . .

MITCH:
May I kiss you, Blanche?

BLANCHE:
Why do you always ask me if you may?

MITCH:
I don't know whether you want me
to or not.

BLANCHE:
Why should you be so doubtful. . . .

MITCH:
That night when we parked by the
lake and I kissed you, you. . . .

BLANCHE:
Honey, it wasn't the kiss I objected
to. I liked the kiss very much. It
was the other little familiarity that
I felt obliged to discourage. I didn't
resent it. Not a bit in the world.
In fact, I was somewhat flattered that
you desired me. But honey, you know
as well as I do, that a single girl,
a girl alone in the world has got to
keep a firm hold on her emotions or
she'll be lost. . . .

MITCH:
Lost.

BLANCHE:
I guess you're used to girls that
like to get lost. . . .

MITCH:
I like you to be exactly the way that
you are, because in all my -- experience
-- I have never known anyone like you. . . .

Blanche laughs.

MITCH:
Are you laughing at me?

BLANCHE:
No, no, no honey, I'm not laughing
at you.
     (she takes his hand)
Come on, let's finish our drink. . . .
We've both been so anxious and solemn

BLANCHE: (Cont.)
tonight that for these last remaining
moments of our lives together I want
to create -- joie de vivre. . . . We're
going to pretend that we are sitting
in a little artists cafe on the left
bank in Paris. Je suis la Dame aux
Camellias. Vous êtes Armand. Do
you understand French?

MITCH:
No . . . no, I don't.

BLANCHE:
Why don't you sit down . . . take off
your coat -- loosen your collar.

MITCH:
I better leave it on.

BLANCHE:
I want you to be comfortable. . . .

MITCH:
No, I'm ashamed of the way I perspire.
My shirt's stickin' to me. . . .

BLANCHE:
Perspiration is healthy. If people
didn't perspire they would die in
five minutes. This is a nice coat!
What kind of material is it?

MITCH:
They call this stuff alpaca.

BLANCHE:
Oh, alpaca!

MITCH:
It's very light weight alpaca.

BLANCHE:
Oh, light weight alpaca.

MITCH:
I don't like to wear a wash coat even
in summer because I sweat through it.

BLANCHE:

Oh. . . .

MITCH:

And it don't look neat on me. A man
with a heavy build has got to be careful of what he puts on him so that he
don't look too clumsy.

BLANCHE:

You're not too heavy.

MITCH:

You don't think I am?

BLANCHE:

You're not the delicate type. You have
a massive bone structure and a very im-
posing physique.

MITCH:

I thank you. . . . Last Christmas I was
given a membership in the New Orleans
Sports Club.

BLANCHE:

Oh . . . good.

MITCH:

It was the finest present I ever was
given. I work out there with the
weights. And I swim and I keep myself
fit. When I started there I was soft
in the belly, but now my belly is hard.
It's so hard now that a man can punch
me in the belly and it don't hurt me.
Punch me! Go on!

She punches lightly at him.

BLANCHE:

Gracious!

MITCH:

See? . . . Blanche, guess how much
I weigh?

> BLANCHE:
> Oh, I'd say in the vicinity of
> one hundred and eighty pounds.

> MITCH:
> Oh, no -- Guess again.

> BLANCHE:
> Not so much?

> MITCH:
> No -- more. . . . I weigh two hundred and
> seven pounds and I'm six feet one
> and one half inches tall in my bare
> feet -- without shoes on. And that is
> what I weigh stripped!

> BLANCHE:
> Oh, my goodness! That's awe-inspiring.

> MITCH:
> (embarrassed)
> My weight is not a very interesting
> subject to talk about.
> (a pause)
> What's yours?

> BLANCHE:
> You guess!

> MITCH:
> Let me lift you!

> BLANCHE:
> Samson! . . . Go on -- lift me!

Mitch lifts her -- holds her up.

> MITCH:
> You're as light as a feather.

He lowers her, but keeps his hands on her waist.

> BLANCHE:
> You may release me now.

> MITCH:
> Huh?

BLANCHE:
I said -- unhand me, sir!
        (he crudely embraces
        her)
Mitch, we're in public! Mitch!

MITCH:
Just give me a slap when I step
out of bounds.

BLANCHE:
That won't be necessary. You're a
natural gentleman, one of the very
few that are left in the world. I
don't want you to think that I'm
old-maid schoolteacherish or anything
like that. It's just -- well -- I
guess it's just that I have old-
fashioned ideals.

He slowly releases her and walks away from her, goes to the
rail and puts one foot on it. She follows.

MITCH:
        (his voice strained)
Where did Stanley and Stella go tonight?

BLANCHE:
I think they were going to a midnight
prevue.

MITCH:
We should all go out together some
night.

BLANCHE:
        (avoiding his suggestion)
You are an old friend of Stanley's?

MITCH:
We was together in the Two Forty-
First.

BLANCHE:
Has he talked to you about me?

MITCH:
Not very much.

BLANCHE:
The way you say that, I suspect that
he has.

MITCH:
Don't you get along with him?

BLANCHE:
What do you think?

MITCH:
I think he don't understand you.

BLANCHE:
That is putting it mildly.
Surely he must have told you how
much he hates me!

She walks down the pier as if alone. Mitch following.

79.   THE PIER   IT IS NARROW-RICKETY   CLOSE TO THE MISTY WATER

MITCH:
I don't think he hates you.

BLANCHE:
He hates me -- or why would he
insult me? The first time I
laid eyes on him, I thought to
myself -- that man is my execut-
ioner! That man will destroy me!

She moves away from him on a wave of feeling. He holds a moment, looking after her. He is very moved by her plight.

MITCH:
Blanche. . . . Blanche. . . .

BLANCHE:
Yes, honey?

MITCH:
Can I ask you a question?

BLANCHE:
Yes -- what?

MITCH:
How old . . .
        (gently)
are you?

BLANCHE:
Why do you want to know that?

MITCH:
I talked to my mother about you
and she said, "How old is Blanche?"

BLANCHE:
You talked to your mother about
me?

MITCH:
Yes.

BLANCHE:
Why?

MITCH:
Because I told her how nice you
were, and I liked you.

BLANCHE:
Were you sincere about that?

MITCH:
You know I was.

* * *

BLANCHE:
Why did your mother want to know my age?

MITCH:
Mother is sick.

BLANCHE:
I'm sorry to hear that -- Badly?

MITCH:
She won't live long -- maybe just a
few months, and she worries because
I'm not settled down before she is --
        (his voice is hoarse
        with emotion)

                    BLANCHE:
You love her very much, don't
you?

Mitch nods miserably.

                    BLANCHE:
I think you have a great capacity
for devotion. You'll be lonely
when she passes on, won't you?

Mitch looks at her, nods.

                    BLANCHE:
I know what that means.

                    MITCH:
          (incredulous)
To be lonely?

                    BLANCHE:
I loved someone, and the person
I loved, I lost.

                    MITCH:
Dead? A man?

                    BLANCHE:
He was a boy, just a boy, when
I was a very young girl. When
I was sixteen I made the discovery, love -- All at once and
much, much too completely.
          (moonlight falls full
          on her face for moment;
          then is clouded again)
-- It was like you suddenly turned
a blinding light on something that
had always been half in shadow --
That's how it struck the world
for me. . . . But I was -- unlucky --
deluded. There was something about
the boy -- a nervousness, a tenderness, an uncertainty. And I didn't
understand. I didn't understand
why this boy that wrote poetry
didn't seem to be able to do anything else. Lost every job. He

BLANCHE: (Cont.)
came to me for help. I didn't know
that. I didn't know anything except
that I loved him unendurably. And
that I had failed him in some
mysterious way. We were very young.
Oh! And his poems -- they all came
back -- little white cards saying
'sorry'. He became silent with me.
At night I pretended to sleep and
I heard him crying. Crying -- the
way a lost child cries.

MITCH:
I don't understand.

BLANCHE:
No. Neither did I -- that's why --
I killed him --

MITCH:
You -- !

BLANCHE:
     (tearing violently
     at the vines)
We drove out one night to a place
called Moon Lake Casino. . . .
     (fade in Varsouviana)
We danced the Varsouviana. Suddenly,
in the middle of the dance floor, the
boy I had married broke away from me
and ran out of the casino. A few
moments later, a shot!
     (Varsouviana cuts off
     abruptly)
-- I ran out, all did, all ran out and
gathered about the terrible thing on
the edge of the lake.
     (her speech becomes
     breathless)
-- Somebody caught my arm. "Don't go
any closer, come back. You don't
want to see!" -- See? See what! --
Then I heard voices say, "Allan,
Allan, the Grey boy!" -- He'd stuck
a revolver in his mouth and fired! --
So that the back of his head had been --

> BLANCHE: (Cont.)
> blown away. . . .
> > (Varsouviana again,
> > building)
> -- It was because on the dance floor,
> unable to stop myself, I'd said to
> the boy, "You're weak. I've lost
> respect for you. I can't pretend
> that I haven't." -- And then the search-
> light that had been turned on the world
> was turned off again and never for one
> moment since has there been any light
> stronger than that yellow lamp.

Mitch goes to her, stands behind her.

> MITCH:
> You need somebody. And I need some-
> body, too. Could it be you and me,
> Blanche?

She turns to him. They embrace, kiss. CUT VARSOUVIANA.

> BLANCHE:
> Sometimes -- there's God -- so quickly.

> DISSOLVE TO:

80. CLOSE SHOT   MITCH

He is in a rage and is being held back by the group of workers,
among them Pablo, who are having difficulty restraining them
from rushing at the CAMERA.

> MITCH:
> Lemme go! I'm going to kill
> you! I'm going to kill you!
> Lemme go -- do you hear -- lemme
> go!

80A. SHOOTING PAST MITCH AND THE GROUP OF WORKING MEN WHO ARE
RESTRAINING HIM --

-- we see Stanley standing alone and at a little distance behind and near him a circle of men have paused at work at their
machines, watching the disturbance.

STANLEY:
Go on -- turn him loose! Go on --
turn him loose! Let him go -- I'm
ready!

FIRST MAN:
(holding Mitch --
simultaneously)
Come on, Mitch -- come on, Mitch!
Let's get out of here -- cool off!

MITCH:
(to the men holding
him)
I'm going to kill him!

STANLEY:
You're going to kill who? You're
too dumb to even know when you're
gettin' wisened up!

MITCH:
Lies! Everyone of 'em -- lies!

STANLEY:
You don't believe me -- ?

MITCH:
No.

STANLEY:
Ask Harry Shaw!

MITCH:
No -- !

STANLEY:
Call up Kiefaber in Auriol.

MITCH:
I don't have to call him up!

STANLEY:
All right -- don't call anybody!

A Foreman enters from the rear and yells:

FOREMAN:
Come on -- cut it out. Fight on
your own time! Let's go -- let's
make a buck around here!

Silence. The men turn, start back to their machines. Stanley
takes a couple of steps toward Mitch and says:

STANLEY:
Okay -- go ahead and marry her --
only hurry it up -- because she's
been in my house for five months
now and her time is up!

Stanley turns and walks away. As he does the machines start
going loud and fast. Mitch turns and walks into a HEAD SIZE
CLOSEUP IN CAMERA.

81.   CLOSE SHOT   BLANCHE   BATHROOM

She is singing as she dries her hair. "PAPER MOON." She
reaches for something. She can't find it. She looks around,
then steps out of the bathroom into the bedroom.

82.   BEDROOM

She spies her glass, full of ice and drink, and she crosses to
it. As she does so, she passes by the opening to the front
room. There she sees Stanley and Stella, who look like they
have been interrupted in an intense conversation.

BLANCHE:
Hello, Stanley.
(her tone is so gay
that it is almost mocking)

She returns to the bathroom, singing. We stay with Stanley and
Stella.

83.   KITCHEN

STANLEY:
Some canary bird. . . .

STELLA:
Now please tell me quietly what

STELLA: (Cont.)
you think you've found out about
my sister.

STANLEY:
You know your Sister Blanche is
no Lily.

STELLA:
What have you heard and from whom?

STANLEY:
That line she's been feeding Mitch.
Our supply man down at the plant
knows all about her and everybody
in the town of Auriol knows about
her. She is as famous in Auriol as
if she was President of the United
States, only she is not respected
by any party.

84.   CLOSE OF BLANCHE IN FRONT OF MIRROR   HAPPY

She is brushing her hair up to fluff it, as she sings:

BLANCHE:
"It's only a paper moon.
Shining over a cardboard sea . . .
But it wouldn't be make-believe
If you believed in me."

85.   THE KITCHEN

STANLEY:
So she moved to the Flamingo, a
second-class hotel which has the
advantage of not interfering with
the private social life of the
personalities there. The Flamingo
is used to all kinds of goings on. . . .
But even the management of the
Flamingo was impressed by Dame Blanche.
In fact they were so impressed they
requested her to turn in her room key --
for permanently. This happened a
couple of weeks before she showed here.

> BLANCHE'S VOICE:
> (o.s.)
> It's a Barnum and Bailey world --
> Just as phoney as it can be.
> But it wouldn't be make-believe,
> If you believed in me."

During this Stella walks away towards the verandah. Stanley
follows Stella out.

86. THE VERANDAH

> STANLEY:
> Sure, I can see how you would be
> upset by this. She pulled the wool
> over your eyes as much as Mitch's.

> STELLA:
> It's pure invention. There's not . . .

> STANLEY:
> Honey, I checked every single story.
> The trouble with Dame Blanche was that
> she couldn't put on her act any more
> in Auriol. They got wised up after two
> or three dates with her and they quit,
> and she goes on to another, the same
> old line, the same old act, the
> same old honey! And as time went
> by, she became the town character.
> Regarded as not just different,
> but downright loco -- nuts.

> BLANCHE'S VOICE O.S.:
> "It's only a paper moon,
> Just as phoney as it can be
> But it wouldn't be make-believe
> If you believed in me!"

87. KITCHEN

Stanley still following Stella.

> STANLEY:
> Which brings me to lie number two.

STANLEY: (Cont.)
She didn't resign temporarily because
of her nerves! No siree, bob! She
didn't. She was kicked out before
the Spring term ended because she
got mixed up with a seventeen-year-
old boy. Well . . . when the boy's dad
learned about it and got in touch
with the High School superintendent. . . .
It was practically a town ordinance
passed against her.

88. THE BATHROOM

door is suddenly thrown open. Clouds of steam pour out.
Blanche thrusts her head out.

BLANCHE:
(in doorway)
Stella!

STELLA:
Yes, Blanche.

BLANCHE:
Can I have another bath towel to
dry my hair with? I just washed it.

STELLA:
Yes, honey.

She crosses to where the towels are kept, going past Stanley
who mutters.

STANLEY:
Her Majesty.

She takes the towel to Blanche.

89. BEDROOM

BLANCHE:
What's the matter, honey?

STELLA:
Matter? Why?

>   BLANCHE:
> You have such a strange expression
> on your face.

>   STELLA:
> Oh . . . I guess I'm a little tired. . . .

>   BLANCHE:
> Why don't you take a nice hot bath
> as soon as I get out?

>   STANLEY:
> How long is that going to be,
> Blanche?

>   BLANCHE:
> Not so terribly long. Possess
> your soul in patience!

>   STANLEY:
> It's not my soul I'm worried about.

Blanche laughs gaily, closes the door.

90.   KITCHEN

as Stella returns.

>   STANLEY:
> Well?

Stella doesn't answer. Crosses to the cake and begins to put
the candles on it.

>   STANLEY:
> How many candles you sticking in
> that cake?

>   STELLA:
> I'll stop at twenty-five.

>   STANLEY:
> Is company expected?

>   STELLA:
> We asked Mitch to come over.

STANLEY:
    (uncomfortably)
Don't expect Mitch over tonight.

STELLA:

<u>Why</u>?

STANLEY:
Stella, Mitch and I were in the
same outfit together; the Two Forty-
First Engineers. We work in the same
plant, and now on the same Bowling-

STELLA:
Stanley Kowalski, did you . . . did you
repeat what . . . that . . . ?

STANLEY:
You bet your life I told him! I'd
have it on my conscience the rest of
my life if I knew all that stuff and
let my best friend get caught.

STELLA:
Is Mitch thru with her?

Blanche's voice is lifted again, serene as a bell.

STANLEY:
I don't know if he's thru with her
or not -- but he's wised up. . . .

STELLA:
But Stanley -- Mitch was going to --
to marry her.

STANLEY:
Well, he's not going to marry her
now. He's not going to jump in a
tank with a school of sharks. . . .

STELLA:
What'll she do . . . what on earth
will she -- do?

STANLEY:
Her future is mapped out for her.

                          STELLA:
            What do you mean?

91.   BEDROOM

Without answer Stanley crosses over to the bathroom door and
pounds on it.

                          STANLEY:
            Hey, canary bird! Toots! Get
            out of the bathroom!

The bathroom door flies open, and Blanche emerges with a gay
laugh. Stanley brushes past her, enters the bathroom, and
closes the door. Blanche is left at the threshold. She shakes
her head with mock sadness about Stanley, and then laughs. . . .

                          BLANCHE:
            Oh, I feel so good after my long
            hot bath! I feel so good and cool
            and rested!

She brushes her hair and twirls around the room in a movement
reminiscent of the one she did before Mitch the first time they
met, on the night of the poker party.

O.S. Stella watching . . . troubled . . . she ducks away.

                                      DISSOLVE TO:

92.   KITCHEN

THE BIRTHDAY PARTY IS SET UP. Stella, Stanley and Blanche are
completing a dismal birthday dinner. Stanley is chewing sullenly on a chicken bone, etc. Stella is embarrassed and sad.
Blanche has a tight artificial smile. Mitch's place is empty.

                          BLANCHE:
            Stanley, tell us a joke. Tell us a
            funny little story to make us all
            laugh. . . . It's the first time in my
            entire experience with men, and I've
            had a good deal of all sorts, that
            I've actually been stood up by any-
            body! I don't know how to take it.
            Tell us a funny story, Stanley.
            Just to help us out!

                STANLEY:
           (licking his fingers)
     I didn't think you liked my stories,
     Blanche.

                BLANCHE:
     I like them when they're amusing,
     but not indecent.

                STANLEY:
     I don't know any refined enough
     for your taste.

                BLANCHE:
     Well -- then let me tell one.

                STELLA:
     Yes, Blanche. You used to know
     lots of good stories.

                BLANCHE:
     Let me see now. I have to run
     through my repertoire. . . . Do you
     all like parrot stories? Well,
     this one is about the old maid who
     had a parrot that cursed a blue
     streak and knew more vulgar expressions
     than Mr. Kowalski.
           (she pauses, smiling at
           Stanley. No reaction)
     And the only way to hush the parrot
     up was to put the cover back --

A phone rings distantly.

                BLANCHE:
           (springs up, listening)
     Oh, that must be upstairs.
           (she sits)

                STELLA:
     Go on, Blanche.

                BLANCHE:
     Mr. Kowalski will not be amused.

                STELLA:
     Mr. Kowalski is too busy making a

STELLA: (Cont.)
pig of himself to think of anything else.
    (to Stanley, viciously)
Your face and your fingers are
disgustingly greasy. Go and wash
up and then help me clear the table.

Stanley hurls a plate to the floor.

STANLEY:
That's how I'll clear the table.
    (on his feet, angrily)
Don't ever talk that way to me!
"Pig -- Polack -- disgusting -- vulgar --
greasy!" -- them kind of words have
been on your tongue and your sister's
too much around here! What do you
two think you are. A pair of queens?
Remember what Huey Long said --
"Every Man is a King." And I am the
king around here, so don't you forget
it!

He hurls a cup and saucer to the floor.

STANLEY:
My place is cleared! You want me
to clear your places?

He stalks out onto the verandah.

BLANCHE:
Stella, what happened while I was
bathing? What did he tell you,
Stella?

STELLA:
Nothing, nothing, nothing.

BLANCHE:
I think he told you something
about Mitch and me! You know
why Mitch didn't come.

Stella shakes her head helplessly.

BLANCHE:
I'm going to call him.

                    STELLA:
    I wouldn't call him, Blanche.

                    BLANCHE:
            (going to the phone)
    Yes I am, I'm going to call him
    on the phone. I intend to be given
    some explanation from someone!

Blanche starts dialing. Stella looks at her miserably then
slowly exits onto the verandah.

93.   EXT. VERANDAH   OUTSIDE STELLA'S FLAT

Stanley is smoking a cigarette. Stella comes out.

                    STELLA:
    I hope you're pleased with your
    doings. I never had so much
    trouble swallowing food in my
    life, looking at that girl's face
    and the empty chair!

                    BLANCHE'S VOICE O.S.:
    Hello . . . Mr. Mitchell please.
    Oh . . . I would like to leave a
    number if I may. Tulane 2121.
    And say it's important. Yes, very
    important. . . . Thank you. . . .

Stella cries quietly. Stanley takes her in his arms.

                    STANLEY:
    Stella, it's gonna be all right
    after she goes and after you've
    had the baby. It's gonna be all
    right again between you and me the
    way it was. You remember the way
    it was? Ah honey, it's gonna be
    sweet just like it used to be.
    We'll get those colored lights
    going again -- the two of us --
    with nobody's sister behind the
    curtain.

O.S. the sound of bellowing laughter comes from the Hubbell's
apartment. Stanley and Stella look up.

                         STANLEY:
                      (chuckling)
                  Steve an' Eunice. . . .

                         STELLA:
                      (warming to him)
                  Come on back in.

She starts back into the kitchen.

94.   INT. KITCHEN   FULL SHOT

Stella enters and starts lighting the candles on the birthday
cake.

                         STELLA:
                  Blanche?

                         BLANCHE:
                      (entering from the bedroom)
                  Yes. Oh, those pretty, pretty candles.
                  Oh, don't burn them, Stella.

                         STELLA:
                  I certainly will.

Stanley enters from the veranda. He picks up pieces of dishes.

                         BLANCHE:
                  No, you ought to save them for baby's
                  birthdays. Oh, I hope candles are
                  going to glow in his life and I hope
                  that his eyes are going to be like
                  candles, like two blue candles
                  lighted in a white cake!

                         STANLEY:
                  What poetry!
                      (he crosses to bedroom door)

                         BLANCHE:
                  I shouldn't have called him. . . .

                         STANLEY:
                  Hey, Blanche, you know it's hot
                  in here with the steam from the
                  bathroom.

BLANCHE:
 (exploding)
I've said I was sorry three times.
I take hot baths for my nerves. Hydro-
therapy, they call it. You healthy
Polack, without a nerve in your body,
how could you possibly know what
anxiety feels like!

STANLEY:
I am not a Polack. People from
Poland are Poles, not Polacks. But
what I am is one hundred percent
American, born and raised in the
greatest country on earth and proud
of it, so don't ever call me a Polack.

The phone RINGS, Blanche rises expectantly.

BLANCHE:
That's for me, I'm sure.

STANLEY:
I'm not sure. You just keep your
seat.
 (answers the phone)
H'lo. Aw. Yeh, hello, Mac.

Blanche has followed and hovers near Stanley, hoping it is for
her. Stella comes up beside her, touches her sympathetically.

BLANCHE:
 (turning on her)
Oh, keep your hands off me, Stella.
What is the matter with you? Why do
you look at me with that pitying look?

STANLEY:
 (bawling as he
 turns on them)
Will you shut up in there!
 (then into phone)
We've got a noisy woman on the place.
No, I don't wanta bowl at Riley's.
I had a little trouble with Riley
last week. I'm the team captain,
ain't I? All right, then, we're not
gonna bowl at Riley's, we're gonna

          STANLEY: (Cont.)
bowl at the West Side or the Gala. . . .
See you!

He hangs up and returns to the table. He reaches in a pocket,
speaks with false amiability.

          STANLEY:
Sister Blanche, I've got a little
birthday remembrance for you.

          BLANCHE:
Oh, have you, Stanley? I wasn't
expecting any.

          STANLEY:
       (holding a little
       envelope toward her)
I hope you like it.

          BLANCHE:
Why, why -- why, it's a --

          STANLEY:
Ticket! . . . Back to Auriol. On the
bus! Tuesday!

The Varsouviana music steals softly in, o.s. Stella rises
abruptly and turns her back. Blanche tries to smile, then she
tries to laugh. Then she gives up both and springs up from the
table. She gasps, sways, then stumbling against furniture,
moves to bedroom.

          STELLA:
You didn't need to do that.

          STANLEY:
Don't forget all that I took
off her.

          STELLA:
You needn't have been so cruel
to someone alone as she is.

          STANLEY:
Delicate she is.

STELLA:
She is. She was. You didn't
know Blanche as a girl. Nobody,
nobody, was tender and trusting
as she was. But people like you
abused her, and forced her to
change.

* * *   STANLEY:
Oh look out will you.

He turns from her, goes to the bureau, and gets his bowling
shirt. Stella follows him.

STELLA:
Do you think you're going
bowling now?

STANLEY:
Sure.

STELLA:
You're not going bowling.
(she catches hold
of his shirt)
Why did you do this to her?

STANLEY:
Let go of my shirt.
(he tries to twist
out of her grasp,
but Stella holds on
and the shirt tears)
You've torn it.

STELLA:
I want to know why? Tell me why?

STANLEY:
(seizing her roughly)
When we first met, me and you,
you thought I was common. How
right you was, baby. I was common
as dirt! You showed me the snap-
shot of the place with the columns.
I pulled you down off them columns
and how you loved it, having them
colored lights going! And wasn't

                              STANLEY: (Cont.)
                    we happy together, wasn't it all
                    okay till she showed here?

He releases her and she turns and walks away from him her body
tense with pain. She reaches for the back of a chair steadying
herself.

                              STANLEY:
                    And wasn't we happy together?
                    Wasn't it all okay until she
                    showed here? Hoity-toity --
                    describing me like an ape.
                              (he suddenly notices
                              the change in Stella)
                    Hey, what is it, Stel? Did I hurt
                    you? What's a matter, baby?

He has crossed to her, is holding her arms to steady her.

                              STELLA:
                         (quietly)
                    Take me to the hospital.

Stanley's arm goes around her supporting her.

                                             FADE OUT.

FADE IN

95.   INT. KITCHEN   STELLA'S FLAT   FULL SHOT   NIGHT

Blanche is on the floor, her head resting in the lap of the
chair, but she is deep in a troubled sleep now. Her hair is
tousled, the bottle of whiskey is empty. O.S. we hear the
Varsouviana ghostly and far away, as Blanche would hear it,
tangling through her dreams. Suddenly there is a LOUD, PREEMP-
TORY KNOCKING at the door. Blanche stirs uneasily. The Varsouviana stops. The KNOCKING CONTINUES. Blanche opens her
eyes, startled and confused.

                              BLANCHE:
                    Who is it, please?

96.   EXT. STELLA'S FLAT   FULL SHOT   MITCH   NIGHT

at the door. He is dressed as we saw him in the plant, and is

unshaved. His face shows all the agony he has gone through in
the last few hours.

>   MITCH:
>   Me. Mitch.

97.   INT. KITCHEN   FULL SHOT

>   BLANCHE:
>   Mitch! -- Just a minute.

She rushes about frantically, hiding the bottle in a closet,
crouching at the mirror and dabbing her face with cologne and
powder. . . . She is so excited that her breath is audible as
she dashes about. At last she rushes to the door and lets him
in.

>   BLANCHE:
>   (as he comes in)
>   Mitch! -- Y'know, I really shouldn't
>   let you in after the treatment I
>   have received from you this evening!
>   So utterly uncavalier! But hello,
>   beautiful!

She offers him her lips. He ignores her and pushes past her
into the flat.

>   BLANCHE:
>   My, my what a cold shoulder!
>   And such uncouth apparel! Why,
>   you haven't even shaved! But I
>   forgive you. I forgive you because
>   it's such a relief to see you. You've
>   stopped that polka tune that I had
>   caught in my head. Have you ever
>   had anything caught in your head?
>   No, of course not, you dumb angel-puss,
>   you'd never get anything awful caught
>   in your head!

He has stalked into the bedroom through the alcove, Blanche
following him and talking as he stares at her.

>   MITCH:
>   Do we have to have that fan on?

                         BLANCHE:
No.

                         MITCH:
I don't like fans.

                         BLANCHE:
Then let's turn it off, honey.
I'm not partial to them!
          (she presses the switch
          -- turning it off)
I don't know what there is to
drink. I -- haven't investigated.
          (she starts for kitchen)

                         MITCH:
I don't want Stan's liquor.

                         BLANCHE:
It isn't Stan's. Some things on the
premises are actually mine! . . . How is
your mother? Is your mother well?

                         MITCH:
Why?

                         BLANCHE:
Something's the matter tonight, but
never mind. I won't cross-examine
the witness. I'll just. . . .
          (she touches her forehead
          vaguely. O.S. the Varsou-
          viana STARTS UP AGAIN)
-- pretend I don't notice anything different about you. That -- music again. . . .

                         MITCH:
What music?

                         BLANCHE:
The polka tune they were playing
when Allan --

O.S. we HEAR a distant REVOLVER SHOT.

                         BLANCHE:
There, the shot! It always stops
after that.

BLANCHE: (Cont.)
    (the polka MUSIC
    DIES out)
Yes, now it's stopped.

        MITCH:
Are you boxed out of your mind?

        BLANCHE:
I'll go and see what I can find
in the way of. . . .
        (she has crossed to the
        closet and found a
        glass and bottle)
Oh, by the way, forgive me for not
being dressed. But I'd practically
given you up! Had you forgotten
your invitation to supper?

        MITCH:
I wasn't going to see you any more.

        BLANCHE:
Wait a minute. I can't hear what
you're saying, and you talk so seldom
that when you do say something, I don't
want to miss a single syllable of it!
What am I looking for around here?
Oh, yes, liquor. Here's something.
Southern Cheer. What can that be I wonder?
        (she comes to him
        with the liquor)
Take your foot off the bed. This room
is almost dainty now. I want to keep
it that way.

        MITCH:
Aren't you leaving here pretty soon?

        BLANCHE:
I wonder if this ought to be mixed with
something? But it's sweet, terribly
sweet. It's a liqueur, that's what it is.
I don't think you'll like it, but maybe
you will, try it.

        MITCH:
I told you already I don't want none of

MITCH: (Cont.)
his liquor. He says you been lapping
it up all summer like a wildcat!

BLANCHE:
What's in your mind? I see something in your eyes!

MITCH:
It's dark in here.

BLANCHE:
I like the dark. The dark is
comforting to me.

MITCH:
I don't think I ever seen you in
the light. That's a fact.

BLANCHE:
Is it?

MITCH:
You never want to go out in the
afternoon.

BLANCHE:
Why, Mitch, you're at the plant
in the afternoon.

MITCH:
Not Sunday afternoon. You never
want to go out till after six and
then it's always to some place
that's not lighted much.

BLANCHE:
There is some obscure meaning in
this but I fail to catch it.

MITCH:
What it means is I've never had a
real good look at you, Blanche.
Let's turn the light on here.

BLANCHE:
Light? Which light? What for?

> MITCH:
> This one with the paper thing on it.

He tears the lantern off the light bulb, and throws it to the floor.

> BLANCHE:
> (picking it up)
> What did you do that for?

> MITCH:
> So I can take a look at you good
> and plain!

> BLANCHE:
> Of course you don't really mean to
> be insulting.

> MITCH:
> No, just realistic.

> BLANCHE:
> I don't want realism, I want magic.

> MITCH:
> Magic?

> BLANCHE:
> Yes, yes, magic. I try to give that
> to people. I do misrepresent things
> to them. I don't tell truth. I tell
> what ought to be truth. And if that's
> sinful - then let me be punished for
> it! <u>Don't turn the light on.</u> . . .

Blanche tries to run into the kitchen, but Mitch grabs her, forces her into the arc of harsh light that spills from the naked bulb. Her hands cover her face. He pulls them down. He looks at her in silence.

98.   CLOSE SHOT   BLANCHE

Her eyes closed, her head thrown back. Her hair is somewhat dishevelled and her makeup is in disrepair. She looks like what she is, a once lovely girl, now in her middle thirties, who has gone through an agonizingly tortured day. Her skin is lustreless, the lines of fatigue pull deep around her mouth and eyes.

99.   BACK TO SCENE

Mitch releases Blanche. He shakes his head slowly in puzzlement
as he looks at her. Finally --

>   MITCH:
> I don't mind you being older than what
> I thought . . . but all the rest of it!
> That pitch about your ideals being so old-
> fashioned and all the malarkey that you've
> been dishing out all summer. Oh, I knew
> you weren't sixteen any more. But I was
> fool enough to believe you were straight.

>   BLANCHE:
> Who told you I wasn't straight? My
> loving brother-in-law?

>   MITCH:
> No! I called him a liar at first.
> Then I checked on the story. I talked
> directly over long distance to this
> merchant in Auriol.

>   BLANCHE:
> Who is this merchant?

>   MITCH:
> Kiefaber.

>   BLANCHE:
> The merchant Kiefaber of Auriol. I
> know the man. He whistled at me. I
> put him in his place. So now for
> revenge he makes up stories about me.

>   MITCH:
> Didn't you stay at a hotel called the
> Flamingo?

>   BLANCHE:
> Flamingo? No! Tarantula was the name of it.

>   MITCH:
> Tarantula?

>   BLANCHE:
> Yes . . . a big spider! That's where I

                    BLANCHE: (Cont.)
brought my victims.
        (pause)
Yes -- I had many meetings with strangers.
After the death of Allan, meetings with
strangers were all that I seemed able to
fill my empty heart with. I think it was
panic, just panic, that drove me from one
to another, searching for some protection
here and there -- in the most unlikely
places. Even at last to a seventeen-
year-old boy. Then somebody wrote the superintendent, "This woman is morally unfit
for her position." True? Yes -- unfit somehow -- anyway. . . . So I came here. There was
nowhere else I could go. And I met you.
You said you needed somebody, I needed
somebody, too. I thanked God for you. You
seemed so gentle. A cleft in the rock of
the world that I could hide in. I guess I
was asking, hoping too much.

                    MITCH:
I thought you were straight.

                    BLANCHE:
What's straight? A line can be straight or
a street. . . . But the heart of a human being?

                    MITCH:
You lied to me, Blanche.

                    BLANCHE:
Don't say I lied to you.

                    MITCH:
Lies, lies, inside and out, all lies.

                    BLANCHE:
Never inside. . . . I never lied in my
heart. I was true in my heart to all
of you . . . always, always!

OUTSIDE THRU WINDOWS WE SEE STREET VENDOR PASS BY.

                    MEXICAN WOMAN:
Flowers. . . .

                    BLANCHE:
What?

                    MEXICAN WOMAN:
Flowers. ...

                    BLANCHE:
Oh, somebody outside.

She goes to door, opens it, stares at the woman.

                    MEXICAN WOMAN:
Flowers. ... Flowers for the dead. ...

                    BLANCHE:
No! No! Not now! Not now!
        (she darts back into
        apartment, slamming door)
I lived in a house where dying old
women remembered their dead men.

                    MEXICAN WOMAN:
        (o.s.)
Wreaths. Wreaths for the dead. ...

                    BLANCHE:
Crumble and fade -- regrets -- recrimina-
tions -- "If you'd done this, it wouldn't
have cost me that!"

                    MEXICAN WOMAN:
        (o.s.)
Flowers for the dead. ...

                    BLANCHE:
And other things, such as blood-stained
pillow slips. "Her linen needs changing."
"Yes, Mother!" But couldn't we get a
colored girl to do it? No, we couldn't
of course -- Everything gone -- but --

                    MEXICAN WOMAN:
        (o.s.)
Flowers. ...

                    BLANCHE:
Death. I used to sit here and she
used to sit over there, and death

> BLANCHE: (Cont.)
was as close as you are. . . .

> MEXICAN WOMAN:
> (crossing the window)
Flowers for the dead. . . .

> BLANCHE:
Death. The opposite is desire.
So how can you wonder? How can
you possibly wonder? Not far from
Belle Reve, before we lost Belle Reve,
was a camp where they trained young soldiers.
On Saturday nights they would go into
town to get drunk. And on the way back
they would stagger onto my lawn and
call. "Blanche! Blanche!" (a pause)
Later the paddy wagon would gather them
up like daisies . . . the long way home. . . .

Mitch crosses quickly to behind Blanche, places his arms about
her waist and turns her about. At first she takes him passionately, then she pushes him away.

> BLANCHE:
What do you want?
> (he reaches for her.
> She throws herself
> into his arms)
Marry me, Mitch!

> MITCH:
No! You're not clean enough to
bring in the house with my mother.

> BLANCHE:
> (loudly)
Go away then. Get out of here
quick, before I start screaming!

He stands still, staring at her. She runs to the door, throws
it open.

> BLANCHE:
Get out of here quick, before I
start screaming!

He backs towards the door.

                    BLANCHE:
          Screaming!

100.   EXT. VERANDAH   OUTSIDE STELLA'S FLAT   NIGHT

       Mitch runs out of the house and clutters down the steps and
       off into the street. Blanche's screams pursue him!

                    BLANCHE:
                     (o.s.)
               Screaming! Screaming!

       People peer in from the street and a crowd begins to collect
       and explore into the courtyard. Amond them are the customers
       from The Four Deuces, convivial and grateful for excitement.
       The music from the bar is behind them, pulsing and agitating
       for climax.

                    PEOPLE IN THE CROWD:
               There? . . . What is it? . . . What's the
               excitement? . . . Look at her! . . . Look
               at her face! Lady, where is it? . . .

101.   MEDIUM SHOT   BLANCHE IN DOORWAY

       suddenly aware of the crowd.

102.   THE CROWD   FEATURING BLANCHE   A POLICEMAN IN B.G.

       pushing his way through.

                    POLICEMAN:
               What is it? What is it?

       Blanche runs into the flat, slamming the door behind her.

103.   INT. STELLA'S FLAT   AS BLANCHE ENTERS

       She bolts the door. Runs to close the courtyard window. The
       Policeman's club strikes against the door.

                    VOICES:
                     (o.s.)
               She was screaming like a maniac. . . .

> VOICES: (Cont.)
> She was screaming murder, Officer. . . .

104. AT THE COURTYARD WINDOW   INT. AS BLANCHE STRUGGLES

To pull the shutters in, shut the window, bolt it. The voices
are continuous:

> POLICEMAN:
> (o.s. -- pounding)
> Lady, open up! This is a police
> officer! Open up!

> BLANCHE:
> Please -- Go away -- I'll be good --

> VOICES:
> You ought to go in there, Officer. . . .
> Maybe she killed somebody.

The music beats louder. She turns to the window on the alley.
There are faces there. Shadows are big on the walls. She is
like a bird behind bars with the cats looking in.

105. BLANCHE AT THE WINDOW TO THE ALLEY   INT.

Faces, and the lights of The Four Deuces behind. She pulls
this window down with difficulty as:

> VOICES:
> (o.s.)
> What happened? . . . What's the
> matter? . . . What happened? . . .
> Lady, somebody bother you? . . .
> Who are they after? . . . Come
> on out, lady! . . .

Then she is met by:

> VOICES:
> (o.s.)
> There she is! . . . There she is! . . .
> I can see her! I see her! . . .

These are at the street window. She goes to it, pulls down the
shade, which blows in at her. She runs to the light, the naked

bulb exposed by Mitch, and turns it off. The only light now
comes from the lamp in the kitchen. She goes there furtively
and crouches by the telephone.

106.   KITCHEN   BLANCHE AT TELEPHONE

> BLANCHE:
> Hello, Hello, Operator!
> > (realizes it is a
> > dial phone. Dials)
> Operator? Operator! Please
> give me Long Distance. . . .

> VOICES:
> > (o.s.)
> Come on out, lady. . . . Oh, leave
> her alone! I'll take care of
> you, honey! Come on out! . . .

> BLANCHE:
> Long Distance! I want to talk
> to Mr. Shep Huntleigh of Dallas.
> Huntleigh. He's so well known
> he doesn't require any address.
> Please understand, I can't, I
> can't. Hurry, please hurry.

DISSOLVE TO:

107.   INT. STELLA'S FLAT   NIGHT

The bottle, now empty, is still in Blanche's hand. A goodly
amount of her fancy clothing is strewn around the apartment.
Blanche is dressed now in a somewhat soiled and crumpled white
satin evening gown and a pair of scuffed slippers. She wears a
rhinestone tiara in her disarranged hair. A mood of hysterical
exhilaration possesses her and she fancies she hears the applause of her old friends at a party at Belle Reve. Light
laughter and voices and nostalgic garden party violins are
heard o.s.

> BLANCHE:
> Listen to me, listen, all of you!

She sets down the bottle. The laughter and voices die down,
only the violins continuing softly o.s.

BLANCHE:
How about taking a swim, a moonlight
swim at the old rock quarry? If anyone's sober enough to drive a car!
Best way in the world to stop
your head buzzing! Only you've
got to be careful to dive where the
deep pool is -- if you hit a rock
you don't come up till tomorrow.

"Good Night Ladies" is heard on the strings.

BLANCHE:
Oh, my goodness! They're playing
"Good Night Ladies." May I rest
my weary head on your shoulders?
It's so comforting. . . .

O.S. we hear the sound of someone trying the door. There is
the sound of a key turning in the lock and the door opens.
Stanley comes in.

STANLEY:
Hiyah, Blanche.

BLANCHE:
How is my sister?

STANLEY:
    (getting beer glasses)
She is doing okay.

BLANCHE:
And how is the baby?

STANLEY:
    (grinning amiably)
The baby won't come before morning,
so they told me to go home and get
a little shut-eye.

BLANCHE:
Does that mean we are to be alone
in here?

STANLEY:
Yep. Just me and you, Blanche.

                    STANLEY: (Cont.)
What've you got these fine feathers
on for?

                    BLANCHE:
Oh, that's right, you left before
my wire came.

                    STANLEY:
You got a wire?

                    BLANCHE:
I received a telegram from an
old admirer of mine.

                    STANLEY:
Anything good?

                    BLANCHE:
I think so. An invitation.

                    STANLEY:
What to?

                    BLANCHE:
A cruise of the Carribean on
a yacht!

                    STANLEY:
Well, well! What do you know!

                    BLANCHE:
It came like a bolt from the blue!

                    STANLEY:
Who did you say it was from?

                    BLANCHE:
An old beau of mine.

                    STANLEY:
The one that give you the white
fox-pieces?

                    BLANCHE:
Mr. Shep Huntleigh. I wore his
ATO pin my last year at college.
I hadn't seen him for a while

BLANCHE: (Cont.)
until last Christmas. Then --
just now -- this wire inviting me
on a cruise of the Carribean!
The problem is clothes. I tore
into my trunk to see what I have
that's suitable for the tropics!

STANLEY:
And come up with that -- gorgeous --
diamond -- tiara?

BLANCHE:
This old relic! It's only
rhinestones.

STANLEY:
Gosh. I thought it was Tiffany's
diamonds.

BLANCHE:
Well, anyhow, I shall be enter-
tained in style.

STANLEY:
It goes to show, you never know
what is coming.

BLANCHE:
Just when I thought my luck had
begun to fail me --

STANLEY:
Into the picture pops this Miami
millionaire.

BLANCHE:
This man is not from Miami.
This man is from Dallas.

STANLEY:
Well, just so he's from somewhere.

He takes off his shirt and tosses it down.

BLANCHE:
Close the curtains before you
undress any further.

                    STANLEY:
               (amiably)
          This is all I'm going to undress
          right now. . . . Seen a bottle-opener?
                    (peering into cabinet)
          I used to have a cousin could
          open a beer-bottle with his teeth.
          That was his only accomplishment,
          all he could do -- he was just a
          human bottle-opener. And then
          one time at a wedding-party --
                    (he finds an opener)
          he broke his front teeth off.
          After that he was so ashamed
          of himself, he used t'sneak
          out of the house when company came. . . .

He opens the beer-bottle. Foam gushes forth. Stanley laughs
happily, letting the beer cascade over his arms and person.

                    STANLEY:
          Rain from heaven!
                    (drinks)
          What'ya say, Blanche?
                    (starts into bedroom)
          Shall we bury the hatchet and
          make it a loving-cup?

                    BLANCHE:
               (terrified)
          No, thank you!

                    STANLEY:
          Aw, get with it, Blanche!

                    BLANCHE:
          What are you doing in here?

                    STANLEY:
               (reaching under
               the bed)
          Here's something I always break
          out on special occasions like this.
          The silk pajamas I wore on my
          wedding night.

                    BLANCHE:
          Oh.

STANLEY:
And when the telephone rings and
they say "You've got a son!" I'll
tear this off and wave it like a
flag! I guess we're both entitled
to put on the dog. . . .
   (she moves again
   to avoid him)
You having a Texas millionaire, and
me having a baby.

BLANCHE:
When I think how divine it is going
to be to have such a thing as privacy
once more -- I could weep with joy!

STANLEY:
This millionaire from Dallas
is not going to interfere with
your privacy any?

BLANCHE:
It won't be the sort of thing
you have in mind. This man is
a gentleman and he respects me.
   (improvising fever-
   ishly)
What he wants is my companionship.
Having great wealth sometimes makes
people lonely. . . .

STANLEY:
I wouldn't know about that. . . .

BLANCHE:
A cultivated woman, a woman of
intelligence and breeding can
enrich a man's life -- immeasure-
ably. I have those things to
offer and time doesn't take them
away. Physical beauty is passing.
A transitory possession. . . . But
beauty of the mind and richness of
the spirit and tenderness of the
heart -- and I have all those things --
aren't taken away, but grow!
Increase with the years! How strange
that I should be called a destitute

BLANCHE: (Cont.)
woman! When I have all of these
treasures locked in my heart. I
think of myself as a very, very rich
woman! But I have been foolish --
casting my pearls before swine.

STANLEY:
Swine, huh?

BLANCHE:
Yes, swine. And I'm thinking not
only of you, but your friend Mr.
Mitchell. He came here tonight.
He dared to come here in his work
clothes, to repeat slander, vicious
stories he had gotten from you!
I gave him his walking papers. . . .

STANLEY:
You did, huh?

BLANCHE:
Then he returned. He returned
with a box of roses to implore
my forgiveness. But some things
are not forgiveable. Deliberate
cruelty is not forgiveable. It
is the one unforgiveable thing
in my opinion, and the one thing
of which I have never, never been
guilty. So I said to him: "Thank
you, but it was foolish of me to
think that we could ever adapt
ourselves to each other. Our
backgrounds are incompatible.
So farewell, my friend! And let
there be no hard feelings."

STANLEY:
Was this before or after the
telegram?

BLANCHE:
What telegram? No! No after!
As a matter of fact, the wire. . . .

STANLEY:
As a matter of fact there wasn't

                STANLEY: (Cont.)
no wire at all.

                BLANCHE:
Oh. Oh!

                STANLEY:
And there isn't no millionaire.
And Mitch didn't come back here
with no roses because I know where
he is --

                BLANCHE:
Oh!

                STANLEY:
There isn't a thing, but imagination
and lies and conceit and tricks! And
look at yourself! Take a look at yourself in that worn-out Mardi Gras outfit,
rented for fifty cents from some rag
picker! And with that crazy crown on!
What kind of a queen do you think you
are --
          (he flings her tiara
          into a corner)
I've been on to you from the start!
You come in here and sprinkle the
place with powder and spray perfume
and cover the light bulb with a
paper lantern and lo and behold
the place has turned into Egypt
and you are the Queen of the Nile
sitting on your throne and swilling
down my liquor! I say Ha! Ha! Ha!
Do you hear me! Ha ha ha!
          (he crosses into
          the bedroom)

                BLANCHE:
Don't come in here --
          (Stanley goes into
          the bathroom)

Now Blanche madly begins to collect her most precious possess-
ions to make an escape. The jewel box, some of her best
dresses, furs -- Then she wildly moves towards the door -- as
she opens it --

108.   THE STREET OUTSIDE STELLA'S FLAT   NIGHT

There is a wild altercation. A drunken white man catches a
negro woman who has stolen his girl's purse. He snatches at
it . . . but she beats him on the head . . . and escapes, root-
ing into it. Meantime two men fall on the drunk and proceed to
manhandle him and strip him of his wallet, watch, etc. . . . .
Blanche slams the door.

109.   THE KITCHEN

Blanche enters and rushes to the telephone.

                    BLANCHE:
            Hello! Hel . . . Operator . . . Operator . . .
            What happened to Long Distance . . . What
            happened? Never mind Long Distance . . .
            give me Western Union -- Hurry, do
            hurry -- There isn't time to be -- Western
            Union? Yes! Take down this message!
            "In desperate, desperate circumstances.
            Caught in a trap! Help me! Caught in . . . "
            Oh --

She drops the phone. . . . Standing beside her, clad in red
pajamas is Stanley. . . . He has overheard her call for help.

She shrinks away from the phone. It clicks . . . steadily . . .
clicks . . .

                    STANLEY:
            You left the phone off the hook.

Stanley hangs it up . . . and then advances toward her. He is
going to close the front door.

                    BLANCHE:
            What are you doing?

Stanley stops.

                    BLANCHE:
            Let me . . . let me get by you. . . . .

                    STANLEY:
            Get by me? Sure Blanche. . . . Go ahead. . . .

> BLANCHE:
> You -- You stand over there!

> STANLEY:
> You got plenty of room to walk
> by me now.

> BLANCHE:
> Not with you there! But I've got
> to get out somehow!

> STANLEY:
> You think I'll interfere with you?

He closes the front door.

> STANLEY:
> Come to think of it -- maybe you
> wouldn't be bad to interfere with. . . .

Blanche runs into the other room. Stanley advances toward her.

> BLANCHE:
> Stay back. Don't you come near
> me another step or I'll --

> STANLEY:
> You'll what?

> BLANCHE:
> Some awful thing will happen!
> It will!

> STANLEY:
> What are you putting on now?

He's advancing on her.

> BLANCHE:
> I warn you, don't. . . . I'm in
> danger!

He takes another step. She smashes a bottle on the table.

> STANLEY:
> What did you do that for?

> BLANCHE:
> So I could twist the broken end
> in your face!

> STANLEY:
> I bet you would do that!

> BLANCHE:
> I would! I will if --

> STANLEY:
> Oh! You want some rough house! All
> right, let's have some rough house!

They have advanced so that we are now able to see the action
in a large mirror only.

> STANLEY:
> Tiger -- Tiger!

He is feigning -- Suddenly he leaps in and seizes her arm --
then he has her --

> STANLEY:
> Drop that bottle-top. Drop it!

He has managed to wrest the bottle top from her -- He throws
it. . . . It smashes into the mirror and the glass shatters --
and the tortured face of Blanche which was big, with it.

> STANLEY:
> We've had this date with each
> other from the beginning!

And on the broken glass we dissolve.

110.   THE STORE   HOT DAY -- SUMMER

Garbage is being collected. Someone is cleaning the front of a
store with a hose. Eunice walks towards the entrance to the
courtyard -- she has a brown paper bag. She enters the courtyard and we see the baby carriage.

110A. CLOSE SHOT

She parts the fly-net. Leans in and kisses a rather pale looking baby -- then starts into the house.

111.   KITCHEN -- STELLA'S FLAT

Eunice enters and listens. A shout from Stanley. He is at the poker table with Steve, Pablo, Mitch.

> STANLEY:
> Drew to an inside straight and made it!

> PABLO:
> Maldita sea tu suerte!

> STANLEY:
> Put it in English!

> PABLO:
> I'm cursing your lousy luck.

> STANLEY:
> (aggressively)
> You know what luck is? Luck is
> believing that you're lucky. Take
> at Salerno. I believed I was lucky.
> I figured that four out of five would
> not come through - but I would . . .
> and I did. I put that down as a rule.
> To hold a front position in this rat
> race you've got to believe you're lucky.

> MITCH:
> (furiously)
> You . . . you . . . you . . . brag . . .
> brag . . . bull . . . bull . . .
>   (turns away from
>   the game -- rests his
>   chin on his arm on back
>   of his chair)

> STANLEY:
> What's the matter with him?

> EUNICE:
> (walking towards bedroom)
> I always did say that men were callous
> things with no feelings, but this does
> beat everything. Making pigs of
> yourselves.

She goes through the curtains into the bedroom.

> STANLEY:
> What's the matter with her? Come
> on. . . . Let's play!

The game resumes in silence.

112. BEDROOM   AS EUNICE ENTERS.

> STELLA:
> How's my baby?

> EUNICE:
> Sleeping like a little angel. Brought
> you some grapes. Where is she?

> STELLA:
> Bathing.

> EUNICE:
> How is she?

> STELLA:
> She wouldn't eat anything. I keep
> telling her we made arrangements
> for her to rest in the country, but
> she's got it mixed up in her mind
> with a cruise to the Islands with
> Shep Huntleigh, an old beau.

> BLANCHE:
> (opening the bathroom
> door and calling)
> Stella!

> STELLA:
> Yes, Blanche?

> BLANCHE:
> If anyone calls, take the number and
> tell him I'll call right back.

> STELLA:
> Yes.

BLANCHE:
And Stella, that cool yellow silk, the
boucle, see if it's crushed. If it's
not too crushed I'll wear it -- and
on the lapel that silver and turquoise
pin in the shape of a sea horse. You'll
find it in the heart-shaped box I keep
my accessories in, and, oh, Stella, try
and locate that bunch of artificial --
    (long, difficult effort
    to remember the name)
-- violets in that box, too, to pin with
the sea-horse on the lapel of the jacket.
    (closes the door)

STELLA:
    (going to jewel box)
I just don't know if I did the right
thing.

EUNICE:
What else could you do?

STELLA:
I couldn't believe her story and
go on living with Stanley.

EUNICE:
    (holding Stella close)
Don't you ever believe it. You've
got to keep on goin', honey. No
matter what happens, we've all got
to keep on going.

BLANCHE:
    (opening door - peeking
    out of bathroom)
Stella? Is the coast clear?

STELLA:
Yes, Blanche.
    (she waits - to
    Eunice hurriedly)
Tell her how well she's looking.

BLANCHE:
    (stepping out of
    the bathroom)

BLANCHE: (Cont.)
Please close the curtains before
I come out.

STELLA:
(going to the curtains)
They're closed.
(she shows Blanche
that they are closed)

STANLEY:
(speaking low, at
the game)
Hey, Mitch, come to!

Blanche steps out. She is in her bathrobe and carries a hair-
brush and brushes her hair. There is a tragic radiance about
her. She speaks with a faintly hysterical vivacity.

BLANCHE:
I have just washed my hair.

STELLA:
Did you?

BLANCHE:
I'm not sure I got the soap out.

EUNICE:
Such fine hair.

BLANCHE:
It's a problem. Didn't I get a call?

STELLA:
Who from, Blanche?

BLANCHE:
Shep Huntleigh . . .

STELLA:
Why, not yet, honey!

BLANCHE:
How strange! I --

At the sound of Blanche's voice, Mitch's arm has sagged and his
gaze is dissolved into space. Stanley barks at him.

STANLEY:
Hey, Mitch!

Mitch returns to the game. The sound of this new voice shocks
Blanche. She makes a little gesture, forming Mitch's name with
her lips, questioningly. Stella nods, and looks quickly away.
Blanche looks perplexed. She glances from Stella to Eunice.
Stella glances away.

                    BLANCHE:
                 (with sudden hysteria)
          What's happened here? I want an
          explanation of what's happened here.

                    STELLA:
                 (agonizingly)
          Hush! Hush!

                    EUNICE:
          Hush! Hush! Honey!

                    STELLA:
          Please, Blanche.

                    BLANCHE:
          Why are you two looking at me like
          that? Is something wrong with me?

                    EUNICE:
          You look wonderful, Blanche. Doesn't
          she look wonderful?

                    STELLA:
          Yes.

                    EUNICE:
          I understand you're going on a trip

                    STELLA:
          Yes, Blanche <u>is</u>. . . . She's going on
          a vacation.

                    EUNICE:
          I'm green with envy.

                    BLANCHE:
                 (exasperated)

BLANCHE: (Cont.)
Help me, you two! Help me get
dressed.

STELLA:
    (taking up dress)
Is this what you want?

BLANCHE:
Yes, it will do. I'm anxious to
get out of here. This place is a trap.

EUNICE:
Such a pretty lavender jacket.

STELLA:
It's lilac-colored.

BLANCHE:
You're both of you wrong. It's
Della Robbia blue.

Blanche is near the table. She sees the grapes.

BLANCHE:
Are these grapes washed?

(CHIMES)

EUNICE:
Huh?

BLANCHE:
Washed! I said -- are they washed?

EUNICE:
I got them from the French Market.

BLANCHE:
That doesn't mean they've been washed.
    (listens to chimes)
Ah, those cathedral bells, they're the
only clean thing in the quarter. Well,
I'm going now.
    (picks up jacket)
I'm ready to go.

(CHIMES FADE)

EUNICE:
    (whispering to Stella)
She's going to walk out before they
get here.

STELLA:
Wait, Blanche.

BLANCHE:
    (glancing towards
    living room)
I don't want to pass in front of those
men.

EUNICE:
    (helping Stella
    bring her back)
Then wait till the game breaks up.

STELLA:
Yes, yes, sit down.
    (leading her to armchair)

BLANCHE:
    (suddenly listening
    as she sits)
I can smell the sea air. My element
is the earth, but it should have been
water -- water -- the blessedest thing
that God created in those seven days.
The rest of my days I'm going to spend
on the sea, and when I die I'm going to
die on the sea. One day out on the ocean
I will die -- with my hand in the hand of
some nice-looking ship's doctor -- a
very young one with a small blonde moustache
and a big silver watch. "Poor lady", they'll
say, "The quinine did her no good. That
unwashed grape has transported her soul to
heaven". And I'll be buried at sea sewn up
in a clean white sack and dropped over-
board at noon -- in a blaze of summer -- and
into an ocean as blue as -- the blue of my
first lover's eyes!

113.   PORCH

A STRANGE MAN appears on the porch, and rings the doorbell. He is followed by a STRANGE WOMAN, severely dressed in a dark tailored suit, and carrying a small black, professional-looking bag.

(DOOR BELL SOUNDS)

114.   BEDROOM

> EUNICE:
> (to Stella, when
> doorbell rings)
> That must be them.

> BLANCHE:
> (on hearing the bell)
> What is it?

> EUNICE:
> (covering)
> Excuse me while I see who's at the door.
> (goes through curtains
> into living room)

> STELLA:
> Yes.

> BLANCHE:
> I wonder if it's for me.

115.   LIVING ROOM

Stanley rises, goes to the door to answer the bell. There is a low exchange between him and the Strange Man.

> STANLEY:
> Doctor?

> STRANGE MAN:
> Yes.

> STANLEY:
> (nods)
> Just a minute. Would you mind
> waiting outside for just a

STANLEY: (Cont.)
couple of seconds. She'll be
right out.
      (turns back into living room)

        EUNICE:
      (at curtain)
Someone is calling for Blanche.
      (enters bedroom)

116.   BEDROOM

        BLANCHE:
It _is_ for me, then! Is it the gentleman
I was expecting from Dallas?

        EUNICE:
      (looking at Stella)
I think it is, Blanche.

        BLANCHE:
I'm not quite ready.

        STELLA:
      (to Eunice)
Ask him to wait outside.
      (to Blanche)
Everything packed?

        BLANCHE:
My silver toilet articles are still out.

Stella hurries to get them, puts them in a hatbox, closes it.
Eunice returns to living room.

117.   LIVING ROOM

Eunice nods to Stanley.

        STANLEY:
      (turns to Doctor)
She'll be here in a minute.

Doctor nods, turns to Strange Woman and tells her the same
thing.

118.   BEDROOM

Eunice is re-entering.

> EUNICE:
> They're waiting in front of the house.

> BLANCHE:
> They? Who's they?

> EUNICE:
> There's a lady with him.

> BLANCHE:
> I can't imagine who this "lady" could be!
> (Stella averts her eyes)
> How is she dressed?

> EUNICE:
> Just -- just a sort of plain-tailored outfit.

> BLANCHE:
> Possibly she's --
> (her voice dies out nervously)

> STELLA:
> Shall we go, Blanche?

> BLANCHE:
> Yes.

They start out of bedroom, carrying bags.

> BLANCHE:
> Must we go through that room?

> STELLA:
> I will go with you.

> BLANCHE:
> How do I look?

> STELLA:
> Lovely!

> EUNICE:
> (echoing)
> Lovely!

Blanche starts into living room, Stella follows. Eunice is passed, then follows.

119.   LIVING ROOM.

> BLANCHE:
> (to men at table)
> Now, please don't get up. I'm only passing through.
> (goes to door)

> STRANGE MAN:
> How do you do.

> BLANCHE:
> (steps onto porch --
> stares at Strange Man)
> You are not the gentleman I was expecting.
> (to Stella)
> That man isn't Shep Huntleigh!

Stella turns quickly into Eunice's arms. Blanche runs into flat. Doctor enters living room, motioning Strange Woman, who also enters.

> STANLEY:
> (as Blanche passes him)
> Did you forget something.

> BLANCHE:
> (shrilly, running
> into bedroom)
> Yes, Yes, I forgot something!

Strange Man has stepped into room. Stands at door. Strange Woman crosses through living room into bedroom.

120.   BEDROOM

> STRANGE WOMAN:
> (confronting Blanche)
> Hello, Blanche.

> STANLEY'S VOICE:
> (o.s.)
> She says she forgot something.

                        STRANGE WOMAN:
That's all right.

Stanley enters bedroom.

121.   C.U. STANLEY   BEDROOM

                        STANLEY:
                        (very close. Seen
                        from Blanche's angle)
What did you forget, Blanche?

122.   MEDIUM SHOT

                        BLANCHE:
I -- I --

                        STRANGE WOMAN:
It don't matter. We can pick it up
later.

                        STANLEY:
Sure, we can send it along with the
trunk.

                        BLANCHE:
                        (retreating)
I don't know you! I don't know
you! I want to be -- left alone --
please!

                        STRANGE WOMAN:
Now, Blanche!

                        VOICES:
                        (echoing and re-echoing)
Now, Blanche! Now Blanche!
Now, Blanche!

                        STANLEY:
You left nothing here but split talcum
and old empty perfume bottles, unless
it's the lantern you want to take with
you.
                        (he tears the lantern
                        off the light bulb)

STANLEY: (Cont.)
You want the lantern?

Blanche cries out, grabs lantern. Strange Woman steps boldly
towards her. Blanche screams and tries to break past the
strange woman. Strange Woman catches her arm. Blanche turns
and wildly scratches at the Woman, who pinions her arms, expertly. Blanche falls, the Woman kneels beside her, holding
her.

                                            CUT TO:

123.   KITCHEN   STELLA AND EUNICE   EUNICE IS HOLDING HER

                            STELLA:
                  Eunice, don't let them do that to
                  her. Don't let them hurt her! What
                  are they doing?
                            (tries to go toward
                            bedroom)

                            EUNICE:
                  No, honey. Stay here. Don't go
                  in there. Don't look.

Mitch springs at Stanley who is standing in the doorway between
the two rooms.

                            MITCH:
                  You! You done this!

                                            CUT TO:

124.   BEDROOM   THE FIGHT SEEN FROM THE OTHER SIDE

                            STANLEY:
                  Quit the blubber!

                            MITCH:
                  I'll kill you.

                            STANLEY:
                  Hold this bonehead!

                            STEVE:
                  Stop it, Mitch.

PABLO:
Yeah. Take it easy.

Pablo and Steve pull Mitch off Stan and out of sight.

STANLEY:
I tell you it aint true what
she said! She asked for some
rough house! I gave her some
rough house!

The Strange Man comes into the shot and kneels beside the
prostrate Blanche. The Woman is still holding her.

STRANGE WOMAN:
These finger-nails will have to be
trimmed. Jacket, Doctor?

STRANGE MAN:
Not unless necessary.
          (he kneels close
          to Blanche)
Miss Du Bois --

BLANCHE:
Please --

STRANGE MAN:
It won't be necessary.

BLANCHE:
          (faintly)
Ask her to let go of me.

STRANGE MAN:
          (to the Woman)
Yes -- let go.

The Woman releases Blanche then rises. Blanche extends her
hands. The man raises her up. He takes off his hat and smiles
at her. She looks at him, wavering at first, then smiling, as
she would at a new beau.

BLANCHE:
Whoever you are -- I have always
depended on the kindness of strangers.

Blanche comes out of the house on the doctor's arm. She walks

by Stella who is on the porch, then past Stanley and out of
Camera. . . . Stella goes to follow her. Stanley intercepts
her and says . . .

> STANLEY:
> Come on honey. . . .

> STELLA:
> (shrinking from him)
> Don't you touch me. Don't you
> ever touch me again. . . .

125. ON THE STREET

Blanche gets into the car with the doctor. It drives off and
we pan with it holding on the courtyard gate - Stella appears
there looking after the car.

126. HIGH SHOT   THE STREET

Blanche's car drives around the corner and disappears.

127. THE COURTYARD

Stella is in tears . . . she goes back slowly towards the baby
carriage, throws back the netting and picks up the infant. . . .
Then she starts back into her home. We hear O.S.

> STANLEY:
> (O.S.)
> Stella!

His tone is harsh and demanding. It is reminiscent (in the
reading) of the cry he gave at the bottom of the steps at the
end of the poker night.

Stella stops. Stanley is heard again from inside the house
. . . more demanding.

> STANLEY:
> Stella!!

Stella looks down at the infant. Crying, she whispers to the
child these words of promise and reassurance.

> STELLA:
> We're not going back in there. Not
> this time. We're never going back.
> Never, never back, never back again.

And then Stella turns and procedes with strength and confidence
up the stairs to Eunice's apartment.

128.   STREET IN NEW ORLEANS

At the back of the shot is the silhouette of the cathedral.
The Cathedral bells that Blanche has referred to as <u>the only</u>
<u>clean thing in the quarter</u> are ringing. The black car carrying
Blanche is coming towards us, turns the corner and goes down a
long dark New Orleans street. It is lost from view.

<u>THE   END</u>

Something of the complexity of modern filmmaking, of the hard and carefully coordinated labor that goes into any production, is suggested by the following two documents.

The first is the initial and closing pages of the final shooting schedule for *The Best Man* (1963). The usual shooting schedule, unless the production is very elaborate, is based on thirty working days. Note that the film is not shot in order of the sequence of scenes. The large number of extras and minor cast numbers needed and the specific days when a location is available and accessible to film equipment are a few factors that help to determine the production sequence as actually drawn up. The problem of the production manager is to arrange the shooting in such a way as to keep costs down efficiently, yet at the same time to permit the director, the principals, and the crew to create the best possible work.

The second item supplements the first. It is a sample from the daily call sheets for Samuel Goldwyn, Jr.'s production of *The Young Lovers* (1963), a low-budget picture with a small cast and limited crew. Note that for the ten numbered scenes only two actors, Peter Fonda and Sharon Hugueny, are involved and only two exterior settings, both on location at the U.C.L.A. campus, which is in Westwood, not far from Hollywood. Yet, including stand-ins, a technical crew of 45 is required, together with 15 vehicles, and a catered lunch for 77. In case of inclement weather, or some other necessity, a cover set—"Schwartz' Classroom"—is indicated. Note that this same studio interior is listed on the advance schedule as the set for the next two working days, September 9 and 10; also given for those two days are the scenes to be shot and their order.

PROD. NO. __914-83__ TITLE __THE BEST MAN(MILLAR/TURMAN PROD)__

DIRECTOR __F SCHAFFNER__ PRODUCER __MILLAR/TURMAN__ ART DIR. __L WHEELER__

PROD BREAKDOWN ASST. __D.MODER__ SCRIPT DATED __8-30-63__

DAYS __30 PLUS__ START DATE __9-16-63__ FINISH DATE __10-25-63__ TYPED __9-3-63__
9 DAYS REHEARSAL

FINAL SHOOTING SCHEDULE

DATE	SET	PAGES	SEQ	SC'NS	CAST
1st DAY 9-16	STAGE #8 INT. RUSSELL SUITE(D) SCS: 11,12 Meet Alice-Jensen enters. Hockstader appears	5			Russell #1,Alice #7,Jensen #2 Hockstader #3
	TOTAL PAGES	5			
2nd DAY 9-17	LOCATION: AMBASSADOR HOTEL INT. CANTWELL HQTRS(D) SC: 16 Cantwell on TV. He & Don exit. Pickup TV for Sc 15A	3			Cantwell #8, Announcer,Don Cantwell #9, bit photographer, Spastic,announc- er #2, 60 extras (attendants,re- porters,photog- raphers, men, women, tv crew, guards, 10 Cantwell girls) tv cameras,news- reel camera, tv boom,big sign "Go with Joe" Books,coffee
	INT. KITCHEN(D) SC: 17 Cantwell & Don meet cleaning woman	1 2/8			Cantwell #8,Don #9,cleaning wo- man bit,3 police etc,4 Russell girls,5 kitchen help

PROD. NO. __914-83__ TITLE _____ THE BEST MAN _____

DATE	SET	PAGES	SEQ	SC'NS	CAST
2nd DAY CONT'D	INT. HOTEL LOBBY(D) SC: 43 After lunch 2 ladies thru lobby to elevator	1			Mrs. Gamadge #5, Mabel #10, Senator bit,boys(men 2)bits,5ad libs, extras from int (men,women, elev operator, desk clerk,bell hops) posters, pictures
	TOTAL PAGES	5 2/8			
3rd DAY 9-18	LOCATION: AMBASSADOR HOTEL INT. BAROQUE ROOM(D) SC: 42 Ladies luncheon.Alice & Mabel do best to knife each other	6 2/8			Alice #7,Mabel #10,Mrs.Gamadge #5,Janet #6,Mrs. Claypoole bit #19, Reporters #1 & #3(35),Mrs. Anderson #77, Mrs.Merwin #20, 32 extras(4 bus- boys,photograph- ers,20 women,8 men)drinks
	TOTAL PAGES	6 2/8			
4th & 5th DAYS 9-19 & 9-20	LOCATION: AMBASSADOR HOTEL INT. BALLROOM(N) SCS: 22,23,24,25,26,27,28,28A 28B,29,29A,29B,29C,29D,30,30A 31,31A Dinner party.Hockstader introduces candidates & wives. Celebrity sings.	9 1/8			Russel #1,Jensen #2,Hockstader #3,Tom #4,Mrs. Gamadge #5,Alice #7,Cantwell #8, Don #9,Mabel #10 Claypoole #11, John Merwin #12 Celebrity #1 & #2,Oscar Anderson #13,Mrs.Claypool #19,Mrs.Merwin #20,Chairman #17 Reporter #51, waiter bit, wives at table dignitaries,men,

PROD. NO. __914-83__ TITLE _____THE BEST MAN_____

DATE	SET	PAGES	SEQ	SC'NS	CAST
4th & 5th DAYS CONT'D					women, 3 waiters orchestra, newsmen, photographers
	TOTAL PAGES	9 1/8			
6th & 7th DAYS 9-23 & 9-24	STAGE #8 INT. RUSSELL SUITE(D) SCS: 13,14 Hockstader talks politics with Bill & tells him of his cancer condition. Mrs. Gamadge enters, passes advice to Alice. Bill exits.	9 4/8			Russell #1,Mrs. Russell #7, Hockstader sc 12 #3,Jensen,#2 Mrs. Gamadge sc 14 #5,Janet reporters in hall,man Luggage clothes,bar set-up
	TOTAL PAGES	9 4/8			
8th & 9th DAYS 9-25 & 9-26	STAGE #8 INT. RUSSELL SUITE(D) SCS: 44,44A Russell bathes as Claypoole pledges support. Hockstader enters. Jensen brings in Bascomb who tells about Cantwell's past in army.	8			Russell #1, Claypoole #11, Jensen #2, Hockstader #3, Bascomb #15,aide (sb)1 valet,1 room service
	INT. CANTWELL HOME(FOR TV SET SC) SC: 18C Mother Cantwell interviewed.	2/8			Interviewer,Mrs. Cantwell, T.V. announcer
	INT. SENATE RM(D)(FOR TV SET SC) SC: 18B Cantwell questions Mafia man	4/8			Cantwell,Mafia man,voice over, Extras?
	TOTAL PAGES	8 6/8			
10th DAY 9-27	STAGE #8 INT. RUSSELL SUITE SC: 47 Bascomb finishes story. Jensen says he has arranged meeting.	6			Russell #1, Hockstader #3, Jensen #2, Bascomb #15, Alice #7

PROD. NO. __914-83__ TITLE _____THE BEST MAN_____

DATE	SET	PAGES	SEQ	SC'NS	CAST
10th DAY CONT'D	As Russell leaves Hockstader has attack,asks for doctor				
	TOTAL PAGES	6			
11th DAY 9-30	LOCATION: BASEMENT BOMB SHELTER INT. BOMB SHELTER(D) SC: 51 Cantwell reads document,greets Marcus & explains his innocence. Marcus rushes out door into newsmen	5 5/8			Russell #1, Cantwell #8, Bascomb #15, 6 newsmen & photographers
	TOTAL PAGES	5 5/8			
12th DAY 10-1	LOCATION: BASEMENT BOMB SHELTER INT. CORRIDOR OUTSIDE BOMB SC: 52 SHELTER(D) Cantwell poses w/Marcus for photographers	7/8			Cantwell #8,Don #9,Bascomb #15 Jensen #2,photographer bit, reporter bit,6 reporters & newsmen
27th DAY 10-22	INT. LIMO(PROCESS)(D) SC: 64 Russell 7 Alice riding to arena	1 4/8			Russell #1,Alice #7,driver?, mockup limo,process plates to cover
	INT. LINEN CLOSET(D) sc; 49 Russell & Cantwell meet. Big discussion as Cantwell asks Russell to withdraw from race. 2 exit to hall	4 4/8			Russell #1, Jensen #2, Cantwell #8,Don #9
	TOTAL PAGES	6 6/8			
28th DAY 10-23	LOCATION: AMBASSADOR HOTEL INT. PALM COURT(D) SCS: 1,2 Russell talks to press	5 1/8			Russell #1, Jensen #2, reporters #1,#2, #3,#4,#5,fan,35 extras(reporters men,women,1

PROD. NO. ___914-83___ TITLE _____THE BEST MAN_____

DATE	SET	PAGES	SEQ	SC'NS	CAST
28th DAY CONT'D					bartender,1 guard,2 waiters) no tv camera
	EXT. PALM COURT(D) SC: 3 Russell tries to call wife on phone. No luck	6/8			Russell #1, Jensen #2,5 reporters,fan, from sc 1, re- porters,man Indian,men, women,elderly lady(SB)6yr old boy(SB)3 Russell girl w.worker, banners,bass drum,mixed but- tons
	TOTAL PAGES	5 7/8			
29th DAY 10-24	LOCATION: AMBASSADOR HOTEL EXT. POOL AREA(D) SCS: 4,5,6,7 Two at pool meet Mrs. Gamadge. They talk, she exits	4 5/8			Russell #1, Jensen #2,Mrs. Gamadge #5,girl bit sc 7,tv in- terviewer sc 7 100 extras (husky woman golfer(SB)men bathers,women bathers,men, women,waiters, tv crew, photogs newsmen,5 Cantwell girls) tv camera tran- sistor radios, private cameras
	INT. HOTEL LOBBY(D) SC: 8 Continuation of pool seq 2 men to elevator	6/8			Mrs. Gamadge, Russell,Jensen, men,women,2 bellhops,from 100 in scs 4-7
	TOTAL PAGES	5 3/8			

PROD. NO. __914-83__ TITLE _____ THE BEST MAN _____

DATE	SET	PAGES	SEQ	SC'NS	CAST
30th DAY	LOCATION: AMBASSADOR HOTEL <u>EXT. AMBASSADOR</u>(D) SC: 40 Jensen entering,meets Lazarus	6/8			Jensen,Lazarus, 45 extras(15 picket line (some colored)5 Cantwell girls, man on stilts,2 attendants,men, women,photogs, newsmen,doorman) cars,Jensen's car,Lazarus car
	EXT. AMBASSADOR HELIPORT(D) SC: 58A Cantwell & Aide board copter	1/8			Cantwell #8, Aide bit,men, women,pilot, copter
	EXT. AMBASSADOR SWIM POOL(N) SC: 35 Hockstader asks Claypoole to be VP. Supporter talks to him	7/8			Hockstader #3, Tom #4,Claypoole #11,supporter bit,40 extras (men,women, servers,see colored help)
	TOTAL PAGES	1 6/8			
POST LAST PRODUCTION	INT. COPTER(D) SC: 58B Cantwell on walkie-talkie	3/8			Cantwell,Aide, Pilot,shoot in flight,copter
	TOTAL SCRIPT PAGES	134 7/8			
		****			

TIGERTAIL PROD., INC.

4th day of shooting   CALL SHEET   Prod. No. 5000

PICTURE: "THE YOUNG LOVERS"   DIRECTOR: SAMUEL GOLDWYN, JR.

SHOOTING CALL: 8:00 A.M.   DATE: FRIDAY, SEPT.6, 1963

SET AND SCENE NO.

     EXT. CAMPUS PARKING ENT. (D) U.C.L.A.
        Scs. 189, 190

     EXT. SMALL PARKING LOT (D) U.C.L.A.
        Scs. 214, 215, 216, 217, 218, 219, 220, 221

COVER SET: INT. SCHWARTZ' CLASSROOM

- -

CAST & BITS	CHARACTER & WARDROBE	HAIRDRESSING	MAKEUP	ON SET
PETER FONDA	EDDIE		7:15	8:00
SHARON HUGUENY	PAM	6:00		8:00

STANDINS: THRU GATE

T. CONNERS   MR. FONDA w/car   7:00
1 WOMAN   MISS HUGUENY w/car 7:00

- -

ADVANCE SCHEDULE

MON. 9/9 & TUES.	INT. SCHWARTZ' CLASSROOM (D)	Scs. 68, 69, 70, 71, 72, 73, 74, 75, 76, 77, 78, 79, 80.	STAGE 4
	INT. SCHWARTZ' CLASSROOM (D)	Scs. 262, 263, 264, 265, 266, 267, 268, 269, 270, 271, 272, 273.	STAGE 4
	INT. SCHWARTZ' CLASSROOM (D)	Scs. 103, 104, 105 188C	STAGE 4
	INT. CLASSROOM	Sc. 188D	STAGE 4

CAMERA	TIME:
1 Camera	6:30
1 Cameraman	6:42
1 Operator	6:42
2 Assistants	6:30

TECHNICAL	
1 Key & 2nd Grip	6:30
4 Co Grips	6:30
1 Greensman	6:30
1 Laborer	6:30

ELECTRICAL	
1 Gaffer & Best Boy	6:30
8 Lamp Opers	6:30
1 Generator	6:30
1 Gen Operator	6:30
1 Booster Lights	6:30

WARDROBE	
1 Ward Man	6:30
1 Ward Girl	6:30

MAKEUP	
1 Makeup Man	6:00
1 Hairstylist	6:00

SOUND	
1 Mixer	6:42
1 Recorder	6:30
1 Mikeman	6:30
1 Cableman	6:30

STILL	
1 Still Man	7:00

PROPERTY	TIME:
1 Property Master	6:30
2 Asst Prop Man	6:30
Tarragoo's car	6:30
Eddie's Motorcycle	6:30
Pam's Car	7:00

RESTAURANT	
77 Lunches	11:30
1 Gals Coffee Box donuts	7:00

HOSPITAL	
1 1st Aid Man	6:30

TRANSPORTATION	
1 Standby Car	6:42
1 Car	7:00
1 Car	7:30
1 Bus (41)	6:30
1 Grip Trk	ON LOC
1 Prop Trk	ON LOC
1 Ward Trk	ON LOC
1 Sound Jeep	ON LOC
1 Elec Trk	ON LOC
1 Generator Trk	ON LOC
P.U. trk	ON LOC
1 LU Driver	6:30

Above the line expenses (cost) cost of staff, talent, and story in preparation and production of a motion picture.

Absolute film (also **abstract film**) a nonrepresentative film whose parts are composed of moving visual patterns.

Abstract music musical accompaniment to a scene or scenes which aims at more than **crutch music**; based upon correspondence or juxtaposition with the structure and rhythm of the images on the screen.

Abstract set a nonrepresentational setting without a definite period or locale.

Academy players directory (**casting bible**) several volumes listing professional actors available for American film productions; includes photographs.

Accelerated motion (also **fast motion** and **speedup motion**) by slowing down the camera mechanism during shooting, the resulting projection of action at standard rate (24 frames per second) will appear to be taking place at greater speed; often used for farce or comic effect, also to emphasize mechanistic order; opposite of **slow motion.**

Accent light a small spotlight focused on a specific detail of a subject; usually placed to one side of the subject or used as backlighting.

Action anything recorded by the camera in a shot; the command, "Action!" beginning a shot, may be given only by the director.

Action director (also **second unit director**) a supplementary director for action scenes and scenes without dialogue which do not require the presence of the director.

Action still a still photograph taken of a scene as it appears in the film, distinguished from other types of still photographs taken during production, such as **art stills, production stills, publicity stills.** See also **Unit still photographer.**

Ad lib extemporaneous dialogue and action not in a prepared script; or working without a script.

Adapt to translate and to change a story, novel, play, or other property for the purpose of making a film.

Aerial shot photograph taken from helicopter, airplane, balloon.

Against the grain (opposite of **on the nose**) any artistic technique in any aspect of the filmmaking process in which one element is used unconventionally, in contrast to audience experience and expectation, to create a sense of conflict, "mixed feelings," and to comment upon the convention violated.

Allusion as in literature, an explicit or implicit reference to another film or films achieved by dialogue, impersonation, music, visual style of shots.

Angle see **Camera angle.**

Animation process by which drawings or objects are photographed so that when shown there will be the illusion of movement.

Answer print (also **first-trial print**) first combined print received from the laboratory and approved as representing the standard for all subsequent prints.

Arc (also **brute**) a large, high-powered carbon light used to illuminate a set for filming.

Arrange to adapt the music created by the *composer* for various voices and instruments.

Art director designs and supervises all sets, exterior and interior, in studio and on location. See also **Production designer.**

Art film used to describe any film, foreign or domestic, ostensibly not intended for large-scale commercial release and distribution.

Art house (or **theater**) a theater specializing in the presentation of art films.

Art still a photograph made of a film actor, not taken from the context of actual filming.

Assemble to begin the editing process by collecting separate shots and arranging them in order.

Assistant cameraman member of camera crew, charged with loading the camera with raw stock and with focusing of lenses.

Assistant director doubles as an assistant to the director and to the unit production manager; generally serves as foreman of the set; specifically charged with handling all bit players and extras, with presence of all players for their shots, notification of all players of their calls, also transportation and set discipline.

Associate producer an immediate assistant to the producer; when the producer is involved in the making of more than one film, he may be charged with the making of one film.

Atmosphere   details of setting, costumes, extras, properties which establish verisimilitude; or aspects of lighting, photography, direction, editing which contribute to convey an emotional mood.

Attitude   the use of **objective** and **subjective** shots by the filmmaker to reveal a meaning or to make a point or statement.

Audience participation shots   any shots in a film in which actors seem to speak to, act, and react to the theater audience or the camera *as camera;* or any scenes or shots in which the audience is explicitly introduced to the process of making the film being seen.

Auteur (French for author)   the filmmaker, in particular, the director, viewed as analogous to the author of a book in the sense that he has authority and control over the creation of the film and responsibility for the finished work, and each work becomes part of his canon; assumes that the director is a responsible artist with a recognizable cinematic manner and style and an artist's concern for specific subjects and areas of experience.

Avant garde   used loosely to describe any films in which form or content or both are experimental.

Back lighting   light directed into the subject and towards the camera from a point behind the subject.

Back projection (also **rear projection**)   projection of a film of an action or setting through a transparent screen, in front of which another action or scene may be filmed. See also **Process shot.**

Background (bg)   that portion of the setting or frame farthest, in real or apparent distance, from the camera.

Background light   light placed on the background to create a visual separation of the subject of a shot from the background.

Background music   music composed and arranged to accompany particular action or dialogue in a film; sometimes prerecorded.

Background players (crowd)   see **Extra.**

Backing   a flat background, which can be a photograph or painting, against which actors are filmed.

Backup schedule   an alternate to the scenes to be shot in regular shooting schedule in the event that, for any reason, the regular schedule cannot be followed.

Balance   when the process of **dubbing** has been completed and the film is a single unit with a single sound track, the editor balances it, equalizing, insofar as possible, the footage in each reel, prior to any preview showing.

Barndoor   a black flap used to block light from shining into the camera lens.

Below the line expenses (cost)   all production expenses involved in filmmaking, including technical facilities, staging and studio costs.

Big closeup   see **Closeup.**

Bit (player)   an actor with a small speaking part.

Bits (of business)   miscellaneous movements, actions, gestures created by the director and actors for dramatic purposes and for characterization.

Blocking (also to **block in**)   rehearsal preparation by the director, assistants, actors, and crew in arranging the composition of a scene, with special emphasis on positions, movements, and gesture of the actors; may involve the use of diagrams or sketches or marking the set with chalk lines or tape; also the initial arrangement of lights. See also **Rough in.**

Blowup   an enlargement of a photograph or a particular part of a photograph, or an enlargement of any printed material.

Body makeup woman   a woman charged with all makeup used for female members of the cast, except those specifically reserved for the makeup artist under union regulations.

Bold   a take which has not been printed, has been put aside, and held in reserve for possible use.

Boom   a mobile suspended microphone, held near actors but out of camera range, to record dialogue. See also **Camera boom.**

Breakdown   an estimated budget for the making of a film, derived from analysis of the script, and subdivided according to estimates of necessary shooting time required, cast and crew, technical resources, and materials.

Bridge music   music designed to accompany and support visual transitions in the film.

Bridging shot   any shot inserted during editing to cover a break in continuity. See also **Insert.**

Broad (also **broadside**)   a reflector light containing two powerful bulbs, creating an even flood covering an angle of roughly sixty degrees.

Brute   see **Arc.**

Budget   the overall estimated and allocated expense for the making of a film, or for any particular aspect of the process; also a daily sheet, issued to cast and crew, indicating which scenes are to be shot on the following day and which people will be required. See also **Call sheet.**

Burnt up   scenes in which set or actors are overlighted.

Busy   anything in action or setting which distracts from the intended focus of interest.

Butterfly lighting   light is placed in front of the subject and shadow reduced to a delicate minimum; used chiefly in closeups, for glamor.

Call sheet   a mimeographed list, prepared by the assistant director and the unit production manager, indicating the requirements and calls for the next day's shooting; includes cast, crew, and equipment required.

Calls   estimated time for various members of cast and crew to report for work.

Cameo part   a bit part in a picture for which a star is cast.

Camera motion picture camera designed to take photographic images on cinematographic film; conventionally a 35 MM camera for commercial filming, but 16 MM cameras, and, occasionally, 8 MM cameras, are also used; capable of using a wide variety of lenses.

Camera angle the position or standpoint of the camera in terms of the scene and the subject being filmed; unless otherwise specified, is usually assumed to be eye level. See also **High angle shot** and **Low angle shot.**

Camera boom (also **crane**) a mobile crane with a platform for the camera which can be used for either fixed or moving shots, and allows for movement horizontally and vertically, backward and forward.

Camera operator second man of the camera crew; operates the camera physically, responsible for frame and focus.

Cameraman (also **cinematographer** and **director of photography**) senior member of the camera crew; supervises all operations of the camera and the lighting of sets and actors; with director creates the composition of the shots.

Cant (**frame** or **shot**; also **oblique angle, slant frame**) a shot made with the camera slightly tilted, to create a special effect or to exaggerate normal angles.

Cast the actors participating in a film, including **stars, featured players, bit players,** and **extras.**

Casting director responsible for keeping records of actors suitable for parts and available for work on a film.

Cheat shot a shot in which a portion of a subject or part of an action is excluded from view to create an illusion or suggest a special effect.

Cinéaste (French for filmmaker) the ordering mind of the director.

Cinema of ideas as in theater of ideas, filmmaking for ideological or social purpose, or films which probe and question intellectual concepts in the context of fiction as well as in the documentary.

Cinéma vérité (also **direct cinema**) deriving from technique of newsreels and documentary filming; deliberate imitation of style and manner of a happening; a conscious attempt to represent an unplanned, accidental filming.

Cinematography the art of recording motion photographically and reproducing it for audiences.

Cinemobile Mark IV a single, 35-foot, bus-like vehicle, created and designed by Fouad Said, containing all necessary equipment, bathrooms, dressing rooms, and space for a staff and crew of fifty, which is rapidly replacing the huge caravans of trucks and vehicles necessary for filming on location; a self-contained unit, this vehicle has been widely and successfully used in filming recent American pictures at a variety of locations.

Clapper (also **number board** and **slate**) a pair of hinged boards which are clapped together at the beginning of each numbered take so that sound and picture can be synchronized in editing; a slate on which the scene number and take number are written and photographed.

Clip   a short section or sequence from a film.

Close medium shot (also **close middle shot, MCS**)   a shot of indefinite distance between a medium shot and a close shot; a close medium shot of a human subject is usually a bust shot.

Closeup (**CU**, also **close shot, CS, tight shot**)   shot in which the camera, actually or apparently, is close to the subject; in terms of an actor, it usually includes area from shoulders to top of head or face only; variations are the large closeup or big closeup, focused on one part of an object or part of the face or anatomy of an actor.

Combined continuity   a complete verbal and numerical record of the finished film, including action, dialogue, sounds, camera angles, footage, and frames, prepared by the **script supervisor.**

Commentary (also **voice over narration**)   descriptive or narrative talk in accompaniment with the film.

Composer   creates music for a film.

Composite print (British: **combined print**)   an edited, completed, positive print of the film, or strip of film, containing all sound tracks.

Composition   the arrangement and real or apparent movement of subjects in frame, shot, scene, or sequence, together with qualities of perspective, lighting, photography. The composition of a single shot is often analyzed analogously to the composition of a painting.

Comprehensive shot   a complete shot of a large area or large-scale action. See also **Establishing shot.**

Continuity   the editorial organization of shots and sequences, with transitions between them, in a film.

Continuity editing   editing which is tied to establishing definite story points; distinguished from **dynamic editing.**

Contrast   the relationship of the elements of brightness in a picture.

Costume designer   designs and creates wardrobe for a film.

Costumers   maintain clothing and wardrobe during production, assist players in dressing, and stand by on set.

Cover   the number of **setups** and **takes** used in filming a scene.

Cover set   a set in readiness for filming in the event that, for any reason, the regular filming schedule cannot be followed.

Coverage   the amount of film, the number of takes and footage, from various angles, allotted by the director in the filming of a scene or sequence.

Crab dolly   a small wheeled platform mount for the camera, which may be moved on level ground by hand; is moved by **grips;** used for easy movement over level ground or on studio sound stage floors; may be moved in any direction (crabbed). See also **Dolly.**

Crane shot (also **boom shot**) a shot taken by a camera from a camera boom.

Credits (also **screen credits**) the names of members of staff, cast, and crew who are officially credited, that is, recognized according to custom, contracts, and union regulations, in the film.

Cross-cut (also **parallel editing**) juxtaposition of two or more separate shots or scenes with parts of each presented alternately so that separate actions are represented as simultaneous.

Crutch music mood pieces supporting scenes; principal problem is timing to end simultaneously with the scene.

Cut (1) an individual strip of film; (2) a transition between two separate shots joined together so that the first shot is instantaneously replaced by the second; (3) as a verb, to trim and join shots together, to edit a film; (4) a shot; (5) an instruction to terminate a shot, given only by the director.

Cutaway a shot apparently taking place at the same time as the main action of a scene; most commonly a **reaction shot.**

Cut-in (also **insert shot**) a shot of some detail of the main action other than the faces of actors involved.

Cut-in scene a scene taken separately and inserted into a film.

Cutout parts of film discarded by the film editor.

Cutter the **film editor;** also refers to his assistants.

Cutting bench a special, vinyl-surfaced table used by film editors.

Cutting on movement a method associated with the **match cut;** when cutting between shots of the same subject in an apparently continuous time sequence, the cut is made on the motion of the subject to reduce audience awareness of the cut.

Cutting piece an illusory blending of widely separated locations or sets into an apparent whole.

Cutting room room or space assigned to the editor and his assistants for editing the film.

Dailies (also **rushes**) film photographed on the previous working day, developed, printed, **rough cut,** and screened on the following day for the benefit of the director and his staff; also daily progress reports on the production.

Day for night shooting night scenes in daylight, using filters and other technical devices to simulate darkness.

Deep focus sharp focus for a **long shot** or **far shot.**

Deep focus lens a lens permitting simultaneous focus for a closeup and a long shot background in the same shot.

Depth of field the distance to and from the camera in which an actor can move or an object can be moved without becoming out of focus.

Depth of focus the extent to which a lens can focus on near and distant objects at the same time.

Dialing　control of the sound during filming by the **mixer;** unwanted sounds can be dialed out.

Dialogue (also **lines, words**)　all spoken words in a film.

Dialogue director (also **coach**)　assigned to rehearsal of lines and prompting of players.

Differential focus　photographing an object in sharp focus with rest of the shot out of focus.

Diffusion screens　screens used to control light and shadow on a set. See also **Reflectors.**

Diffusor　material which is used to soften a beam of light.

Direct cut　a cut, but stipulated direct cut in script directions to emphasize this particular form of transition rather than to leave it optional; often used at a place where, conventionally, the editor might use another transition.

Directional movement　real or apparent movement of the subjects of a shot or scene as blocked and arranged by the director as a part of his composition and **structured rhythm;** movement, within a frame, may be left (**l**) or right (**r**), towards the background (**bg**) or foreground (**fg**) of the shot; also applied to arrangements of static objects on a set which may be photographed in such a way, by moving the camera, by lens adjustment, or by changing the angle, as to make objects seem to move, as, for example, when the camera imitates the **point of view** of a moving character; also applied to the relationship of movements and motion in separate shots and scenes linked together in editing.

Director　responsible for all aspects of filmmaking from the beginning of production to release.

Dissolve (also **lap dissolve** and **mix**)　the merging of one shot into the next, produced by superimposition of the two shots and a fade out of the first and a fade in of the second; usually a laboratory process, but can be done in the camera while shooting.

Documentary film　a nonfiction film on subjects of general interest.

Dolly　a wheeled platform serving as a camera mount which can be manhandled in any direction; sometimes called **trolley** when mounted on tracks.

Dolly in (also **track in**)　moving the camera towards the subject, decreasing the distance of the shot.

Dolly out (also **track out**)　moving the camera backwards, away from the subject, increasing the distance of the shot.

Dolly shot (also **travelling shot, tracking shot**)　a moving shot, usually made of a moving subject. See also **Following shot, Running shot, Trucking shot.**

Domestic release　commercial release of a film to be shown in theaters in the U.S. and Canada.

Double　see **Stunt double.**

Dress extra an **extra** reporting for work in his own tuxedo or full dress, her own evening gown.

Dubbing (also **mixing** and **rerecording**) process of combining all sound tracks, including music, sound effects, and dialogue, into one synchronized sound track for the film; also the process of synchronizing foreign language dialogue for foreign language versions of a completed film.

Dupe negative a negative made from a positive print.

Dynamic editing a style of editing suitable to action scenes and characteristic of documentary filmmaking where the film is "made" in editing; its quality is rapid pace and maximum visual impact in combinations of shots.

Dynamic frame any device or technique which serves to make the screen itself appear either to enlarge or decrease in size.

Editor (also **cutter**) responsible to the director for entire process of editing and assembling the film, from first takes to final **work print**, including all technical aspects, optical and sound.

Establishing shot a shot which serves to locate the action for the scene to follow.

Expressionism in cinema refers to a filmmaking movement in post-World War I Germany; characterized by deliberate artifice in lighting, costumes, and sets, by symbolic or mime-like acting, by fantasy or strong elements of the fantastic.

Exterior (**EXT.**) shooting done outdoors, on location, or on the lot of the studio.

Extra (also **screen extra**) a member of the cast used for background purposes and authenticity; if the extra acts or reacts in a scene, a silent bit, he receives additional pay. See also **Stand-in.**

Eye level (also **horizontal**) the standard camera angle, assumed unless otherwise specified by the director or the script.

Eyepiece viewing lens attachment to camera permitting the operator to see exactly what the camera lens will record. See also **Viewer.**

Fade the screen is blank (dark) with no image projected; a fade, in context of a film, usually serves as a distinct break in continuity, clearly setting off one sequence of shots from another; a slow fade calls for a very gradual diminishment of light and the image until the screen is blank.

Fade in the gradual appearance of a picture on the screen.

Fade out the gradual disappearance (fading) of picture and images from the screen, ending with a blank screen.

Far shot (also **very long shot, extreme long shot, distance shot**) a shot which includes not only the entire setting, but also the details of a distant background.

Fast motion (**effect**) see **Accelerated motion.**

Fast tempo the overall sense of timing, of "fast and slow" scenes and sequences in a film, is determined not by the speed of photography or by the physical speed or movement of subjects filmed, but by narrative and visual context and, chiefly, by the editorial craft in cutting. The effect of fast tempo might be achieved through cross-cutting or by dynamic editing.

Favoring (also **featuring** and **centering on**)   in any two shot or group shot, this direction calls for photography which will stress the significance of one or more of the characters involved.

Featured player   an actor with a major part who receives screen credit (billing), but who is ranked below the stars.

Feeler print   a print made from the edited negative of the work print with all effects inserted, but before final mixing.

Fill light   light placed so as to control the shadows cast by the **key light.**

Film grain   the size of the particles composing the light-sensitive layer of a film; a shot or print is said to be grainy when these particles are clearly visible in projection.

Filters   transparent glass or gelatin placed in front of or behind the camera lens to alter the light qualities or, in color filming, the tone relationships; among the standard filters used are *neutral density filters*, a gray filter uniformly cutting down on the light hitting the lens; *polarizing filters*, used especially to decrease sunlight and reflections on glass and water; *diffusion filters*, which serve to soften hard lines and are used for facial closeups; *fog filters*, which create a foggy effect; for black-and-white films, a *color filter*, which lightens its own color and darkens its compliment; and *color-compensating filters*, used to control illumination and give good color rendition.

Final negative   the edited negative from which the composite print is made.

Fine grains   duplicate negatives of the film ordered from the laboratory for technical and editorial use.

Fixed (also **static**) **camera**   shooting from any angle or distance when the camera remains in a fixed position throughout the shot; distinguished from **mobile** or **moving camera.**

Fixed frame   a shot in which the camera is fixed (static) and in which there is no background movement.

Flash forward   shot, scene, or sequence interrupting the ongoing time sequence of a film by introducing action or events to come; it may refer forward to scenes which will be viewed or may imply future time and events outside the chronology of the film.

Flash shot   a shot of very few frames and short duration, therefore almost subliminal in effect; often used as an insert within the context of an ongoing shot or scene to represent a fragment of subjective memory or an intimation or intuition of future time.

Flashback   a shot, scene, or sequence, introduced into the chronological sequence of a film and breaking that sequence by referring to time past; it may refer back to action already seen or may introduce narrative elements or subjective memory of the past into the imagined present of the film.

Flip (also **flipover wipe** and **flip frame**)   a transitional device in which the frame of one shot revolves 360 degrees, and flips over, ending its revolution with the frame of the next shot.

Floor   any part of a studio where shooting is in progress; the ground level of any set, exterior or interior.

Focus   to adjust the lens of a camera (or projector) in order to keep a sharply defined image.

Following shot   a shot in which the camera moves or seems to move to follow a moving actor or object. See also **Running shot.**

Footage   a length of film measured in feet; often used loosely to refer to a shot, scene, or sequence of a film.

Foreground (**fg**)   that part of the scene immediately in front of the camera.

Foreshadowing   cinematic or narrative (or both) means of preparing the audience to accept as probable some future action or event.

Form cutting   the framing in a following shot of a subject or compositional arrangement which has a shape or contour in some way similar to an image in the shot preceding it; the relationship and juxtaposition of the two can serve as a simple comparison (as in a simile in poetry), or, by association, within the context of the film, or by allusion, can be raised to the higher power of metaphor and symbol.

Frame (sometimes **still**)   a single photograph in the series printed on a length of cinematographic film; in photographing a scene or shot the frame of the shot, seen through the eyepiece of the camera, or the **viewer,** determines the staging areas (background and foreground, left and right) and the composition of the shot or scene; anything which can be seen is said to be *in frame;* anything in the scene or shot which cannot be seen is *out-of-frame* or *off-frame* (of); see also **Off-camera** and **On-camera;** the average ninety-minute feature film is made up of 129,000 separate frames or 8,100 feet of film.

Frame line   the dividing line separating each single frame from the next.

Frame slant   a shot in which the camera is slightly tilted on its axis so that the image appears on the screen off center, in a tilted position. See also **Cant.**

Freeze shot   the repetition of a single frame for an extended time, done either in camera while photographing or by editing, so that, when seen in projection, the shot appears to freeze, to be a still photograph. See also **Zoom freeze.**

Front lighting (also **pancake lighting**)   the light source is from approximately the same position and angle as the camera; serves to flatten out planes and angles.

Full shot   a shot of indeterminate distance, from any angle, but fully including the subject of the shot; when applied to actors, the shot calls for the full body to be in frame.

Gaffer   the electrical foreman of the set; also may be used, loosely, to designate any foreman of any production department or crew.

General shot   any shot from any angle in which a complete action or a large part of the set is visible.

Glass shot   a shot in which part of the background or setting is painted or photographed on glass or other transparent material, which is placed between the camera and the subject so that it will merge with the full-size set being photographed.

Gobo (also **nigger**)   a black screen, mounted adjustably, used to control light falling on the camera.

Greensman (also **nurseryman**)   charged with all trees, plants, shrubbery, and flowers not in vases on exterior or interior sets; responsible for required seasonal changes.

Grip   a skilled set laborer, general, all-purpose set assistant; the foreman is known as the **key grip** or **head grip.**

Group shot   a shot of unspecified distance and angle, concentrating upon three or more characters.

Hand-held camera (HH)   use of a camera—a 16 MM camera whose film will subsequently be blown up to 35 MM—without any conventional fixed or mobile mounting; characteristic of documentary and direct cinema filming; *effect* of hand-held camera can be imitated with conventional camera mounting; though held by hand, the camera can be firmly controlled by means of body braces, shoulder rests.

Hatchet lighting   light source placed ninety degrees from the camera to create a half-shadow effect on the subject.

Head-on shot   a shot in which the action appears to come directly towards the camera; most often used in relation to **trucking shot.**

Heavy   a movie villain.

Hi hat   a small, low mount for the camera for very **low angle** shooting, or for shooting a few inches off the floor.

High angle shot (also **high shot**)   a shot taken by any means from an elevated angle in terms of the subject; sometimes referred to as **shooting down** or **looking down.**

Implicit music   music for film which, in addition to supporting the physical sense of action (see also **Kinetic music**), also serves to fit with visual image and dialogue to convey a parallel or corresponding mood, and likewise to accentuate visual techniques and transitions.

In sequence   shooting on a schedule which follows the sequence and order of the shooting script; this is very seldom done, for reasons of economy and efficiency.

Incidental music   music apparently coming from a real sound source in the scene, as for example, radio, jukebox, musical instrument.

Inkie   an intensely bright incandescent lamp.

Insert   (1) a shot, usually a closeup, used to reveal a **title** or any subject in detail; (2) any material cut into a scene, though not shot in the making of the scene, by the editor; (3) also a camera car used for mobile photography.

Intercut   a short cut used within a larger sequence. See also **Cross-cut.**

Interior (INT.)   any set which represents an indoor situation; distinguished from **exterior.**

Interpolated shots   see **Insert.**

Intertitles (also **titles,** distinguished from the **main title** or **titles and credits**) any shot of any written or printed material inserted in any scene or sequence of a film.

Invisible cutting (also **invisible editing**)   unobtrusive cutting by means of **match cuts** or by **motivation,** intended to distract audience attention from awareness of editing.

Iris in   to open up the photographed image from a pinpoint or small portion of the frame until the whole frame is filled with the picture.

Iris out   to close down the photographed image to a pinpoint or small portion of the frame.

Irising   a gradual opening up or closing down of the photographed image from or to a pinpoint; can be done in camera by means of an *iris diaphragm* or by **masking;** can be accomplished in laboratory by optical or chemical means; a transitional device for linking one scene to another.

Juicer   any electrician working on the set.

Jump cut (distinguished from a **match cut**)   in perjorative sense, refers to any poorly made match cut; used as a deliberate artistic device, it represents the cutting out of footage which would give the sequence a conventional continuity; also a cut in which the camera angle changes slightly on the cut, giving an impression of a jump in action.

Key light   the main source of light illuminating the subject of a shot.

Kinesthetic involvement   the result of artistic techniques designed to involve the audience in sharing physical and psychological feelings of the film.

Kinetic music   music designed to accompany and express the actions shown in a scene or sequence.

l   left; stage left or frame left.

Lap dissolve   see **Dissolve.** See also **Overlap shot.**

Lay behind   musical term; music to be subdued and unobtrusive in accompaniment to a scene.

Lens turret   a rotating device on the camera which carries two or more lenses which may be turned swiftly into position during shooting.

Library shot   any shot taken from a film library for use in a film; a shot not taken for a particular film, but used in it. See also **Stock shot.**

Lighting the set   with very few exceptions all sets, exterior and interior, in studio and on location, must be **lit,** that is, illuminated by lights and controlled by reflectors, diffusion screens.

Location   any place outside a studio and its lot where exterior or interior shooting takes place; such shooting is said to be *on location; local* location is within easy driving distance of the studio; any other location is classified as *distant.*

Long lens   a lens with a focal length greater than normal, therefore including a narrow angle of a scene; incorrectly called a **telephoto lens.**

Long shot (ls)   shot taken at a distance from the action or subject, conventionally not less than fifty yards and often at a greater distance; a long shot need *not* be a **full shot** including a complete setting or action.

Loop film (also **cyclic film**)   a short film with its ends joined together which can be run through a projector without interruption in continuous repetition.

Looping   process by which actors replace lines made on the original sound track, for purposes of clarity and inflection, in a studio sound recording room; a loop film is prepared and projected and the actor repeats his lines, timing (**synchronizing**) his words with his filmed lip movements; frequently used, wrongly, for **dubbing.**

Lot   any land owned by a studio and situated near sound stages where shooting may take place; also a term for the entire studio; something is located as happening *on the lot* or *off the lot.*

Low angle shot (also **camera looking up**)   the camera is situated below the subject of the shot, shooting upward.

Low key   (1) when only a few highlights are used to illuminate the subject and a large portion of the set is shadowy, the lighting is called *low key;* (2) similarly the subject may be shot in low key by stopping down the lens opening of the camera; (3) finally, a dark print, in color or black and white, is low key.

Low truck shot   a moving shot taken from a low angle.

Main title (also **title and credits**)   the title of the film; usually shown in combination with the screen credits.

Makeup artist   responsible for all makeup; except, when making up female players, union regulations confine the makeup artist's activities to area from top of head to apex of breastbone, from fingertips to elbows; also responsible for creation of all character effects, as, for example, wounds, scars, aging; and responsible for mustaches, beards, and male wigs.

Map location   convention, established by earliest filmmakers and followed ever since, in which the frame is viewed as analogous to a map; thus right-to-left movement indicates movement east to west and vice versa, and the top of the frame may suggest north, the bottom, south; from this beginning developed more sophisticated means of directional cutting, using a rhythm of lines of movement within a shot, scene, and sequence.

Married print   see **Combined print.**

Mask   a shield or shape placed in front of the camera lens to eliminate (that is, mask out) some part of the shot.

Mask shot   shot made with lens covered to limit what can be filmed; most often used (analogous to insert shot) to simulate a shot seen through an object, as, for example, a keyhole or crack, telescope, gun sight, binoculars, or camera.

Master film   the final edited negative from which all theatrical prints are made.

Master scene   the overall scene, as indicated in the shooting script and by the director, considered as a unit, without regard to the breakdown of the scene into separate shots and takes or the cutting within the scene by the editor.

Master shot   a single shooting or take of an entire piece of dramatic action.

Match cut   a carefully unobtrusive cut designed to blend the action of two shots so closely together that the effect of cutting is minimized.

Matte shot   a special effects process whereby two separately shot sequences are combined harmoniously into one print, giving the effect of being done at one time and in one location; related to **process shot.**

Meal penalty   a union regulation requiring that on all location shooting the entire film company must be fed at precisely specified hours and with high quality food; failure to meet this regulation requires that the producer must pay a penalty to all workers.

Medium (or **middle**) **close shot** (**MCS**) or **closeup** (**MCU**)   a shot of indeterminate distance between a medium shot and a close shot; basically a close shot in which a larger part of the subject than usual is visible.

Medium long shot (**MLS**)   shot of indefinite distance between medium and long, tending towards the long shot but retaining the medium shot's characteristics of clear identity of persons and at least part of the immediate setting.

Medium shot   by convention a shot made from between five and fifteen yards' apparent distance and including a subject or group in entirety.

Metteur en scène (French; also *réalisateur*)   director, filmmaker.

Middle shot (**mid-shot**; also **American shot**)   a medium shot which focuses on the subject from the knees up.

Mise en scène (French)   scenery, setting, and staging; involves, for the director, direction of actors in delivery of lines and in blocking (planning) their movements; also includes planning individual camera shots.

Mixer   on the set, a member of the sound crew who operates a sound console in conjunction with the camera; charged with obtaining clear and distinct sound recording during shooting; during dubbing, any one of several sound men who dial in and dial out sounds from the various tracks, creating the sound track for the film.

Mobile (also **motion**) **camera**   the capacity of the camera to be changed in distance and angle between shots, or to move or seem to move during a single shot.

Model shot   any shot in which a model or an object or objects is photographed.

Montage   (1) term used by Sergei Eisenstein to describe rhetorical arrangement of shots (sometimes single frames) in juxtaposition with each other in order to produce or imply another unit independent of the separate elements forming it; defined by Ernest Lindgren in *The Art of the Film* as "the combination in art of representative fragments of nature to form an imaginative whole which has no counterpart in nature"; (2) French term for the editing process; (3) American term for an assembly of short shots used to indicate a passage of time and events within that time span.

MOS (also **wild picture**)   any shots, scenes, or sequences taken without sound; when used in script directions it calls for a silent unit.

Motivation   establishing probability or causality for anything in the film whether in narrative of script, action, and characterization of actors, or in the editing cuts and transitions.

Moving shot (also **running shot**)   any shot in which the camera, by any means, follows with actors or objects moving in that scene.

Moviola   originally a trade name, now used for all brands of the special projection machine used by film editors; machine allows the editor to run the film at various speeds, backwards and forwards, to stop on any single frame, and to view the film closely through a magnifying device.

Muddy scene   a scene which is inadequately or badly lighted.

Multiple exposure (double exposure)   two or more exposures made on the same series of frames.

Multiple images   special effects method which produces any number of images of the same shot or subject in a frame, or a variety of separate images in the same frame and shot.

Music editor (also **music cutter**)   assigned as technical aid and assistant to the composer.

Mute negative   negative of sound film not including the sound track.

Mute print   positive print of sound motion picture not including the sound track.

Narrative editing   see **Continuity editing.**

Negative cost   the total expense of making a film.

Negative cutter   a specialist at the photographic laboratory, responsible for matching the original negative, frame by frame, with the final work print created by the film editor, to create the master film.

Negative cutting   the editorial work done at the photographic laboratory to match the original negative with the final work print.

Neorealism (Italian: *réalismo*)   post-World War II movement in Italian cinema, lasting into the 1950s; characterized by a direct and simple style of filmmaking, and use of natural settings and unprofessional actors.

New Wave (French: *nouvelle vague*)   a contemporary movement in French filmmaking, based upon the concept of the director as *auteur*; developed by critics writing for *Cahiers du Cinéma*, some of whom have since proved theory in practice, directing distinguished films.

Newsreels   filmed shorts of recent news events widely shown in theaters prior to the development of television and TV news programs; significant in the development of the documentary film.

Nonsynchronous sound (distinguished from **synchronous sound** in which a sound effect is precisely matched to the visual image apparently producing the sound)   the use of the sound without the visual image, the sound substituting for and implying the visual image; also applied to unrealistic sound in which the sound does not derive directly from the visual image but comments on it, as, for example, a scene showing the stockmarket with stockbrokers shouting, but the sound is of barking dogs and roaring beasts.

Objective camera   by careful application of various techniques, the director seeks to divert audience attention away from any sense of filmmaking and to present the subject in a seemingly objective manner, as if the camera were merely recording events.

Off-camera (also **off-frame, of,** and **off-screen, os**)   any action or dialogue or sound taking place out of view in a particular shot, scene, or sequence.

On-camera (also **on-screen**)   action, dialogue, or sound happening in frame, directly experienced by the spectator in a particular shot, scene, or sequence.

On the nose   any aspect of a film, visual, auditory, or narrative, presented in an explicit and conventional fashion; perjoratively, a cinematic cliché.

Optical effects   any effects carried out or created in the optical department of a film-processing laboratory; in addition to a variety of laboratory effects, many effects usually created by camera or editing can be created in the laboratory by complex processes.

Optical printer   a device which makes it possible for images from one film to be photographed on another film.

Optical zoom   a simulated **zoom shot** created in the laboratory.

Out-take   any take that is not used in the completed film.

Overlap   in sound or dialogue; a sound or words from one shot or scene intruding upon another, either carried over from a previous scene or anticipating the next.

Overlap shots   a series of shots of the same action from different angles with the effect of extending the time and distance covered by the action.

Overlay   one sound track superimposed on another in dubbing.

Overshooting   the practice by most film directors of shooting and printing far more film of a given scene than can be used in the finished film, for the purpose of allowing maximum flexibility and creativity during editing; an average feature film, 8,100 feet, is reduced by editing from 200,000 feet of printed takes.

Over-shoulder shot   shot, sharing the viewpoint of a character, but including a portion of the character's back and shoulders in the foreground.

Package   subject of film to be made, together with basic staff, cast, and crew available and interested to work on it; and frequently including a draft of the screenplay, along with a breakdown.

Paint in   to add objects, by various means, to a photographed scene as a special effect.

Pan (also **panoramic shot**)   to rotate the camera head on its pivot or axis in a horizontal plane in order either to keep a moving subject in view or to move across a stationary scene. See also **Swish-pan.**

Pan down/pan up (British)   to move the camera in a vertical plane, down or up, towards the subject. See also **Tilt shot.**

Parallel editing (also **parallel action**)   an editing technique of presenting separately shot sequences of action happening in different locations as related to each other by shifting the audience viewpoint back and forth between the separate sequences. See also **Cross-cut.**

Peep show (also **kinetoscope**)   one of the earliest forms of motion picture involving the use of a vertically moving, sprocketed film strip, seen by a single viewer through a slit or eyehole.

Photofloods   small, bright lights used for general illumination.

Photoplay   in early days (1914), a euphemism for movies, result of a contest for an appropriate term; a film version of a stage play, with minimal adaptation for cinema.

Pickups   shots filmed after the completion of the regular shooting schedule and during the editing phase of production; refers to minor material, not involving extensive reshooting, but merely shots needed for transitions, continuity.

Playback   use of a recorded sound track during shooting or in looping in order to synchronize action, sound, lip movements, and dialogue.

Point of view (POV)   an aspect of **subjective camera;** calls for the camera to simulate, by position, angle, and distance, the view of a subject in the scene of action taking place in that scene; unlike the over-shoulder shot, a point of view shot does not usually include the observing subject or subjects in its frame.

Polecats   single ceiling-to-floor poles used as mounts for light fixtures.

Position camera position is defined as static (fixed) or moving.

Prescoring any music **scored** before production of a film.

Print a positive copy of negative film; a **take** indicated to be sent to the laboratory for processing and reproduction.

Process shot (also **back projection, rear projection**) a scene shot against the background of a moving picture, which is projected through a transparent screen behind the actions being filmed; thus the process shot joins together the two separate units of film in one unit; a conventional example is the shot of two actors in an automobile with a shot of moving traffic projected behind them for verisimilitude.

Producer financier, and responsible overall for the making of a film, from idea through theatrical release, domestic and foreign.

Production designer an art director with exceptional responsibility and control, including costumes, props, makeup, decorations, and style, as well as sets.

Production manager see **Unit production manager.**

Production still any still photograph taken of any aspect of a film in production.

Prop any object seen or used on any set except painted scenery and costumes.

Prop box wheeled, portable, piano-size boxes containing all materials necessary for props and their maintenance; also applied to any portable vehicle, including moving van, used by the prop man.

Prop man (also **property master**) responsible for all objects used in the action of a film, excluding scenery and costumes.

Property the story of subject matter of a film to be produced; or a finished film.

Post-synchronize (British; **looping** [U.S.]) recording dialogue with projected film.

Publicity still any still photograph taken before, during, or after the shooting of a film for the purposes of publicity and advertising, including display photographs often used at the entrance of theaters.

Pull back (PB) a camera direction indicating that the camera moves, or seems to move, back away from the subject.

Put in (a special effect) to create an effect by augmenting or increasing something actually photographed; for example, flames of a fire may be *put in* a scene.

Quartz light (also **halogen**) specially designed incandescent light capable of extremely high intensity and heat; thus a powerful source of illumination.

Quick cutting editing of film in short shots for an effect of rapidity.

Raw stock film that has not yet been used, exposed, or processed.

Reaction shot a shot featuring the response or reaction of one or more characters to an action already seen or about to be seen.

Reduction (opposite of enlargement and **blowup**)   process by which a film made in one width is produced in a smaller width; for example, 35 MM is *reduced* to 16 MM or 8 MM prints.

Reel   a strip of film on a spool; standard reel is 2,000 feet for American 35 MM projectors.

Reflector light   a light with a built-in reflector; may be either a spotlight for concentrated light beam or floodlight with evenly diffused illumination.

Reflectors   reflecting boards used to control, boost, and direct sunlight or lighting.

Relational editing   editing of separate shots to link them together associatively and intellectually.

Release print   a film for general theatrical showing.

Release script (British)   script version of the finished film. See also **Combined continuity.**

Remake   another filmed version of a previously produced property.

Rembrandt lighting   dramatic and shadowed lighting; term is attributed to Cecil B. De Mille upon receipt of a telegram complaining that sender "couldn't even see the characters' faces half the time" in a De Mille film. "Tell him it's Rembrandt light," De Mille replied.

Retakes   takes made again of unsatisfactory material already shot and viewed in rough form.

Reverse angle shot   a shot made in opposite direction, that is, *reversed*, from the preceding shot.

Reverse motion   camera photographing with film running backward so that when projected the actions or movements appear in reverse sequence; important for special effects.

Riffle book (also **flip book** and **kineograph**)   an early (1868) patented precursor of the motion picture in which a succession of parts of a movement are depicted on pages of a book so that by swiftly thumbing the pages, the viewer enjoys the illusion of a moving image.

"Roll it" (also **"roll 'em"**)   a director's cue for the start of filming or projection of a film.

Rough cut print   a first assembly of the total film in rough form and without music and dubbed sound effects.

Rough in   arrangement and blocking of lighting on the set prior to shooting.

Running lines   rehearsing dialogue.

Running shot   a shot in which the camera moves or seems to move keeping up with a moving actor or object.

Running time   the length of time a film will take to be projected at standard projection speed.

Rushes   see **Dailies.**

Scenario (also **production script**)   see **Script.**

Scene a series of **shots** taken at same setting or location from any number of camera angles and positions.

Scoring call assignment of musicians and conductor for purpose of recording the music track for a film.

Scoring stage special sound stage designed for scoring the music track of a film during projection of the sequences to be scored.

Screenplay preproduction, written version of film including settings, scenes, characters, dialogue, and usually some indicated camera directions.

Scrim framed netting used in order to soften, diffuse, or eliminate light on the set.

Script (shooting script) a version of the screenplay as revised and prepared for production.

Script supervisor (also **script clerk**) keeps track of everything happening during shooting, that is, logs the shooting in terms of the shooting script; serves as reminder and prompter; prepares combined continuity when filming and editing are complete.

Second unit a self-contained production unit for the filming of scenes and sequences not requiring the director or principals of the cast.

Seconds assistants to the assistant director.

Sequence a number of scenes linked together by time, location, or narrative structure to form a unit of a motion picture.

Serials brief one- or two-reel films involving the same central characters, and presented on a continuing basis; traditionally each unit ending with an unresolved problem or situation (a cliffhanger) which is resolved at the outset of the next episode.

Series short films involving the same chief characters, and each film a complete episode in itself.

Set any place, exterior or interior, on location or in a studio, designated and prepared for shooting in the production of a film.

Set decorator furnishes and decorates the set.

Set dresser responsible for details of settings and locations during production.

Set painter responsible for painting, maintaining, aging all painted parts of the set, also for eliminating reflections.

Setup relationship between the location of the camera, the area of the set or scene, and the actors; a single camera position.

Shadowmakers devices in many sizes and shapes used by cameramen to create shadows and to filter light.

Sharpness the extent or relative degree in which details in a shot are presented with photographic clarity and definition; when details are clear and distinct, easily identified and perceived, they are said to be *sharp*.

Shoot to film a shot, scene, sequence, or entire motion picture.

Shoot up/down   to shoot from a low angle or a high angle on the subject.

Shooting ratio   the ratio of film shot to the final footage of the completed film.

Shooting schedule   an advance schedule of work assignments, together with sets, cast, costumes, and equipment required.

Short   any standard film of less than 3,000 feet in length.

Shot   (1) a single continuous unit of film taken at one set and from one camera setup; (2) a single photograph or frame; (3) a notation of camera angle, distance, movement involved in one setup; (4) a printed **take;** editorially, any consecutive strip of frames; (5) **cut** is sometimes used for any shot or part of a take in editing.

Shotgun microphone   a special microphone designed to pick up and isolate particular sounds against a noisy background.

Skip framing   a laboratory simulation of accelerated motion; printing only a portion of the original negative frames gives effect of speeded-up action; opposite of **double framing,** which slows down action.

Slow motion   effect of slowing down natural action or rhythms; either by filming actions at faster rate than usual, then projecting at standard rate, or by optical effects in the laboratory.

Sneak preview   an unannounced trial showing of a new film before a regular theater audience.

Soft focus   effect derived from shooting slightly out of focus.

Sound   an integral part of all but silent films consisting of dialogue, music, and sound effects.

Sound boom   a boom for placing the recording microphone close to the actors in a scene.

Sound crew   all technicians on the set charged with the recording of dialogue and sounds and the dialing out of unwanted noise during shooting; a separate unit from the camera crew, but working in close coordination with them.

Sound effects editor   responsible for overseeing the preparation of separate tracks and for the final dubbing of the sound track.

Sound montage   use of dialogue, music, or sound effects to relate separate settings or sequences.

Special effects   technical tricks in photography or processing designed to create illusions; anything added to the film after shooting, in the laboratory or in editing.

Special effects expert   handles the design, mechanics, and engineering of any required special effects which cannot be created in camera or by laboratory.

Splicing   joining together separate pieces of processed film.

Split screen (also **half-wipe**)   frame in which two or more images are simultaneously seen.

Spotlight any light which projects an intense and narrow beam.

Stand-in an extra who takes the place of an actor during times of light arrangement and camera adjustment.

Star a principal member of the cast with a leading dramatic role in the film; a major box-office attraction, not necessarily an actor or actress.

Static position a setup in which the camera is in a fixed position and does not move or seem to move; for example, though actors move about within the frame or move out of the frame, the camera does not move with them or follow, but continues throughout the shot to shoot from an established angle, recording the same fixed frame.

Steal a shot to photograph subjects who are not aware of being filmed.

Step outline (also **synopsis**) a brief story outline indicating the dramatic structure of a screenplay yet to be written.

Stock shot (**stock footage**) use of film not specifically photographed for the motion picture being produced.

Stop camera (also **stop photography**) two separate camera operations film the same shot, the two shots becoming one shot in viewing.

Stop printing the repetition of a single frame or image, created in laboratory, to **freeze** or stop action.

Story preproduction, it is the narrative line of the script augmented by the storyboard; in filming and after, the story is the organization of shots and sequences into continuity.

Story analyst a professional reader, preparing synopses and analyses of published material and recommending likely film properties.

Storyboard (also **continuity sketches**) a preliminary, cartoon-strip form version, in sketches, prepared from the shooting script, breaking down action into a controlled sequence of possible shots.

Straight cut (also **direct cut**) a cut called for where, by convention, another kind of editorial linking or transition might be expected.

Stretch out a bus-type limousine for transportation to and from locations.

Structured rhythm (also **structural rhythm**) generally applied to the overall sense of harmonious order of a film, deriving from the director's artistry and control; in film the elements are multiple, including and combining the basic narrative structure of the story, the patterns and arrangements of sound, music, and dialogue, the composition of light and shadow, the angles and movement of the camera, the editorial devices for separating and joining shots, scenes, and sequences; more specifically, structural rhythm in film refers to the purely visual aspects of the director's art, ranging from the composition of individual frames and shots to the relationships, established by likeness and contrast, of sequences, and their significance within the complete aesthetic experience of the film.

Studio driver all-purpose professional vehicle driver; also drives cranes, fork-lifts, trucks, tractors.

Studio stock   wardrobe, props, and other materials in possession of a studio.

Stunt   any piece of action requiring the use of a professional stuntman.

Stunt coordinator   experienced stuntman who acts as foreman of any group of stuntmen.

Stunt double   a stuntman who bears a close photographic resemblance to a particular actor.

Stuntman   a professional performer of all potentially dangerous action—leaps, falls, horse falls, fights, fainting—in a film.

Subjective camera (also **subjective shots**)   shots created so that the audience views them as if from the literal or subjective point of view of a character; shots indicative of the filmmaker's feelings and attitudes towards characters, objects, events, when the process of filmmaking has been established, explicitly or implicitly, as part of the cinematic experience.

Subtitles   (1) in silent films, the insertion of printed dialogue, comment, and description into filmed scenes or between scenes on subtitle cards; (2) in foreign language films not dubbed into English, the use of white letters on some dark part of the frame to give a translation of dialogue; (3) any title other than the main title.

Sun gun   small, battery-powered unit used chiefly in documentary filming for night shooting, following a subject from exterior to interior, and as a fill light in sunlight.

Superimposition   two or more shots within the same frame, an effect achieved either by camera or in laboratory; may apply also to sounds on tracks.

Survey   search for and establishment of the locations for various shots to be used in a film.

Swish-pan (also **whip shot**)   a rapid panning movement of the camera from one viewpoint or position of the set to another with the effect of blurring intermediate details in movement.

Synchronous sound   sound timed and simultaneous with visual images.

Take   each separate recording made of a shot while filming; a shot may consist of any number of takes; when any take is converted into a positive print from the negative, it becomes a **print**; also, in acting, a strong reaction.

Telephoto lens (also **true telephoto lens**)   a lens with an exceptionally long focal length, able to focus on a very narrow angle of a scene.

Tests   preliminary examinations, often by shooting film, prior to actual production, designed to check costumes (*wardrobe tests*), makeup, and talent (*screen tests*).

Theme   a musical sequence, analogous to *leitmotif*, associated in a film with a character, an action, a place; in film overall, the basic idea or subject of the film.

Thin (1) in sound, a sound too weak or vague for its purpose; (2) in acting, a two-dimensional role; (3) in writing, a part of the narrative which is not strongly created or a character not sufficiently developed.

Tilt shot (tilt up/tilt down) shot made by moving camera on its pivot or axis in a vertical plane.

Title any written or printed material used in the context of a film, as distinguished from the **main title** announcing the title of the film itself.

Tracking shots (also **trucking, travelling;** sometimes **dollying**) shots in which a mobile camera, mounted on tracks, a truck or other vehicle, or a dolly, moves with the subject or moves towards or away from the subject of a shot.

Trailer (also **theatrical trailer**) a short sequence of film used to advertise a feature film, and often derived from it, for theatrical showing.

Treatment intermediate stage in development of script, basically narrative in form, between step outline and screenplay.

Trim to cut or shorten in editing.

Trim can (also **out-take**) a film can where marked and numbered frames, cut out of a sequence in editing, are kept.

Trims and outs all frames of unused film left over at any stage of editing; these are stored in studio vaults for any possible future use.

Trucking shot loosely, any moving shot with camera on mobile mounting; strictly, a moving shot with camera mounted on a truck or van.

Two-shot shot of two characters, the camera usually as close as possible while keeping both in the shot.

Typage acting use of stock photographs from a film library of faces which, when cut into a dramatic sequence, seem to be reacting to the filmed situation and events.

Undershooting filming sequences with too little footage to permit adequate editorial coverage.

Unit production manager executive officer for the producer; from beginning is charged with execution of all the producer's plans, with budgeting, personnel, scheduling, picking locations, serving as manager and foreman for all crews and departments.

Unit still photographer member of production staff responsible for taking all action, production, publicity, and art still photographs.

Utility man lowest ranking titled member of a production crew; charged with running errands and general janitorial duties on the set.

Viewer a small hand-held lens device with frame lines precisely fitting the subject to be shot, permitting the director and the cameraman to examine possible shots without having to move the camera; the camera operator also has a similar instrument attached to his camera.

Voice over (VO) dialogue, comment, or narration coming from off-screen.

Wardrobe department charged with all aspects of costumes and clothing.

Whip shot (also **zip pan**) see **Swish pan.**

White telephone film   a type of film popular in the thirties, characterized by great luxury, opulent settings; often a musical film.

Wide angle lens   a lens of shorter focal length than is standard; creates an exaggerated perspective, increasing the apparent distance between the foreground and background of a shot.

Wigwag   an automatic red warning light which flashes outside the door of studio sound stages whenever sound is being recorded on the set.

Wild lines   dialogue not recorded on camera.

Wild sound (also **wild track**)   any sound not recorded to synchronize precisely with the picture taken; may be recorded during shooting or separately.

Wipe   a link between two shots, both sharing the screen briefly before the second image replaces the first; there are a wide variety of possible wipes in terms of direction; a *half-wipe* is a split-screen effect; a *soft wipe* has a slightly blurred edge between the two cuts.

Work print (also **copy print, cutting copy**)   any initial version of the uncompleted film used for editing, dubbing, preliminary screenings.

Wrangler   a handler for horses used in a film.

Zoom (shot)   a shot made by using a lens of varying focal lengths, permitting the change from wide angle to long lens or vice versa during an uninterrupted shot; camera can *zoom in* or *zoom out;* not as dimensional as an equivalent dolly shot with fixed lens but moving camera; *zoom in* effect can be simulated in laboratory with **optical zoom** in which an area of a frame can be progressively enlarged.

Zoom freeze   a zoom shot ending with a **freeze,** or apparent still photograph.

BIBLIOGRAPHY

Film Art, History

Altshuler, Thelma C. *Responses to Drama: An Introduction to Plays and Movies*. Boston: Houghton Mifflin, 1967.

Amelio, Robert, with Anita Owen and Susan Schaefer. *Willowbrook Cinema Study Project*. Dayton: Pflaum, 1970.

Anderson, Joseph L., and Donald Richie. *Japanese Film: Art and Industry*. New York: Grove, 1960.

Armes, Roy. *The Cinema of Alain Resnais*. New York: Barnes, 1968.

———. *French Film*. New York: Dutton, 1970.

———. *Screen Series: French Cinema*. New York, Barnes, 1970.

Arnheim, Rudolf. *Film as Art*. Berkeley: University of California, 1957.

———. *Visual Thinking*. Berkeley: University of California, 1969.

Baker, Fred. *Events: The Complete Scenario of the Film*. New York: Grove, 1970.

Balazs, Bêla. *Theory of the Film*. New York: Roy, 1953.

Balcon, Michael. *Twenty Years of British Films, 1925–1945*. Falcon, 1947.

Ball, Robert Hamilton. *Shakespeare on Silent Film*. New York: Theatre Arts, 1968.

Balshoffer, Fred J., and Arthur C. Miller. *One Reel a Week*. Berkeley: University of California, 1968.

Barbour, Alan G., with Alvin H. Marrill and James Robert Parish. *Karloff*. Kew Gardens, N.Y.: Cinefax, 1969.

Bardeche, Maurice, and Robert Brasillach. *History of Motion Pictures*. New York: Norton, 1938.

Barnouw, Erik, and S. Krishnaswamy. *Indian Film*. New York: Columbia University, 1963.

Barr, Charles. *Laurel and Hardy*. Berkeley: University of California, 1968.

Barry, Iris. *D. W. Griffith: American Film Master*. New York: Museum of Modern Art, 1965.

Battcock, Gregory. *The New American Cinema*. New York: Dutton, 1967.

Baxter, John. *Hollywood in the Thirties: A Complete Critical Survey of Hollywood Films from 1930–1940*. Paperback Library, 1970.

————. *Science Fiction in the Cinema*. New York: Barnes, 1970.

————. *Science Fiction in the Cinema: A Complete Critical Review of SF Films from A TRIP TO THE MOON (1902) to 2001: A SPACE ODYSSEY*. New York: Paperback Library, 1970.

Bazin, André (tr. by Hugh Gray). *What is Cinema?* Berkeley: University of California, 1967.

Behimer, Rudy, with Terry-Thomas and Cliff McCarty. *The Films of Errol Flynn*. New York: Citadel, 1969.

Bellone, Julius (ed.). *Renaissance of the Film*. New York: Macmillan, 1970.

Bennett, Joan, and Lois Kibbee. *The Bennett Playbill*. New York: Holt, Rinehart and Winston, 1970.

Benoit-Lévy, Jean. *The Art of the Motion Picture*. New York: Coward-McCann, 1946.

Bluestone, George. *Novels into Film*. Berkeley: University of California, 1966.

Blum, Daniel, and John Kobal. *A New Pictorial History of the Talkies*. New York: Grosset & Dunlap, 1970.

Bobker, Lee. *Elements of Film*. New York: Harcourt, Brace & World, 1969.

Bogdanovich, Peter. *The Cinema of Alfred Hitchcock*. New York: Museum of Modern Art, 1963.

————. *The Cinema of Howard Hawks*. New York: Museum of Modern Art, 1962.

————. *The Cinema of Orson Welles*. New York: Museum of Modern Art, 1961.

————. *John Ford*. Berkeley: University of California, 1970.

Bowser, Eileen. *Film Notes*. New York: Museum of Modern Art, 1969.

Brownlow, Kevin. *How It Happened Here*. New York: Doubleday, 1968.

————. *The Parade's Gone By*. New York: Alfred Knopf, 1968.

Butler, Ivan. *Religion in the Cinema*. New York: Barnes, 1969.

Calder-Marshall, Arthur. *The Innocent Eye: The Life of Robert J. Flaherty*. New York: Harcourt, Brace & World, 1963.

Cameron, Ian (ed.). *The Films of Jean-Luc Goddard*. New York: Praeger, 1970.

————. *The Films of Robert Bresson*. New York: Praeger, 1970.

————. *Second Wave*. New York: Praeger, 1970.

————, and Elizabeth Cameron. *Dames*. New York: Praeger, 1969.

————, and Robin Wood. *Antonioni*. New York: Praeger, 1969.

Carey, Gary. *Lost Films*. New York: Museum of Modern Art, 1970.

Carmen, Ira H. *Movies, Censorship, and the Law*. Ann Arbor: University of Michigan, 1966.

Casty, Alan Howard. *The Dramatic Art of Film.* New York: Harper & Row, 1970.

――――. *The Films of Robert Rossen.* New York: Museum of Modern Art, 1969.

Ceram, C. W. *Archaeology of the Cinema.* New York: Harcourt, Brace & World, 1965.

Clarens, Carlos. *Horror Movies.* Berkeley: University of California, 1968.

――――. *An Illustrated History of the Horror Film.* New York: Putnam, 1967.

Cocteau, Jean. *Cocteau on the Film.* New York: Roy, 1954.

Conway, Michael, and Mark Ricci. *The Films of Marilyn Monroe.* New York: Citadel, 1964.

――――, Dion McGregor, and Mark Ricci. *The Films of Greta Garbo.* Introduced by Parker Tyler. New York: Citadel, 1963.

Cowie, Peter. *The Cinema of Orson Welles.* New York: Barnes, 1965.

――――. *International Film Guide, 1964.* New York: Barnes, 1965.

――――. *International Film Guide, 1965.* New York: Barnes, 1966.

――――. *Screen Series: Sweden.* New York: Barnes, 1970.

――――. *Seventy Years of Cinema.* New York: Barnes, 1969.

――――. *Three Monographs: Antonioni, Bergman, Resnais.* New York: Barnes, 1963.

Crowther, Bosley. *The Lion's Share.* New York: Dutton, 1957.

――――. *Movies and Censorship.* New York: Public Affairs Committee, 1962.

Deming, Barbara. *Running Away From Myself: A Dream Portrait of America Drawn from the Films of the Forties.* New York: Grossman, 1969.

Deschner, Donald. *The Films of Spencer Tracy.* New York: Citadel, 1969.

Dickens, Homer. *The Films of Gary Cooper.* New York: Citadel, 1970.

――――. *The Films of Marlene Dietrich.* New York: Citadel, 1969.

Dickinson, Thorold, and Catherine De la Roche. *Soviet Cinema.* London: Falcon, 1948.

Dimmitt, Richard B. *Actor's Guide to the Talkies.* 2 vols. Metuchen, N.J.: Scarecrow, 1967.

――――. *Title Guide to the Talkies.* 2 vols. Metuchen, N.J.: Scarecrow, 1965.

Donner, Jorn. *The Personal Vision of Ingmar Bergman.* Bloomington: Indiana University, 1964.

Douglass, Drake. *Horror.* New York: Collier Books, 1969.

Dunne, John Gregory. *The Studio: A Cinéma Vérité Study of Hollywood at Work.* New York: Farrar, Straus & Giroux, 1968.

Durgnat, Raymond. *The Crazy Mirror: Hollywood Comedy and the American Image.* New York: Horizon, 1969.

――――. *Eros in the Cinema.* New York: Fernhill, 1966.

――――. *Films and Feelings.* Cambridge, Mass.: M.I.T., 1967.

――――. *Luis Buñuel.* Berkeley: University of California, 1970.

————. *Nouvelle Vague: The First Decade.* Loughton (Essex), Eng.: Motion Publications, 1966.

————, and John Kobal. *Greta Garbo.* New York: Dutton Pictureback, 1965.

Eisenstein, Sergei M. *Film Form.* New York: Harcourt, Brace, 1949. Paperback by Meridian, New York, 1957.

————. *The Film Sense.* New York: Harcourt, Brace, 1942. Paperback by Meridian, New York, 1957.

———— (ed. by Jay Leyda). *Film Essays and a Lecture.* New York: Praeger, 1970.

Eisner, Lotte H. (tr. by Roger Greaves). *The Haunted Screen: Expressionism in the German Cinema and the Influence of Max Reinhart.* Berkeley: University of California, 1969.

Enser, G. S. *Filmed Books and Plays, 1928–1967.* New York: British Book Centre, 1969.

Essoe, Gabe. *The Films of Clark Gable.* New York: Citadel, 1969.

————. *Tarzan of the Movies: A Pictorial History of More Than Fifty Years of Edgar Rice Burroughs' Legendary Hero.* New York: Citadel, 1968.

An Evaluative Guide to Films on Jobs, Training and the Ghetto. New York: American Foundations on Automation and Employment, 1970.

Everson, William K. *The American Movie.* New York: Atheneum, 1963.

————. *The Bad Guys: A Pictorial History of the Movie Villain.* New York: Citadel, 1964.

————. *The Films of Laurel and Hardy.* New York: Citadel, 1969.

————. *A Pictorial History of the Western Film.* New York: Citadel, 1969.

Feldman, Joseph, and Harry Feldman. *Dynamics of the Film.* New York: Hermitage, 1952.

Fenin, George N., and William K. Everson. *The Western.* New York: Orion, 1962.

Feyen, Sharon. *Screen Experience: An Approach to Film.* Dayton: Pflaum, 1970.

Films 1968: A Comprehensive Review of the Year. New York: Catholic Office for Motion Pictures, 1968.

Finkler, Joel. *Stroheim.* Berkeley: University of California, 1970.

Fischer, Edward. *The Screen Arts.* New York: Sheed and Ward, 1960.

Five Catalogues of the Public Auction of the Countless Treasures Acquired From Metro-Goldwyn-Mayer. 5 vols. Los Angeles: David Weisz, 1970.

Ford, Charles. *Histoire du Western.* Paris: Pierre Horay, 1964.

Franklin, Joe. *Classics of the Silent Screen: A Pictorial Treasury.* New York: Bramhall House, 1959.

Fulton, A. R. *Motion Pictures: The Development of an Art Form From Silent Films to the Age of Television.* Norman: University of Oklahoma, 1960.

Gessner, Robert. *The Moving Image: A Guide to Cinematic Literacy.* New York: Dutton, 1970.

Gibson, Arthur. *The Silence of God: Creative Response to the Films of Ingmar Bergman.* New York: Harper & Row, 1969.

Gifford, Denis. *British Cinema—An Illustrated Guide.* New York: Barnes, 1968.

Gilson, Rene. *Jean Cocteau.* New York: Crown, 1969.

Gish, Lillian (with Ann Pinchot). *The Movies, Mr. Griffith and Me.* Englewood Cliffs: Prentice-Hall, 1969.

Goodman, Ezra. *The Fifty Year Decline and Fall of Hollywood.* New York: Simon and Schuster, 1961.

Gow, Gordon. *Suspense in the Cinema.* New York: Barnes, 1968.

Graham, Peter. *A Dictionary of the Cinema.* New York: Barnes, 1964.

————. *New Wave: Critical Landmark.* New York: Doubleday, 1968.

Graham, Sheilah. *Confessions of a Hollywood Columnist.* New York: Morrow, 1969.

————. *The Garden of Allah.* New York: Crown, 1970.

Grierson, John. *Grierson on Documentary.* Berkeley: University of California, 1970.

Griffith, Richard. *The Cinema of Gene Kelly.* New York: Museum of Modern Art, 1962.

————. *Fred Zinneman.* New York: Museum of Modern Art, 1958.

————. *Marlene Dietrich: Image and Legend.* New York: Museum of Modern Art, 1959.

————. *The Movie Stars.* New York: Doubleday, 1970.

————. *Samuel Goldwyn: The Producer and His Films.* New York: Museum of Modern Art, 1956.

————. *The World of Robert Flaherty.* London: Gollancz, 1953.

————, and Arthur Mayer. *The Movies.* New York: Simon and Schuster, 1957.

————, and Paul Rotha. *The Film Till Now.* New York: Funk and Wagnalls, 1949.

Guarner, Jose Luis. *Rossellini.* New York: Praeger, 1970.

Guback, Thomas H. *The International Film Industry: Western Europe and America Since 1945.* Bloomington: Indiana University, 1970.

Guiles, Fred Lawrence. *Norma Jean: The Life of Marilyn Monroe.* New York: McGraw-Hill, 1969.

Hampton, Benjamin B. *A History of the Movies.* New York: Covici, Friede, 1931.

Henri, Jim. *The World's Most Sensual Films.* Chicago: Merit Books, 1965.

Henderson, Robert M. *D. W. Griffith: The Years at Biograph.* New York: Farrar, Straus & Giroux, 1970.

Heyer, Robert, and Anthony Meyer. *Discovery in Film.* Paramus, N.J.: Paulist, 1969.

Hibbin, Nina. *Screen Series: Eastern Europe.* New York: Barnes, 1970.

Higham, Charles. *Hollywood in the Forties.* New York: Barnes, 1968.

————, and Joel Greenberg. *Hollywood In The Forties: A Complete Critical Survey of Hollywood Films 1940–1950.* New York: Paperback Library, 1970.

Hofmann, Charles. *Sounds for Silents.* New York: D. B. S. Publications, 1970.

Houston, Penelope. *The Contemporary Cinema.* Baltimore: Penguin, 1963.

Huaco, George. *The Sociology of Film Art.* New York: Basic Books, 1965.

Huettig, Mae D. *Economic Control of the Motion Picture Industry.* Philadelphia: University of Pennsylvania, 1944.

Hughes, Robert (ed.). *Film Book 1.* New York: Grove, 1959.

Hull, David Stewart. *Films in the Third Reich.* Berkeley: University of California, 1969.

Hunnings, Neville. *Film Censors and the Law.* New York: Hillary, 1967.

Huss, Roy, and Norman Silverstein. *The Film Experience: Elements of Motion Picture Art.* New York: Harper & Row, 1968.

Isaksson, Folke, and Leif Furhammar. *Politics and Film.* London: November Books, 1970.

Ivens, Joris. *The Camera and I.* New York: International Publishers, 1969.

Jacobs, Lewis. *The Rise of the American Film.* New York: Teachers College, Columbia University, 1967.

———— (ed.). *The Emergence of Film Art.* New York: Hopkinson and Blake, 1969.

————. *Introduction to the Art of the Movies.* New York: Noonday, 1960.

———— (ed.). *The Movies As Medium.* New York: Farrar, Straus & Giroux, 1970.

Jarratt, Vernon. *The Italian Cinema.* New York: Macmillan, 1951.

Jarvie, I. C. *Movies and Society.* New York: Basic Books, 1970.

Jensen, Paul. *The Cinema of Fritz Lang.* New York: Barnes, 1969.

————, and Arthur Lennig. *Karloff and Lugosi: Titans of Terror.* New York: Atheneum, 1971.

Kitses, Jim. *Horizons West: Anthony Mann, Budd Boetticher, Sam Peckinpah: Studies of Authorship Within the Western.* Bloomington: Indiana University, 1970.

Knight, Arthur. *The Liveliest Art: A Panoramic History of the Movies.* New York: Macmillan, 1957.

Kracauer, Siegfried. *From Caligari to Hitler.* New York: Noonday, 1959.

————. *Theory of Film.* New York: Oxford University, 1960. Paperback by Galaxy, New York, 1965.

Kuhns, William. *Themes: Short Films for Discussion.* Dayton: Pflaum, 1970.

————, and Thomas F. Giardino. *Behind the Camera.* Dayton: Pflaum, 1970.

————, and Robert Stanley. *Teaching Program: Exploring the Film.* Dayton: Pflaum, 1970.

————, and Robert Stanley. *Exploring the Film.* Dayton: Pflaum, 1970.

Kyrou, Ado (tr. by Adrienne Foulke). *Luis Buñuel.* New York: Simon and Schuster, 1963.

Lahue, Kalton C. *Collecting Classic Films.* New York: Amphoto, 1970.

————. *Continued Next Week.* Norman: University of Oklahoma, 1964.

————. *A World of Laughter: The Motion Picture Comedy Short, 1910–1930.* Norman: University of Oklahoma, 1966.

Larsen, Otto N. *Violence and the Mass Media.* New York: Harper & Row, 1970.

Lauritzen, Einar. *Swedish Films.* New York: Museum of Modern Art, 1962.

Lawson, John Howard. *Film: The Creative Process.* New York: Hill and Wang, 1964.

Lebel, J. P. (tr. by P. D. Stovin). *Buster Keaton.* New York: Barnes, 1967.

Levin, Martin (ed.). *Hollywood and the Great Fan Magazines.* New York: Arbor House, 1970.

Limbacher, James I. *Using Films: A Handbook for the Program Planner.* New York: Educational Film, 1967.

Linden, George. *Reflections on the Screen.* Belmont, Calif.: Wadsworth, 1970.

Lindgren, Ernest. *The Art of the Film.* New York: Macmillan, 1948. 3rd ed. 1968.

Lindsay, Vachel. *The Art of the Moving Picture.* Introduction by Stanley Kauffmann. New York: Liveright, 1970.

Low, Rachel. *The History of the British Film (1896–1906, 1906–14, 1914–18).* London: Allen & Unwin, 1948–50.

MacCann, Richard Dyer. *Film and Society.* New York: Scribner's, 1964.

————. *Hollywood in Transition.* Boston: Houghton Mifflin, 1962.

———— (ed.). *Film: A Montage of Theories.* New York: Dutton, 1966.

Madsen, Axel. *Billy Wilder.* Bloomington: Indiana University, 1969.

Manoogian, Haig P. *The Film-Maker's Art.* New York: Basic Books, 1966.

Manvell, Roger. *The Film and the Public.* Baltimore: Penguin, 1955.

————. *Films.* Harmondsworth (Middlesex), Eng.: Penguin, 1950.

————. *New Cinema in Europe.* New York: Dutton, 1965.

————. *New Cinema in the USA: The Feature Film Since 1946.* New York: Dutton Picturebacks, 1968.

————, and John Huntley. *Technique of Film Music.* New York: Hastings House, 1957.

McBride, Joseph (ed.). *Persistence of Vision.* Madison: Wisconsin Film Society, 1968.

McGuire, Jerimiah. *Cinema and Value Philosophy.* New York: Philosophical Library, 1968.

McVay, J. Douglas. *The Musical Film*. New York: Barnes, 1968.

Michael, Paul. *The Academy Awards: A Pictorial History*. New York: Bonanza Books, 1964.

————. *The American Movies Reference Book: The Sound Era*. New York: Prentice-Hall, 1969.

————. *Humphrey Bogart: The Man and His Films*. Indianapolis: Bobbs-Merrill, 1965.

Milne, Tom (ed.). *Losey On Losey*. New York: Doubleday, 1968.

————. *Rouben Mamoulian*. Bloomington: Indiana University, 1969.

Montagu, Ivor. *Film World: A Guide to Cinema*. Baltimore: Penguin, 1965.

————. *With Eisenstein in Hollywood*. New York: International Publishers, 1969.

Morella, Joe, and Edward Epstein. *Judy*. Introduction by Judith Crist. New York: Citadel, 1969.

Moussinac, Leon (tr. by D. Sandy Petrey). *Sergei Eisenstein*. New York: Crown, 1970.

Murphy, George (with Victor Lasky). *Say . . . Didn't You Used to Be George Murphy?* New York: Bartholomew House, 1970.

Museum of Modern Art Film Library. *Film Notes, Part I, The Silent Film*. New York: Museum of Modern Art, 1949.

Mussman, Toby (ed.). *Jean-Luc Goddard*. New York: Dutton, 1968.

Negri, Pola. *Memoirs Of A Star*. New York: Doubleday, 1970.

Nemcek, Paul. *The Films Of Nancy Carrol*. New York: Lyle Stuart, 1970.

Nemeskurty, Istvan. *Word and Image*. Budapest: Corvina, 1969.

Nicoll, Allardyce. *Film and Theatre*. New York: Crowell, 1936.

Nilsen, Vladimir. *Cinema as Graphic Art*. New York: Hill and Wang, 1959.

Nitsch, Hermann. *Orgies Mysteries Theatre*. Darmstadt: Marz Verlag, 1969.

Nizhny, Vladimir. *Lessons With Eisenstein*. New York: Hill and Wang, 1963.

Nowell-Smith, Geoffrey. *Luchino Visconti*. New York: Doubleday, 1968.

O'Leary, Liam. *The Silent Cinema*. New York: Dutton, 1965.

Osborne, Robert. *Academy Awards*. New York: Schwords, 1969.

Pechter, William S. *Twenty-four Times a Second*. New York: Harper & Row, 1970.

Perry, George. *The Films of Alfred Hitchcock*. New York: Dutton Picturebacks, 1965.

Powdermaker, Hortense. *Hollywood, the Dream Factory*. Boston: Little, Brown, 1950.

Quirk, Lawrence. *The Films of Joan Crawford*. New York: Citadel, 1969.

Ramsaye, Terry. *A Million and One Nights*. New York: Simon and Schuster, 1926.

Randall, Richard S. *Censorship of the Movies*. Madison: University of Wisconsin, 1968.

Ray, Man. *Self Portrait*. London: Andre Deutsch, 1963.

Reed, Rex. *Conversations in the Raw: Dialogues, Monologues, and Selected Short Subjects.* New York: World, 1970.

Renan, Sheldon. *An Introduction to the American Underground Film.* New York: Dutton, 1967.

Rhode, Eric. *Tower of Babel: Speculations on the Cinema.* New York: Chilton, 1967.

Richardson, Robert. *Literature and Film.* Bloomington: Indiana University, 1969.

Richie, Donald. *The Films of Akira Kurosawa.* Berkeley: University of California, 1970.

————. *George Stevens: An American Romantic.* New York: Museum of Modern Art, 1970.

Ringgold, Gene (with DeWitt Bodeen). *The Films of Cecil B. De Mille.* New York: Citadel, 1969.

Robinson, David. *Buster Keaton.* Bloomington: Indiana University, 1969.

————. *The Great Funnies.* New York: Dutton, 1968.

————. *Hollywood in the Twenties.* New York: Barnes, 1968.

————. *Hollywood in the Twenties: A Complete Critical Survey of Hollywood Films from 1920–1930.* New York: Paperback Library, 1970.

Robinson, W. R. (ed.). *Man and the Movies.* Baltimore: Penguin, 1969.

Rondi, Gian L. *Italian Cinema Today.* New York: Hill and Wang, 1965.

Rosenberg, Bernard, and Harry Silverstein. *The Real Tinsel.* New York: Macmillan, 1970.

Ross, Lillian. *Picture.* New York: Rinehart, 1952.

Ross, T. J. (ed.). *Film and the Liberal Arts.* New York: Holt, Rinehart and Winston, 1970.

Rotha, Paul. *Rotha on the Film.* New York: Oxford University, 1958.

Roud, Richard. *Godard.* New York: Doubleday, 1968.

Ruesch, Jurgen, and Weldon Kees. *Nonverbal Communication: Notes on the Visual Perception of Human Relations.* Berkeley: University of California, 1969.

Sadoul, Georges. *French Film.* Falcon, 1953.

Salachas, Gilbert. *Federico Fellini.* New York: Crown, 1969.

Samuels, Charles (ed.). *A Casebook on Film.* New York: Van Nostrand, 1970.

Sarris, Andrew. *The American Cinema: Directors and Directions.* New York: Dutton, 1968.

————. *Interviews With Film Directors.* New York: Avon, 1967.

———— (ed.). *The Film.* Indianapolis: Bobbs-Merrill, 1968.

Scheuer, Stephen H. (ed.). *Movies on T.V.* 4th ed. New York: Bantam, 1968.

Schramm, Wilbur, with Philip H. Coombs, Friedrich Kahnert, and Jack Lyle. *The New Media: Memo to Educational Planners.* Paris: UNESCO, 1967.

Schrelvogel, Paul. *Films in Depth* (separate booklets for study, including the following titles: *An Occurrence at Owl Creek Bridge, No Reason to Stay, Overture–Overture/Nyitany, The Language of Faces, Orange and Blue, Toys, Timepiece, Night and Fog, Sunday Lark. Flavio, The Little Island, A Stain on His Conscience*). Dayton: Pflaum, 1970.

Schumach, Murray. *The Face on the Cutting Room Floor*. New York: Morrow, 1964.

Sharp, Dennis. *The Picture Palace and Other Buildings for the Movies*. New York: Praeger, 1969.

Shelby, H. C. *Stag Movie Review*. Canoga Park, Calif.: Viceroy, 1970.

Sherman, Eric, and Martin Rubin. *The Director's Event: Interviews with Five American Film-Makers*. New York: Atheneum, 1970.

Shipman, David. *The Great Movie Stars: The Golden Years*. New York: Crown, 1970.

Sitney, P. Adams (ed.). *Film Culture Reader*. New York: Praeger, 1970.

Snider, Robert L. *Pare Lorentz and the Documentary Film*. Norman: University of Oklahoma, 1968.

Sohn, David A. *Film: The Creative Eye*. Dayton: Pflaum, 1970.

Solmi, Angelo (tr. Elizabeth Greenwood). *Fellini*. New York: Humanities, 1968.

Spottiswoode, Raymond. *A Grammar of the Film: An Analysis of Film Technique*. Berkeley: University of California, 1950.

Springer, John. *The Fondas*. New York: Citadel, 1970.

Stack, Oswald. *Pasolini on Pasolini: Interviews with Oswald Stack*. Bloomington: Indiana University, 1969.

Steene, Birgitta. *Ingmar Bergman*. New York: Twayne, 1968.

Steiger, Brad. *Monsters, Maidens, and Mayhem: A Pictorial History of Hollywood Film Monsters*. Chicago: Camerarts, 1965.

Stephenson, Ralph, and Jean R. Debrix. *The Cinema as Art*. Baltimore: Penguin, 1965.

Stewart, David C. *Film Study in Higher Education*. Washington, D.C.: American Council on Education, 1966.

Strick, Philip. *Antonioni*. Loughton (Essex), Eng.: Motion Publications, 1965.

Sussex, Elizabeth. *Lindsay Anderson*. New York: Praeger, 1970.

Swindell, Larry, *Spencer Tracy*. New York: World, 1969.

Tabori, Paul. *Alexander Korda*. London: Oldbourne, 1959.

Talbot, Daniel (ed.). *Film: An Anthology*. Berkeley: University of California, 1966.

Taylor, John Russell, *Cinema Eye, Cinema Ear: Some Key Film-makers of the Sixties*. New York: Hill and Wang, 1964.

Thomas, Bob. *Selznick*. New York: Doubleday, 1970.

———. *Thalberg: Life and Legend*. New York: Doubleday, 1969.

Thorp, Margaret. *America at the Movies*. New Haven: Yale University, 1937.

Truffaut, François. *Hitchcock.* New York: Simon and Schuster, 1967.

Tyler, Parker. *Classics of the Foreign Film: A Pictorial History.* New York: Citadel, 1962.

————. *The Hollywood Hallucination.* Introduction by Richard Schickel. New York: Simon and Schuster, 1970.

————. *The Three Faces of the Film.* New York: Yoseloff, 1960.

————. *Underground Film: A Critical History.* New York: Grove, 1970.

Verdone, Mario. *Roberto Rossellini.* Paris: Editions Seghers, 1963.

Walker, Alexander. *The Celluloid Sacrifice: Aspects of Sex in the Movies.* New York: Hawthorn, 1967.

————. *Stardom.* New York: Stein and Day, 1970.

Ward, John. *Alain Resnais, or the Theme of Time.* New York: Doubleday, 1968.

Warshow, Robert. *The Immediate Experience.* New York: Doubleday, 1962.

Weaver, John T. *Forty Years Of Screen Credits.* Metuchen, N.J.: Scarecrow, 1970.

Weinberg, Herman G. *Joseph von Sternberg.* New York: Dutton, 1967.

————. *The Lubitsch Touch: A Critical Study of the Great Film Director.* New York: Dutton, 1969.

————, with preface by Fritz Lang. *Saint Cinema: Selected Writings 1929–1970.* New York: Drama Book Specialists, 1970.

Weise, E. (ed. and tr.). *Enter: The Comics—Rodolphe Topffer's Essay on Physiognomy and the True Story of Monsieur Crepin.* Lincoln: University of Nebraska, 1965.

White, David Manning, and Richard Averson (eds.). *Sight, Sound, and Society—Motion Pictures and Television in America.* Boston: Beacon, 1968.

Wilde, Larry. *Great Comedians Talk About Comedy.* New York: Citadel, 1969.

Willis, John. *Screen World 1949–* . Annual, 21 vols. New York: Crown, 1970.

Wollen, Peter. *Signs and Meaning in the Cinema.* Bloomington: Indiana University, 1969.

Wood, Robin. *Arthur Penn.* New York: Praeger, 1970.

————. *Hitchcock's Films.* New York: Barnes, 1965.

————. *Hitchcock's Films: A Complete Critical Guide to the Films of Alfred Hitchcock.* New York: Paperback Library, 1970.

————. *Howard Hawks.* New York: Doubleday, 1968.

Wood, Tom. *The Bright Side of Billy Wilder, Primarily.* New York: Doubleday, 1970.

Youngblood, Gene. *Expanded Cinema.* New York: Dutton, 1970.

Zalman, Jan. *Films and Film-Makers in Czechoslovakia.* Prague: Orbis-Prague, 1968.

Zinman, David. *Fifty Classic Motion Pictures: The Stuff That Dreams Are Made Of.* New York: Crown, 1970.

Screenplays and the Process of Filmmaking

Agee, James. *Agee on Film.* Boston: Beacon, 1964.

Agel, Jerome (ed.). *The Making of Kubrick's 2001.* New York: New American Library, 1970.

Alton, John. *Painting with Light.* New York: Macmillan, 1949.

Antonioni, Michelangelo. *Screenplays of Michelangelo Antonioni.* New York: Orion, 1963.

Baddeley, W. Hugh. *The Technique of Documentary Film Production.* New York: Hastings House, 1963.

Beckett, Samuel, and Alan Schneider. *Film By Samuel Beckett.* New York: Grove, 1969.

Bellocchio, Marco. *China Is Near.* New York: Orion, 1969.

————. *Viridiana, The Exterminating Angel, Simon of the Desert.* New York: Orion, 1969.

Bergman, Ingmar. *Four Screenplays of Ingmar Bergman.* New York: Simon and Schuster, 1960.

Bobker, Lee. *Elements of Film.* New York: Harcourt, Brace & World, 1969.

Boyer, Deena (tr. by Charles Lam Markmann). *The Two Hundred Days of 8½.* Afterword by Dwight Macdonald. New York: Macmillan, 1964.

Burder, John. *The Technique of Editing 16MM Films.* New York: Hastings House, 1968.

Capote, Truman, with Eleanor and Frank Perry. *Trilogy.* New York: Macmillan, 1969.

Carrick, Edward. *Designing for Moving Pictures.* New York: Studio, 1947.

Carson, L. M. Kit. *David Holzman's Diary: A Screenplay.* New York: Noonday, 1970.

Cassavetes, John, and Al Ruban. *Faces.* New York: New American Library, 1970.

Clair, René (tr. by Piergiuseppe Bozzetti). *Four Screenplays: Le silence est d'or, La beauté du diable, Les belles-de-nuit, Les grandes manoeuvres.* New York: Orion, 1970.

Cocteau, Jean (ed. by Robert Morris Hammond). *Beauty and the Beast.* New York: N.Y.U., 1970.

————. (tr. by Lily Pons). *The Blood of a Poet.* New York: Bodley Head, 1947.

————. (tr. by Carol Martin-Sperry). *Two Screenplays: The Blood of a Poet, The Testament of Orpheus.* New York: Orion, 1968.

Cross, Brenda (ed.). *The Film Hamlet: A Record of its Production.* London: Saturn, 1948.

De Sica, Vittorio. *Miricale in Milan*. New York: Orion, 1968.

Dreyer, Carl (tr. by Oliver Stallybrass). *Four Screenplays*. London: Thames and Hudson, 1970.

Duras, Marguerite (tr. by Richard Seaver). *Hiroshima Mon Amour*. Picture editor Robert Hughes. New York: Grove, 1961.

Eastman, Charles. *Little Fauss and Big Halsy*. New York: Pocket Books, 1970.

Eisenstein, Sergei M. *Ivan the Terrible*. New York: Simon and Schuster, 1962.

Eisler, Hans. *Composing for the Films*. New York: Oxford University, 1947.

Eliot, T. S., and George Hoellering. *The Film of Murder in the Cathedral*. New York: Harcourt, Brace, 1952.

Fellini, Federico (tr. by Howard Greenfield; ed. by Tullio Kezich). *Federico Fellini's Juliet of the Spirits*. New York: Ballantine, 1965.

———. *La Dolce Vita*. New York: Ballantine, 1961.

——— (tr. by Judith Green). *Three Screenplays: I Vitelloni, Il Bidone, The Temptations of Doctor Antonio*. New York: Orion, 1970.

Ferguson, Robert. *How to Make Movies: A Practical Guide to Group Film-Making*. New York: Viking, 1969.

Fielding, Raymond. *The Technique of Special Effects Cinematography*. New York: Hastings House, 1965.

Fonda, Peter, with Dennis Hopper and Terry Southern. *Easy Rider*. New York: New American Library, 1969.

Foote, Horton. *The Screenplay of To Kill a Mockingbird*. New York: Harcourt, Brace & World, 1964.

Fry, Christopher. *The Bible*. New York: Pocket Books, 1966.

Gassner, John (ed.). *Best Film Plays of 1943/44*. New York: Crown, 1945.

———. *Great Film Plays*. New York: Crown, 1959.

——— (ed. with Dudley Nichols). *Best Film Plays of 1939/40*. New York: Crown, 1941.

Geduld, Harry M. (ed.). *Film Makers on Film Making: Statements on their Art by Thirty Directors*. Bloomington: Indiana University, 1967.

Gelmis, Joseph. *The Film Director as Superstar*. New York: Doubleday, 1970.

Godard, Jean-Luc. *The Married Woman*. New York: Berkeley, 1965.

Goode, James. *The Story of The Misfits*. Indianapolis: Bobbs-Merrill, 1963.

Gordon, George N., and Irving A. Falk. *Your Career In Film Making*. New York: Julian Messner, 1969.

Herman, Lewis. *A Practical Manual of Screen Playwriting: For Theater and Television Films*. New York: World, 1966.

Higham, Charles. *Hollywood Cameramen: Sources of Light*. London: Thames and Hudson, 1970.

———, and Joel Greenberg. *The Celluloid Muse: Hollywood Directors Speak*. New York: New American Library, 1970.

Hopper, Dennis. *The Last Movie*. New York: New American Library, 1970.

Isaksson, Ulla. *The Virgin Spring*. New York: Ballantine, 1960.

Kantor, Bernard R., with Irwin A. Blacker and Anne Kramer (eds.). *Directors at Work*. New York: Funk and Wagnalls, 1970.

Larson, Rodger, Jr. *A Guide for Film Teachers to Filmmaking by Teenagers*. New York: Cultural Affairs Foundation, 1968.

Leyda, Jay. *Films Beget Films*. New York: Hill and Wang, 1964.

Livingston, Don. *Film and the Director*. New York: Macmillan, 1953.

Maddux, Rachel, with Stirling Silliphant and Neil D. Issacs. *Fiction Into Film: A Walk in the Spring Rain*. Knoxville: University of Tennessee, 1970.

Madsen, Roy. *Animated Film*. New York: Interland, 1969.

Manoogian, Haig P. *The Film-Maker's Art*. New York: Basic Books, 1966.

Manvell, Roger. *Three British Screenplays: Brief Encounter, Odd Man Out, and Scott of the Antarctic*. London: Methuen, 1950.

Mascelli, Joseph V. *The Five C's of Cinematography: Motion Picture Filming Techniques Simplified*. Los Angeles: Cine/Grafic Publications, 1965.

———— (ed.). *American Cinematographer Manual*. Hollywood: American Society of Cinematographers, 1966.

Maysies, Albert, and David Maysies. *Salesman*. New York: New American Library, 1969.

McGowan, Kenneth. *Behind the Screen: The History and Techniques of the Motion Picture*. New York: Delacorte, 1965.

Mercer, John. *An Introduction to Cinematography*. Champaign, Ill.: Stipes, 1970.

Miller, Arthur. *The Misfits*. New York: Viking, 1961.

Miller, Merle, and Evan Rhodes. *Only You, Dick Darling, or How to Write One Television Script and Make $50,000,000*. New York: Bantam Books, 1964.

Montagu, Ivor. *With Eisenstein in Hollywood*. New York: International Publishers, 1969.

Naumburg, Nancy (ed.). *We Make the Movies*. New York: Norton, 1937.

Nilsen, Vladimir. *The Cinema as a Graphic Art*. New York: Hill and Wang, 1959.

Nurnberg, Walter. *Lighting for Photography*. New York: Hastings House, 1956.

Oringel, Robert S. *Audio Control Handbook*. New York: Hastings House, 1956.

Osborne, John. *Tom Jones*. London: Faber, 1964.

———— (ed. Robert Hughes). *Tom Jones: A Film Script*. New York: Grove, 1964.

Pennebaker, D. A. *Bob Dylan—Don't Look Back*. New York: Ballantine, 1968.

Petrow, Mischa. *Efficient Film-Making Practices: Rules, Forms & Guides.* New York: Drama Book Specialists, 1970.

Pincus, Edward, and Jairus Lincoln. *Guide to Filmmaking.* New York: New American Library, 1969.

Provisor, Henry. *8MM/16MM Movie-Making.* New York: Chilton, 1970.

Pudovkin, V. I. *Film Technique and Film Acting.* New York: Grove, 1960.

Quigley, Martin, Jr. (ed.). *New Screen Techniques.* Quigley, 1953.

Rattigan, Terence. *The Prince and the Showgirl.* New York: New American Library, 1957.

Reisz, Karel. *The Technique of Film Editing.* New York: Hastings House, 1968.

Renoir, Jean. *The Rules of the Game.* London: Lorrimer, 1970.

Rilla, Wolf. *A–Z of Movie Making.* London: Studio Vista, 1970.

Robbe-Grillet, Alain. *Last Year at Marienbad.* New York: Grove, 1962.

———. *L'Immortelle.* Paris: Editions de Minuit, 1963.

Serling, Rod. *Patterns.* New York: Simon and Schuster, 1957.

Shoman, Vilgot (tr. by Martin Minow and Jenny Bohman). *I Am Curious (Blue).* New York: Grove, 1970.

———. *I Am Curious (Yellow).* New York: Grove, 1968.

———. *I Was Curious—Diary of the Making of a Film.* New York: Grove, 1968.

Skillbeck, Oswald. *ABC of Film and TV Working Terms.* New York: Focal, 1960.

Smallman, Kirk. *Creative Film-Making.* New York: Macmillan, 1969.

Sontag, Susan. *Duet for Cannibals: A Screenplay.* New York: Farrar, Straus & Giroux, 1970.

Southern, Terry. *The Journal of The Loved One: The Production Log of a Motion Picture.* With photography by William Claxton. New York: Random House, 1965.

Souto, H. Mario Raimondo (ed. by Raymond Spottiswoode). *The Technique of the Motion Picture Camera.* New York: Communications Arts Books, 1967.

Spottiswoode, Raymond. *Film and Its Techniques.* Berkeley: University of California, 1951.

Taylor, Theodore. *People Who Make Movies.* New York: Doubleday, 1967.

Trapnell, Coles. *Teleplay.* San Francisco: Chandler, 1966.

Truffaut, François, with Helen G. Scott. *Hitchcock.* New York: Simon and Schuster, 1966.

Vadim, Roger. *Les Liaisons Dangereuses.* New York: Ballantine, 1962.

Vardac, A. Nicholas. *Stage to Screen: Theatrical Method from Garrick to Griffith.* New York: Blom, 1949.

Visconti, Luchino (tr. by Judith Green). *Three Screenplays: White Nights, Rocco and His Brothers, The Job.* New York: Orion, 1970.

———. *Two Screenplays: La Terra Trema, Senso.* New York: Orion, 1970.

Wanger, Walter, and Joe Hyams. *My Life With Cleopatra.* New York: Bantam, 1963.

Warhol, Andy. *Blue Movie.* New York: Grove, 1970.

Wexler, Norman. *Joe.* Introduction by Judith Crist. New York: Avon, 1970.

Wilder, Billy and I. A. L. Diamond. *Irma La Douce.* New York: Midwood-Tower, 1963.

Published screenplays are now becoming available, in various forms, for study and appreciation.

(a.) Under the general editorship of Robert Hughes, a highly regarded film editor, Grove Press has released a series of scenarios, "reconstructed from the finished film," and offering many illustrations from the film. A section of "Interviews and Criticism" in each volume is a useful gathering of material. Among the screenplays so far published in this series are *The 400 Blows* by François Truffaut, *Masculine Feminine* by Jean-Luc Goddard, *L'Aventura* by Michelangelo Antonioni, and *Rashomon* by Akira Kurosawa.

Simon and Schuster has two separate series of screenplays. These series are presented under two general titles—"Modern Film Scripts" and "Classic Film Scripts." The Modern Film Scripts series includes such works as Truffaut's *Jules and Jim,* Godard's *Alphaville,* De Sica's *The Bicycle Thief,* Bergman's *The Seventh Seal,* Kurosawa's *Ikiru,* and *The Third Man,* written by Graham Greene and directed by Carol Reed. The Classic Film Series makes available such films as *Grand Illusion, Potemkin, L'Age d'or, Un chien andalou, The Blue Angel, Les enfants du Paradis,* and *M.*

Some Critical Works

Adler, Renata. *A Year In The Dark.* New York: Berkeley, 1970.

Agee, James. *Agee on Film: Reviews and Comments.* Boston: Beacon, 1964.

Alpert, Hollis. *The Dreams and the Dreamers.* New York: Macmillan, 1962.

———, and Andrews Sarris. *Film 68–69: An Anthology by the National Society of Film Critics.* New York: Simon and Schuster, 1969.

Boyum, Jay Gould, and Adrienne Scott. *Film as Film: Critical Responses to Film Art.* Boston: Allyn and Bacon, 1970.

Crist, Judith. *The Private Eye, the Cowboy, and the Very Naked Girl.* New York: Holt, Rinehart and Winston, 1968.

Crowther, Bosley. *Great Films: Fifty Golden Years of Motion Pictures.* New York: Putnam, 1967.

Ephron, Nora. *Wallflower At The Orgy.* New York: Viking, 1970.

Kael, Pauline. *Going Steady.* Boston: Atlantic-Little, Brown, 1970.

———. *I Lost It at the Movies.* Boston: Little, Brown, 1965.

————. *Kiss Kiss Bang Bang.* New York: Bantam, 1969.

Kauffmann, Stanley. *World on Film.* New York: Harper & Row, 1967.

Lejeune, C. A. *Chestnuts in Her Lap, 1936–1946.* London: Phoenix, 1947.

Lewis, Leon, with William David Sherman. *Lanscape of Contemporary Cinema.* Buffalo: Buffalo Spectrum, 1967.

Macdonald, Dwight. *Dwight Macdonald on Movies.* Englewood Cliffs: Prentice-Hall, 1969.

Manvell, Roger, and others (eds.). *Shots in the Dark.* New York: British Book Centre, 1952.

Sarris, Andrew. *Confessions of a Cultist.* New York: Simon and Schuster, 1970.

Schickel, Richard. *Movies.* New York: Basic Books, 1964.

———— (ed. with John Simon). *Film 67/68: An Anthology by the National Society of Film Critics.* New York: Simon and Schuster, 1968.

Simon, John. *Acid Test.* New York: Stein and Day, 1963.

————. *Private Screenings: Views of the Cinema of the Sixties.* New York: Macmillan, 1967.

Sontag, Susan. *Against Interpretation.* New York: Farrar, Straus & Giroux, 1966.

Tyler, Parker. *Magic and Myth in the Movies.* New York: Holt, Rinehart and Winston, 1947.

Zinsser, William K. *Seen Any Good Movies Lately?* Introduction by Elia Kazan. New York: Doubleday, 1958.

Notes and Suggestions for Further Research

One of the basic problems facing the student, who is not a specialist in films and has no plans for being a professional, is where to begin. Above and beyond the many books, some of them with fine bibliographies and references, the student must seek out certain useful reference books and periodicals.

To search out articles and reviews of pictures, the student is directed to *The Reader's Guide to Periodicals* in the library, where this material is to be found under the heading of "Moving Pictures."

In addition to the "key" reviews of films by the small number of establishment reviewers centered in and around New York—reviews in the New York *Times, The New Yorker, New Republic, Commonweal, Life, Time, Newsweek,* the New York *Post, Cue, The Village Voice, New York Magazine, The New Leader,* the New York *Daily News,* etc.—there are regular reviews in many if not most of the big national "slick" magazines as well. Among those regularly offering film reviews are *Vogue, Cosmopolitan, Cavalier, Playboy, Redbook, Good Housekeeping, Psychology Today,*

Ladies Home Journal, and *Esquire*. Similarly, on an irregular basis, there are articles about films, actors, and directors, etc., in most of these magazines.

Some of the chief quarterlies now offer some film criticism and review on a fairly regular schedule. Among these are *Contempora*, *The Hudson Review*, *Partisan Review*, *Georgia Review*, *Trace*, and *The Yale Review*. More infrequently film criticism is found in other quarterlies such as *The Virginia Quarterly Review* and *The Kenyon Review*.

Among the many serious publications devoted exclusively to the study of films and readily accessible in this country are *Cahiers du Cinéma*, *Cinema*, *Continental Film Review* (London), *Film Comment*, *Film Culture*, *Film News*, *Film Quarterly*, *International Film Art News*, and *Sight and Sound* (London). (See "Selective List of U.S. Film Magazines" below.)

For films produced and released over the past ten years, *Film Facts* offers a basic listing of cast and credits, together with a summary of the chief reviews. In the annual index there is a listing of all awards and prizes garnered by these films.

For more professional reaction to films within the film industry, see such trade publications as: *Daily Cinema* (London), *Daily Variety*, *Film Daily*, *Hollywood Reporter*, and *Motion Picture Daily*.

A great deal of film criticism, together with articles, interviews, and general information, is to be found in local newspapers throughout the country.

There are certain very useful reference books available for the interested student. Among these are *Foremost Films of 19 , A Yearbook of the American Screen 1939– *, edited by Frank Vreeland (Chicago: Pitman).

The most ambitious and extensive encyclopedia of film, in six volumes up to 1967, unfortunately for most students still untranslated from the Italian, is *Film-lexicon Degli Autori e Delle Opere* (Rome: Edizioni di Bianco e Nero).

There is, as yet, a shortage of reference books, encyclopedias, and dictionaries of film in English. Among those, in various languages, commonly used by students of film are:

Bessy, Maurice, and Jean-Louis Chardans. *Dictionnaire du Cinéma et de la télévision*. Paris: J.-J. Pauvert, 1965. Illustrated.

Boussinot, Roger (ed.). *L'encyclopédie du cinéma*. Paris: Bordas, 1967. Illustrated.

Cameron, James Ross, and Joseph S. Cifre. *Cameron's Encyclopedia: Sound Motion Pictures*. Coral Gables, Fla.: Cameron, 1959.

Enciclopedìa dello Spettàcolo. 9 vols. Rome: Maschere, 1954–62.

Enciclopedìa dello Spettàcolo, 1955–1965. Rome: Unione editorale, 1966. Illustrated.

*Enciclopedìa dello Spettàcolo, 1963– . 6 vols. Venice: Istituto per la
collaborazióne culturale, 1963– . Illustrated.
Guide to Government-Loan Film. Alexandria, Va.: Serina, 1969. Contains
more than 900 synopses of films from 53 federal agencies, plus 2,000
titles and sources.
Guide to Military-Loan Film. Alexandria, Va.: Serina, 1969. Contains
synopses of 1,430 16MM service films.
*The International Film and Television Council Directory of Organizations
and their National Branches*. London: International Film and Television Council (Rome), 1963. Published in French and English in par-
allel columns on opposite pages.
*Motion Pictures from the Library of Congress Paper Print Collection, 1894–
1912*. Berkeley: University of California, 1969.
Multi-Media Instructional Materials Catalog. New York: Universal Education and Visual Arts, 1970.
Saldoul, Georges. *Dictionnaire des films*. Paris: Editions du Seuil, 1965.
Standards for Cataloguing, Coding and Scheduling Educational Media.
Washington, D.C.: N.E.A. Publication, 1970.
Theatrical Variety Guide. Los Angeles: Theatrical Variety Publications,
1966. "The dictionary of the entertainment industry issued on behalf
of American Guild of Variety Artists."

An extremely valuable guide for schools, film groups, and students is
James L. Limbacher's *Feature Films on 16: A Directory of 16 MM Sound
Films Available for Rental from Major Distributors in the United States*
(New York: Continental 16, 1966).

Also useful is *The Filmviewer's Handbook* by Emile G. McAnany, S.J.,
and Robert Williams, S.J. (Glen Rock, N.J.: Paulist Press, 1965).

Specifically related to the interests of the general and appreciative audience to whom this textbook is addressed are *The Motion Picture and the
Teaching of English* by Marion C. Sheridan, with Harold H. Owen, Jr.,
Ken Macrorie, and Fred Marcus (New York: Appleton-Century-Crofts,
1965); and *Film Study in Higher Education*, edited by David C. Stewart
(Washington, D.C.: American Council on Education, 1966). Both of these
books contain a great deal of information useful to the student of film,
including addresses and locations of archives and libraries.

Some important basic reference works

Current Film Periodicals in English. New York: Adam Reilly, 1970. Lists
more than 100 magazines and newspapers devoted to all aspects of
film, with subscription information, description of contents, and information for writers.

Dimmitt, Richard B. *An Actor Guide to the Talkies.* Metuchen, N.J.: Scarecrow, 1967. 2 vols. Vol. 1 lists 8,000 films between 1949 and 1964 in alphabetical order. Typical entry gives title, date, and names of characters together with name of actor playing each. Vol. 2 is an alphabetical index of actors with a reference to each film in Vol. 1 in which the actor has played.

————. *A Title Guide to the Talkies.* Metuchen, N.J.: Scarecrow, 1965. 2 vols. Lists 16,000 feature films from 1927 to 1963 in alphabetical order. Typical entry gives date, company, director, and source.

Halliwell, Leslie. *The Filmgoer's Companion.* 2nd ed. New York: Hill and Wang, 1967. A useful compendium of information listed alphabetically. Includes entries on actors, directors, individual films, etc., as well as larger topics and specialized movie terminology. Inevitably, each user will find omissions, but this is perhaps the best handbook available and is recommended for anyone interested in film.

Michael, Paul (ed.). *The American Movies Reference Book: The Sound Era.* Englewood Cliffs: Prentice-Hall, 1969. Excellent illustrations. Non-technical, but a very thorough listing of titles, credits, dates, awards, with helpful bibliography.

The New York Times Film Reviews, 1913–1968. 6 vols. New York: The New York Times, 1970.

Sarris, Andrew. *The American Cinema: Directors and Directions, 1929– .* New York: Dutton, 1968. An entry for each director treated. Includes a list of his films with dates and brief (one to four pages) critical comment.

Schewer, Steven. *Movies On T.V., 1969–1970.* New York: Bantam, 1969.

Spottiswoode, Raymond (ed.). *The Focal Encyclopedia of Film and Television Techniques.* New York: Hastings House, 1969. Well illustrated with charts and drawings. Thorough and extremely useful.

Wagner, Robert, and David Parker. *A Filmography of Films About Movies and Movie Making.* Rochester: Eastman Kodak, 1970.

The Yearbook of Motion Pictures. New York: *The Film Daily,* 1918–1957. A key source of statistics, survey articles, lists of films (with credits), awards, distributors, etc.

Selective List of U.S. Film Magazines

(Prepared by Thomas Atkins, Professor of Drama at Hollins College, and Editor of *Cinema Critic.*)

Cinéaste 27 West 11th Street, New York, N.Y. 10011. Editor: Gary Crowdus. Illustrated quarterly. $.60 per issue; $2.00 four issues.

Offbeat magazine focusing chiefly on *cinéma engagé*—films which protest or explore social problems, new trends in ideological and political use of film. Articles, interviews with "radical filmmakers," book reviews, abstracts of U.S. and foreign film magazines not readily available at newsstands, news of festivals and film events, unclassifieds carrying information wanted, film magazines and equipment for sale, rent, trade.

Cinema   9661 Wilshire Boulevard, Beverly Hills, Calif. 90212. Editor: Paul Schrader. Illustrated triyearly. $1.25 per issue; $5.00 four issues.

In the past *Cinema* has been stronger on visuals than on text, with covers featuring sexy starlets and pictorial tributes inside to big Hollywood or foreign screen personalities; recent issues indicate an upgrading of the contents to appeal to academia. Interviews, articles, current film reviews. New feature: "Lost Films."

Film Comment   100 Walnut Place, Brookline, Mass. 02146. Editor: Richard Corliss. Illustrated quarterly. $1.50 per issue; $6.00 four issues.

Under its founder and former editor, Gordon Hitchens, *Film Comment* was noted for elucidating social causes related to cinema: censorship, blacklisting, propaganda and documentary film, civil liberties in mass media, etc. The first issue edited by its new head, Richard Corliss, suggests that in the future the magazine may become less socially engaged, more concerned with film criticism and aesthetics—that is, more like other film magazines. Articles, interviews with directors, current film reviews, book reviews, and news of film schools and festivals. New feature under Corliss: "Film Favorites," in which critics analyze their favorite American films.

Film Culture   G.P.O. Box 1499, New York, N.Y. 10001. Editor: Jonas Mekas. Illustrated quarterly. $1.00 per issue; $4.00 four issues.

Published since 1955, *Film Culture* has become the official journal of the New American Cinema—*avant garde*, experimental filmmakers (Kenneth Anger, Stan Brakhage, Bruce Conner, Ed Emshwiller, Ron Rice, Jack Smith, Andy Warhol, *et al.*) whose works are distributed by such organizations as Film-Makers' Cooperative in New York and Canyon Cinema in San Francisco. Articles by and about experimental filmmakers, historical articles and documents, Herman G. Weinberg's column "Coffee, Brandy and Cigars," occasional book reviews. Special issues devoted to single topics: D. W. Griffith, Erich von Stroheim, Andrew Sarris on American directors, with chronology, 1915–1962, etc. Annual Independent Film Award made to outstanding creative filmmaker.

Filmfacts   P.O. Box 213, Village Station, N.Y. 10014. (Now a publication of The American Film Institute, 1815 H Street, N.W., Washington, D.C. 20006.) Editor: Ernest Parmentier. Illustrated fortnightly. $25.00 annual subscription.

Now in its tenth year, publishes information on every motion picture (domestic and foreign) released in the U.S. Story synopsis, reviews from major critics, complete cast and production credits. Annual film awards supplement.

Film Heritage   University of Dayton, Dayton, Ohio 45409. Editor: F. Anthony Macklin. Illustrated quarterly. $.60 per issue; $2.00 four issues. Small academic journal, with conservative reputation, publishing critical reviews of current films and revaluations of older films, occasional interviews with directors, bibliographies, and book reviews.

Film Library Quarterly   Film Library Information Council, 101 Putnam Avenue, Greenwich, Conn. 06830. Editor: William Sloan. Illustrated quarterly. Subscription included with membership in FLIC: individual voting membership $10.00, individual nonvoting $8.00, student $5.00. Informative journal publishing articles and reviews on "aspects of library film and media services, the documentary, avant-garde, and short film." News of film schools, conferences, and information about film distributors.

Filmmakers Newsletter   80 Wooster Street, New York, N.Y. 10012. Editor: Suni Mallow. Illustrated monthly. $.75 per issue; $4.00 eleven issues. Aims to provide independent and student filmmakers with hard-core information about filmmaking techniques and equipment, distributors, festivals, conferences, film schools. Articles by and about independent filmmakers. Lists equipment for sale, rent, trade; jobs wanted or positions open for filmmakers; plus calendar of independent film events.

Film News   250 West 57th Street, New York, N.Y. 10019. Editor-publisher: Rohama Lee. Illustrated bimonthly. $6.00 six issues. Recently celebrated its thirtieth anniversary of providing information about new audiovisual materials and equipment. Addressed primarily to educators using film in schools and libraries, each issue features articles about conferences, festivals, technical innovations, and educational experiments; plus 20 to 50 short reviews of films and filmstrips, brief comments on film and TV books, abstracts of film and TV periodicals, and a calendar of educational film events. Special feature: descriptive listings of films according to topics—Black-themed films, films about the American Indian, etc.

Film Quarterly   University of California Press, Berkeley, Calif. 94720. Editor: Ernest Callenbach. Illustrated quarterly. $1.25 per issue; $5.00 four issues. Addressed chiefly to the film scholar and student, this magazine emphasizes film history/aesthetics and has a somewhat highbrow and stuffy reputation. Critical and historical articles, interviews with directors, reviews of current features and short films, and book reviews; occasionally runs two differing opinions of same film. In recent ad for overseas readers, ***Film Quarterly*** described itself as a publication of "intricate analysis, rigorous argument, lengthy articles and reviews"; it uses a difficult vocabulary and makes "no attempt to be popular."

Film Society Review   American Federation of Film Societies, 144 Bleecker Street, New York, N.Y. 10012. Editor: William A. Starr. Illustrated monthly. $.50 per issue: $5.00 twelve issues (included in membership dues: $10.00 or $25.00 annually).

Official magazine of the American Federation of Film Societies, prints reviews of current films, excerpts from major critics, abstracts of U.S. and foreign film magazines, book reviews, news of film festivals, Supplement to *FSR, Film Society Bulletin*, carries AFFS news and listings of latest film offerings from distributors' catalogues. Primary audience: campus and community film societies, libraries, museums.

New Cinema Review   80 Wooster Place, New York, N.Y. 10012. Editor-publisher: Suni Mallow. Illustrated monthly. $.75 per issue; $4.00 eleven issues.

Motto: "We review only special films"—independent/*avant garde*/experimental films made outside of Hollywood and the major studios. Interviews with experimental filmmakers, articles on the state of the *avant garde* here and abroad, rental information about films reviewed, and listings of independent film screenings around the country.

Selected Film Distributors

Many of these companies have branch offices around the country; only the main office is listed. Most send free catalogues on request.

Brandon Films & Audio Film Center (recently merged under Crowell-Collier and Macmillan) 34 MacQuesten Parkway South, Mount Vernon, N.Y. 10550.

Canyon Cinema Cooperative   Room 220, Industrial Center Building, Sausalito, Calif. 94965.

Columbia Cinematheque   741 Fifth Avenue, New York, N.Y. 10022.

Contemporary Films/McGraw-Hill   Princeton Road, Hightstown, N.J. 08520.

Film-makers' Cooperative   745 Lexington Avenue, New York, N.Y. 10016.

Films Incorporated   35-01 Queens Boulevard, Long Island City, N.Y. 11101.

Grove Press Film Library   214 Mercer Street, New York, N.Y. 10012.

Institutional Cinema Service   915 Broadway, New York, N.Y. 10010.

Janus Films   745 Fifth Avenue, New York, N.Y. 10022.

Museum of Modern Art Film Library   11 West 53rd Street, New York, N.Y. 10019.

Pyramid Films   Box 1048, Santa Monica, Calif. 90406.

Radim Films   17 West 60th Street, New York, N.Y. 10023.

Roa's Films   1696 N. Astor Street, Milwaukee, Wis. 53202.

Twyman Films   329 Salem Avenue, Dayton, Ohio 45401.

United Artists   729 Seventh Avenue, New York, N.Y. 10019.
United Films Inc.   1122 So. Cheyenne, Tulsa, Okla. 74119.
United World Films   221 Park Avenue, New York, N.Y. 10003.
Walter Reade 16   241 East 34th Street, New York, N.Y. 10016.
Warner Bros., Inc.   Nontheatrical Division, 666 Fifth Avenue, New York, N.Y. 10019.
Willoughby-Peerless Film Library   115 West 31st Street, New York, N.Y. 10001.

Reference Source

Feature Films on 8mm and 16mm: Directory of Feature Films Available for Rental, Sale and Lease in the United States, compiled and edited by James L. Limbacher. Continental 16, 241 East 34th Street, New York, N.Y. 10016. 2nd ed., $7.50.